MOZART
The Man and his Works

'Mozart is the most inaccessible of the great masters'
Schnabel

'On the heights it is warmer than one thinks in the valleys'
Nietzsche

W. J. TURNER

Mozart

THE MAN AND HIS WORKS

This edition has been revised and edited by
CHRISTOPHER RAEBURN

BARNES & NOBLE INC., NEW YORK

First published in the U.S.A. 1966
by Barnes & Noble Inc., New York, N.Y.

Printed in Great Britain

Introduction

I HAVE GONE TO the original sources for the material of this book, and all the translations from the German, French, Italian, and occasional Latin, are my own so I must take the responsibility for their accuracy. In translating the letters of Leopold and Wolfgang I have tried to be accurate and to reflect the spirit of the originals rather than dress them in smooth or graceful English.

My object has been to present a sufficiently full and accurate account of the man revealed as far as possible in his own words. This picture will be found to differ considerably from most of those current, especially in the English language.

Aesthetic criticism has also been an important part of my task, but I have not attempted any formal analysis of particular compositions as this is a matter for specialist study. It has been undertaken notably by T. de Wyzewa and G. de Saint-Foix whose first two volumes dealing with the period of 1756–77 were published in 1912. The third volume, prepared after the death of Wyzewa by M. de Saint-Foix, published in Paris in 1936, only brings this examination up to the year 1784, two years before the composition of *Figaro*. [Volumes IV and V were completed by Saint-Foix alone, and published in 1939 and 1946 respectively. C.R.]

W. J. T.

Introduction to Revised Edition

WHEN W. J. Turner's *Mozart, the Man and his Works* originally appeared, it had an instantaneous success. Despite the passage of twenty-five years, it still retains its quality of infectious enthusiasm for the subject; it was for the author, above all, a labour of love arising from his passion for both Mozart and his music.

The book was written at a period when many of Mozart's works were still being rediscovered, and before a comprehensive edition of his Letters had appeared in English. In the intervening years millions of people have become familiar with Mozart's music, through innumerable performances and the media of the wireless and the gramophone, culminating in the world-wide celebrations commemorating his bicentenary in 1956.

Nevertheless, Turner's work can stand very much as it first appeared. Certain minor inaccuracies have emerged in the light of modern research and they have been corrected. There may appear to be too much reliance on the findings of Wyzewa and Saint-Foix, but their study, despite its limitations, has not yet been superseded by any work which can be accepted as a definitive analysis of Mozart's music.

As Turner explained in his own Preface, his translations are intended to reflect the spirit of the Mozart Correspondence rather than to put it into impeccable English, and I have altered his version only where it may have been misleading.

Apart from the omission of a few passages which now seem redundant, the addition of certain modern references and a new bibliography, the book remains as it was written. The author would be gratified, were he alive, to know how widely appreciated Mozart is today, and his work once again will win Mozart many new friends.   C.R.

Acknowledgment

I ONLY LEARNED of Miss Emily Anderson's forthcoming edition of the letters of the Mozart family after I had made my own translations; but I have to acknowledge her friendly courtesy in discussing several matters with me.

Contents

List of Illustrations

CHAPTER ONE

Birth and Parentage

IN A LETTER dated Salzburg, February 9, 1756, Leopold, the father of Mozart, writes to Jakob Lotter in Augsburg:

> On the evening of January 27, at 8 o'clock, my wife was happily delivered of a boy . . . the boy is named Joannes Chrysostomus Wolfgang Gottlieb.

In the baptismal entry *Theophilus* was written, not *Gottlieb*; but finally the Latin form, Amadeus, was used. Mozart at first used to sign himself: 'J. G. Wolfgang', but after 1770 he always subscribed himself: 'Wolfgang Amadeus', and 'Wolfgang' was the name he was known by in his family. There is something peculiarly significant in Mozart's second name of 'God-lover' (*Theophilus*, *Gottlieb*, *Amadeus*), as will be made clear to the discerning who read this book. Mozart's father, Leopold, born on November 14, 1719, in Augsburg, was thirty-seven years old, and his wife, Anna Maria Pertl, born on December 25, 1720, at Schloss Huttenstein, was thirty-six years old at the birth of their son.

Mozart's father's family had been in Augsburg since the beginning of the seventeenth century, where they were all small craftsmen. His paternal great-grandfather and grand-father were bookbinders. His father, Leopold, had two brothers, who continued their father's trade as bookbinders; but Leopold himself, possibly through the influence of his godfather, Canon Johann Georg Grabherr, became a choirboy in the monastery of St Ulrich, Augsburg. On October 13, 1777, he writes to Mozart, who is then in Augsburg, that he well remembers singing a cantata at St Ulrich, when the Hofrat Ofele married 'the beautiful Lepin, a merchant's daughter, who sang well, played the clavier and had 30,000 florins'. Leopold also played the organ, for Mozart, in a letter to his father, dated Munich, October 10-11, 1777, writes:

> Do you recall the name Freysinger . . . he says he knows you quite well and studied with you. He remembers Messenbrunn, especially, where you (this was quite new to me) played the organ quite incomparably. He said: 'It was astounding how the hands and feet flew, crossing one another, but incomparable. He was an excellent man. My father thought highly of him. And how he mocked the priests when they wanted him to turn monk! . . .'

The last remark must have slightly surprised Mozart, who knew his father only as a strict and devout Catholic; but Leopold, in a letter to his son, dated Salzburg, December 15, 1777, refers to his own youth when he writes:

> May I ask whether Wolfgang has not forgotten to confess. God comes before everything; from Him must we expect our earthly happiness and have care always for the Eternal: young people hear such things unwillingly – I know it, I was also young; but God be thanked I always came to myself again after all my youthful follies, flew from all danger to my soul and kept always God and my Honour and the dangerous consequences of sin before my eyes.

Leopold, in 1737, at the age of eighteen, was entered as a student at Salzburg University. This may be accounted for by the fact that the Benedictine order to which the monastery of St Ulrich, Augsburg, belonged had founded and still partly maintained the University of Salzburg. There Leopold studied jurisprudence as well as music, and he won distinction in an examination in 1738. The University of Salzburg was specially noted for its support of music, and music must have been Leopold's principal study, for in 1740 he took a position with Count Johann Baptiste of Thurn, Balfassina and Taxis, the Dean of the Cathedral, in the double rôle, as was customary in those days, of valet and musician. The Count was a music lover and to him Leopold dedicated, in the same year of 1740, his first engraved work, the 'Sonate Sei per Chiesa e da Camera a tre (Due Violini e Basso)'. In 1743 Leopold became fourth violinist in the Archbishop Sigismund of Salzburg's Court chapel; by 1758 he had risen to second violinist and in 1763 he became vice-Kapellmeister to

Jos. Franz Lolli, who succeeded, in that year, Joh. Ernst Eberlin as Kapellmeister. In addition to the instrumental chapel, there was a vocal chapel, consisting of thirty solo and choir singers and fifteen choirboys, whose function it was to perform the church music. From 1744 Leopold taught these boys the violin, and from 1777, after the death of the Cathedral organist, Anton Cajetan Adlgasser, the clavier as well.

Leopold Mozart was also a composer and it was his duty to provide music for the services of the church when required. His pay, outside anything he might get from private lessons, was four hundred gulden a year until 1762, when it was raised to five hundred. As Schurig curtly says, Leopold, after his marriage on November 21, 1747, found this salary 'scanty'. But it must be remembered by English or American readers that the small towns of Germany and Austria have always given better value for the same money than has ever been obtainable in any English or American town or city. Further, in the eighteenth century in Salzburg no part of a man's income went in dog-licences, wireless sets and licences, movies, automobiles, or any other of the new pleasures of the twentieth century; nor was it then necessary to travel twenty or thirty miles from one's home in order to get air to breathe and find a little unspoiled nature.

As a composer Leopold was industrious and capable. Here is a letter to his friend and publisher, Lotter, in Augsburg, dated December 29, 1755:

> Have you a good subject for an oratorio? If I had time I would compose another for Lent. Have you *Christus begraben*,[1] which I composed last year? We have to produce two *Oratoria* every Lent, and where are we to find subjects enough? It must not be *de passione Christi*, but it might be some penitential story. Last year, for instance, we produced one on Peter's Repentance, and another is now being composed on David in the Wilderness.

The famous teacher and theorist, Marpurg (1718–95), of Berlin, in his *Historisch-kritische Beyträge zur Aufnahme der*

---

[1] '*Christus begraben:* Cantata for three voices: Magdalena, Nicodemus, Joseph von Arimathea. Chorus of disciples, and friends of our Lord. Words by S. A. W. [ieland]. Music by J. G. L. Mozart' was printed in Salzburg in 1741; so he must have composed on this subject twice.

Musik, Vol. III (p. 183 f.), published Berlin, 1757, has a section on Leopold Mozart – possibly written by Leopold or based on material supplied by him – which reads as follows:

He has made himself known in all kinds of composition, though none has been printed, and only in 1740 he, himself, engraved six Sonatas *à tre* on copper, chiefly for practise in the art of engraving. In July 1756, he published his 'Violin School'. Among the manuscript compositions of Herr Mozart which have become known are principally many contrapuntal and other church pieces; further, a great number of Symphonies, some for four, some for all customary instruments; over thirty Serenades, containing solos for various instruments. He has also composed many Concertos, especially for the flute, oboe, bassoon, French horn, trumpet, etc.; innumerable Trios and Divertimentos for various instruments; twelve Oratorios and a number of theatrical pieces, even pantomimes and occasional music, such as Soldiers' music with trumpets, kettle-drums, drums and fife, besides the usual instruments; Turkish music, music for a steel clavier; and, finally, a Sledge Drive music with five harness-bells; not to speak of Marches, so-called Night-pieces and many hundreds of Minuets, Opera-dances and such-like things.

It is worth quoting here a description of Leopold's musical sledge-drive given in a programme printed by himself for a performance at the *Collegium Musicum* in Augsburg on December 29, 1755:

MUSICAL SLEDGE DRIVE

Introduced by a prelude, consisting of a pleasing *andante* and a spirited *allegro*.

Then follows:

A prelude with trumpets and drums.

After this:

The Sledge Drive, with the sledge-bells and all the other instruments.

After the Sledge Drive:

The horses are heard rattling their harness.

And then:

> The trumpets and drums alternate pleasantly with the oboes,
> French horns and bassoons, the first representing the
> cavalcade, the second the march.

After this:

> The trumpets and drums have another prelude, and:
> The Sledge Drive begins again, but stops suddenly, for all the
> party dismount and enter the ballroom.
> Then comes an *adagio*, representing the ladies shivering with cold.
> The ball is opened with a minuet and trio.
> The company endeavour to warm themselves by country dances.

Then follows the departure, and, finally:

> During a flourish of trumpets and drums the whole party mount
> their sledges and drive homewards.

There were fanatical pedants in those days as well as in these,
so it is no wonder that after the performance of one of these
occasional pieces of Leopold's in Augsburg he received the
following anonymous letter:

> *Monsieur et très cher ami!*
> May it please you to compose no more absurdities such as Chinese
> and Turkish music, sledge drives and peasant weddings, for they re-
> flect more shame and contempt on you than honour, which is re-
> gretted by the individual who herewith warns you and remains,
> > Your sincere Friend.
> *Datum in domo verae amicitiae.*

This letter, as Leopold himself believed, was probably sent by a
rival musician.

Leopold did not cease composing in order to devote himself
wholly to the training of his two gifted children, as was once
believed; nor are his compositions as worthless as early biographers of Mozart have supposed. Mozart, in a letter to his
father from Vienna dated March 29, 1783, asks Leopold to send
some of his church music, and repeats his request on April 12,
1783, saying:

> I beg you, when it is warmer, to search under the roof and send us
> some of your church music; you have nothing to be ashamed of –

Baron van Swieten and Starzer know as well as you and I that taste is always changing – and even – that the change of taste unfortunately extends as far as church music; which, however, should not be – whence it comes also that the true church music is to be found under the roof – and even worm-eaten. . . .

Schubart, in his *Aesthetik der Tonkunst*, prefers Leopold's church music to his chamber music, mentions him as the man who had 'placed music in Salzburg on its then excellent footing' and declares that he 'showed great knowledge of counter-point, but was somewhat old-fashioned'. Otto Jahn examined a Litany, *De Venerabili*, in D major, composed in 1762, and sent to Munich in 1774 by Leopold, together with a grand Litany by his son. Of this work Jahn writes:

> It is written for solos, chorus and the usual small church orchestra of the day, and shows throughout the learning of a musician skilled in the use of traditional forms. The harmony is correct, the disposition of the parts skilful and the contrapuntal forms are handled boldly; nor does the composer fail to introduce regular, well-worked-out fugues in the proper places; *'Cum Sancto Spiritu'* and *'Et vitam venturi saeculi'* in the Mass; *'Pignus futurae Gloriae'* in the Litany.
>
> But there is no originality or inventive power either in the composition as a whole or in isolated passages. Leopold Mozart's sacred music gives him a right to an honourable place among contemporary composers, but to no higher rank.

Apart from the music of Leopold's printed in his own lifetime, a selection was made and published in the *Denkmäler der Tonkunst in Bayern*.[1] This 'excavation', says Schurig, has only an historical interest and is a mere act of piety to the father of a great artist; but elsewhere Schurig, commenting on Mozart's letter to his father about his church music which I have already quoted, expresses his opinion that Mozart spoke with conviction when he praised his father's church music, and goes on to say that Leopold was: 'a super-pious Catholic, not from diplomacy but in a sort of fatalistic belief. In his church compositions rather than elsewhere is the expression of his inner life, also true art.'

Everything depends on the point of view. My own opinion is that Leopold Mozart as a composer was as good as is the average

[1] IX Jahrgang II Bd. (published by Breitkopf and Härtel, Leipzig, 1908).

well-known and accepted composer of the day – and I mean of any day. 'In Leopold Mozart lived and stirred not a spark of genius,' writes Schurig. Well, the same may with equal truth be written of the majority of artists – writers, painters and musicians – who achieve a contemporary celebrity. But from another point of view there is, sometimes, in some of these men, a spark of talent, though not the burning fire of genius. I think this spark was in Leopold.[1]

Herman Abert, who made a much more thorough study of the music of Leopold's contemporaries and predecessors than did Otto Jahn, has a more favourable opinion and says of Leopold:

> What distinguished him . . . chiefly from his contemporaries was that instead of dealing with the higher problems of nature, fable and story, he, like his countryman, Schubart, in his songs, plunged boldly into the daily life of the common people. Sturdy peasants, jolly hunters, soldiers with drums and fifes, postillions, a gay sledge-party – these were things after his own heart, and, above all, he did not overlook in them the harsh, comic sides, as his 'ladies shivering with cold' in the 'Sledge Drive' and the 'bewailing of the bridal wreath' in the 'Peasants' Wedding' show. . . .

Of Leopold's *divertimenti* and symphonies Abert remarks that they show an undoubted kinship with the work of his son, both as regards the 'demoniacal' and the *'cantabile'* traits of his art:

> Only the son, from the beginning, heightened the light, social tone of the whole of this kind of music into something noble and spirited, while the father remained within the limits of the sturdy, common citizen. But also, in details, distinctly perceptible ties link both together here and there. For example, in rhythm Leopold inclines to syncopation as a means of excitement; in melody he has the tendency to a spicing with retards, chromatic *appoggiaturas*, etc., and often remarkably moving, tortuous figuration; in harmony, finally, besides the . . . characteristic use of the minor key, the predilection for whole series of sixths for the expression of quiet dreaming or passionate urge. All these are traits which, immensely heightened and spiritual-ized, repeat themselves in the son and not, like the immediate similarities with the father, merely in the youthful works. . . .

Abert, rightly, points out that it is hard to understand that

[1] Wyzewa and G. de Saint-Foix are of the opinion that Leopold's compositions are models of artistic probity and technically excellent', but without originality or life.

anyone should have denied the influence on such a susceptible nature as Mozart's of the one musician nearest at hand – namely, the father. To conclude with this necessary account of Leopold's accomplishment as a composer, I shall just mention the three Sonatas for Clavier, composed (according to Seiffert) in the years 1762–3, which have survived print in Haffner's *Œuvres mêlées*, published in Würzburg. Faisst,[1] in his *Beiträge zur Geschichte der Claviersonate*, printed in the periodical *Cäcilia*, 1846, says of these Sonatas that they might well be the work of Leopold's son so great is their likeness in form and spirit, and other critics have found in them points of favourable comparison with Domenico Scarlatti and Philipp Emanuel Bach.

I said that I, personally, believed there was a spark of true talent in Leopold Mozart, though certainly not the burning fire of genius, and here I will quote what might be considered as suggesting such a musical spark – namely, the following bars from the first movement of No. 3 of the six *divertimenti* for two violins and violoncello, belonging, probably, to the year 1760, which I have taken from Abert:

This is the place for a slight digression upon musical standards. That there are many different elements in music besides the three fundamentals of melody, harmony and rhythm – though these may be reduced to tone and time, or, simply, to tone, since it is impossible to hear a tone without some time duration – is certain. Musical talent is not, as one may at first be inclined to think, a simple, but is a complex talent. The idea that a musician of genius is simply a man with a peculiar and specialized gift for combining or relating tones which are mere tones in the abstract without relation to life or anything else is an illusion. That this faculty can exist in a man without reference to other qualities

[1] *Faisst*, Immanuel Gottlob Friedrich (b. 1823, d. 1894), organist, composer and theoretical writer.

or gifts is true, just as the mathematical faculty can; but such an unrelated faculty does not, by itself, make a musician of genius – it only makes a musician. The faculty itself varies enormously in degree; that is a matter of common experience, and it explains why even among musicians of genius some have this pure musical faculty to a greater degree than others. Gluck, for example, had it less than Haydn. It is even possible for a musician of no genius – say, a Sterndale Bennet, or even a Max Reger – to have this musical faculty more strongly developed than a composer whose work is, nevertheless, superior to theirs; superior, that is, by virtue of other qualities of which this faculty is the instrument.

In a great musician of genius every human quality must enter, and he will be great in so far as his musical faculty is at the service of and expresses his human nature and, therefore, according also to the depth and capacity of that nature. Music *is* the man. But not only is it the man, it is – in the case of the greatest artists – a universe and that is what Schopenhauer really meant when he said that 'music is the world over again'. It was also what Goethe was alluding to when he makes Werther say, in a letter to his friend, that he is always being praised for his intelligence and his knowledge whereas it is his heart – which nobody ever mentions – that is the really remarkable thing about him. During the past hundred years men have been apt to assume that they varied individually to a greater degree as regards intelligence or specific gifts than, say, in the qualities of the heart. A comic illustration of this is Charles Kingsley's well-known:

'Be good, sweet maid, and let who will be clever.'

These lines are always quoted as if it were more within individual control to be good than to be clever, whereas, in truth, one is born more or less 'good', as one is born more or less 'clever'; education and experience can only develop what natural powers in these directions exist already. The qualities of the heart are as many and as various as those of the head, and no great artistic genius is possible without possessing the qualities of both highly and richly developed. We shall come, in the course of this book, to realize that where Mozart surpassed his father – as, indeed, perhaps he surpasses all the great musicians of genius before or since – is in his possession not only of a greater degree of purely musical talent than has been possessed by any man, but, also, in the combination in him of such a variety of human qualities of head and heart in so high a degree of vitality that we may say of him that he had a truly Shakespearean nature.

In order that this problem of artistic genius may not have been made to appear too simple in the foregoing analysis, I must now add that there is a still unmentioned element of mystery in it. What this element is may best be suggested by indicating that in artistic genius there is a specific love, in addition to, although linked with, our ordinary human loves. The prototype of human love is the love of God, and men's and women's capacity to love one another and nature depends on this primary love of God dwelling within them. But in the great artist of genius there is also another prototype, which, in the case of musicians, I may best define by calling it not the love of God, but the love of the God of Music; and it is from this specific love that musical talent derives. 'Do you think that I make music for my pleasure?' wrote Berlioz once bitterly, in a letter. This phrase suggests the difference I am trying to make clear between the enjoyment or pleasure in music and the love of it. True love is always a source of pain as well as of joy, and the passionate, concentrated love of music in a great musician of genius, such as Mozart, may be likened in its intensity to personal love, for which reason I describe it not as the love of music, but of the God of Music.

And just as God loves those who love Him, so Music loves those who are its true lovers and showers its riches upon them. Finally – and most mysterious of all – there is some hidden connexion in great creative musical genius between the love of God and this love of the God of Music. The one enriches the other as if there were a marriage between them.

The differences between the character and nature of Leopold and of his son will come out more clearly in the narrative of Mozart's life; but the reader will have already gathered that Mozart's father, Leopold, was no ordinary man. As a musician he was on a level with the majority of the best-reputed of his contemporaries, both as a composer and as an executant, and it remains now to say something of his work as a teacher.

In 1756, the year in which his great son was born, Leopold published his *Versuch einer gründlichen Violinschule*,[1] which very soon made him famous among all contemporary musicians and proved that he was not only a practical musician, but a fine theorist and teacher. His lengthy correspondence with his publisher, Lotter, shows how exceptionally scrupulous in all matters of detail Leopold was. I shall quote a few sentences at random from this celebrated Violin Method, for the light they throw on Leopold and, hence, also, on the sort of training his son was likely to get from him:

> Nothing can be more ridiculous than to seem afraid even to grasp the violin firmly; or merely to touch the strings with the bow—held perhaps with but two fingers—and to attempt so expressive an up-bow to the very bridge of the violin so that a note here and there is all that is heard in a whisper without any notion of what it means, as if in a dream.

> It is dispiriting to go on playing at random without knowing what you are about.

> To advance before the pupil is ready is the greatest error that either masters or pupils can fall into. The former often lack patience to wait for the right time or they let themselves be carried away by the pupil, who thinks he has done wonders when he can scrape out a minuet or two. . . .

> These are the passages for practice. The more distasteful they are the better I shall be pleased. I have striven to make them so.

Among many interesting remarks, apart from actual technical instruction, are his references to *tremolo* and *rubato*. He censures players who:

> '. . . tremble upon every long note or cannot play a couple of bars simply without introducing senseless and ridiculous tricks and fancies.

[1] 'Essay at a Fundamental Method for the Violin', first published by J. J. Lotter in Augsburg, 1756; further editions 1769–70, 1787, 1791, 1804; translated into French 1770; into Dutch 1766.

. . . shake on every note as if afflicted with a fever.

. . . disdain to keep uniform time in the accompaniment of a concerted part and strive to follow the principal part. . . .

. . . spoil the *tempo rubato* of an experienced artist by waiting to follow him. . . .'

He has a particular dislike to what he calls 'virtuosos of the imagination'. Such 'virtuosos of the imagination' are still as plentiful today as they were in Leopold's time, and Leopold is bitingly sarcastic about them. A 'virtuoso of the imagination', he says:

. . . often gives to a semiquaver in an *adagio cantabile* the time of half a bar, before recovering from his paroxysm of feeling; and he cares nothing at all for the time; he plays in recitative.

Leopold was no enemy to true expression, for he recognizes that the aim of the performer lies in what Philipp Emanuel Bach described as 'good execution' – namely, 'the power of expressing musical ideas to the ear correctly and with full effect'. As one of the means to this in violin playing, Leopold indicates the bowing as the 'medium by the judicious use of which it is possible to communicate the pathos of the music to the audience'. It is interesting to note that Italian singers have not changed since Leopold Mozart's day, for he refers to the fact that it is true that when playing for some Italian singers:

. . . who learn everything by heart and never adhere to time or measure, one has often to pass over whole bars to save them from open shame.

Everybody can remember occasions when conductors have been adversely criticized for not giving singers time to breathe, when all that they were doing was to try to make them sing more strictly in time, instead of dragging, as all incompetent singers do habitually, just as they did in Leopold's day.

Among contemporary criticisms of Leopold's Violin Method, the following may be worth citing:

Marpurg, in his *Historisch-kritische Beyträge*, compares Leopold with Geminiani:[1]

> What Geminiani did for the English nation, Mozart has accomplished for the German, and their works are worthy to live side by side in universal approbation . . . a thorough and gifted virtuoso, a sensible and methodical teacher and a learned musician. . . .

Schubart, in his *Aesthetik der Tonkunst*, said:

> His 'Method' . . . is written in good German and with admirable judgment. The examples are chosen well and the system of fingering is not in the least pedantic. The author inclines to the school of Tartini,[2] but he permits greater freedom in the use of the bow.

It is also worth quoting the opinion of Goethe's musical adviser, Zelter,[3] who has the following claims to our interest nowadays:

(1) He told Goethe that Berlioz' *Huit Scènes de Faust* – which the young French composer had sent in admiration to the German poet – were horrible nonsense;
(2) he criticized the poet's *Werther* to the effect that Werther should have shot Albrecht instead of himself;
(3) he re-wrote some of J. S. Bach's music with the notion that he was improving it; and
(4) he was the teacher of Mendelssohn.

Zelter was enthusiastic over Leopold's Violin Method, adding to his praise: 'it is well-written, too.' This is worth remarking, because it is abundantly clear that Leopold Mozart was not only a man of superior culture, but a man of considerable general intellectual force. One has to bear this very clearly in mind when considering the character of his son. The nineteenth-century notion of the 'child-like' Mozart, the pure, lovable, unconscious, naïve, innocent genius, is completely at variance with the facts. I doubt if in the history of men of genius there is another ex-

---

[1] *Geminiani*, Francesco (b. Lucca, 1667; d. Dublin, 1762); famous violinist and composer, author of *The Art of Playing the Violin*, published in English, London, 1731–4.
[2] *Tartini*, Giuseppe (b. 1692; d. Padua, 1770); famous violinist and composer and originator of improvements in the construction and technique of the bow.
[3] *Zelter*, Carl Friedrich (b. Berlin, 1758; d. 1832); director of the Berlin Singakademie and founder of the German Liedertafeln.

ample of a father having so great and persistent an influence on
his son as Leopold's, and the cool, calculating, sharp, sarcastic
turn of mind of Leopold, his inclination to biting satire, his
scepticism in all material affairs, his extreme man-of-the-world-
ness – all these qualities (except the latter) are visible also in his
son, as we shall see in due course from his letters. Mozart was as
sharp and severe in his criticism of men and women and as
realistically penetrating in his judgment as his father; he even
shared his practical sagacity; but what he utterly lacked was his
father's caution. This lack of caution was not due, however, to
defect of judgment, to simple-mindedness – no man of genius
was ever less simple-minded than Mozart – but to the possession
of a positive quality to a quite inordinate degree, namely, sensibility. Some sensibility the hard-headed Leopold must, of course,
have had or he would not have been an artist. He was even capable
of enthusiasm, since he wrote a letter to the poet Gellert which
moved Gellert to the following answer:

> I should be indeed insensible if the extraordinary kindness with
> which you have honoured me had left me unmoved ... I accept your
> love and friendship, my dear sir, with the same frankness with
> which they are offered. Do you, indeed, read my works and en-
> courage your friends to do the same? Such approbation, I can truly
> say, was more than I could have dared to hope for from such a
> quarter. Does my last poem, '*Der Christ*', meet with your approval?
> I venture to answer myself in the affirmative, since I am encouraged
> in this by the subject of the poem, your own noble spirit – as un-
> wittingly you display it in your letter – and by my consciousness of
> honest endeavour.

Leopold has been described by some writers as a pedant and a
bigot. It is quite clear from his own letters that he was neither.
He was a devout Catholic, being born in Catholic South Germany, but, also, by conviction; yet, nevertheless, he became a
freemason towards the end of his life. He was not superstitious,
and, speaking of a ghost-story, said: 'It must be only an hysterical
illusion.' He remonstrates with his daughter when ill for risking
endangering her health rather than abstain from going to Mass;
while writing, on one occasion, that he had 'invariably found that
begging sisterhoods were the signs of much moral degradation

concealed under the cloak of hypocrisy'. But one of his most characteristic utterances was the following:

> Accept it as a universal truth that all men tell lies and add to the truth, or take away from it, just as it suits their purpose. Especially must we believe nothing which, if known, would add to the reputation of the speaker or flatter his interlocutor, for that is sure to be false.

This saying, which is worthy of La Rochefoucauld and undeniably true, was not of much assistance to his son. Mozart, as we shall learn, could see through men just as clearly as his father; there was nothing wrong with his head. What was wrong with him was his heart and his general sensibility, which was, indeed, extreme. The old Biblical utterance that the truly virtuous shall be light of heart, if applied to Mozart, would make him out to be one of the most virtuous of men, for his natural buoyancy and gaiety of heart were quite extraordinary. It was this sheer lightheartedness and vivacity which made him do rash things and involve himself in difficulties and responsibilities which his more cautious father would have avoided. After all, a man is not a man of genius for nothing. Men of such genius as Mozart's must be conscious of it. It must be an exhilarating element in their lives to a degree of which we can hardly conceive. It may amount, indeed, to what we might call an intoxication of the spirit to which lesser men can only aspire through being in love or in drink. Mozart was gay and, in a sense, reckless. That Mozart was aware of his genius is abundantly clear from his letters. In fact, he took it so for granted that when writing to his father from Vienna on August 17, 1782, when he was twenty-six years old, he mentions without any surprise or even comment, when talking about his prospects and whether he would have to leave Germany and go to France or England, how the Archduke Maximilian, speaking of him, said: 'Such people only come into the world once in a hundred years.'

As to his sensibility, we have a piece of astonishing contemporary evidence. J. A. Schachtner, who died in 1795, four years after Mozart, had been Court trumpeter at Salzburg since 1754 and had known the family well since Mozart's childhood.

Shortly after Mozart's death he wrote to Mozart's sister a letter answering questions which she had put to him. Her fourth question and his answer are as follows:

Fourth question:
What particular qualities, maxims, rules of life, singularities, good or evil propensities had he?

Answer:
He was full of fire; his inclinations were easily swayed; I believe that had he been without the advantage of the good education which he received he might have become a profligate scoundrel—he was so ready to yield to every attraction which offered.

When reading this, one cannot help being reminded of Keats':

Men of genius are great as certain ethereal chemicals operating on the mass of neutral intellect—but they have not any individuality, any determined character. . . .[1]

Schachtner's letter is the source of so much of the authentic information about Mozart as a child that it must be quoted in full. I, therefore, give the rest of it here:

Salzburg,
April 24, 1792.

Honoured and gracious Madam,
Your very welcome letter reached me, not at Salzburg, but at Hammerau, where I was visiting my son. . . .
From your habitual obligingness towards everyone and especially towards the Mozart family, you may judge how sorry I was that I could not at once discharge your commission. To the point, then!
Your first question: 'What favourite pastimes, out-side his occupation with music, your late-lamented brother had as a child?' is not to be answered, since as soon as he began to give himself up to music his mind was as good as dead to other things[2] and even his childish

---

[1] Letter to Benjamin Bailey, November 22, 1817. See the rest of this letter; also, in his letter to George and Thomas Keats, December 21, 1817, the passage on 'negative capability'.

[2] It is noteworthy that Leopold writes to his son from Salzburg, February 16, 1778:
'My son! in all your affairs you are hot-headed and hasty. Your character now is wholly altered from what you were as a child and youth. As a boy and child you were serious rather than childish and when you were at the clavier or otherwise occupied with music nobody dared make the least joke. Your very countenance was so serious that many observant persons . . . prophesied your early death on account of your precocious and reflective expression. Now, it seems to me, you answer hastily in a joking tone on the slightest provocation.'

games and toys to be interesting to him had to be accompanied with music. When we (he and I) carried his toys from one room into another, the one who went empty-handed had always to sing and fiddle a march. Before he began to study music he was so keenly alive to any bit of fun enlivened with a spice of mischief that he would forget about eating and drinking and everything else. As you know, he became so extremely fond of me (being devoted to him) that he would ask me ten times a day whether I loved him, and if I jokingly answered: 'No', immediately bright tears came into his eyes, so tender and affectionate was his good little heart.

Second question: 'How did he behave as a child with the great when they admired his talent and proficiency in music?' In truth he betrayed very little pride or veneration for rank[1] for he could have shown both by playing before the great who understood little or nothing of music, but he never wanted to play unless there were musical connoisseurs among his audience or unless he were deceived into thinking that there were.

Third question: 'What studious occupation did he like best?' Answer: In this respect it was much the same to him what he was set to learn, he only wanted to learn and left the choice to his beloved father. It seemed as if he realized that he could find in the world no teacher or guide like his ever-memorable father.

Whatever he was given to learn he gave himself so completely to that that everything else, even music, was laid aside. For example, when he was learning arithmetic tables, stools, walls and even the floor were chalked over with figures.

Fourth question. . . .[2]

Let me add some remarkable and astonishing facts relating to his fourth and fifth years of whose truth I can guarantee. Once I went with his father to your home after the Thursday service and we found the four-year-old Wolfgangerl busy with the pen.

Father: 'What are you doing?'

Wolfg.: 'Writing a concerto for the clavier, the first part is almost done.'

Father: 'Let me see.'

Wolfg.: 'It's not quite finished.'

---

[1] In a most interesting letter from Salzburg, dated February 16, 1778, Leopold writes to his son:

'It is your good heart which causes you to give your complete trust and love to anyone who unreservedly praises you, esteems you and lauds you to the skies: whereas, as a boy, your modesty was so extreme that you began at once to weep when you were overpraised. The greatest art is to learn to know yourself and then, my dear son, do as I and study other people so as to know them well. You know it has ever been my study and it is indeed a fine, useful, even essential study.'

[2] Already quoted, see p. 16.

Father: 'Never mind, let me see it, it must be something very fine.'
Your father took it from him and showed me a daub of notes for
the most part written over dried ink-blots. (*N.B.* The little Wolfgangerl dipped his pen every time to the bottom of the inkwell so
that a blot fell every time he touched the paper but that did not disturb him, he rubbed it off with his hand and went on writing.) We
laughed at first at this apparent nonsense but then your father began
to note the theme, the notes, the composition, his study of the sheet
became more intent until at last tears of wonder and delight fell from
his eyes.

'Look, Herr Schachtner,' he said, 'how correct and orderly it is;
only it is of no use because it is so very difficult that nobody could
play it.' Then Wolfgangerl struck in: 'That is why it is a concerto,
one must practise it until one can do it; look! this is how it goes.' He
played but could only bring out enough to show us what he intended.
He had then the notion that playing concertos and working miracles
were the same thing.

Once more, gracious Madam! You will doubtless remember that I
had a very good violin which Wolfgangerl on account of its soft and
full tone always called 'butter-fiddle'. One day, soon after you came
back from Vienna (early in 1763) he played on it and could not
praise it enough; a day or two after I came to see him again and
found him playing with his own violin; he said: 'What is your butter-
fiddle doing?' and went on playing to his fancy. At last he reflected a
little and said: 'Herr Schachtner, your violin is half a quarter of a
tone lower than mine, that is if it is tuned as it was when I last
played on it.' I laughed at this but your father, who knew the extraordinary ear and memory of the child, begged me to get my violin
and see whether he was right. I did and right he was.[1]

Some time before this, the day after your return from Vienna,
Wolfgang having brought with him a small violin which he got as a
present from Vienna, then came in our then excellent violinist Herr
Wenzl who was a beginner at composition.

He brought six Trios with him which he had prepared in the absence of your father, to have his opinion on them. We played these
Trios, your father taking the bass part on the viola, Wenzl the first
violin, and I the second. Wolfgangerl begged to be allowed to play
the second violin but your father reproved him for his silly request
since he had not had the slightest instruction on the violin and your
father thought he was not in the least prepared for playing.

---

[1] It must be said for the benefit of non-musicians that such accuracy of ear and
retentiveness of memory although, of course, exceptional are not quite as rare as
might be supposed. Many musicians totally lacking in genius – to say nothing of
genius of Mozart's order – have possessed this faculty. See my remarks on pp. 8–9.

Wolfgang said: 'One does not need to have learnt to play the second violin', and when your father told him to go away and not disturb us further Wolfgang began to cry bitterly and toddled off with his little violin. I interceded for him to be allowed to play with me and at last his father said: 'Play with Herr Schachtner but so softly that you are not heard or you must go away at once.' Wolfgang played with me. Soon I perceived with astonishment that I was quite superfluous; I put my violin quietly down and looked at your father down whose cheeks tears of wonder and delight were rolling, and so he played all six Trios. When we had finished Wolfgang grew so bold with our applause that he declared he could play first violin. We let him try as a joke and we almost died of laughter to hear him play with incorrect and uncertain execution certainly but without breaking down.

In conclusion: 'Of the delicacy and fineness of his ear.'

Almost up to his tenth year he had an insurmountable dread of the trumpet when it was played alone without other instruments; if one merely held out a trumpet towards him it was as if one had pointed a loaded pistol at his heart. His father wanted to rid him of this childish fear and asked me once in spite of his objections to blow towards him but, my God! I had to desist. Wolfgang no sooner heard the clanging sound than he turned pale, began to totter and would have fallen into convulsions had I not stopped.

This is all I can say, I think, in answer to your questions. Pardon my scrawl, I am too cast down to do better.

I am, honoured Madam,
With the greatest esteem and regard,
Your most obedient servant,
(Sgd.)   ANDREAS SCHACHTNER,
Court Trumpeter.

Mozart's mother, Anna Maria Pertl[1] (written also as Bertl or Bertel), was the daughter of Wolfgang Nikolaus Pertl, steward of the Convent of St Gilgen by St Wolfgang-See, and Rosina Altmann. Her letters – all of which I have carefully read – confirm her reputation of being a cheerful, happy-natured woman, perhaps less intellectual than her husband though more tolerant and humorous but, nevertheless, with a real love of music[2] and a lively

---

[1] Born December 25, 1720, at Huttenstein, near St Gilgen, in the Salzkammergut, married Leopold Mozart November 21, 1747, died Paris, July 3, 1778.
[2] She writes to Leopold from Mannheim on January 3, 1778:
'Here, on account of the death of the Elector, all is in deepest mourning, no Opera (which is a great grief to me), comedy, play, concerts, sledge-drives, music, everything has been suspended.'

interest in politics.[1] It is not to be imagined that so exacting a man as Leopold, who did not marry until he was twenty-eight, would have married a stupid woman and from her portrait now in the Mozarteum at Salzburg one can see that she was a woman of character and capacity. In my opinion Mozart owed more of his character to his mother than to his father. From all the evidence she seems to have been gay and lovable and although a capable, industrious and unselfish wife and mother – in short, a true, sound-natured woman – not at all authoritative and domineering but lively and accommodating. She seems to have had the Salzburg bias to the droll and comical.[2] Schubart in his *Aesthetik der Tonkunst* writes:

> The Salzburg mind is addicted to low comedy. Their popular songs are so drolly burlesque that one cannot listen to them without dying of laughter. The clownish spirit shines through them all, though the melodies are often fine and beautiful.

Who can fail to see this characteristic in the operas of Mozart?[3] This side of his genius he certainly got from his mother and the well-known Salzburg proverb:

> He who comes to Salzburg becomes in the first year stupid, in the second year idiotic (*einfex*) and in the third a true Salzburger,

might have been written by Mozart himself in one of his letters, it is so exactly in his spirit.

Leopold and Anna Maria had seven children, of whom only two survived; a daughter, Maria Anna (called Nannerl or Marianne in the family), born on July 30, 1751,[4] and the son, Wolfgang, born on January 27, 1756. Nannerl, who was thus five years older than Wolfgang, showed very early a decided talent

[1] Her letters to her husband from Mannheim and Paris are full of references to politics.

[2] The buffoon (Hanswurst) on the Viennese stage, the creation of Stranitzky, was given the Salzburg dialect.

[3] Another feature inherited from his mother by Mozart was his long and prominent nose. Mozart's father and mother were considered the best-looking bridal couple of their time in Salzburg.

[4] Nannerl survived her brother; she married in 1784 Baron von Berchthold zu Sonnenberg, Hofrath of Salzburg and Warden of St Gilgen. On his death in 1801 she returned to Salzburg and taught music. She became blind in 1820 and died on October 29, 1829.

1. Maria Anna Mozart in Gala Dress, 1763

2. Mozart in 1777 as a Knight of the Golden Spur

for music and Leopold taught her the clavier. The teaching of his sister made a great impression on Wolfgang; when he was only three years old he used to seat himself at the clavier and amuse himself striking thirds with great delight.

When Wolfgang was four years old his father began to teach him minuets and other pieces on the clavier and in a short time he could play them with perfect correctness and in the proper time. In his fifth year he began to compose little pieces which he played to his father and which he then wrote down.[1]

In addition to the memoir sent by Mozart's sister in December 1799 to Messrs Breitkopf, another source of reliable information about Wolfgang's earliest studies is the music-book provided by her father for Marianne's exercises which was presented by the Grand Duchess Helene in 1864 to the Salzburg Mozarteum. It contains minuets and other little pieces, also longer ones such as a theme with twelve variations, and passages from the composers Agrell, Fischer and Wagenseil written in the hand of Leopold and his musical friends. The book has the title:

Pour le Clavecin. Ce livre appartient a Marie Anna Mozart, 1759,

but unfortunately there are a number of pages missing. However, to the eighth minuet there is a note by Leopold:

The preceding minuet was learnt by Wolfgangerl in his fourth year.

There are other similar observations – e.g.:

This minuet and trio Wolfgangerl learnt in half-an-hour at half-past nine o'clock on January 26, 1761, one day before his fifth birthday.[2]

A second book, intended for Wolfgang, is complete. Some details of it were given in the *Mitteilungen für die Berliner Mozart-gemeinde* published in Berlin in March, 1908, and Abert gives a

[1] Schlichtegroll's *Nekrolog*, an annual obituary of eminent persons compiled for the year of Mozart's death, 1791, by Professor Schlichtegroll, which appeared in 1793 and 1794 – described as containing 'an authentic biography of my brother' by Marianne Mozart.
[2] Otto Jahn says: 'They are simple, easy pieces in two parts but requiring an independence of the hands not possible without a degree of musical comprehension surprising in so young a child.'

B

thorough analysis of it. On the back of the first page is written:

> To my dear son Wolfgang Amadée on his sixth birthday from his father Leopold Mozart. Salzburg, October 31, 1762.

One of the first[1] compositions of Mozart's that we possess is a minuet transcribed into Marianne's book by Leopold with the note that it was composed by his son in January 1762. Here it is:

Minuet in F. (*K.*2)

---

[1] Abert and others consider the Minuet in G (K.1) to be Mozart's first. This is on the authority of his sister Marianne who has written on the MS. (now in the Municipal Museum at Salzburg) that it was composed by her brother and 'written by his own hand in his fifth year'.

Wolfgang's music-book, given to him in 1762 by his father, has been painstakingly examined by Abert. It consists of 135 pages and includes examples of songs and dance music from popular collections; also pieces by Philipp Emanuel Bach, Telemann, Kirchhoff, Schmidt, Hasse, etc. Not only the old dances – *allemandes*, *courantes*, etc. – are included but what were then the new dance forms of minuet and polonaise. 'The book shows,' says Abert, 'how much stronger on Mozart's early development was the influence of the North German school than was formerly suspected.'

CHAPTER TWO

The Prodigy Children

(1762–6)

LEOPOLD DECIDED TO show his two wonder-children to the
world. In January 1762, he took Nannerl (aged eleven) and Wolfgang (aged six) on their first experimental journey to Munich.
They stayed three weeks and played before the Elector. In September of the same year they set out for Vienna, breaking the
journey at Passau where the Bishop wanted to hear the prodigies
and then rewarded them with – one ducat! They also stayed at
Linz, giving a concert under the patronage of Count Schlick. A
Count Herberstein[1] and a Count Pfalz also heard them there and
promised to spread the news about them in Vienna. The information about these tours comes chiefly from Leopold's letters to
Lorenz Hagenauer, a Salzburg business man in whose house the
Mozarts lodged. Hagenauer was a good friend of the family and
lent Leopold most of the money for his various tours. His house,
in which Mozart was born, still stands in the Getreidegasse and
the floor occupied by the Mozarts has been turned into a museum
where the portraits and many other interesting Mozartiana are
now exhibited. Extracts from Leopold's letters to Hagenauer will
give the best account of this second tour, the first one to Vienna:

Linz,
October 3, 1762.
. . . This delay [in Passau] for which His Grace's favour is re-
sponsible is also responsible for costing me the eighty gulden I had

[1] In 1785 this Count Herberstein, then Bishop of Passau, told Mozart how he
remembered his extreme concern as a child on seeing a beggar fall into the water.

made in Linz. . . . Wolfgang had the honour to perform before His Grace, but not the girl, and for this he received a whole ducat, that is four gulden and ten kreutzer.

. . . On the 26th we left Passau with Count Herberstein in the morning and arrived at 5 o'clock in the evening at Linz. . . .

The children are happy and just as if they were at home. The boy[1] is as intimate with everybody, especially with the officers, as if he had known them all his life.

Vienna,
October 16, 1762.

On the feast of St Francis in the afternoon at 4.30 we left Linz by the so-called 'Water-ordinary'[2] and arrived the same night by dark at Mauthausen. The following Tuesday at midday we reached Ibbs where our Wolferl[3] . . . played so well on the organ that the Franciscan fathers . . . with a guest . . . left their eating and ran to hear open-mouthed with astonishment. By night we were at Stein and Wednesday the 6th at 3 o'clock in Vienna. We had much rain and wind on the journey. Wolfgang had already a cold in Linz but in spite of all discomfort, early rising, unusual food and drink and the wind and rain, remained, thank God! well.

I must mention that we got through the customs quickly and without payment owing to Wolferl who made friends with the officer, showed him his clavier . . . and played him a minuet on his little fiddle. . . .

The Countess von Zinzendorf is busy on our account and all the ladies have lost their hearts to the children. When I was alone in the Opera on the 10th I heard the Archduke Leopold[4] saying from his box there was a boy in Vienna who played the clavier wonderfully, etc. The very same evening about eleven I received a command to go to Schönbrunn. . . .

I had the firm intention to let you know as soon as we came from Schönbrunn but we had to go direct from Schönbrunn to the Prince von Hildburghausen . . . now there is only time to tell you that we were so graciously received that as I tell it it will be reckoned a fairy tale. Let it suffice that Wolferl sprang on the lap of the Empress,[5] put his arms around her neck and vigorously kissed her. We were with her from three till six. . . .

---

[1] Leopold always used the South German expression *Der Bub* for the five-year-old Wolfgang.
[2] No doubt the boat service on the Danube between Linz and Vienna.
[3] Wolfgangerl.
[4] Later, the Emperor Leopold II of Austria.
[5] Maria Theresia.

Vienna,
October 19, 1762.

. . . The treasurer paid me one hundred ducats with the statement that Her Majesty will soon send for us again. . . .

Would you like to know what Wolferl's dress looks like? It is of the finest cloth, lilac-coloured; the vest of silk of the same colour, the coat and waistcoat embroidered with broad gold braid. It was made for the Archduke Maximilian. Nannerl has the Court dress of a Princess of white embroidered and hand-trimmed taffeta.[1]

Wolfgang fell ill with scarlet fever and the Viennese nobility sent their doctors and much attention was paid to Leopold and his children,[2] but Leopold complains to Hagenauer (November 24, 1762) that through this illness they lost four weeks which have cost them one ducat a day. After making a journey to Pressburg in Hungary on December 11th Leopold and his two children returned from Vienna to Salzburg early in January. There was now a slight change in his position, for the Kapellmeister at Salzburg, Ernst Eberlin, died in 1762 and Joseph Lolli became Kapellmeister in his place, Leopold Mozart being now appointed vice-Kapellmeister.

The success of this tour decided Leopold to make a more ambitious one. As their possible public was almost exclusively the nobility they left Salzburg again on June 9, 1763, to pay a round of visits to the German Courts and principal cities with Paris as the ultimate goal. Again, I shall extract from Leopold's letters to Hagenauer the most interesting details of this tour:

Wasserburg,
June 11, 1763.

. . . Two hours from Wasserburg one of the back wheels broke in pieces . . . to amuse ourselves we went to look at the organ and I explained the use of the pedal to Wolferl whereupon he began to try it – pushing away the stool and standing he preluded using the pedal as if he had practised it for months. Everybody was astonished and

[1] Leopold had the two children's portraits painted in these gala clothes which were presented to them by the Empress. These portraits are reproduced in Plates 1 and 4.
[2] Wolfgang became very fond of the Archduchess Marie Antoinette and once when she had picked him up after a fall he said: 'You are very good, I will marry you.' 'Why?' asked the Empress who was standing by. 'From gratitude,' he answered, 'she was good to me but her sister stood by and did nothing.'

what many achieve after much labour comes to him as a new gift of God.

From Wasserburg they proceeded to Munich where they played before the Elector of Bavaria and the Archduke Clemens. Wolfgang played a concerto on the violin and extemporized two cadenzas. Leopold received one hundred gulden from the Elector and seventy-five from the Archduke. They then left for Augsburg. They remained there fifteen days and gave three concerts at which the audience was 'almost entirely composed of Lutherans'. From Augsburg they went to Ludwigsburg which was the summer residence of the Duke of Württemberg whose capital was Stuttgart. The Italian Jommelli[1] was Kapellmeister to the Duke and had raised the standard of music in Stuttgart to a high level. Leopold mentions his salary of four thousand gulden yearly and appointments to Hagenauer and says: 'What do you think of that for a Kapellmeister!' He did not succeed in getting the Duke to hear his children, for which he blamed Jommelli, declaring that he used his influence all for Italian music and musicians and did not believe a German musician could have real talent; but this seems to have been only imagination on Leopold's part for there is much evidence that Jommelli was an amiable man and not biased against Germans. In Ludwigsburg Leopold heard Nardini[2] play the violin and wrote enthusiastically to Hagenauer:

Tell Herr Wenzel that I have heard a certain Nardini play and that for beauty, cleanness and evenness of tone and for expressive *cantabile* nothing finer is to be heard.

From Ludwigsburg they went to Schwetzingen, the summer residence of the Elector Palatine, Karl Theodor, to whom they had introductions from Prince von Zweibrücken and Prince Clemens of Bavaria. The Court assembled to hear them on July 18th from five till nine o'clock and they made a great impression. Here Leopold heard for the first time the famous Mannheim orchestra; he writes:

---

[1] *Jommelli*, Niccolò (b. Naples, 1714; d. Naples, 1774), celebrated composer of the Neapolitan school.
[2] *Nardini*, Pietro (1722–93), famous violinist and composer, pupil of Tartini. Solo violinist and leader of the Stuttgart Court orchestra, 1753–67.

Schwetzingen,
July 19, 1763.

. . . I had the pleasure to hear besides good singers a remarkable flautist, Herr Wendling. The orchestra is without question the best in Germany – respectable young men, well-behaved, neither tipplers, gamblers nor boors, as praiseworthy for their behaviour as for their playing. . . .

Mainz,
August 3, 1763.

. . . We took a trip from Schwetzingen to Heidelberg to see the castle. . . . In the Church of the Holy Spirit Wolfgang played the organ to such effect that the Dean as a remembrance ordered his name to be inscribed upon it.

They did not appear at Court in Mainz owing to the illness of the Elector Joseph Emmerich von Breitbach but gave two concerts and made two hundred florins and then proceeded to Frankfurt.

Frankfurt,
August 20, 1763.

Our concert was on the 18th. It was good. All were astounded. On the 22nd, 25th and 26th we gave others. Wolfgang is quite extraordinarily lively but also naughty. Nannerl is no longer suffering in comparison; all speak of her and admire her skill.

I have bought a pleasing clavier from Herr Stein in Augsburg that has been of great service for practice on the journey.

Once since we have been travelling – I think it was in Augsburg – Wolfgang when he awoke in the morning began to weep. I asked him why and he replied that it was because the never saw Herr Hagenauer, Wenzel, Spitzeder, Deibel, Leitgeb, Vogt, Nazerl and other friends.[1]

The effect made in Frankfurt by the children may be gathered from the following newspaper notice which appeared on August 30, 1763:

The general astonishment awakened in all hearers by the never before seen or heard of ability of the two children of Herr Leopold Mozart, Kapellmeister at the Court of Salzburg, has necessitated the threefold repetition of the single concert originally intended. . . .

The little girl who is in her twelfth and the boy who is in his seventh year will not only play concertos on the clavecin or harpsi-

---

[1] Salzburg friends of the Mozart family. This charming touch reminds one of what one keeps forgetting—that Mozart on this tour was a child of seven.

chord and concertos by the greatest masters, but the boy will also play a violin concerto, will accompany symphonies on the clavier – the manual or keyboard being covered with a cloth – with as much facility as if he could see the keys; further, he will name exactly all tones singly or in chords given on the clavier or on any other instrument, bells, glasses, clocks, etc. Finally, he will improvise from his head on the harpsichord or organ in the most difficult keys as requested for as long as desired in order to show that he understands how to play the organ as thoroughly as the harpsichord though it is quite a different matter.

It is noteworthy that Goethe, then fourteen years old, a native of Frankfurt, heard Mozart at one of these concerts as he relates to Eckermann many years later:

> I saw him as a seven-year-old boy when he gave a concert. . . . I was about fourteen years old and I remember still quite distinctly the little fellow with his powdered wig and sword.

From Frankfurt they travelled to Coblenz, Bonn, Cologne and Aachen where the Princess Amalie, a sister of Frederick the Great, tried to persuade Leopold to take his children to Berlin. He writes to Hagenauer from Brussels on October 17, 1763:

> If the kisses which she bestowed on my children, especially on Master Wolfgang, had been *louis d'or* all would have been well but neither the hotel nor the post-horses can be paid with kisses. . . . Prince Karl [von Lothringen] has promised to hear my children but has not yet done so. He does nothing but hunt, eat and drink and so has no money. . . .
> If you have been astonished in Salzburg at my children you will be absolutely astounded when, if God wills, we return. . . .

From Brussels they travelled by post-horses, arriving on November 18, 1763, at Paris, where they lodged with the Bavarian Ambassador, Count von Eyck, whose wife was a daughter of Count Arco, the Chamberlain at Salzburg. They were introduced to the Court at Versailles where the most important person was Madame de Pompadour.[1] Leopold writes to the wife of Hagenauer at Salzburg as follows:

[1] Madame de Pompadour, mistress of Louis XV (1710–74). The Seven Years' War, in which France lost India and Canada to England, had just finished (1763). Rousseau (1712–78) had published *La Nouvelle Héloïse* (1760), *Émile* and *Le Contrat Social* (1762).

Paris,
February 1, 1764.

One must not always write to men but also remember the beautiful and devout sex. Whether the Paris ladies are beautiful I cannot surely say for they are contrary to nature, like the Berchtesgadner dogs, so painted that to the eyes of an honest German even a naturally beautiful person becomes insufferable through this detestable ornamentation.[1] . . . It is to be noted that here it is not the custom to show homage to the King or to any member of the Royal Family by bending the knee or head but one remains standing upright without the slightest movement . . . you can imagine what a sensation it must have caused the French when the King's daughter not only in her apartment but also in public on seeing my children let them kiss her hands and returned their kisses. . . .[2]

No doubt you would like to know what Madame the Marquise de Pompadour looks like? She must have been very beautiful for she still looks well. She is tall and stately, stout but well-proportioned, blonde and has some likeness to the Kaiserin about the eyes. She is very proud and has a remarkable mind. Her rooms in Versailles are like a paradise . . . and in Paris in the Faubourg St Honoré she has a wonderful house newly built. The room where the clavier stood, which was completely gilt and elaborately lacquered and painted, contains a life-size portrait of her and of the King.

What else! There is a permanent conflict between Italian and French music. All French music is worthless but they are beginning to alter it thoroughly . . . and in ten or fifteen years I hope to see the present French taste extinguished.[3] The Germans play mostly compositions of the masters, among whom Schobert,[4] Eckard[5] and Honnauer for clavier and Hochbrucker and Mayr for harp are very popular. Le Grand, a French clavier player, has quite given up his style and his sonatas are now according to our taste. Schobert, Eckard, Le Grand and Hochbrucker have brought their printed sonatas to us and made a present of them to my children. Four

[1] The 'honest' German has returned to life in the Third Reich (1932–   ). I find his bigotry more detestable than the very ancient and, to me, charming fashion for women of painting the face. [I leave W. J. T.'s note as it originally appeared in 1938. C. R.]

[2] An oil painting by Michel Barthélemy Ollivier, of Mozart at the clavier in the salon of Prince Conti, is in the Louvre at Paris.

[3] It is worth remembering that Rameau (1683–1764) died in Paris in the September of this year which Leopold is writing.

[4] Schobert, Johann (b. c. 1720; d. 1767), educated at Strasbourg, sometime organist at Versailles. According to Burney he was one of the few composers of his time not influenced by Philipp Emanuel Bach.

[5] Eckard or Eckardt, Johann Gottfried (b. Augsburg, 1735; d. Paris, 1809), a famous pianist and composer considered by Burney and Grimm to be superior as a pianist to his rival Schobert. He was also a brilliant miniature painter.

sonatas by Monsieur Wolfgang Mozart are now at the engravers.

Imagine the sensation these sonatas will make in the world when one sees on the title page that it is the work of a seven-year-old child and how when a proof is wanted of this incredible capacity, as has already happened, he will put a bass immediately to any minuet without touching the clavier and also, if wished, a second violin part! You will be able to hear how good these sonatas are. There is one *andante* of quite exceptional merit and I can assure you, Frau Hagenauer, that God daily performs new miracles with this child. . . . He accompanies and transposes at sight and reads any piece, French or Italian, that is put before him.[1]

My girl plays the most difficult pieces of Schobert and Eckard . . . with incredible clarity. . . .

These four sonatas, the first printed works of Mozart, were entitled:

> *Sonatas[2] pour le Clavecin qui peuvent se jouer avec l'accompagnement de Violon, dediées à Mme Victoire de France par J. G. Wolfgang Mozart de Salzburg âgé de sept ans. Œuvre première, à Paris aux addresses ordinaires.*

Another set of sonatas[3] were published with a dedication to the Comtesse de Tessé, lady-in-waiting to the Dauphinesse. This dedication was by Grimm,[4] author of *Correspondance Littéraire*, a German settled in Paris. He was for a time secretary to the Duke Orléans and had become an influential personage and rendered Leopold Mozart valuable assistance. Of this dedication Leopold writes to Hagenauer:

Paris,
April 1, 1764.

. . . In several days the Sonatas which Wolfgang has dedicated to Mme la Comtesse de Tessé will be ready. They would have been

---

[1] Lest this be thought paternal exaggeration the following notice by Suard (*Mélanges de littérature*, II, p. 337) may be quoted:

'He was from six to seven years old. I heard him play on the clavier at the *Concert Spirituel* and in private houses. He astonished all music-lovers by the facility and precision with which he executed the most difficult pieces. He accompanied at sight. He improvised on his instrument and produced the happiest melodies and already showed a profound feeling for harmony.'

[2] K. 6 and 7. Wyzewa and Saint-Foix give a careful analysis of these and the following Sonatas.

[3] K. 8 and 9.

[4] *Grimm*, Friedrich Melchior, Baron von (1723-1807), not be to confused with the brothers Grimm, collectors of fairy-tales, etc.

ready sooner but the dedication by our best friend, Herr Grimm, was not acceptable to the Comtesse and had to be altered. It is a pity ... the Comtesse and my boy were very vividly described in it but the fact is she will not have herself praised. ...

In this same letter he announces with satisfaction to Hagenauer that he will shortly receive from the Bankers, Turton & Baur, two hundred *louis d'ors*; also that he has had permission to give two public concerts in the *Théâtre de M. Félix, Rue St Honoré*, which is reserved by the King for the opera, plays and the *Concerts Spirituels*. He also mentions that a Baron von Bose, whom Leopold describes as being 'all that a truly noble man shall be in this world', has presented Wolfgang with Gellert's *Geistliche Oden und Lieder* in which he has inscribed:

Take, little seven-year-old Orpheus, this book from the hand of your admirer and friend. Read it often and know its divine songs; lend them in blessed hours of grace your irresistible harmonies so that the senseless scorners of religion may mark and perceive so that they hear and fall down and worship God.

(*Sgd.*)   FRIEDRICH KARL,
Baron von Bose.

Finally, he mentions the services of Grimm:

Mr Grimm alone, to whom I had a letter from a Frankfurt merchant, has done everything. He has fixed up the Court; he has looked after the first concert. He himself has paid me eighty *louis d'ors* for three hundred and twenty tickets he has disposed of and also defrayed the cost of the wax candles – there were more than sixty table candles. This Grimm has obtained the permission for the concert and will now look after the second for which one hundred tickets are distributed. See what a man can do who has sense and a good heart! He is from Regensburg. ...

Monsieur de Mechel, a copper engraver, is working day and night to engrave our portraits which Herr von Carmontelle, an admirer, has painted extremely well.[1] Wolfgang plays the clavier. I stand behind and play the violin and Nannerl has one arm on the clavier and with the other holds the music as she sings.

On April 10, 1764, Leopold and his wife and two children left Paris for London. At Calais they saw the sea for the first time and

[1] This charming picture by Carmontelle is now in the *Musée de Chantilly*. See Plate 5.

crossed not in the usual packetboat, which was full, but in a boat he chartered, arriving in London on April 23rd.

London,
May 28, 1764.

... On April 27th we were from six to nine o'clock with the King and Queen[1] in ... St James's Palace. The present was only twenty-four guineas but the favour which His Majesty and the Queen showed us is not to be described; one would never, in short, think that these friendly people were King and Queen of England – the way we have been received here surpasses everything. Eight days later we were walking in St James's Park. The King and Queen drove past and although we were in other clothes they recognized us. ... The King opened the window, nodded and smilingly greeted us, especially Master Wolfgang.

... On May 19th we were brought to Court and were from six to ten o'clock with the King and Queen. .... The King put before Wolfgang not only pieces by Wagenseil but also by (Christian) Bach, Abel, and Handel. He has played them all at sight. He played on the King's organ in such a way that they preferred it even to his clavier playing; he accompanied the Queen in a song and a flautist in a solo; finally, he took the bass of a Handel aria and improvised a most beautiful melody on it to the astonishment of all. In a word what he knew when we started from Salzburg is a mere shadow of what he knows now. It surpasses all imagination.

The Mozarts gave a concert on June 5th in a hall at Spring Gardens, near St James's Park, at the hour of twelve o'clock, out of which Leopold made a large profit, being able to send Hagenauer at Salzburg one hundred guineas on June 28th. He allowed Wolfgang to play at a charity concert in aid of the Lying-in Hospital on the Surrey side of Westminster whose foundation stone was laid in the following year (1765) but soon after this Leopold caught a severe chill and was ill for some time, retiring to Chelsea whence he writes:

Chelsea,
August 9, 1764.

... It is one of the loveliest prospects in the world. Wherever I look I see nothing but gardens and beyond the most beautiful houses. ...

[1] King George III and Queen Charlotte of Mecklenburg-Strelitz. The King was a great admirer of Handel's music and the Queen played and sang.

During his father's illness Wolfgang began composing symphonies,[1] and his sister relates that he said to her once as she was sitting near while he worked: 'Remind me to give something really good to the horn.'

They returned to Town in October and lodged in Frith Street, Soho. They were invited to Court again and on January 18, 1765, were published:

> *Six Sonatas pour le clavecin qui peuvent se jouer avec l'accompagnement de Violon ou Flaute traversière très humblement dediées à Sa Majesté Charlotte Reine de la Grande Bretagne, composées par J. G. Wolfgang Mozart âgé de huit ans Œuvre III London. Printed for the Author and Sold at his Lodgings at Mr Williamson in Thrift [Frith] Street, Soho.*

From the Queen, who had accepted the dedication, Leopold received fifty guineas, but the novelty of the child prodigies was wearing off. A concert was postponed to make room for Dr Arne's oratorio *Judith* and finally took place on February 21st at six o'clock in the small Haymarket theatre and Leopold informs Hagenauer that he has only made a profit of one hundred guineas,[2] being less than he expected. For a final concert on May 13th, announced as their last appearance before leaving London, Leopold was obliged to reduce the price for seats from half-a-guinea to four shillings. On this occasion Wolfgang played on a two-manual harpsichord which Tschudi[3] had made for the King of Prussia. The Italian opera under Giardini was then flourishing in London, and one of the favourite singers of the time, Manzuoli,[4] became a friend of the Mozarts and gave Wolfgang singing lessons. But the most important musical acquaintance made by the Mozarts was

---

[1] Mozart composed three symphonies during his stay in England:

B Flat, K.17	.	Chelsea, July–September, 1764.
E Flat, K.18	.	London, December–January, 1764–5.
D K.19	.	London, January–April, 1765.

The symphony in E Flat (K.18) is, according to Wyzewa and Saint-Foix, a copy of an overture by Abel.

[2] Let the young and inexperienced reader not be disturbed by this constant preoccupation of Leopold with money. The money was needed; his was miserable pay at Salzburg with no hope of more but only the prospect of an indigent old age.

[3] *Tschudi*, Burkat (b. Switzerland, 1702; d. London, 1773), celebrated harpsichord maker and founder of the house of Broadwood. He was the younger son of a noble Swiss family and came to England in 1718 as an ordinary journeyman joiner.

[4] *Manzuoli*, Giovanni (b. Florence, 1725), a successor of the famous Farinelli.

that of Johann Christian Bach,[1] the youngest son of J. S. Bach, whose opera seria *Adriano in Siria* was first produced in London at the King's Theatre on January 26, 1765, and was no doubt heard by Wolfgang, to whom he showed great kindness. Christian Bach was music-master to the Queen and it is related that he used to take Wolfgang on his knee and go through a sonata with him, playing each a bar in turn so precisely that one would not have suspected two performers. Also he began a fugue which Wolfgang completed.

A scientific examination of Wolfgang's powers was made by the Hon. Daines Barrington and the circumstantial report was published in *Philosophical Transactions*, 1770, Vol. XL, and reprinted in Barrington's *Miscellanies* (1781).[2] I take the following extracts from the latter:

... At seven years of age his father carried him to Paris where he so distinguished himself by his compositions that an engraving was made of him.[3] The father and sister who are introduced are exceedingly like their portraits; so is also little Mozart, who is styled: '*Compositeur et Maître de Musique âgé de sept ans*'. After the name of the engraver follows the date which is in 1764; Mozart was therefore at this time in the eighth year of his age.

Upon leaving Paris, he came to England where he continued more than a year. As during this time I was witness of his most extraordinary abilities as a musician, both at some public concerts and likewise having been alone with him for a considerable time at his father's house, I send you the following account, amazing and incredible almost as it may appear.

I carried to him a manuscript duet, which was composed by an English gentleman to some favourite words in Metastasio's opera of *Demofoonte*. The whole score was in five parts – viz. accompanyments for a first and second violin, the two vocal parts and a bass. I shall here likewise mention that the parts for the first and second voice were written in the counter-tenor cleff; the reason for taking notice of which particular will appear hereafter.

My intention in carrying with me this manuscript composition

---

[1] *Bach*, Johann Christian (b. Leipzig, 1735; d. London, 1782).
[2] It was published by J. Nichols and fronting the account of Mozart is a charming engraving of the seven-year-old child by T. Cook, with verses from Homer's *Hymn on Mercury*.
[3] This must be the engraving of Carmontelle's picture and it is interesting to have an eye-witness's testimony to its likeness.

was to hear an irrefragable proof of his abilities as a player at sight, it being absolutely impossible that he could ever have seen the music before.

The score was no sooner put upon his desk than he began to play the symphony in a most masterly manner, as well as in the time and stile which corresponded with the intention of the composer. I mention this circumstance because the greatest masters often fail in these particulars on the first trial. The symphony ended he took the upper part, leaving the under one to his father.

His voice, in the tone of it, was thin and infantine but nothing could exceed the masterly manner in which he sung.

His father, who performed the under part in this duet, was once or twice out, though the passages were not more difficult than those in the upper one; on which occasions the son looked back with some anger, pointing out to him some mistakes and setting him right.

He not only, however, did complete justice to the duet by singing his own part in the truest state and with the greatest precision: he also threw in the accompanyments of the two violins, wherever they were most necessary and produced the best effects. It is well known that none but the most capital musicians are capable of accompanying in this superior stile.

. . . When he had finished the duet he expressed himself highly in its approbation, asking with some eagerness whether I had brought any more such music.

Having been informed, however, that he was often visited with musical ideas, to which, even in the middle of the night, he would give utterance on his harpsichord; I told his father that I should be glad to hear some of his extemporary flights.

The father shook his head at this, saying that it depended entirely upon his being as it were musically inspired, but that I might ask him whether he was in humour for such a composition.

Happening to know that little Mozart was much taken notice of by Manzuoli, the famous singer who came over to England in 1764, I said to the boy that I should be glad to hear an extemporary *Love Song*, such as his friend Manzuoli might choose in an opera.

The boy on this (who continued to sit at his harpsichord) looked back with much archness,[1] and immediately began five or six lines of a jargon recitative proper to introduce a love song.

He then played a symphony which might correspond with an air composed to the single *affetto*.

It had a first and second part, which, together with the symphonies was of the length that opera songs generally last: if this ex-

[1] Connoisseurs will never understand the amusements of genius but it does not matter so long as they are sincere.

temporary composition was not amazingly capital, yet it was really above mediocrity, and showed most extraordinary readiness of invention.

Finding that he was in humour, and as it were inspired, I then desired him to compose a *Song of Rage* such as might be proper for the opera stage.

The boy again looked back with much archness and began five or six lines of a jargon recitative proper to precede a *Song of Anger*.[1] This lasted also about the same time with the *Song of Love*; and in the middle of it he had worked himself up to such a pitch that he beat his harpsichord like a person obsessed, rising sometimes in his chair.[2] The word he pitched upon for this second extemporary composition was, *Perfido*.

After this he played a difficult lesson, which he had finished a day or two before; his execution was amazing considering that his little fingers could scarcely reach a sixth on the harpsichord.

His astonishing readiness, however, did not arise merely from great practice; he had a thorough knowledge of the fundamental principles of composition as, upon producing a treble he immediately wrote a bass under it which when tried had a very good effect.

He was also a great master of modulation and his transitions from one key to another were excessively natural and judicious. . . .

The facts which I have been mentioning I was myself an eye-witness of. . . . Witness as I was myself . . . I must own that I could not help suspecting his father imposed with regard to the real age of the boy, though he had only a most childish appearance, but likewise had all the actions of that stage of life.[3]

For example, whilst he was playing to me a favourite cat came in, upon which he immediately left his harpsichord, nor could we bring him back for a considerable time.

He would also sometimes run about the room with a stick between his legs by way of horse. . . .

It must be repeated here that musical precocity is no indubitable sign of genius but only of a certain musical talent. Samuel Wesley, William Crotch and the father of the Duke of Welling-

[1] This worthy intellectual, Barrington, is a model of the intellectuals or 'high-brows' of all time; but he is a good model, one to which contemporaries of his kind should look up to if this attitude were within their capacity.

[2] Here we have the most illuminating piece of information. It is precisely in this passion that the *prodigy* Mozart showed his chief difference from other prodigies who have never fulfilled their early promise.

[3] Barrington made inquiries and obtained proof of Mozart's having been born in 1756 from the register in Salzburg. This examination was made in June 1765.

ton[1] were all musical prodigies almost as remarkable in their way as Mozart. It is a part of the materialistic philosophy of a certain type of mind common in every age among the educated (who of course display in this the fact that they are semi-educated, or what the Germans call *halbgedildete Leute*) to be always asking for a sign. These signs are to be supplied only on the lower planes, never on the higher ones. That is the reason why the true superiority of musicians such as Mozart, Schubert, Berlioz and Beethoven is even to this day invisible to a great many musicians and connoisseurs. The prowess of child prodigies has its proper uses and among them may be mentioned the fact that the seven-year-old Mozart's musical capacity was accepted in Vienna during the heyday of Jewish proselytization to Christianity as evidence that at the age of seven the circumcised had acquired the capacity of deciding to become baptised.[2]

Before leaving London Leopold presented to the British Museum a manuscript composition by Wolfgang for four voices, entitled *God is our Refuge*, which was acknowledged as follows:

Sir,
  I am ordered by the Standing Committee of the Trustees of the British Museum to signify to you, that they have received the present of the Musical performances of your very ingenious son, which you were pleased lately to make Them, and to return you their thanks for the same.

(Sgd.) M. MALY,

British Museum.   Secretary.
July 19, 1765.

The Mozart family left London on July 24, 1765, for Canterbury, where they stayed with Sir Horace Mann and finally left England on August 1st for The Hague at the pressing solicitation of the Dutch Ambassador, speaking for Princess Caroline of Nassau-Weilburg, sister of the Prince of Orange. They went from Calais to Lille when Wolfgang was ill with a severe cold. On the

---

[1] *Wellesley*, Garrett Colley, Earl of Mornington (b. 1735; d. 1781), composer of glees and madrigals.
[2] Hanslick *Geschichte der Konzertwesens in Wien*, Vienna, 1869. This has reference only to the age at which a child may be considered to be rational. There was no Jewish blood in Mozart as far as is known.

way to The Hague Wolfgang played upon the organ of the church
of St Bernard in Ghent and also in Antwerp Cathedral. No sooner
had they got to The Hague than Marianne and then Wolfgang fell
ill. Leopold writes to Hagenauer:

> Hague,
> November 5, 1765.
>
> . . . My poor daughter if not quite lost is in the last extremity . . .
> she caught cold the second day after our arrival, namely September
> 12th. At first it seemed slight . . . but on the 26th . . . she seemed to
> have fever in the throat . . . the doctor himself lost hope . . . on
> October 21st she . . . received the Last Sacrament. She was so weak
> she could hardly speak. Had anyone been able to hear the conversa-
> tion which we three, my wife, I and my daughter had together many
> evenings . . . he could hardly have refrained from tears. During
> them Wolfgang occupied himself in another room with his music.
>
> On October 21st the Princess of Weilburg sent to me the noble
> old Professor Schwencke who soon showed that he understood his
> craft better . . . the whole time my daughter was delirious and in her
> sleep talked English, French, German in such a way that in spite of
> our trouble we often had to laugh. That had the effect of relieving
> Wolfgang a little of his sadness on account of his sister. . . .

> Hague,
> December 12, 1765.
>
> . . . My daughter was hardly a week out of bed when [Wolfgang]
> fell ill and in four weeks was scarcely recognizable being reduced to
> nothing but bone and skin . . . on the 30th he was in danger but on
> December 1st better. After this he slept for about eight days and
> never spoke till at last his strength returned. Then he spoke day and
> night but quite unintelligibly. . . .

In Holland Wolfgang composed six sonatas[1] for piano and violin for the Princess of Nassau-Weilburg which were engraved; also
variations on the song *Wilhelmus von Nassau*[2] and other trifles
which were also published.[3] Wolfgang played in concerts at The
Hague and Amsterdam and Leopold's *Violin Method* was translated into Dutch and published with a dedication to the Prince of
Orange. From Holland they returned to Paris, arriving on May

[1] K.26–31.
[2] K.25.
[3] *Galimathias musicum in F* (K.32).

10th, and the two children, Marianne and Wolfgang, again played several times at Versailles. Wolfgang also composed on June 12th a Kyrie[1] for four voices with stringed accompaniment. Leaving Paris on July 9th with six post-horses they went to Dijon, staying there fourteen days at the request of the Prince of Condé on the occasion of the assembly of the Estates of Burgundy; then on to Lyons where they stayed a month, arriving at Geneva in the midst of the civil war.

In the following letter to Hagenauer Leopold remarks:

Munich,
November 10, 1766.

. . . You perhaps know that quite near Geneva the celebrated Voltaire[2] has a place called Fernay where he lives. . . from Lausanne we went to Berne and then to Zürich.[3] We stayed only eight days at the former and fourteen at the latter. In both places we had an opportunity to make the acquaintance of the intelligentsia;[4] at the latter the two learned Herr Gessners[5] made our stay very pleasant and our departure sad. . . . Thence via Winterthur to Schaffhausen. Here also our two weeks' stay was very pleasant.

In Donaueschingen His Highness [Prince Joseph Wenzeslaus von Fürstenberg] received us with extraordinary kindness . . . we were there twelve days; for nine days we had music from five to nine every night. . . . The Prince gave me twenty-four *louis d'or* and to each of my children a diamond ring. The tears streamed from his eyes as we took our leave of him. In short we all wept together at parting and he asked me to write often to him.

Then we went hell-for-leather via Messkirch, Ulm, Günzburg to Dilligen . . . after a day in Augsburg we arrived the night before last in Munich. . . .

[1] K.33.
[2] Voltaire (b. 1694; d. 1778).
[3] The Mozarts gave a concert at Zurich as they did in most of the larger towns where they made a prolonged stay.
[4] Leopold's word is *Gelehrten*.
[5] The physicist Johannes Gessner and the poet Salomon Gessner. The latter presented Leopold and his wife with a copy of his works, inscribed:

'Accept this gift, dear friends, in the same friendly spirit in which I offer it. May it preserve my memory fresh among you. May you, venerable parents, long enjoy the sight of the happiness of your children wherein consists the most precious fruit of their education; may they be as happy as their merit is extraordinary! In the tenderest youth they are an honour to their country and the admiration of the world. Happy parents! happy children! . . .

(*Sgd.*) 'SALOMON GESSNER
'Zürich, August 3, 1766.'

P.S. We beg you or rather your wife to find us a good maid-servant. . . .

God (the for me, unworthy man, all too-good God) has given to my children such talents as incite me – apart from the obligations of a father – to devote everything to their good education. Every moment that I lose is lost for ever and if ever I have realized how invaluable time is for the young it is now. You know that my children are accustomed to work. Should they become used to idle-ness my whole edifice is overthrown. Habit is an iron shirt and you yourself know how much my children, especially Wolfgang, have to learn. Who knows what our return to Salzburg brings. Perhaps we shall be received in such a way that we shall gladly take up our pack and set off again. At any rate I bring the children back to their Fatherland. If they are not wanted I am not to blame. . . .

On the way to Munich, at Biberach, at the request of Count Fugger von Babenhausen, Wolfgang competed on the organ with Sixtus Bachmann who was two years his senior and this compe-tition aroused great interest. In Munich Wolfgang was again taken ill and on his recovery the family returned to Salzburg at the end of November 1766, after an absence of more than three years.[1]

---

[1] They had left Salzburg on June 9, 1763.

CHAPTER THREE

Mozart's Development
as a Child

Age 7–10 (1763–6)

MOZART LEFT SALZBURG on his great European tour as a child prodigy at the age of seven and returned to Salzburg at the age of ten. During this period, as we have seen, he visited most of the principal towns of South Germany, of France, of Belgium and of Holland besides staying over a year in England. Apart from his public concerts he was frequently playing at Courts and in private houses. He also met most of the eminent musicians and composers in every city and was everywhere taken by his father to the opera and to the principal churches where there was music worth hearing. In addition he composed a quantity of music which comprises, in the old Köchel catalogue, numbers from K.6 to K.33; in addition to which we must add, according to Wyzewa and Saint-Foix, the twenty-five *Petites pièces de musique* (K. *Anhang* 109ᵇ) composed at Chelsea between April and December 1764, and the three Sonatas by Johann Christian Bach in D, G and E flat (K.107), arranged as Concertos with accompaniment of two violins and a figured bass.

It is worth briefly reviewing the chief musical contacts which he made during this three-year tour, some of which I have already mentioned in the previous chapter. At Stuttgart he heard the famous violinist Nardini and the orchestra under Jommelli. At Schwetzingen he heard the Mannheim orchestra, reputed the

best in Germany, the creation of J. W. A. Stamitz.[1] At Brussels
he was introduced to the sonatas of J. G. Eckard[2] who had settled
in Paris in 1758. Eckard was a pupil of Philipp Emanuel Bach
who took from his master the newly-conceived sonata form and
contributed to its evolution, namely to its principle of thematic
development and to its three-movement construction. Eckard
made much use of the Alberti[3] bass which enters largely into Wolfgang's sonatas composed in Paris and London. The sonata was a
musical product of mixed Italian-German origin and in the
eighteenth century music was as international as it is now, the influence of any inventive or originating mind spreading quickly
among all the musicians throughout Europe. More gifted as a
composer than Eckard was Schobert[4] who had settled in Paris in
1760 and had many of his compositions printed there. It was a
musical period in which the pianoforte was about to be substi-
tuted for the harpsichord, the sonata had already taken the place
of the suite and homophony was encroaching upon counterpoint.

---

[1] *Stamitz*, Johann Wenzl Anton (1717–1757), a Bohemian violinist and composer:
his brother, Anton Thaddeus, was a cellist in the Mannheim band.

[2] See note p. 30.

[3] *Alberti*, Domenico (b. Venice, 1710; d. Rome, 1740): he probably did not invent
the Alberti bass but he made such persistent use of it that it bears his name. It consists of breaking the notes of a chord conveniently for the left hand on the keyboard.
It is the popular tum-ti tum-ti bass.

[4] See note p. 30.

These are a few bars from the first *allegro* of the Sonata in C (K.6) composed by Wolfgang at Brussels on October 14, 1763.

Here we find that Alberti bass and the Sonata as a whole, according to Wyzewa and Saint-Foix, shows distinct traces of the style of Eckard, whose Six Sonatas for the Harpsichord were printed at Paris in May 1763, and were among the sonatas played in public by Wolfgang, so Leopold informs us.

Another composition of the seven-year-old Wolfgang written between June and October 1763, and probably also at Brussels, must be quoted, as it shows more than precocious skill. The manuscript written in Wolfgang's own hand is in the Mozarteum at Salzburg:

Andante (incomplete) in B flat for Harpsichord (K.9 b).

We know from Leopold's letters that Wolfgang met Eckard and Schobert in Paris and played their sonatas. Schobert was harpsi-chordist in the service of the Prince de Conti and possibly Schobert himself is among the figures in the salon of the Prince shown in the painting by Ollivier.[1] The French harpsichord players such as Le Grand and Charpentier were at this time all publishing sonatas in the German style, just as their theatrical music was under the influence of Italy. Schobert is claimed as a French composer by Wyzewa and Saint-Foix although his name suggests a Germanic origin[2] and he was educated at Strasbourg. However, his music was influenced by the French tradition and had a grace and sensitiveness which made it more attractive to

[1] Original in the Louvre.
[2] Grimm says: 'Schobert était Silésien.'

Wolfgang than the more learned and scholastic work of Eckard. According to Wyzewa and Saint-Foix, Schobert was the first composer to write sonatas for harpsichord with a violin part and is thus the creator of the modern sonata for pianoforte and violin. One of the signs of his influence on Wolfgang is that after his visit to Paris Wolfgang only published sonatas '*pouvant se jouer avec l'accompagnement du violon*'. It was from Schobert, according to the same authority, that Mozart got the practice of often using the minuet form for the finale of his sonatas.

But it was not so much the form of Schobert that influenced Wolfgang as the spirit, for the most striking characteristic of Schobert was his sensibility, with an inclination to the minor keys and to strongly pathetic and emotional expression and *tempo rubato*. Wyzewa finds in the first Sonata in D of Op. III of Schobert, published in Paris in 1764, hints of the Schubert of the 'Erl-King' and the 'Wanderer'. This access of sensibility in music was something rather new and we may find here, as we like, either the influence of Rousseau[1] or consider that it was just part of the general development of the Romantic spirit, the urge to a more natural and free expression of which Rousseau was only one of the manifestations. Musical historians and critics are apt to forget – if they ever knew – that Goethe's *Sorrows of Werther* was published in 1774 when Mozart was only eighteen years old and that, so far from belonging to a formal and so-called classical age or to the stiffest period of eighteenth-century routine or its final decadence in rococo triviality, Mozart was born in the *Sturm und Drang* period and belongs as completely and characteristically to the European Romantic revival as William Blake, who was born in 1757, the year after Mozart's birth. It was Mozart's father, Leopold, who belonged to the pre-Revolutionary epoch; whereas Mozart was twenty-four years younger than Beaumarchais[2] and

[1] *Rousseau*, Jean Jacques (b. Geneva, 1712; d. near Paris, 1778), author of the celebrated *Confessions*, *Emile* and *Le Contrat Social* (1762). Rousseau was also a composer and writer on music; his best-known composition was *Le Devin du Village*, produced at the Paris Opera on March 1, 1753, and often repeated until 1829 when some wag (supposed to be Berlioz who, however, denied it) gave it its death-blow by throwing an immense powdered perruque on the stage.

[2] *Beaumarchais*, Pierre-Augustin Caron de (1732–1799), author of the famous satire on the old régime, *Le mariage de Figaro* (1780).

the French Revolutionary spirit was in full flood during his life-time. Nearly all Lessing's[1] finest literary work, for example, was published during Mozart's childhood and the German writers of this new age – Klopstock, Wieland, Herder, etc. – were all Mozart's seniors.

The fact is that the picture some musical writers have been pleased to draw of Mozart as a highly-refined and sophisticated product of aristocratic eighteenth-century dilettantism, the last and over-delicate flower of salon culture, is historically as well as psychologically false. This, certainly, was the environment in which he was born but the seeds of revolution had already been sown. Voltaire had long ago done his great work, and was looked upon by Mozart's father as very little better than the devil, while Rousseau's *Le Contrat Social* was published when Mozart was six years old. Mozart's whole social outlook was entirely different from his father's and the difference in temperament is strikingly shown even when as an eight-year-old child in Paris in 1764 he was attracted to the music of Schobert by an affinity of nature, whereas his father, Leopold, did not approve of Schobert, des-cribing him as 'low and not at all what he should be. . . .'

Mozart is hardly likely to have come into contact with Rameau, whose *Castor et Pollux* was the piece with which the Paris opera reopened on January 23, 1764, for Rameau was an old man of eighty-one; his music was already out of fashion and Italian opera had become the vogue; the operas performed in Paris during the winter of 1763-4 while the Mozarts were there – which were more to the taste of the public – were by Duni,[2] Philidor[3] and Mon-signy.[4] It is worth noting that Philidor's famous *Le Sorcier*, just performed at the *Comédie-Italienne* on January 2, 1764, with enor-mous success, was influenced to some extent by Gluck's *Orphée*

---

[1] *Lessing*, Gotthold Ephraim (1729–1781), perhaps the greatest German writer between Luther and Goethe.

[2] *Duni*, Egidio Romoaldo (b. Naples, 1709; d. Paris, 1775).

[3] *Philidor*, François André Danican (b. Dreux, 1726; d. London, 1795), is con-sidered by some authorities to surpass his contemporaries Monsigny and Grétry as an operatic composer. He was a chess prodigy and at the age of eighteen was equal to the best masters and earned his living at the game. He wrote a well-known treatise, *Analyse du jeu des échecs*, which was translated into English.

[4] *Monsigny*, Pierre Alexandre (1729–1817), one of the best of French comic opera composers.

which had appeared in Vienna in 1762, but was not to be heard in Paris in the revised form until 1774. Monsigny had been inspired to the composition of comic opera by Pergolesi's[1] *La Serva Padrona*, which was first produced in Paris in 1746 but met with its real success on its revival there in 1752. The capriciousness of fame is shown in the fact that such an eminent musicologist as Professor Edward J. Dent considers Pergolesi to be inferior in comic opera to his contemporaries Leo and Logroscino, composers whose work is now known only to scholars and historians. But the idea that the best works are those which are most frequently performed one or more hundred years after they were written is as naïvely untrue as the idea that the best works are those which are most popular during their author's lifetime. The truth is contrary to both these superstitions and it is this – that there is always a general tendency for the best works to disappear from public sight or hearing and to be replaced by inferior ones; it is by dint of a constant effort made by the few that the best survives from generation to generation. Duni is said to have remarked to Pergolesi after the performance of his *L'Olimpiade*: 'Your opera is far too good to succeed', and whether true or not of this particular work this remark expresses an everlasting truth. Even today Mozart's *Die Entführung aus dem Serail* is more popular than the finer *Così fan Tutte*, for example.[2]

In England the Mozarts must have heard a great deal of the music of Handel who had only died five years before their arrival in London. We know that Wolfgang heard the overture to *Esther* and that during his visit Handel's *Messiah*, *Judas Maccabeas*, *Alexander's Feast*, *Israel in Egypt* and *Samson* were performed at Covent Garden, while Handel was the favourite composer at the Court of George III. But perhaps the chief influence on the child was that of John Christian Bach with whom Wolfgang was brought into close personal contact. Of all the sons of John Sebastian this, the youngest and so-called 'English' Bach, was the most Italianate; so that the Italian influence which was prevailing in Opera in Paris was reinforced in London, especially as the

[1] *Pergolesi*, Giovanni Battista (1710–1736).
[2] [This is probably still true, but much less so than when Turner wrote it. *C.R.*]

opera in London was wholly Italian, there being no English opera whatsoever.

Another composer he made contact with was Abel,[1] a pupil at the Thomasschule of J. S. Bach. Wolfgang actually transcribed in his own hand a symphony by Abel. This work in E flat (K.18) was for long considered as an original work by Mozart but was discovered by Wyzewa and Saint-Foix to be a transcription, without the change of a single note, of the last of the six overtures published by Abel as his Op. VII. An interesting fact is that in Mozart's transcript there are parts for two clarinets which in Abel's published score are written for oboes; but Wyzewa and Saint-Foix believe that this alteration was made later by Abel owing to the rarity in those days of the clarinet, whereas it is known that there were two clarinet players at the opera in London in 1763 used in J. C. Bach's *Orione*. Abel and J. C. Bach were close friends and collaborators and their influence is to be seen in Wolfgang's sonatas and symphonies composed in London. Of the symphonies composed by Wolfgang in London I shall quote only the first few bars of the Symphony in D (K.19) which was written in the spring of 1765 for two violins, alto, bass, two oboes and two horns. The horns are only used for doubling but the oboes have a definitely characterized part. This is the opening rhythmic subject:

[1] *Abel*, Karl Friedrich (b. Cöthen, 1725; d. London, 1787), a famous *viola da gamba* player and composer.

It is worth remarking that in these London symphonies – the first he composed – Mozart makes much use of alternations of *forte* and *piano* and occasionally of *mezzo forte, forte piano* and *sempre piano* marks, gives a certain independence to the alto and distinguishes the 'cellos from the double bass. From the careful analysis made by Wyzewa and Saint-Foix of these early compositions of Mozart, Abert drew the conclusion that Mozart arrived in London in 1764 a child of genius of nine years of age and left it in 1765 aged ten an accomplished master of the contemporary craft of composition equal to any living composer of the time. The extraordinary impressionability of Mozart, which is one of his outstanding characteristics, is shown by the way in which he was always being affected by and absorbing the music he met with and reflecting it in his own work. It is the opinion of Wyzewa and Saint-Foix that in Holland, after his departure from London, Wolfgang first came across the early clavier sonatas of Joseph Haydn which were first published by Breitkopf in 1766. It is certain that Haydn, who in this year was thirty-four years of age, was already well known as a composer outside his own country and symphonies and quartets of his were to be had in print in Amsterdam, Paris and London. The official gazette, *Wiener Diarium*, speaks of Haydn in 1766, as *der Liebling unserer Nation* (the darling of our nation) and compares him with Gellert, at that time not only Leopold Mozart's but the nation's most esteemed poet.[1]

It is worth mentioning here some observations made by Hermann Abert, based more or less on Wyzewa and Saint-Foix's exhaustive studies of Mozart's early music, but which even a cursory examination of Mozart's music and personality would support. 'The young Mozart,' he says, 'is not to be placed wholly in either of the two main groups into which most great composers fall; neither in form nor in expression does he appear as a conscious innovator but he is also just as free from having a fixed goal in the light of tradition. He is, indeed, the most impression-

---

[1] The habit of bracketing Haydn and Mozart together as if they were contemporaries overlooks this great discrepancy in their ages; actually Haydn belonged to the generation of Mozart's father, Leopold.

able of all the great composers. There was not a single musical influence of his age which he did not feel and in his youth, like the young Goethe, he gave himself up to them without reservation or plan, like a butterfly flitting from flower to flower.'

But this sensibility, as Abert properly takes care to add, was no sign of chaos or of lack of individuality. It was rather the discovery of himself in others and a sign of his quite extraordinarily catholic and universal nature. Mozart was never a mere imitator but he was so exceedingly many-sided that he found himself everywhere in the world of music that surrounded him.

CHAPTER FOUR

Salzburg and Vienna

Age 11–12 (1767–8)

LET US CONSIDER for a moment this prodigy of nature, Wolfgang Mozart, now returned to his home in Salzburg, a child of ten who is already not only an accomplished musician but a master-musician.

We know nothing of what literary or general instruction he received in Salzburg on his return but his musical instruction continued and he was soon kept busy with composition. On the exercises his father set him his lively fancy made him give names to parts such as *il Signor d'Alto, il Marchese Tenore, il Duca Basso,* and this same fancy constructed on his return journey homewards an imaginary kingdom, named by him *Rücken,* inhabited by children, of which he was King. What he imagined was so real to him that he got the servant, who happened to be a good draughtsman, to make a map of it which he furnished with names of places.

Wolfgang's study of counterpoint, directed by Leopold, was based on Fux's[1] *Gradus ad Parnassum* and his exercise book of eighty-two pages, now in the Mozarteum, consists chiefly of examples of two and three part counterpoint. His musical activity during the year 1767 in Salzburg may be judged from the fact that within this period he composed – at the command of the Archbishop Sigismund and on commission from other residents –

---

[1] *Fux*, Johann Joseph (b. Styria, 1660; d. Vienna, 1741), composer and theorist with a marvellous knowledge of counterpoint. His *Gradus* was published first in Latin in 1725, in German 1742, Italian 1761, French 1773, English 1791.

3. Mozart in 1782–3

4. Mozart in Gala Dress, 1763

one part of the oratorio *Die Schuldigkeit des ersten Gebotes*,[1] a
Latin cantata, a German cantata for Lent, an offertory, a *Licenza*
or festival music for the anniversary of the Archbishop's conse-
cration, a symphony, a serenade and a cassation (instrumental
music for the open air). In addition to these works the catalogue
made by his father in 1768 mentions the following compositions,
now lost – namely, six *Divertimenti* in four parts for various
instruments; six trios for two violins and violoncello and a number
of minuets, marches and fanfares for trumpets and kettle-drums.

It is not my intention to analyse these works or give detailed
particulars of them although I shall mention that the Latin
cantata was a sort of academic comedy presented at the Salzburg University on May 13, 1767, entitled *Apollo et Hyacinthus
seu Hyacinthi Metamorphosis*[2] which consisted of long, detached
airs and duets, recitatives, choruses and overture with a Latin
text. Mozart's Latin at eleven years old may be judged from the
following letter he wrote to Madame Hagenauer two years later,
which shows he was still studying it:

Dear Friend,
I beg your forgiveness for taking the liberty of troubling you with
these few lines; but since you said yesterday that you understood
everything and that I might write Latin to you as much as I liked I
cannot refrain from sending you at once some Latin lines: when you
have read them please send the answer back by one of your servants
for ours cannot wait. But you must send me the answer in a letter.

> *Cuperem scire, de qua causa, aquam plurimis adolescentibus ottium
> usque adeo aestimatur, ut ipsi se nec verbis nec verberibus, ab hoc
> sinant abduci.*

(*Sgd.*)   WOLFGANG MOZART

A quotation from the cantata entitled 'Grab-Musik, 1767' (K.42),
a dialogue between the Soul and an Angel, may be given as an

---

[1] *The Obligation of the First Commandment* (K.35), printed in Salzburg 1767. First
part, music by Herr Wolfgang Mozart aged ten years, second part by Herr Johann
Michael Heiden (Haydn), Court *Konzertmeister*, third part by Herr Anton Cajetan
Adlgasser, Court Composer and Organist. The autograph of this score in Mozart's
boyish writing was found by F. Pohl in the Royal Library at Windsor (A.M.Z.,
1865, p. 225).
[2] K.38. Manuscript autograph at Berlin, composed for two sopranos, two altos,
one tenor and choruses with accompaniment of two violins, two altos, two oboes,
two horns and bass.

C

example of what Mozart was composing at the age of eleven: the autograph is in Berlin:

On September 11, 1767, Leopold and his whole family set out on a visit to Vienna where the approaching marriage of the Arch-duchess Maria Josepha with King Ferdinand of Naples gave hope of festivities at which opportunities for making known the talents of Wolfgang might be plentiful. The letters from Leopold to Hagenauer provide the particulars of this journey. On September 22nd he writes from Vienna: 'Of our doings here I have nothing to report yet. Every day there is an opera seria or buffa or a comedy.' On the 29th he writes: 'Hasse's[1] opera *Partenope* is good but the singers are nothing special, particularly for such a festival . . . the dancing, however, is superb, the principal being the Frenchman, Vestris.'[2]

Unfortunately an attack of small-pox broke out in Vienna and the Archduchess Josepha caught it. This held up all their expectations: 'do not be surprised,' he writes from Vienna on October 14th, 'if we take out four hundred or even five hundred gulden. *Aut Caesar aut nihil!* A day will perhaps come that will alone pay for everything. We have not yet played anywhere because we have not yet played at Court.' His next news on October 17th was that the Archduchess had become 'a heavenly bride!' Leopold had been advised when in Paris to follow the example of the Duke of Orleans and have his children vaccinated but he wrote on February 22, 1764: 'I prefer to leave it all in God's hands; let him in his divine mercy dispose as he will of the life of this wonder of nature.'

Now, however, he and his family fled, but too late, from Vienna to Olmütz from whence he writes on November 10, 1767:

> *Te Deum laudamus!* Wolfgangerl has happily recovered from the small-pox. And where? In Olmütz. And where? In the house of His Excellency Count Leopold Anton von Podstatzky. . . . We reached Olmütz on Monday, 26th. To our disgust we had to put up with a bad, damp room in the '*Schwarzen Adler*' since all the others were taken. We were obliged to have a fire and, more vexation, the stove smoked so that we were almost blinded. At ten o'clock Wolfgang complained about his eyes. I noticed that his head was hot, also his cheeks, which were very red, while on the contrary his hands were icy cold. His pulse was also not normal. We gave him some *Schwarz-pulver* and put him to sleep. He was rather restless all night and still more hot and dry in the morning. We got two better rooms and wrapped Wolfgang in furs. . . . His temperature increased. We gave him *Mark-grafenpulver* and *Schwarzpulver*. Towards evening

[1] *Hasse*, Johann Adolph (b. Hamburg, 1699; d. Venice, 1783), the most popular German opera composer of the first half of the eighteenth century, a pupil of Porpora and A. Scarlatti.
[2] *Vestris*, Gaëtan Apolline Balthasar (b. 1729; d. 1808). He worked under Noverre, and in 1778 he danced in Mozart's ballet written for Noverre in Paris, *Les petits riens* (K.Anh.10[299b]).

he became delirious and remained so the whole of October 28th.

After Church I went to Count von Podstatzky, who received me most graciously, and told him that my little one was ill and I feared he might have small-pox whereupon he said he would take us in as he was not afraid at all of it. He called his housekeeper, instructed him to get two rooms ready and sent for a doctor. . . .

In the afternoon at four o'clock we wrapped Wolfgang in shawls and furs, put him in the carriage and took him to the Count's. On the 29th he had small red pock marks but we doubted he had small-pox as he seemed less ill. He took nothing but a powder every six hours and always *Skabiosentee*.

On the 30th and 31st on my birthday the small-pox came fully out and as soon as this happened all distemper was gone. And thank God he felt better. He was astonishingly swollen and had a thick nose. When at last he saw himself in the mirror he said: 'Now I look like Mayrl!', by which he meant the musician Mayr.

. . . I cannot describe the kindness and goodness with which we have been treated. I will ask how often it has happened that a whole family and child in such circumstances have been taken in and cared for out of pure humanity. This act will do no little honour to Count von Podstatzky in the biography of our little one that I intend to publish some day for I consider that a new epoch in his life begins now. . . .

No sooner had Wolfgang recovered from small-pox than his sister Marianne caught it; when she recovered they returned to Vienna. Wolfgang had to be careful of his eyes for some time – he had been blind for many days – and relieved his convalescence by learning to play cards and fencing. He was at all times very fond of bodily activity; as soon as he could compose again he wrote a little aria for the daughter of his physician, Wolf.[1]

They arrived back in Vienna on January 10, 1768, and were received at Court by the Empress Maria Theresia. 'His Majesty the Emperor,' writes Leopold to Hagenauer from Vienna on January 23, 1768:

came into the ante-chamber where we were waiting until they had had their coffee and himself led us in. There were present only Prince Albert of Sachsen-Teschen and the Archduchesses . . . you cannot imagine with what kindness the Empress spoke with my

[1] Leopold refers to this in a letter to his son ten years later, dated May 28, 1778, when he writes: 'From Ollmütz came Dr Wolf for whose daughter Wolfgang composed an aria. . . .'

wife about the children's illness and our great tour, pressing her hand and stroking her cheeks compassionately while the Emperor spoke with me and Wolfgang about musical and other matters and made Nannerl blush very often. You must not conclude from this affability that we shall get an exceptional present.

Leopold's realistic clear-headedness was not deceived; in spite of her geniality the Empress presented them with no more than a fine but valueless medal. Since the death of her husband the Empress had ceased to visit the opera or to give musical parties and musical commissions depended now upon her son, the Emperor Joseph, who was notoriously parsimonious. The Mozarts, however, had many friends at Court – namely, Count von Dietrichstein, the Master of the Horse, Fräulein Josepha Guttenburg, 'the Empress's right hand', the Court physician L'Augier, a talented and accomplished music-lover whose house was the meeting place of learned and cultured society, and, especially important, the Duke Johann Karl of Braganza, a man of spirit and character who had distinguished himself in the Lisbon earthquake and in the Austrian Army and to whom Gluck[1] dedicated, later, in 1770, his opera *Paride ed Elena*. It was now the carnival season and nothing was thought of but balls, masquerades and dances which it was the habit – according to Leopold – of the Court to farm out, sharing the profits with the contractors. Quite apart from this seasonal form of legitimate gaiety the Mozarts had other obstacles to contend with. One of them was the general low level of taste of the majority of the nobility and wealthy classes.

The pictures that some writers have drawn, looking back upon the eighteenth century from the depressing standpoints of their contemporary scenes in the nineteenth and twentieth centuries, are much too rose-coloured. The majority, as at all times and everywhere in the past (and as it will be in that Utopian future so dear to the young and enthusiastic), is always the same as in this respect – that its *niveau*, its habitual level, is lower than that of the truly superior minority. There is only one change which time and occasion brings with varying intensity and that is the degree

---

[1] *Gluck*, Christoph Willibald Ritter von (b. 1714; d. Vienna, 1787).

and extent of the majority's education. There are ages of wide-spread or lesser-spread culture; there are countries and towns more illiterate than others. The spread of education and literacy may add rather more opportunities to the many but it chiefly adds a new and even more potent barrier to the activity of the few; because for every one new and better-equipped appreciator of music, poetry or any other form of art it produces one hundred additional 'high-brows', intellectuals, connoisseurs, dilettantes – call them what you will – who are mere egoists devoid of either understanding, respect or love and who are the bitterest enemies of art and of artists although their talk is of nothing else. They have knowledge – the knowledge of dates, of periods, of aesthetic theories – and they have seen and heard everything but ex-perienced nothing.[1] Of all audiences this is the worst for the genuine artist but it comprises ninety per cent of what is described as the cultured audiences everywhere. The real tastes of such people are shown in their enthusiasms; they are never enthusi-astic about art; they know too much and their only pleasure is in airing their knowledge; but when it comes to their real pleasures on lower levels then they are not critical at all but extravagantly enthusiastic. In the twentieth century the real pleasures of such cultured people – 'high-brows', intellectuals, etc. – remain what they have always been. Let Leopold Mozart himself describe them. He writes to Hagenauer:

Vienna,
February 3, 1768.

The Viennese – to speak generally – are not eager for anything serious and sensible and have little or no understanding of it; that they care for nothing but utter trash, burlesques, harlequinades, ghost tricks, farces and devil's antics is well known and their theatres furnish proof of it daily. You may see a fine gentleman, even with an order on his breast, laughing till the tears run down his face and applauding with all his might some senseless buffoonery or simple joke while in a most affecting scene where the situation and action are irresistibly fine and stirring and where the dialogue is of the

---

[1] 'What is a connoisseur?' asked Oscar Wilde rhetorically, and replied with pro-found truth: 'A man who knows the price of everything and the value of nothing.' One might add 'date' to 'price'.

highest order he will chatter so loud with a lady that his better-disposed neighbours cannot hear a word. . . .

This, Leopold tells Hagenauer, is the chief cause of their difficulties; another is the character of the Court with its parsimonious Emperor. He also describes amusingly the fear of small-pox which prevented Prince Kaunitz, a well-known musical connoisseur, from doing anything for them, as he ran from all who showed a trace of it and Wolfgang, adds Leopold, 'has still many red spots, small, it is true, but clearly visible in the cold weather'. In this same letter of February 3, 1768, Leopold continues:

As I now reflected over these matters and thought on how much money I had spent and that to return home now without further waiting would be great cowardice, there was a new development. I found that all the clavier-players and composers in Vienna were opposed to us with the single exception of Wagenseil[1] who being ill, however, could be of little use to us. The tactics these people used were to avoid carefully any opportunity of seeing us and of learning the extent of Wolfgang's capacity. And for what reason? In order that when asked whether they had heard the boy and what they thought of him they might be able to reply that they had not heard him and that what was said of him could not be true, but must be an imposture or humbug and that what he was given to play was prepared and it was ridiculous to suppose he could compose. You see that is why they avoid us, for if they saw and heard him then they could not talk thus without endangering their honour.

But I set a trap for one of these gentry. I persuaded someone to give us private notice of when he would be present and to induce him to bring an exceptionally difficult Concerto which should be put before Wolfgang. We arrived and he had the opportunity of hearing his Concerto played by Wolfgang as if he knew it by heart. The astonishment of this clavier-player and composer, his expression and his exclamations in his amazement made us all realize the truth of what I have already told you. In the end he said: 'As an honest man I can only say that this boy is the greatest musician living in our time in the world. I could not have believed it.'

And so to convince the public of what it has before it I determined

---

[1] *Wagenseil*, Georg Christoph (b. Vienna, 1715; d. 1777), famous clavier-player and composer, music-master to the Empress Maria Theresia. When Wolfgang, aged six, in Vienna on his first visit, was playing before the Court, he inquired: 'Is not Herr Wagenseil here? He knows all about it,' and when Wagenseil came forward said to him, 'I am playing one of your concertos, you must turn over for me.'

on something quite exceptional, to wit, that Wolfgang should compose an opera. Can you imagine the outcry that arose among the composers? 'What! shall we hear Gluck[1] today and tomorrow see a boy of twelve years of age at the harpsichord and conduct his own opera?' Yes, and in spite of all braying idiots! I have even brought Gluck on to our side, at least so far that even if he is not wholehearted he can't let it be noticed since our protectors are also his. And in order to secure the actors, who habitually cause most vexation to the composer, I have spoken with them myself and one of them will keep me informed. The first idea to let Wolfgang write an opera came to me in truth from the Emperor himself since he twice asked Wolfgang whether he would like to compose an opera and conduct it himself. Wolfgang replied eagerly: 'Yes. . . .' But it will not be an opera seria, for no more are being given and they are not popular, but an opera buffa. Not a short one but one lasting two-and-a-half to three hours. For opera seria there are no singers. Even Gluck's tragic opera *Alceste* has been performed by opera buffa singers. Now Gluck is writing an opera buffa. The opera buffa singers are excellent.[2] . . . What do you think of this? Is not the renown of having written an opera for Vienna the best way to win credit not only in Germany but also in Italy?'

A few words on opera seria, opera buffa and singspiel are needed here, as these terms will often recur. At this stage, however, I shall only say briefly what is necessary. Opera seria means roughly serious opera, which in the early eighteenth century had a rather stereotyped form, consisting of recitatives and arias with the leading rôles taken by *castrati* (i.e. artificial male sopranos); opera buffa was a more popular form derived from the lighter *intermezzi* with which opera seria was interspersed, its structure was also made up of recitatives and arias but bass voices were introduced and given important rôles. The difference between opera buffa and singspiel is that the latter is a German form in which the music plays a less important dramatic and a more lyrical part; also in singspiel there is usually, though not always, spoken dialogue in the place of the recitative *secco*[3] or *stromentato*[4] of opera buffa.

[1] Gluck's *Alceste* had been produced in Vienna on December 16, 1767, i.e. only about a month before the time of Leopold's writing.
[2] Leopold names eight singers, all Italian.
[3] *Secco*: dry or bare; i.e. in free verbal rhythm spaced with accompanying chords.
[4] *Stromentato*: instrumental; i.e. with a more musical rhythmic accompanying pattern.

All these forms were in full development in Italy, Germany and France in Mozart's childhood.

The novelty of *Alceste* which Leopold and Wolfgang had heard in Vienna during this visit consisted chiefly in the genius of Gluck. In principle he was only composing an opera seria in accordance with the ideas of Benedetto Marcello who in his *Teatro alla Moda* (1720) appealed for dramatic propriety in opera. Marcello was a poet as well as a composer and his ideals in opera have been those of every great operatic composer at all times. They can be simply summed up in one sentence from Gluck's celebrated preface to *Alceste* which runs as follows:

I endeavoured to reduce music to its proper function, that of seconding poetry by enforcing the expression of the sentiment and the interest of the situation without interrupting the action or weakening it by superfluous ornament.

I have elsewhere[1] remarked that there is only one word wrong in this famous sentence of Gluck's and that is the word 'reduce', which should be changed into 'heighten' or 'raise'. For music can have no higher goal than expression; when it becomes mere abstract pattern or 'ornament' it sinks to the level of the decorative, which in all the arts is on a lower plane than the expressive.

But Gluck's use of the word 'reduce' is an unwitting sign of the limitations of his musical genius – which is a matter I shall have cause to speak about when I am dealing with the great operas of Mozart's maturity.[2] It suffices to say here that in dramatic truthfulness and power of expression Gluck's *Alceste*, when first produced in Vienna on December 16, 1767, was far superior to all contemporary operas. Yet it did not escape the fate of most great works on their first appearance, as we learn from Sonnenfels, in his *Gesammelte Schriften*, who mimics the gossip of the nobility in the boxes of the Vienna Opera-house as follows:

What! this is meant to be pathetic? Well, perhaps we shall shed a few tears presently – from *ennui*.

Come, this is throwing money away! It is too absurd, a fool of a woman dying for her husband!

[1] *Berlioz, the Man and his Works* (Dent, 1934).
[2] See note p. 309.

This is typical of the stuff talked by the 'snobs' throughout the ages.

Through the recommendation of the Emperor and the influence of his Court friends Leopold was able to get a contract from Affligio,[1] the *entrepreneur* who held the lease of the theatre, for Wolfgang to compose an opera to a text by Marco Coltellini who had been 'Theatrical Poet' in Vienna since 1758 and had written librettos for Gassmann,[2] Hasse and Salieri.[3] Coltellini delivered the text and Wolfgang set to work on his first opera, *La Finta Semplice* (K.51), to try to get it completed by Easter 1768, and in due course finished his score of three acts containing twenty-five numbers, written on five hundred and fifty-eight pages.

Even before the opera was finished the usual intrigues inseperable from theatrical enterprise began. Affligio put them off from Easter to Whitsuntide and as soon as one difficulty was disposed of another arose. At length Affligio declared that he would put on Wolfgang's opera if Leopold insisted but would take care to have it hissed off the stage. In the meantime Leopold's long absence from Salzburg was endangering his position as first violin and assistant *Kapellmeister*; he was told he might stay away as long as he liked but that he would no longer be paid during his absence. He writes to Hagenauer:

Vienna,
July 30, 1768.

. . . Nothing but our honour keeps us here; otherwise we should long since have been in Salzburg. Would you like the whole of Vienna to be saying that Wolfgang was not able to finish the opera or that it had turned out so badly that it could not be produced or that his father, not he, had written it? Would you care to have such lies spread in all countries. . . .

What does His Majesty the Emperor say to it all? On this point I can only touch briefly . . . the theatre is leased or rather given over

[1] *Affligio*, Giuseppe, one of the tribe of impresarios so necessary to the theatre; an adventurer who obtained a commission in the army by swindling and ended his life in the galleys for forgery. He had a good run on other people's money and was probably superior to most of his critics.

[2] *Gassmann*, Florian Leopold (b. Bohemia, 1729; d. Vienna, 1774), composer, and in 1772 appointed Court *Kapellmeister* by the Emperor Joseph II.

[3] *Salieri*, Antonio (b. Legnago, 1750; d. Vienna, 1825), a pupil of Gassmann, composer and Court *Kapellmeister* after Gassmann's successor, Bonno.

to Affligio who must pay annually one thousand gulden which the Court otherwise would have to pay. The Emperor and his whole family have the right of free entry. Consequently the Court cannot say a word to this Affligio as he takes all the risks. . . .

The singers, who in any case scarcely know their notes . . . and must learn by ear, now began to say they could not sing their arias (which they had already heard in our room, approved of and applauded) as they were not suitable, the orchestra that it would not be conducted by a boy, etc., etc.

Meanwhile others declared the music was not worth a groat . . . because the boy did not sufficiently understand Italian. When I heard this I let it be known in important quarters that Hasse and the great Metastasio[1] had declared that these caluminators might come to them and hear from their own lips that thirty operas had been produced in Vienna which in no single number reached the level of this boy's, which they both admired extremely.

As to the idea that the father not the boy had composed it . . . I took the opportunity to open a volume of Metastasio and put the first aria I came to before Wolfgang. He took his pen and wrote, without reflection, in the presence of the onlookers, music to it with many instruments at an astounding pace. He did this in the presence of the *Kapellmeister* Bonno, the Abbé Metastasio, Hasse, the Duke of Braganza and Prince Kaunitz. . . .

Had it been an opera seria . . . I should have departed and presented it to His Grace (the Archbishop of Salzburg) but as it is an opera buffa and one that requires special buffa character I must save our honour here, cost what it will. . . .

I am responsible to Almighty God in this affair, otherwise I should be the most ungrateful creature. And if ever I were responsible for convincing the world of this miracle it is just now when one ridicules all that is wonderful and denies all miracles. They must be convinced. Was it not a great joy and a great victory for me to hear a Voltairean[2] say to me in amazement: '*Now I have for once in my life seen a miracle. And it is the first.*' Just because this marvel is so visible and undeniable they would suppress it. They will not allow God to have the glory of it. They think to themselves that in a few years it will pass into the category of the normal and cease to be a miracle of God. . . .

---

[1] *Metastasio*, Pietro (b. Rome, 1698; d. Vienna, 1782), Italian poet and the most famous of all opera librettists. Burney describes him at the age of seventy-four (in 1772) thus: 'For that time of life he is the handsomest man I ever beheld. There are painted on his countenance all the genius, goodness, propriety, benevolence and rectitude which constantly characterize his writings. I could not keep my eyes off his face, it was so pleasing and worthy of contemplation.'

[2] Grimm, in Paris, speaking of Wolfgang in 1764, when he was eight years old.

You may well wonder why Prince Kaunitz and others, even the Emperor himself, do not order the opera to be produced . . . actually Prince Kaunitz against the wishes of the Emperor had induced Affligio to bring the French comedians here which cost him over seventy thousand gulden . . . for which Affligio puts the blame on Prince Kaunitz who, however, hoped . . . to get the Emperor to make good the loss with the result that His Majesty has not been inside a theatre for many weeks . . .

On September 21st Leopold lodged a formal complaint against Affligio's non-fulfilment of his contract to the Emperor through the Court Director of Music, Count Johann Wenzel Spork, but it was fruitless. It has been estimated[1] that Leopold brought back to Salzburg about seven thousand gulden from his three years' tour through Europe, to say nothing of the costly presents, most of which the sensible Leopold sold although some remained in the family, notably the two rings – given to Wolfgang respectively by the Empress Maria Theresia at Schönbrunn and by the Prince Archbishop at Augsburg – which are now in the Mozarteum. Although the year of 1768 spent in Vienna must have been expensive, it is thought that enough remained of the gains of the prodigy children's tour to finance the later visits to Italy made by Leopold and Wolfgang, for which he was already preparing in Vienna.

In the meantime Wolfgang received a commission which must have partly compensated for the non-performance of his opera buffa La Finta Semplice. This came from a Dr Anton Mesmer[2] who had built a little theatre in his garden and some time in the late summer of 1768 had the commissioned work, Bastien und Bastienne (K.50), performed there. In addition to these two operas Wolfgang composed three symphonies between the departure from Salzburg and his return there from Vienna, namely:

Symphony in F (K.43) for two violins, two altos, 'cellos, bass, two obes (or flutes) and two horns;

[1] By Schurig.
[2] This was the celebrated Friedrich Anton Mesmer (1733–1815), promulgator of the theory of animal magnetism who added the word 'mesmerism' to our language and is one of the long line of distinguished Austrian physicians who, culminating in our time in Siegmund Freud, have added to the gaiety of the world.

Symphony in D[1] (K.45) for two violins, alto, 'cello, bass, two
  oboes, two horns, trumpets and kettle-drums, dated Vienna,
  January 16, 1768;

Symphony in D (K.48) for seven violins, alto, bass, two obes, two
  horns, trumpets and kettle-drums, dated Vienna, December
  13, 1768.

Another commission came Wolfgang's way. It was for a Mass
from an acquaintance of the Mozarts, the famous Jesuit, Father
Ign. Parhammer, who had been zealous in purifying the country
after the emigration of Protestants from Salzburg in 1733. He was
Director of the Orphan Asylum where the musical education of
the orphans was only secondary to their religious instruction, so
much so, in fact, that they were occasionaly employed in the opera.
For Father Parhammer, on the occasion of dedicating a new chapel,
Wolfgang composed a Solemn Mass with four trumpets, which
was performed in the presence of the Emperor as the following extract from the *Wienerischen Diarium* of December 10th records:

On Wednesday 7th His Imperial Majesty with the Archdukes
Ferdinand and Maximilian and the Archduchesses Maria Elizabeth
and Maria Amelia visited the Orphan Asylum in the Rennweg to
be present at the festival service and dedication of the newly-
erected Chapel. . . .[2]

The entire music, sung by the choir of orphans, was newly-
composed for the occasion by Wolfgang Mozart the twelve-year-old
son of the Salzburg Kapellmeister, Herr Leopold Mozart, well
known for his extraordinary talent; it was conducted by the composer himself with the utmost correctness and received with general
applause and admiration.

The music of this Mass is lost so that Mozart's earliest extant
Mass is the *Missa brevis* in G for four voices, quartet and organ
(K.49), composed afterwards in the month of December 1768.

Shortly after this the Mozarts left Vienna and returned to Salzburg.

[1] This Symphony in D was later transformed into the Overture to *La Finta
Semplice*. In this work Wyzewa and Saint-Foix see the disappearance of Paris and
London influences to give place to German and Viennese ones.

[2] The notice goes on to say that the royal party was received by His Eminence the
Cardinal Archbishop and attendant clergy 'amid the liveliest fanfares of trumpets
and drums and the firing of guns and cannon'. The world has sadly deteriorated
since the days when Orphan Asylums were opened in this manner.

CHAPTER FIVE

First Operas and other Compositions

Age 13 (Salzburg, 1769)

SIGISMUND, COUNT OF Schrattenbach, Archbishop of Salzburg, was a very different man from his successor, the Archbishop Hieronymus, who was to play such an unpleasant part later in Mozart's life. He was proud of his Salzburg prodigy and gave orders for Wolfgang's opera to be performed in the palace. The programme, which Köchel discovered, was as follows:

La Finta Semplice Dramma Giocoso per Musica
Da rappresentarsi in corte per ordine di S. A. Reverendissima
Monsignor
Sigismondo Arcivescovo
e Prencipe
di Salisburgo
Prencipe del S.R.I.
Legato Nato della S.S.A.
Primate della Germania e dell antichissima famiglia
dei conti di SCHRATTENBACH. etc., etc.
Salisburgo Nella Stamperia di Corte 1769

Personaggi:

Fracasso, Capitano Ungarese	Ninetta Cameriera
Il Sig. Giuseppe Meisner.	La Sig. Maria Anna Fösömair.
Rosina Baronessa Sorella di	Don Polidoro Gentiluomo sciocco
Fracasso, la quale si finge	Fratello di Cassandro
Semplice	Il Sig. Francesco Antonio
La Sig. Maria Maddalena	Spizeder.
Haydn.	Don Cassandro Gentiluomo sciocco

Giacinta, sorella di Don
  Cassandro e Don Polidoro
La Sig. Maria Anna
  Braunhofer.

ed Avaro Fratello di Polidoro
Il Sig. Giuseppe Hornung.
Simone Tenente del Capitano
Il Sig. Felice Winter.

Tutti in attual servizio di S. A. Reverendissima, etc.
La Musica è del Signor Wolfgango Mozart in Età di Anni dodici.

Of the libretto of Mozart's first opera I shall give no details. Most of these contemporary books for Italian operas were, as Wyzewa and Saint-Foix put it, 'veritable *tours de force* from the point of view of futile complication'. *La Finta Semplice* (K.51) is a masterpiece from this point of view, which 'Mozart himself [aged twelve!] had some difficulty in understanding'. As for the music which Wolfgang composed in four months (April to July 1768) it consists of twenty-one airs, three finales, one duet and one chorus. The manuscript is in Berlin. The libretto was not one to stir the interest of Wolfgang (two out of the four male characters are described as 'stupid') and it is worth remarking that Wyzewa and Saint-Foix consider that, although Mozart put poetry and charm into some of the lover's airs, what he expressed with most justness and 'remarkable musical beauty' are the comic sentiments, the cowardice and drunkenness of the old Cassandro, the droll spleen of the valet Simone and the remarks of the soubrette Ninetta to whose music he gives the light and lively form of *petites chansons*. It may be worth quoting a few bars from one

beautiful air given to Rosine, No. 15 in which strings and bassoons
are combined with delightful effect.

After the performance of *La Finta Semplice* the Archbishop
appointed Wolfgang to be *Konzertmeister* and this was entered in
the Court Calendar of 1770.

The singspiel *Bastien und Bastienne* was a one-act opera of the
new kind of which Rousseau's *Le Devin du Village*[1] was the prototype, influencing Philidor's *Le Sorcier* and Monsigny's *Rose et
Colas* which had been produced with great success in Paris during
the Mozarts' visit there. A German variety of this new form of
simple, natural and less conventionalized opera – which had
developed in Italy out of the popular intermezzos played between
the acts of the more exalted and ambitious opera seria as a sort of
sop to the groundlings – had been introduced to Vienna by J. A.
Hiller.[2] These were Wolfgang's models when he composed
Bastien und Bastienne in 1768, but whether before or after *La
Finta Semplice* is not quite certain. The likeliest is that it was
composed partly before and partly afterwards.

The text of Wolfgang's singspiel was based on a parody of
Rousseau's *Le Devin du Village*[3] which had been performed first
in 1752 before King Louis XIV at Fontainebleau and then before
the *Académie Royale de Musique* in Paris on March 1, 1753, with
enormous success. Everybody from the King downwards was
soon singing *J'ai perdu mon serviteur*, and even twenty years later,
in 1774, Rousseau's singspiel rivalled Gluck's *Orfeo* in success
with the Paris public.

The parody of Rousseau's work appeared at the *Théâtre des
Italiens* on September 26, 1753, with the title *Les Amours de
Bastien et Bastienne*. Rousseau had aimed at natural feeling and
unity of tone, expressed in flowing melodies and intelligible reci-

[1] See p. 46 n. 1.
[2] *Hiller*, Johann Adam (b. Prussia, 1728; d. 1804), originator of the Leipzig
Gewandhaus concerts, formerly *Concerts Spirituels*, founded the German *Singspiel*
based on the simple *Lied* (song) as the French operettas were based on the French
chanson. Successor to Doles as Cantor and Director of Bach's *Thomasschule* in
Leipzig.
[3] The origin of this piece is described by Rousseau himself in the eighth book of
his *Confessions*.

tatives with a certain general character of Arcadian idealism.
Rousseau's plot is as follows:

> Colette, a village maiden, inconsolable for her faithless swain,
> goes to a soothsayer who tells her that Colin has been seduced by
> the lady of the manor but still loves Colette and will return to her.
> She must punish him and inflame his desire by assumed indifference.
> The soothsayer informs Colin that Colette loves another, whereupon
> he begs for help and the soothsayer undertakes to summon Colette
> by magic. Colette appears and plays the prude, whereupon Colin
> rushes off in despair but she recalls him and scenes of reconciliation
> follow in which the soothsayer is rewarded and the villagers share
> in the joy of the lovers.

The parody was written by Harny in collaboration with the
gifted singer and actress Madame Favart and as a parody it carried Rousseau's naturalism still further and made the characters
real peasants. Madame Favart appeared (and was the first to do
so on the stage) in linen peasant clothes, with bare arms and
wooden sabots and made a sensational hit. The character of the
parody may be judged from the first air of Collette, which in
Rousseau's original has the words: '*J'ai perdu tout mon bonheur*',
whereas Bastienne sings: '*J'ai perdu mon ami*', to the tune of a
popular song, '*J'ai perdu mon âne*'. In 1764 a German translation
was made by Weiskern and this was the text used by Mozart
with certain alterations made by Schachtner. Compared with its
predecessors and contemporaries in German singspiel Mozart's
has a more pastoral and less burlesque character. It was composed with an orchestral part for two violins, alto, two oboes,
two horns, two flutes and bass and consists of eleven arias, two
duets (the duets are confined to the singing of the melody in
thirds when the two characters sing together) and a trio which is
of a more developed type. The recitatives were composed later
(1769) in Salzburg. *Bastien und Bastienne* is a charming work and
may still be heard with pleasure. I have heard it performed by an
Italian marionette opera company with excellent effect.

Instead of quoting any of the music of *Bastien und Bastienne* I
shall give the principal theme of the opening allegro of the Symphony in D (K.48) composed in Vienna at the end of 1768 just
before returning to Salzburg.

Wyzewa and Saint-Foix remark that here we may find a trait characteristic of Mozart at this period, i.e. of giving to the violins sudden and frequent leaps upwards or downwards. The andante is a true German *Lied* but with a variation section treated contrapuntally, the minuet, according to the same authorities, shows the influence of Joseph Haydn, the trio is bizarre in rhythm, the finale has a multiplicity of ideas and the whole work 'is new, deeply original with a breadth of inspiration that we shall not find again during the succeeding period even in the instrumental works of Mozart's first sojourn in Italy'.

Apart from his musical compositions practically nothing is known of how Wolfgang was ocupied during his thirteenth year (1769) spent in Salzburg. Among the works of this period is a *Missa Brevis* in D minor (K.65) composed in January 1769, and a Mass in C (K.66) composed in October of the same year for his friend Dominikus Hagenauer who had become a priest and was the son of Leopold's Lorenz Hagenauer. This latter Mass was the first which broke to some extent with the older style of ecclesiastical music and showed the influence of the developments which had taken place in operatic and symphonic music. It may be interesting to see a few bars from the *Missa Brevis* in D minor written for four voices, two violins, bass and organ. Here is the opening of the *Kyrie* and of the *Dona nobis*:

In addition to these Wolfgang composed the Cassation[1] in G (K.63) for two violins, two altos, bass, two oboes (or flutes) and two horns; he also wrote many others which have not survived. Cassations and serenades were a Salzburg speciality and his fellow-citizens frequently called upon Wolfgang to compose this sort of charming and delightful music for their festival occasions. As early as 1684 in a travel book published in Nuremberg a Dr Browne remarks on the fact that in Vienna 'not a night passed without one hearing a *Nachtmusik* under our windows'.

Towards the end of the year 1769 Leopold was preparing to take his son to Italy and on December 13, 1769, Leopold and Wolfgang, now aged thirteen and eleven months, left Salzburg on their first Italian tour.[2]

---

[1] There is considerable doubt about the derivation of this word, but in the eighteenth century it was used for a piece of instrumental music played in the open air, and some derive it from the German *Gasse* – a street. Perhaps it implies a farewell. This work is also described as Divertimento (Final-Musik).

[2] In the Salzburg Court Calendar of November 27, 1769, appeared the following announcement:

'*Hodie Dominus Wolfgangus Mozart iuvenis 14 annorum cum facultate abeundi Italiam literam decretoriam accepit, quod sit in posterum Concert-Maister cum promisso quod post reditum ex Italia iam sit competentem huic officio pensum percepturus.*'

CHAPTER SIX

The First Italian Tour

Age 13–15 (December 13, 1769 – March 28, 1771)

THIS FIRST ITALIAN tour, unlike the grand European tour, was undertaken by Leopold and Wolfgang alone, leaving Wolfgang's mother and sister at home in Salzburg. Wolfgang is approaching his fourteenth birthday and now we shall have his own letters home as well as his father's to quote from.

In the eighteenth century musicians from all parts of Europe went to Italy as the head-spring and fountain of musical life just as in the nineteenth century they went from all parts of the world to Germany. Owing to the number and independence of large and important cities with their rival princely and episcopal courts there existed throughout Italy a magnificent and widespread organization for the production of music. Music had become the national art and the taste for it was more generally diffused among the population than in any other country. Music, as known in Europe since the Dark Ages following on the collapse of the Roman Empire, originated in Italy – notation and all – and was an entirely new art. The richly-endowed monasteries and churches rivalled the court theatres in their support of music and, indeed, the musical instruction of the young was largely given in religious institutions. In Venice alone there were four special foundations in which boys and girls received musical tuition preparatory to their service in the Church, namely, the *Ospedale della Pietà*, intended for foundlings; the *Ospedaletto*, of which Sacchini[1] was at

---

[1] *Sacchini*, Antonio Maria (b. near Naples, 1734; d. Paris, 1786), famous opera and church composer, son of a fisherman, studied at San Onofrio, Naples, through the influence of Durante, whose pupil he became for composition at the same time as Jommelli and Piccinni.

this time Kapellmeister; *Gli Mendicanti*; and *Gl'Incurabili* of which Galuppi[1] was head. Similar institutions in Naples were *De Poveri di Gesu-Christo*; *Della Pietà de Turchini*; *S. Onofrio*; *Loretto*. Such institutions, mostly dating from the sixteenth century, were true *conservatoires* of music, giving excellent and thorough instruction in singing, instrumental music and composition. In addition to these ecclesiastical establishments were a number of aristocratic academies, the fruit of the Renaissance, such as *Degli Arcadi* in Rome, *Della Crusca* and *Degli Elevati* in Florence, and – particularly valuable regarding music – the two famous academies of Bologna: *Dei Filomusi* (founded by Banchieri in 1615) and *Dei Filarmonici* (founded in 1666 by Carratis). The latter had the greatest reputation of all at the time of the Mozarts' Italian tour and to belong to it was perhaps the highest honour a musician could obtain.

Mozart was the last great German musician to study in Italy. Among his predecessors in this journey on their youth to the Mecca of music were Schütz[2] (in 1609 and again in 1629), Handel, Hasse, Gluck, and J. C. Bach. Haydn was the first great exception to this Italian training and it is notable that Haydn does not count as an opera composer.

Leopold had furnished himself with a letter of introduction from the composer, Hasse, to the Abbé Ortes in Bologna from which I take the following:

> I have made the acquaintance of a certain Herr Mozart, Kapellmeister to the Bishop of Salzburg, a gifted and cultured man of the world who, as I believe, understands not only music but other matters. He has a daughter and a son. The former plays the clavier extremely well and the latter who cannot be more than twelve or thirteen is already at this age both a composer and Kapellmeister. I have seen his compositions; they are certainly good and I have noticed nothing in them of a twelve-year-old boy. I have no reason to doubt that they are his own. I have tested him in various ways and he has done things which for such an age are somewhat incomprehensible and would be remarkable in a grown-up man.

[1] *Galuppi*, Baldassare (b. near Venice, 1706; d. 1785), famous opera composer, collaborated with Goldoni.

[2] *Schütz*, Heinrich (b. 1585; d. 1672), perhaps the most notable of all German composers before J. S. Bach.

As the father now wants to bring him to Italy . . . and has asked me for a letter of recommendation I take the liberty to give him one to you [here follows the request to Ortes to help with advice and introductions]. Herr Mozart is a highly cultivated and polished man, his children are well brought up. The boy is, in addition, beautiful, lively, charming and behaves in such a way that one absolutely cannot help loving him. One thing is certain: if his development keeps pace with his age something wonderful will come of him. Only the father must not over-indulge him or spoil his nature with the incense of excessive praise. That is the only danger I fear. I have written you a long letter, receive it in goodwill. . . .

This letter is of exceptional interest for several reasons. In the first place it was written by Hasse, then about sixty-nine years old, the most famous of living German composers and a man of exceptional musical gifts, some of whose operatic melodies have great beauty.[1] Secondly it is written in the deliberately cool tone of a professional musician giving an expert opinion. The gush which is pronounced by music-lovers and dilettantes of all sorts upon musical performances and musical compositions is quite worthless as a criterion, since such people are not really equipped to give a reliable judgment in such matters – no matter how genuine their emotions may be. Here we have a greatly talented musician of vast experience who thoroughly understands his art and who at his time of life must have already met with such numbers of prodigies and musically gifted people as to be able to discount ninety per cent of what the laity think is talent and discern whether there showed in this boy signs of something truly unusual on the highest plane. With true understanding Hasse puts his finger on the deciding point: 'If his development keeps pace with his age something wonderful will come of him.' Hasse did not quite live to see the wonders that came, for he died in Venice, an old man of eighty-four, in 1783, three years before the production of *Figaro*.

Armed with this and other letters the Mozarts arrived at Innsbruck where, on December 16th, Wolfgang played at sight at the house of Count Künigl a concerto put before him as a test and

[1] Two of his airs from the opera *Artaserse* – *Pallido è il sole* and *Per questo dolce amplesso* – were sung every night to Philip V of Spain for ten years by Farinelli, the greatest castrato singer of all time.

received twelve ducats, to which feat the *Innsbrucker Ordinari Zeitung* gave due notice. They travelled over Steinach, Brixen and Bozen to Rovereto where Leopold found an old acquaintance, an official named Cristani, who had studied the violin with him in Salzburg. Leopold writes to his wife from Verona on January 7, 1770, that this Cristani, whom she will remember, said as soon as they entered that Wolfgang resembled his mother whose face he had not forgotten.[1] In Rovereto Wolfgang played at the house of Baron Todeschi; also he played on the organ at the principal church and the rumour of his prowess which had spread through the town brought such a crowd that a way had to be made for them to get into the choir.

And now I shall print the first letter of Wolfgang's which has survived – excepting that already quoted, and of uncertain date, about his Latin to Frau Hagenauer. It is an enclosure to his father's letter from Wirgl dated December 13, 1769:

Dearest Mother,
  My heart is completely ravished from sheer joy because this journey is so jolly because it is so warm in the coach and our coach-man is a splendid man who when the road permits goes like the wind. Papa will have written the description of our journey, the reason I have written Mama is to show that I know my duty and that I am with the deepest respect your faithful son,

(*Sgd.*) WOLFGANG MOZART.

Carissima sorella mia
Siamo arivati a wirgel.[2]

One of the most extraordinary of the many unusual traits of Mozart is his docility, filial obedience and respect for his parents. This he maintained throughout his life and the reader will often be astonished at his letters to his father written long after he was a fully grown-up and independent man. It is an absolutely genuine and integral part of his nature and in no way a formality; nor does he ever abate one jot of his individual independence but

---

[1] A fact worth noting especially in view of my contention that Mozart's temperament came rather from his mother than his father.
[2] Written thus in Italian in the original (i.e. 'Dearest Sister, We have arrived at Wirgl').

acts as he himself thinks right, however much his father is in opposition; but we shall see how he will take great pains to explain patiently to his father what he does and why he does it. I lay particular stress on this since this characteristic has far-reaching consequences in his creative work with which I shall deal when the time comes. In the meantime I would point out to people of this age who gape at and swallow whole post-Freudian psycho-analyses pushed to absurdity, just as their forefathers did with their post-Mesmer hypnotic fancies, that Mozart had neither a father- nor a mother-complex but a merely natural love for each of his parents, neither excessive nor deficient. This perfect poise is no doubt rare, rarer even than 'normal' eyesight, but it cannot be called unnatural. Its significance in Mozart is cardinal, for Mozart's amiability and docility were not negative – i.e. not due to a lack of vitality – but were the result of an extraordinary balance and harmony of opposites in his nature which, as we shall see, plays a decisive rôle in his creative genius.

Leopold writes twice from Innsbruck and once from Bozen. In his letter of December 17, 1769, from Bozen, we meet with the simple code which the Mozarts used in their correspondence when they thought discretion was advisable. This was certainly due to Leopold – whom Hasse did not call a man of the world for nothing. It is quite clear that Leopold was well-versed in the intriguing duplicity of the world and quite a match for all the politicians he met with among musicians, officials and other hangers-on to courts and institutions. Sometimes what Leopold thinks worthy of coding seems laughable to us, as in this letter where he used it merely to tell his wife that the usual fee they get is twelve ducats. From the Inn of the *Due Torri* at Verona Leopold writes:

Verona,
January 7, 1770.

... In Verona it was seven days before the nobility could arrange a concert ... because there was opera daily. These gentlemen to whom we were recommended are Il Marchese Carlotti, Il Conte Carlo Emilei, Il Marchese Spolverini, Marchese Donisi, Conte Giusti del Giardino, Conte Allegri. We had a permanent invitation from Carlotti, also from Locatelli.[1] We have dined twice with Carlotti, with Emilei and with Giusti, who has a beautiful garden and picture gallery. You will find it perhaps in Kaysler's Travels. Yesterday we dined with Locatelli. . . .

The Receiver-General for Venice, Sgr Lugiati, requested the gentlemen to ask me to allow Wolfgang's portrait to be painted.[2] . . . Yesterday it was started and today after Church he must sit again for it. . . . Later we went to the church San Tomaso to play on its two organs, and although this decision was only taken while at table and was made known by a couple of notes to the Marchese Carlotti and Count Pedemonte yet on our arrival there was such a crowd that we had scarcely room to get out of the coach . . . when it was over the uproar was still greater because everyone wanted to see the little organist. As soon as we were in the coach I ordered it home; locked our room and began to write this letter otherwise we should have had no peace. . . .

Tomorrow we are going with Locatelli to see the Amphitheatre and other sights. . . . Was it fine and not cold in Salzburg during the Christmas holidays? We have had it very cold for eight days and imagine! everywhere we eat there is neither a stove nor heating in the dining-room. One's hands get blue with cold. I would rather eat in a cellar,[3] more of this subject, which is our greatest trial another time. . . .

Leaving Verona they arrived at Mantua on January 10, 1770. Wolfgang made a serious impression on more than one of the ladies of Mantua. A Signora Bettinelli wept at his departure and a Signora Sartoretti sent him a pomade for his hands which had suffered from the cold and a vase with a beautiful bouquet and tied in its red ribbon a poem written by herself and (with an eye on Leopold, no doubt) four ducats.

At Mantua, in the Philharmonic Society's hall, a concert was given with Wolfgang as the principal performer. Leopold writes to his wife:

[1] *Locatelli*, Michelangelo, a wealthy merchant, from the same family as Pietro Locatelli, the famous violinist and composer.

[2] This is the portrait: *Mozart* at the clavier, in 1770 (see p. 107), painted by della Rosa. Lugiati called Wolfgang, in a letter to his mother about the portrait, a '*raro e portentoso giovane*'.

[3] Everywhere in Austria and in Germany the cosiest place to have meals is in the famous cellars of the town-halls, hotels, etc. Our English word 'cellar' has unfortunately damp and depressing associations utterly alien to the gay and delightful German *Keller* which perhaps ought to be translated by the word 'tavern'.

Milan,
January 26, 1770.

On the sixteenth in Mantua there was the usual weekly concert.
. . . I wish you could have seen the little theatre (*teatrino*) . . . I have
never in my life seen anything more beautiful. It is not a theatre but
a hall built like an opera-house with boxes. Where the stage should be
is a platform for music and behind the music again a gallery for
listeners built like a box. The crowd, the calls, the applause, uproar
and bravos, in short the general admiration is not to be described. . . .

I must tell you that neither for this concert nor the one in Verona
was there payment. Entry is free; in Verona only for the nobility,
since they are supported by them alone; in Mantua, however,
nobility, military and reputable *bourgeoisie* are admitted as it has a
grant from the Empress. From this you will realize that we shall not
become rich in Italy but you know it is enough if we pay our travelling expenses. This I have managed so far. In the six weeks since we
left Salzburg we have paid out seventy ducats, for even though
one lives *a parte* and mostly does not eat at home still the food at
night, the firewood and room cost so much that one never comes out
of an inn under six ducats for a stay of nine or eleven days. I thank
God I left you at home. Firstly you would not have stood the cold,
secondly it would have cost a terrible lot for we should not have had
the choice of lodging we now have; for example, in the Augustine
monastery of San Marco where, although we pay, we are better off,
more comfortable and near to His Excellency Count Firmian.[1] Every
night our beds are warmed so that Wolfgang at bedtime is always
happy. We have a Brother Alfonso to wait on us.

As an example of the sort of concert given by Wolfgang in
Italy on this tour the programme of the concert at Mantua may
be worth quoting in its original Italian:

*Serie delle Composizioni musicali da eseguirsi nell' Accademia
pubblica Filarmonica, la sera del dì 16. del corrente Gennajo, in
occasione della venuta del espertissimo giovanetto Sig. Amadeo Motzzart*

1. Sinfonia di composizione d'esso Sig. Amadeo.
2. Concerto di Gravecembalo esibitogli, e da lui eseguíto all'improvviso.
3. Aria d'un Professore.
4. Sonata di Cembalo all'improvviso, eseguíta dal Giovine, con
   variazioni analoghe d'invenzion sua, e replicata poi in tuono
   diverso da quello in cui è scritta.

[1] *Firmian*, Count Karl Joseph (1716–1774), Governor-General of Lombardy from
1759, described by Winckelmann as 'one of the greatest, wisest, most humane and
learned men of his time and country'.

5. Concerto di Violino d'un Professore.
6. Aria composta, e cantata nell'atto stesso dal Sig. Amadeo all'improvviso, co' debiti accompagnamenti eseguíti sul Cembalo, sopra parole fatte espressamente; ma da lui non vedute in prima.
7. Altra Sonata di Cembalo composta insieme, ed eseguíta dal medesimo sopra un motivo musicale, propostogli improvvisamente dal primo Violino.
8. Aria d'un Professore.
9. Concerto d'Oboè d'un Professore.
10. Fuga musicale composta, ed eseguíta dal Sig. Amadeo sul Cembalo, e condotta a compiuto termine secondo le leggi del Contrappunto, sopra un semplice tema per la medesima, presentatogli all'improvviso.
11. Sinfonia dal medisimo concertata con tutte le parti sul Cembalo sopra una sola parte di Violino, postagli dinanzi improvvisamente.
12. Duetto di Professori.
13. Trio, in cui il Sig. Amadeo ne sonerà col Violino una parte all'improvviso.
14. Sinfonia ultima di composizione del suddetto.

It is worth remarking on the amount of improvising that Wolfgang was always set to do. His capacity in this respect was clearly phenomenal and it is not surprising that a savant in Verona wrote of him as a 'wonder-work of nature'. I shall now transcribe for the benefit of those, like myself, who are curious to see the unbowdlerized, unimproved original matter as it came from the writer's hands a letter – the first written to his sister which we possess – in which Wolfgang's queerly spelt (even for an Austrian) German is to be seen mixed with Italian as it came fresh from his hand, not as it was originally printed by Nissen in 1828. The matter of this letter is not important, so I do not translate it; what is important is the evidence it gives of Wolfgang's extraordinary vivacity. The mixture of languages – German, Italian, French and even, but rarely, English – is a characteristic of a great many of his letters:

Verona,
al sette di Jannuarro [1770].

Allerliebste Schwester,
Einen spang langen habe ich gehabt, weil ich so lang auf eine Antwort vergebens gewartet habe; ich hatte auch ursache weil ich

deinen brief noch nicht emfangen habe. ietzt hört der teutsche
tölpel auf und fängt das wälsche tölperl an.[1] Lei è piu franco nella
lingua italiana di quel che mi hó imaginato. lei mi dica la cagione,
perchè lei non fù nella comedia che anno giocato i cavalieri? adesso
sentiamo sempre Opere: che è titolata: il Ruggiero.[2] Oronte, il padre
di Bradamanta, è un prencipe: fà il sign. afferi:[3] un bravo cantante,
un paritono,[4] mà gezwungen, wen er in Falset hinauf, aber doch
nicht so sehr, wie der Tibaldi zu Wien. Bradamante, figlia d'orionte,
inamorata di Ruggiero mà: si soll den Leone heyrahten, sie will ihm
aber nicht: fà una povera Baronessa che ha avuto una gran dis-
grazia, mà non so che? Recita: unter einem fremden Nam, ich weiss
aber den Namen nicht: ha una voce passabile, e la statura non sarebbe
male, ma distona come il diavolo. Ruggiero un ricco principe, in-
namorata di Bradamanta, un Musico, canta un poco Manzolisch[5] ed
à una bellissima voce forte ed è già vecchio ha cinquante cinque anni
ed à una leuffige gurgel. Leone, soll die Bradamente heyrathen,
reichissima est; ob er aber asser dem Theatro reich ist, das weis ich
nicht, fà una donna, la moglie di Afferri. à una bellissima voce, ma è
tanto sussuro nell theatro che non si sente niente[6] Irene fà una sorella
di Lolli dell gran Violinisto, che abbiamo sentito a Vienna. à una
schnosselte voce, e canta sempre um ein viertil zu tardi, o troppo à
buon ora. ganno fà, un signor, che non sò come egli si chiama, è la
prima volta che lui Recita. Zwischen einen jeden act is ein Balet:
es ist ein braver Tanzer da, der sich nenet: Monsieur Ruesler. er
ist ein teutscher, und tanzt recht brav, als wir dass letzte Mahl: aber
nicht gar dass letzte mahl: in der opera waren, haben wir den Mr
Ruesler in unseren balco heraufkomen lassen: dan wir haben den
balco des Marquis Carlotti frey, dan wir haben den schlüssel darzu:
und mit ihm geredet: apropos: Alles in der Mascara iezt, und was das
comote ist, wen man seine Larve auf den Hut hat, und het has
privilegium den hut nicht abzuziehen, wen einer mich grüsst, und
nimer beym namen nennen, sondern allzeit, servitore umilissimo,
giora Mascara. Cospeto di Baco, dass spritzt: was aber das rareste
ist, ist dieses: das wir um 7^{ben} uhr gegen halber 8 uhr schon zu bette
gehen. Se Lei indovinasse questo, io dirò certamente, che Lei sia la
Madre di tutti indovini. küsse anstatt meiner der mama die Hand,

---

[1] 'Now the German blockhead stops and the Italian blockhead starts' – an early
and rather simple example of the habit of playing with words which was almost a
mania of Mozart's.
[2] An opera by P. Guglielmi, libretto by C. Mazzolà.
[3] Name of a singer.
[4] Baritone.
[5] A reference to Manzuoli which shows that Wolfgang had not forgotten this
singer whom he heard in London at the age of nine.
[6] 'But there is such a noise in the theatre one can hear nothing.' This is an interesting observation showing how little Italian audiences have changed.

und dich küsse ich zu tausend mahl, und versichere Dich, dass ich
werde bleiben immer

dein aufrichtiger Bruder,

WOLFGANG MOZART.

Portez vous bien, et aimez moi toujours.

In this letter, written just before his fourteenth birthday we
may notice how critical Mozart is of the singers he hears and
how concisely he expresses himself.

In Mantua they heard Hasse's opera *Demetrio* and Wolfgang
writes to his sister from Milan on January 26, 1770:

> The *prima donna* sings well but lifelessly . . . the *seconda donna*
> looks like a grenadier and also has a powerful voice and really does
> not sing badly. . . . The principal man sings well but his voice is
> uneven, he is called Caselli,[1] the second man is already old and I
> didn't like him. . . . A tenor named Otini sings not badly but does
> not sustain his tone, like all Italian tenors. He is a good friend of
> ours; I don't know the other's name, he is still young but nothing
> out of the way. *Primo ballerino* good, *Prima Ballerina* good and it is
> said she is by no means a fright but I have not seen her close to, the
> rest, however, are much as usual. In Cremona . . . the orchestra
> good[2] and the first violinist is called Spagnoletto. *Prima donna*, not
> bad, already old I think, looks a fright, doesn't sing as well as she
> acts and is the wife of a violinist who plays in the opera . . . the
> opera is *La Clemenza di Tito*.[3] *Seconda donna* on the stage no fright,
> young, but nothing special. *Primo uomo* . . . a pretty voice and a
> beautiful *cantabile*. The two other *castrati* young and passable. . . .
> *Ballerino primo* good, *Ballerina prima* good and a real horror. . . . In
> Milan . . . we have not yet been to the opera. . . .

For the two young *castrati* Wolfgang composed in Milan two
Latin motets to which probably belong the *Quaere superna* (K.143)
and the *Offertorium* (K.117). Count Firmian, who had presented
Wolfgang with the works of the poet Metastasio,[4] gave a *soirée* at
his Palace inviting the Duke of Modena and his daughter and
the Cardinal Archbishop of Milan. In order to show his capacity

---

[1] *Caselli*, Vincenzo, a castrato.

[2] Wolfgang writes very curtly, omitting most verbs. I have tried to retain his style
everywhere when translating, even at the cost of writing uncouth English.

[3] By Hasse, text by Metastasio. This text, adapted by C. Mazzolà, was later set
also by Mozart.

[4] Turin edition in nine volumes.

to write an opera – Piccinni was at that moment in Milan from Paris, preparing for the performance of his new opera *Cesare e Cleopatra* (*Cesare in Egitto*) – Wolfgang composed the great recitative and aria in E flat (K.77) *Misero me et Misero pargoletto*[1] for soprano, two violins, two altos, two oboes, two bassoons, two horns and contrabass. Of this astonishing production Wyzewa and Saint-Foix remark:

> In truth this piece is one on the greatest scale that he has produced in this style and one of those in which the precocity of his genius appears most astonishing. The recitative and the air are made one by means of brief repeats in the air of the rhythm in the accompaniment to the recitative; and already this latter gradually becomes more melodic and takes a more definite form to lead into the magnificent burst of music in the air.

Wolfgang tells his sister in his letter of January 26th that he had just finished this aria before writing to her.

The success of this and other arias composed by Wolfgang had the desired result of obtaining for him a commission to compose a new opera for the next season for which the best singers were to be engaged and he was to get about one hundred ducats and free quarters during its production in Milan.[2] The libretto was to be sent on to him, the recitatives had to be forwarded to Milan in October, and at the beginning of November the composer himself was to be there to complete the opera and prepare for its production at Christmas. These conditions were most convenient, for they enabled the Mozarts to continue their tour.

Wolfgang's mother must have shown some concern about his health, for Leopold writes:

Milan,
February 17, 1770.

We are, thank God, both well. That the winter, as you say, is not so dangerous in Italy as the summer I can well believe. But if one does not ruin one's health through disorderly and superfluous eating and drinking and also has no inner organic weakness then there is

---

[1] From Metastasio's *Demofoonte*.
[2] One of the musicians to test Wolfgang's quality in Milan was the famous *Sammartini*, Giovanni Battista (b. 1700; d. 1775).

nothing to worry about. We are everywhere in God's keeping. Wolfgang will not be injured either by eating or drinking. You know how moderate he is and I can assure you that I have never seen him more careful of his health than in this country. He avoids everything that he doesn't think good for him, has very little to eat many days and yet is fat and healthy and the whole day long is lively and gay.

With this same letter of his father's Wolfgang encloses a note to his sister:

Milan,
February 17, 1770.
... Mariandel I am so glad you have been so terrifically jolly ... *Addio* ... farewell, I kiss Mama's hand a thousand times and to you I send a hundred loving smacks or pats on your wonderful horse-face. To make an end I am thine ...

'Wolfgang in Germany, Amadeo in Italy' – as he writes in another letter.

On the way from Milan to Parma, at Lodi on March 15th, dated seven o'clock in the evening, Wolfgang composed his first String Quartet (K.80). Of this work in G major Wyzewa and Saint-Foix write:

Though one must not suppose that the child had composed the whole of this quartet in a single evening (at the inn at Lodi): this time, as usual, he has sat down to write a work only when he already had it, almost entirely completed, in his head; at most he will have improvised the minuet because, unlike the other movements, there are so many erasures that his father has been obliged to copy out again the whole of the trio.

This quartet consists of three movements only, in the Italian style, as follows: *Adagio, Allegro, Menuetto e trio*. Wolfgang added a finale (*Rondo*) in 1773. And the same authorities say that although Wolfgang must already have been familiar with the first quartets of Jos. Haydn, Starzer, Stamitz, Hoffmann and Michael Haydn[1] – superior in form if not in content to the quartets of Boccherini and Sammartini – yet this first quartet of his is entirely Italian in character.

They arrived at Bologna on March 24th and on that day both Leopold and Wolfgang wrote home about the celebrated singer

[1] See footnote p. 136.

in Parma, Lucrezia Agujari, known as *La Bastardella*, who invited them to supper and sang three arias for them. Leopold writes:

That she could sing the C in *altissimo* I could not have believed if I had not heard it with my own ears. The passages Wolfgang has written down were in her aria and she sang these somewhat softer than the deeper notes but as clearly as an octave pipe in an organ. Short trills and all were note for note as Wolfgang has written out. Also she has good alto notes down to G. She is not pretty but not ugly, has at times a wild look in her eyes like people who are subject to fits, and limps with one leg. Otherwise she has a good presence also a good character and reputation....

Wolfgang's letter to his sister is as follows:

[Bologna]
March 24, 1770.

O you Industrious One!

While I was lazy so long I thought it didn't matter so long as I again became industrious for a bit. Always on days when the German post comes the food and drink tastes better to me. I beg of you to tell me who sings in the Oratorio, also what its title is. Write also how the Haydn minuets please you and if they are better than the first. I am glad from the bottom of my heart to hear that Herr von Amann is well again: tell him, I beg you, that he must be careful; he must take things quietly, tell him that, I beg of you, and also say that I often think of how we played[1] ... and tell him also that I often recall how many times he has said to me: 'Shall we divide?' and how I always replied: 'As before.' Next time I shall send you a Minuet which Mr Pick danced in the theatre and which is danced by everybody at the *feste di ballo* in Milan, just to show you how slowly they dance. The Minuet is in itself very good. It comes, naturally, from Vienna, also is certainly by Teller or Starzer. It has a lot of notes. Why? because it is a theatre minuet which goes slowly. The Minuets of Milan and most Italian ones have many notes, go slowly and with many bars, e.g. the first section has sixteen, the second has twenty and even twenty-four bars.

At Parma we met a singer, the celebrated Bastardella, and heard her splendidly in her own home. She has (1) a fine voice, (2) a

[1] Here follows a reference to some game of their own devising. Leopold writes a postscript to his wife in his letter from Milan on Carnival Tuesday: 'The misfortune of Basily (von Amann) upset us very much, especially Wolfgang, who shed many tears, you know how sensitive he is.'

luscious larynx, (3) an unbelievable range. I heard her sing the
following:

In Bologna on March 26, 1770, Field-Marshal Count Pallavicini
arranged a brilliant concert, attended by one hundred and fifty
persons, in order to introduce Wolfgang to the nobility, including
the Cardinal Legate Antonio Colonna Branciforte and the greatest Italian musician of the time, Padre Martini.[2] Leopold writes
to his wife the next day:

[1] This is written by Mozart in the old soprano clef, i.e. two tones lower than the
treble clef.

[2] *Martini*, Giambattista, commonly called Padre Martini (b. Bologna, 1706; d.
1784), composer, scholar and mathematician, one of the most learned musicians of
history. Burney estimated his library at Bologna to consist of 17,000 volumes.
Author of *Storia della Musica*, three volumes (1757–1781), and *Esemplare o sia
Saggio fondamentale pratico di contrappunto fugato*, two volumes (1774–5).

D

Bologna,
March 27, 1770.

. . . I wish you might know Count Pallavicini. He and Count Firmian are a pair of noblemen who possess similar tastes, modes of thought and are equally amiable, courteous and generous. . . .

What pleases me especially is that Wolfgang is more admired here than in any of the other Italian towns since this is the seat and residence of so many masters, artists and scholars. He is also most in request here and this increases his fame throughout Italy since Padre Martini is the god of the Italians and he speaks of Wolfgang with such admiration and has personally tested him. Twice we have visited Padre Martini and each time Wolfgang has composed a fugue of which P. Martini has only supplied him with the *ducem* or *quida* in a few notes. We have visited the Cavaliere Broschi, better known as Signor Farinelli,[1] at his estate outside the town. We have seen Spagnoletta[2] . . . Manfredini[3]

. . . Farewell, I kiss you and Nannerl a thousand times, remember me to all Salzburg, I am your true and sleepy husband,

(*Sgd.*) MZT.

[March 28]: It was not a bad idea to send us the Ball-Minuet to Bologna to be arranged for clavier because there is nobody in Salzburg who could do it. It has given Wolfgang the greatest pleasure. . . . He will himself write next time; I wrote yesterday as he was already in bed . . . he is now asleep and the post is going.

From Bologna they went to Florence, arriving on March 30th and presenting a letter from Count Firmian to Count Rosenberg,[4] the Austrian ambassador at the Tuscan court, on April 1st. A concert was arranged for the next day. Leopold writes to his wife:

Florence,
April 3, 1770.

. . . We stayed until ten o'clock. It went as usual and the admiration was all the greater since the musical director, the Marquis

---

[1] See footnote p. 74.

[2] Gius. Useda from Milan.

[3] A famous singer (castrato), and brother to Vincenzo Manfredini (b. 1737; d. 1799), maestro di capella and author of *Difesa della musica moderna*.

[4] *Orsini-Rosenberg*, Count Franz Xaver Wolf (b. 1723; d. 1796), was Imperial Ambassador the court of Tuscany from 1766 to 1772. In 1776 he was appointed Chief Chamberlain to the Viennese Court and Director of the Court Theatres, and subsequently played an important part in Mozart's career.

Ligniville,[1] is one of the first contrapuntalists in Italy and put before Wolfgang the most difficult fugues and gave him the hardest subjects which Wolfgang developed and played as one eats a piece of bread. Nardini accompanied. Today we see Manzuoli. The castrato Niccolini is also here. I am very troubled that we must depart next Friday to go to Rome. I wish you could see Florence and its surroundings. You would say that here one should live and die. . . .

In Florence Wolfgang met and became very friendly with an English boy of his own age (fourteen) named Thomas Linley who was a pupil of the violinist Nardini. Linley's promising career was cut short by his accidental death by drowning in 1778.

The Mozarts arrived in Rome on April 11th, the Wednesday of Holy Week, and Leopold writes to his wife:

Rome,
April 14, 1770.

. . . In Rome they say that they have had rain for four months and we truly had an experience of it for on Wednesday and Thursday we went in fine weather to hear the *Miserere* in the Sistine Chapel at St Peter's and were . . . overtaken by such rain that our cloaks have never been so soaked. Of the horrible journey here I shall say little. Imagine a mostly unbuilt country and horrible inns . . . filth and nothing to eat except, with luck, here and there some eggs and cabbage. . . .

You will perhaps have heard of the celebrated *Miserere* in Rome which is so highly treasured that the musicians are forbidden under threat of excommunication to let a single part of it be taken out of the Chapel or to copy it or give it to anyone. *We alone have it*. Wolfgang has written it down . . . we shall bring it home with us and as it is one of the secrets of Rome we will not let is pass into other hands so as not to incur directly or indirectly the displeasure of the Church. . . .

This celebrated feat of Wolfgang's refers to the *Miserere* of Dom. Greg. Allegri (1582–1652). He wrote it out from memory on returning to their inn after a single hearing on the Wednesday and when the performance was repeated on the Good Friday he took the manuscript with him and hiding it in his hat made some

---

[1] *De Ligniville*, Marchese Eugenio, Duca di Conca, Director of Music at the Court of Tuscany from 1765 to 1790, was an expert in Canon writing and Wolfgang copied out a number of his Canons and experimented himself (see K. *Anhang* 238) in composing them.

corrections. This feat became known and made a great sensation and he was called upon to produce his copy in the presence of the papal singer, Cristofori, who was amazed at its correctness. Leopold's news, however, excited consternation in Salzburg, Wolfgang's mother and sister believing that he had sinned in transcribing the *Miserere* and Leopold writes, in reply to their misgivings, from Naples on May 19, 1770:

> . . . When we read your ideas about the *Miserere* we both had to have a good laugh. There is nothing in the least to be worried about. It is taken in quite another way here. All Rome knows of it. The Pope himself knows that Wolfgang has written down the *Miserere*. There is nothing to be afraid of; it has brought him great honour. . . . You must not fail to show this letter everywhere and let His Grace the Archbishop know of it. . . .

In Rome they presented their letters of introduction and were welcomed by the Chigi, Barberini, Bracciano, Altemps and other important families on whom Wolfgang's playing and improvising made a great impression since, as Leopold writes:

> Rome,
> April 21, 1770.
> . . . the deeper we penetrate into Italy the greater grows the astonishment. Wolfgang does not stand still but develops so from day to day that the greatest connoisseurs and masters cannot find words to express their admiration. . . .
>
> We have met an incredible number of English here, among others Mr Beckford[1] who met us at Lady Effingham's in London, with whom early today we went walking, in company with other English people, in the gardens of the Villa Medici belonging to the Grand Duke of Florence
>
> We have changed our first lodging and Herr Marcobruni has brought us to the house of the Papal Courier Uslenghi in the Piazza del Clementino. Here we are very comfortable, both mother and daughter cannot do enough for us. The Master is in Portugal and they look on us as the Heads of the house; we eat together, have a large room which is very healthy as it gets the morning sun. When friends visit us we can use all the other rooms and as the daughter is a beginner learning to play we are not without a harpsichord. . . .
>
> Yesterday we were at Prince Chigi's where among others was the

[1] Probably *Beckford*, Peter (b. 1740; d. 1811), a well-known sportsman and raveller and the author of *Familiar Letters from Italy*, published in 1805.

so-called King of England or Pretender and the secretary of state, Cardinal Pallavicini. . . .

In Rome Wolfgang composed two arias: *Se ardir e speranza* (K.82) and *Se tutti i mali miei* (K.83) to words taken from Metastasio's *Demofoonte*, both for soprano voice with orchestra. He also composed a Symphony in D (K.81) which appears in Breitkopf's catalogue in 1775 as by his father; but Wyzewa and Saint-Foix declare it to be Wolfgang's work on internal evidence: 'There is not a note of this symphony which could have emanated from the heavy and banal invention of Leopold Mozart,' and explain the confusion as due to a misunderstanding of Wolfgang's possible reference to a symphony by his father in his letter to his sister dated April 23, 1770, which must refer to another work.[1] He also composed a Contredanse in B flat for two violins, bass, two oboes and two horns (K.123). It is interesting to read the particulars written by Leopold in sending this dance to Salzburg on April 14th:

> Wolfgang is well and sends a Contredanse. He would like Herr Cirillus Hofmann [dance-master at the Salzburg Court] to devise the steps to it and in such a way that only two persons dance when the two violins play as a prelude and then let the whole company dance together each time the whole orchestra plays. What would be most beautiful would be for five different couples to dance in turn the solos as there are five solos and five *tuttis*.

This is an early example of the interest Mozart took in dancing, of which he was passionately fond all his life. Arithmetic was another of his pleasures as the following letter indicates:

Rome,
April 21, 1770.

Cara sorella mia,
    I beg you to find the Art of Reckoning which you wrote out for me and which I have lost. So will you please copy it with examples and send it to me. . . . I am just working on the aria *Se ardir e speranza*.

Nonsense rhymes and drawings of places and people appear

[1] E. F. Schmid confirms in *Mozart Jahrbuch*, 1958, that the symphony is by Wolfgang.

frequently in Wolfgang's letters, which also occasionally contain expressions of such grossness that the reader at first can hardly believe his eyes. These latter, one comes to realize, are invariably a sign of his being in extraordinarily high spirits, so much so that his pen flies to absurdity, extravagance and coarseness of phrase out of the sheer animal vitality of the writer. This quality in Mozart is not to be mistaken. It appears in these earliest letters of the boy of fourteen and indeed in his father's letters one is constantly coming across the remark: 'Wolfgang is indescribably lively.'

Of these boyish epistles, written from Rome, there are a number which are mere postscripts to his father's letters, such as:

> Rome,
> April 14, 1770.

I am, God be praised and thanked, apart from my miserable pen, well and kiss Mama and Nannerl a thousand times. I only wish that my sister were in Rome for this city would surely please her well since the church of St Peter's is the real thing[1] and so are many things in Rome. The finest flowers are now of the past – this very moment papa has said it. . . . Now I have just drawn St Peter with the keys, St Paul with the sword, and St Luke together with my sister. I have had the honour of the kissing of St Peter's foot at St Peter's and as I have the misfortune to be so little I have been lifted up to the said old guy.

> Rome,
> April 28, 1770.

I kiss my sister's face and my mother's hand. I have as yet seen neither scorpions nor spiders, one talks and hears nothing of them. . . .

> Rome,
> May 2, 1770.

I am, God be thanked and praised, well and kiss my mother's hand and my sister's face, nose, mouth, neck, my bad pen and backside if it is clean.

Sometimes he signs his letters:

> *Wolfgango in Germania*
> *Amadeo in Italia.*

---

[1] *Regulair*, Wolfgang writes. His German is strewn with French or pseudo-French words.

He also used the following expression to describe the year 1771:

hinten wie vorn und in der Mitte doppelt.[1]

From Rome they travelled to Naples in company with some Augustine monks, as the road was by no means safe, owing to bandits, arriving in Naples on May 14th. They gave a concert on May 28th and made many friends in Naples, among them the English ambassador, Sir William Hamilton, and his wife who played the clavier 'with great feeling and trembled when she had to play before Wolfgang' – as Leopold tells his wife in a letter dated May 19th. In Naples they heard opera buffa at the *Teatro Nuovo*, which was then dominated by Piccinni and Paisiello, and at the San Carlo they heard Jommelli's opera, *Armida Abbandonata*, at its first performance on May 30th. The impresario, Amadori, introduced by Jommelli, offered Wolfgang a libretto which he was obliged to refuse owing to his contract to write an opera for Milan.

Naples and its beautiful surroundings were a joy to them. Leopold writes to his wife:

Naples,
May 26, 1770.

This is the third letter I have written to you from Naples. The situation of this town daily pleases me better and the town itself on the whole is not bad if the people were not so godless and some of them so stupid . . . and the superstition!![2]

Naples,
May 29, 1770.

. . . Up till now we have had to endure no heat because there has been so much rain; yesterday there was a terrible wind and rain and it is something rare for Naples that the heat is not greater by now. Nevertheless we shall return home rather dark because of the air and also when the sun shines one realizes forthwith that one is in Naples. You know that Wolfgang has always wanted to be brown. . . .

Wolfgang can hardly wait for the holidays, he begs you now and then to write twice a week, especially when there is anything new: it is only in Salzburg that news is quickly written. . . .

[1] 'Behind as in front and doubled in the centre.'
[2] Wolfgang's playing at the *Conservatoire della Pietà* so astonished the gentry that they thought there was magic in the ring he wore and when he took it off and played without it they redoubled their applause.

Naples,
June 5, 1770.

. . . It is still always very cold in the mornings and at night and on
June 2nd we had fearful rain. . . . Our concert was very successful.
. . . The Princess of Francavilla has made us a good present and we
still have a few stray small expectations. You will be vexed that I do
not let you know our receipts in detail. I don't give them because in
Salzburg they consider only what we get and don't think of the
expenses, for very few know what travelling costs. It is enough if I
tell you that, God be praised, we lack nothing for our journeys to be
made in decent comfort. . . .

Naples,
June 9, 1770.

. . . The situation of this place, its fruitfulness, liveliness, curiosi-
ties and a hundred beauties make my departure from Naples very
sad; the filthiness, the swarms of beggars, the detestable, yes godless
people, the bad upbringing of the children, the unbelievable
wantonness even in the churches, however, has the effect of lessening
one's regrets. . . .

Rome,
June 27, 1770.

Yesterday at eight o'clock in the evening we arrived at Rome. We
made this journey, which took four and a half days with the Vit-
turino, by the Post in twenty-seven hours but we have decidedly
flown. . . . As we only slept for two hours during the twenty-seven
and only had four baked cold *hendl* and a piece of bread to eat you
can imagine how hungry, thirsty and sleepy we were. Our good
Frau Uslenghi gave us an excellent gently-cooked Rice and we took
nothing besides but a couple of soft-boiled eggs each and as soon as
we entered our room Wolfgang sat down on a chair and fell so fast
asleep that I completely undressed him and put him in his bed
without his making the slightest sign of waking . . when he awoke
after nine o'clock in the morning he did not know where he was and
the whole night through he lay without stirring from where I had
put him.

From Wolfgang's letters from Naples, which are usually much
briefer than his father's, I select the following:

[To his sister][1]

---

[1] This letter, like many others, begins in Italian and continues in German. Some
of his letters to his sister are entirely in Italian. Leopold's letters are all in German.

Naples,
May 19, 1770.

... Write and tell me how is Herr Canary. Does he still sing? Does he still pipe? Do you know why I think of the canary? Because in our lobby there is one that makes a noise just like ours. . . . Yesterday we put on our new clothes; we looked as beautiful as angels. . . . Naples is beautiful but it is more populous than Vienna and Paris; in the impudence of its people I am not sure that London does not surpass Naples; for here the beggars have their own leaders or heads who receive twenty-five ducats in silver monthly from the King to keep them in order.

Amicis sings at the opera. We have been with her. Caffaro composes the second opera, Majo the third but nobody knows yet the composer of the fourth. Go regularly to the Litany at the Mirabell and hear the *Regina coeli* or the *Salve Regina*, sleep soundly and have no bad dreams. Give H. von Schidenhofen my most horrible greeting *tralaliera*, *tralaliera*. And tell him he must learn to play the Repetiter-Minuet on the clavier so that he does not forget to *do* it. Let him *do* it so that it *does* me good when I *do* accompany him. *Do* give my respects to all good friends and *do* be fit and *do* not die so that you *do* not fail to write and I *do* write again to you and let us always so *do* until we *do* all and still I *do* remain he who will *do* until there is no more to *do*.

[To his mother and sister]

Naples,
May 22, 1770.

I am, God be praised and thanked, well and kiss mama's hand and both of you I kiss a thousand times.

[To his sister]

Naples,
May 29, 1770.

The day before yesterday we were at the rehearsal of Signor Jommelli's opera which is well written and truly pleased me. Signor Jommelli spoke to us and was very civil. We also went to a church to hear music by Signor Ciccio di Majo, the music was beautiful. He also spoke to us and was very amiable. Signora De Amicis sings marvellously. Thank God we are well, I especially when a letter comes from Salzburg. I beg you to write to me every post, even if you have nothing to write I would like to have it just so as to have a letter every post-day. It would not be a bad thing if you wrote me sometimes a letter in Italian.

[To his sister]

Naples,
June 5, 1770.

. . . Now I begin to describe my daily life:

At nine o'clock, sometimes at ten o'clock I wake and then we go out and have breakfast at a restaurant (*trattore*), after eating we write and then go out and then lunch but on what? On meat-days, half a chicken or a small piece of roast meat, on fast days a little fish, and afterwards we go to sleep.[1] *Est-ce-que vous avez compris?* Let us talk Salzburgish, it's more sensible. We are, thank God, well, papa and I. I hope you and mama are also well. Naples and Rome are two sleepy cities. Wonderful handwriting! Isn't it? Write to me and don't be so lazy. Otherwise you will have a beating from me. *Quel plaisir! Je te casserai la tete.* I am delighted with the portraits. . . . The opera here is by Jommelli; it is good but too clever and old-fashioned for the theatre. De Amicis sings incomparably as does Aprile also who has sung in Milan. The dances are miserably pretentious. The King[2] is a raw Neapolitan product and at the opera stands always on a footstool so as to seem taller than the Queen. The Queen is beautiful and courteous and has greeted me in the most friendly way six times on the Molo (that is the place where one goes walking). I kiss Mama's hand.

[To his mother and sister]

Naples,
June 16, 1770.

I am still lively and perpetually jolly as usual and like travelling: now I have gone to the Mediterranean sea. I kiss Mama's hand and Nannerl a thousand times and am

your son Stefel and your brother Hansl.

[To his sister]

Rome,
July 7, 1770.

I have been astonished that you can compose so well. In a word the song is excellent. Try to compose more. Send me soon the other minuets by Haydn. *Mlle. j'ai l'honneur d'etre votre très humble serviteur et frère Chevalier de Mozart – Addio.*

On July 8th the Pope conferred on Wolfgang the Order of the Golden Spur which Gluck had received in recognition of his

[1] This letter starts in German, continues in Italian and then goes into Salzburg dialect.

[2] Ferdinand IV of Naples (1751–1825). 'What the King is,' writes Leopold to his wife from Rome on June 30th, 'is better told than written.'

opera *Antigono* produced in Rome in 1756, the year of Wolfgang's birth, when Gluck was forty-two. This order brought with it the title of *Ritter* or *Chevalier* which Gluck always used. Wolfgang used it for a few years at the instigation of his father, who wrote to his wife:

> Rome,
> July 7, 1770.
>
> What I last wrote to you about the order was correct. It is the same that Gluck has . . . he must wear a fine golden cross that he has received and you can imagine how I laugh when I hear people address him as: *Signor Cavaliere*. We are to have an audience for this with the Pope tomorrow.

Leopold made Wolfgang sign his compositions *Del Sign. Cavaliere W. A. Mozart* and later advised him to wear his order in Paris; but Mozart let it drop completely when he grew up and it is never heard of again.[1] The pedagogic Otto Jahn comments on this fact: 'Mozart was too simple-natured and too essentially a musician to set any store by outward distinctions,' which is as inept a remark as possible. Mozart was *not* simple; on the contrary, he was much too clever and realistic not to understand that a title only makes an artist look ridiculous in the eyes of the politicians and powers-that-be who confer it and who take care never to confer any but low-grade distinctions on artists – whom they correctly despise for taking them. Has it ever been heard that a poet or a composer was made a Prince or a Duke in recognition of his genius? No, it has never been and it never should be heard of. As for the rank and file it is certainly fitting that decent men of talent should have social recognition but *Ritter Mozart* makes as ludicrous a combination as would *Sir* William Shakespeare.

Wolfgang had arrived at the age of puberty. His father writes from Rome on July 4th to his mother: 'Wolfgang has visibly grown in Naples,' and again on July 21st from Bologna: 'If Wolfgang keeps on growing he will return home rather big.' On August 25th Leopold tells his wife that Wolfgang's clothes are all too

---

[1] [An explanation may be found in the incident told on p. 171. *C.R.*]

small for him but he must have patience until they go to Milan when fresh ones can be made:

> . . . He has now no singing voice, it has completely gone; it has neither high nor low notes and not five pure tones. This vexes him very much for he cannot sing his own things which often he would like to sing to himself . . .

They had left Rome on July 10th, travelling via Vivita Castellana, Loretto and Sinegaglia to Bologna where they arrived on July 20th and were invited to pass the hot season at the country house of Count Pallavicini. Wolfgang made friends with the son of the Count, who was his own age, and whom Leopold describes as very intelligent, playing the clavier and speaking three languages. In Bologna they met Mysliwecek (1737–81) who was to compose an opera for Milan, after Wolfgang. Here Wolfgang received the libretto for his opera which was by a Turin poet named Cigna-Santi and was entitled *Mitridate, Re di Ponto*.

During this summer at Bologna Wolfgang wrote a number of compositions but it was his almost daily intellectual intercourse with Padre Martini, with whom he made a number of studies in counterpoint, that was most profitable to him. One of the fruits of this association was the *Miserere* (K.85) for alto, tenor and bass with figured continuo showing trace of the influence of Allegri's Roman *Miserere*. The last three sections of this work, *Quoniam*, *Benigne* and *Tunc acceptabis*, are not by Mozart but possibly are by Martini.

The Mozarts attended a festival of the famous Bologna Philharmonic Society on August 13th at which Burney was present and he writes in his *Travels*:

> I must not forget to inform my musical readers that I recognized in Herr Mozart's son the little German whose precocious and supernatural talent amazed us all in London some years ago when he was a mere child. Since his arrival in Italy he has been much admired in Rome and Naples.

The Bologna Philharmonic Society, founded in 1666, had been given a position of unique authority in church music by a bull of Pope Benedict XIV in 1749 and only its members could be Kapellmeisters in Bologna churches, while for the rest of the Papal domains its membership dispensed with any examination. Members had to be twenty years of age, to have been admitted into the first class of composers and to have been one year in the second class of cantori and suonatori. The Society elected Wolfgang a member, although he was only fourteen years old, on his accomplishment of a prescribed task which was to write on a Cantus firmus from the Gregorian Antiphony a contrapuntal elaboration in duple time for four, five or eight voices *a capella* strictly according to rule, adhering to the old church modes. Leopold describes the event in the following letter to his wife:

Milan,
October 20, 1770.

On the evening of the 18th at five o'clock we arrived, God be praised, safe and sound in Milan. We had to wait a whole day in Parma because the rivers were so swollen on account of the astonishingly heavy rain that it was impossible to cross them. . . . For three weeks I have had severe rheumatism in my right arm and I took this with me on the journey. Instead of getting worse it got better although it has not quite gone. I used nothing and have used nothing. It will go as it came. The movement of the carriage did me no good but I kept thinking: one must drive away evil with evil. . . .

We were delayed a couple of days in Bologna because the *Accademia Philharmonica* elected Wolfgang unanimously. . . . He had to appear in the Academy Hall on October 9th at four o'clock in the afternoon. Then the *Princeps accademiæ* and the two *Censores* (who are old *Kapellmeisters*) in the presence of members gave him an antiphon from the Antiphonary which he had to set in four parts in a neighbouring room into which he was locked. When it was ready it was examined by the Censors and all the *Kapellmeisters* and composers who voted on it by means of white and black balls. As all the balls were white he was called in and everyone clapped and wished him well as he entered and he was proclaimed a member by the *Princeps*. He returned thanks and the ceremony ended. . . . I was on the other side of the hall in the Library all the time. Everyone was astonished that he was ready so soon for many have taken three hours on an antiphon of three lines. You must know that this kind of composition is by no means easy as many things are excluded. . . . He finished it in exactly half-an-hour.

Mozart's test-piece is still in the archives of the Bologna Philharmonic Society where it was found by Gaspari in a volume of various test-pieces, chiefly by Martini's pupils. The Cantus firmus *Cibavit eos in adipe* (K.44) is another exercise made by Mozart under Martini and the piece published as Wolfgang's own test-piece (K.86) is one of two workings out of the same test in this volume written out in Mozart's hand.

One or two letters written home by Wolfgang about this period deserve quoting:

[To his mother]
July 21, 1770.

I congratulate Mama on her birthday and wish that she may live many hundred years still and always remain in good health for which I am always asking God and pray every day and will always pray every day for both of you. . . . I kiss Mama's hand a thousand times and remain until death,

Your true son.

[To his sister]

. . . May you live hundreds of years still and die when you are a thousand. . . . I have not time to write more. The pen is not worth a fig, like he who guides it. The title of the opera I have to compose at Milan is not yet known. I have got the *Thousand and One Nights* in Italian as a present from our hostess in Rome; it is most amusing to read.[1]

[To Lorenz Hagenauer]
Bologna,
July 28, 1770.

I follow in the trail of the other congratulations and confirm all that my dear father most sincerely has wished for you and present my compliments to you and to dear Frau Hagenauer,

Your most obedient servant,
(*Sgd.*) WOLFGANGO AMADEO MOZART.

[To his sister]
Bologna,
August 4, 1770.

I regret sincerely from my heart that Miss Martha is so ill and I pray every day for her that she may get well; tell her from me she should not take too much exercise or eat very salt things. Apropos!

---

[1] This is one of the very rare occasions when Mozart mentions a book. Leopold, on the contrary, makes many references to books and was a very well-read man.

have you given Robinig[1] my letter? You say nothing about it; I beg you, when you see him, to tell him not to forget all about me. I can't write any better for this pen is a note-pen[2] and not a letter-pen. My violin now has new strings and I play every day; but I only put this in because Mama asked once if I still played the violin. I have been more than six times alone to churches and functions. I have already composed four Italian symphonies besides Arias of which I have written certainly five or six, also a motet.[3]

Does Herr Deibl[4] come often and honour you with his amusing talk? And noble Herr Karl v. Vogt,[5] does he still deign to listen to your insufferable voice? Herr von Schidenhofen must busy himself helping you in writing minuets or he shall get no more sweets. . . .

Addio, farewell: my only diversion at present is walking and Capriol and *spaccat-machen*. Italy is a land of sleep, one is always sleeping. . . .

[To his mother and sister]

Bologna,
August 21, 1770.

I am still active and in truth very gay. Today I had the pleasure of riding on a donkey; for it is the custom in Italy so I thought I must also try it. We have the honour of the acquaintance of a Dominican friar who is considered holy. I don't quite believe it for he often takes a cup of chocolate at breakfast, then a good glass of strong Spanish wine; and I myself have had the honour to eat with this holy one who after he had drunk a whole glassful of strong wine at table on top of plain wine had two good slices of melon, peaches, pears, five cups of coffee, a whole plateful of nails, two full plates of milk and lemons. With industry he might do all this but I don't believe it because it would be too much but he takes a great deal for tea[6] in the afternoon.

[To his sister]

Bologna,
September 8, 1770.

So as not to fail in my duty I shall also write a few words. . . .

I am just reading *Telemachus*[7] and am already in part two, meanwhile farewell. I kiss Mama's hand.

[1] *Sigmund Robinig* (1760–1823), son of a rich merchant.
[2] i.e. for writing musical notation.
[3] These symphonies are K.95, 97, 81 and 84. The arias are K.143, 88, 78, 79, 77, 82, 83. The motet is K.117.
[4] *Franz Deibl*, oboeist and violinist in Salzburg.
[5] *Karl Vogt*, violinist of the Salzburg Court Chapel.
[6] *Jause*, Austrian dialect for afternoon meal.
[7] *Télémaque* by Fénélon.

Bologna,

September 22, 1770.

... The six Minuets of Haydn[1] please me better than the previous twelve, we have often had to play them to the Countess[2] and we wish we could introduce into Italy the taste for German minuets since their own last almost as long as a whole symphony. Excuse my bad writing, I could do better but I am in a hurry. . . . I kiss Mama's hand.

[To his mother]

Bologna,

September 29, 1770.

In order to make the letter longer I shall add a few words. I am sorry from my heart that poor Miss Martha has to suffer and bear patiently so long an illness, I hope that with God's help she will soon be better, if not one must not let oneself be too cast down for the will of God is always for the best and God will know best whether it is better to be in this world or another,[3] but she must console herself meanwhile that now she is coming from the rain into the fine weather. I kiss Mama's hand, farewell, *addio*.

(*Sgd.*) WOLFGANG MOZART.

[To his sister]

Bologna,

October 6, 1770.

... It gladdens my heart that you have been so merry. I wish I had been with you. I hope Miss Martha is better. Today I played the organ for the Dominicans. Give for me my best wishes to Fr. Hagenauer and Miss Theresia. . . . *Addio*, farewell, a hand-kiss to Mama. . . .

[To his mother]

Milan,

October 20, 1770.

My dear Mama. I cannot write much as my finger hurts through writing so many Recitatives: I beg you to pray for me that my opera goes well and that we can then be once more happy together. I kiss Mama's hand a thousand times and to my sister I had a lot to say, but what? That only God and I know, if it be God's will then I shall

[1] Michael Haydn.
[2] Countess Pallavicini.
[3] The reader must not make the mistake of thinking these are conventional expressions of Mozart's. This attitude, which he had from childhood, he never lost, for it was completely personal and had nothing to do either with his being a Catholic or, later on, a Freemason.

soon say it to her by word of mouth, mean-while I kiss her a
thousand times. My compliments to all good friends. We have lost
the good Martha yet we shall with God's help find her in a blessed
state. . . .[1]

Two days before this last letter was written – namely, on
October 18th – they arrived in Milan from Bologna. Wolfgang
had to work on the libretto of his opera *Mitridate*, *Re di Ponto*, a
version by Cinquo-Santi of Racine's tragedy. The usual intrigues
inseparable from the theatre set in, in addition to all sorts of
difficulties with the singers, which however Leopold's tact and
Wolfgang's infinite adaptability overcame. Leopold writes to his
wife:

Milan,
October 27, 1770.

. . . Our lodging is not far from the theatre and consists of a large
room with a balcony and three windows. There is a stove in the
room. The bedroom is the same size, with two large windows but no
stove. Thus, if we don't freeze we are sure not to have stinking air.
The bed is as broad as nine good-sized men. . . .

We wish you both good health and especially cheaper times as
you are always giving me the depressing news that everything gets
dearer. What will finally happen to Salzburg if nobody thinks out
some means of introducing a sounder policy? For with such small
incomes we shall become no better than beggars. The poor Court
officials have scarcely the wherewithal to still their hunger and as
their children learn nothing because they lack the means so they grow
up idlers and in twenty years the town will be full of a crowd of
useless people living in want who will be a burden to the Court and
to the public. In a few years, even from year to year, it will be seen
that I am speaking the truth. If one wants people to marry and the
town to be populated one must first of all know how to give these
people work and means to live. To people the place with beggars is
easy.[2] One must be able to give them work and profit; then it is
good to increase the population. And that does not seem to me im-

---

[1] Leopold in this same letter writes to his wife: 'I shall not reopen the wound by
writing a letter of condolence to Herr and Frau Hagenauer. What cannot be altered
one must leave in God's keeping, what else is there to do?'

[2] A hit at the Church's policy. The notion spread by many of Mozart's biographers that his father was a narrow-minded bigot is absolutely false. The rest of
this letter applies to all Europe and England today. Politicians everywhere continue
to neglect realities for abstract principles and party strife.

possible, although Salzburg is very small and is shut in right and left. . . .

We kiss your hand a billion times and I am your old

(*Sgd.*) MOZART.

Milan,
November 3, 1770.

Wolfgang thanks you for your good wishes for his birthday and hopes, if the good God allows us to see another happy one, to make return to you in perfect joy and happiness all you have wished him.

I have nothing further to write than that we are, thank God, both well and wish it were already the New Year or at least Christmas; for until then there is much to ponder and do. . . . Patience! . . . we shall, with God's help happily bite our way through the unavoidable vexations which every *Kapellmeister* has to endure from the *virtuoso canaille*, just as Hanswurst gnawed through the Dreckberg.

Milan,
November 10, 1770.

. . . If our good friends from time to time can supply a joke in your letter it will be welcome for Wolfgang is now so occupied with serious matters[1] and consequently very serious; I am delighted if something amusing comes his way. . . .

We have, thank God, won the first battle and beaten one enemy who . . . tried to persuade the *Prima Donna* to sing none of Wolfgang's arias . . . but there is another storm in the theatrical heaven which we see far off brewing. . . . You must not be at all surprised, these are unavoidable troubles which the greatest masters meet with . . . one must not take them too much to heart. . . .

Milan,
November 17, 1770.

. . . In the afternoon we usually take a walk for I do not wish Wolfgang to write immediately after eating unless under the greatest necessity. . . .

Milan,
December 1, 1770.

I received safely your letter of the 16th. On the 16th I wrote in haste and so forgot to tell you that your letter of the 9th filled with your and Nannerl's good wishes arrived safely. It made Wolfgang melancholy when he read it and he said: 'Mama and Nannerl pity me thoroughly because papa has written in the previous letter such comic catchwords.'

---

[1] The composition of the opera *Mitridate*.

You believe the opera is already written. You are quite wrong. If it depended on our son then two operas would be ready but in Italy everything goes on in the most idiotic way. You will hear all in good time. It would be too tedious to write it. . . .

Yesterday as we were returning home we heard something which seemed unbelievable and which I could not have believed to be possible to hear in Italy, namely, two beggars, a man and woman, in the street singing an entire song in fifths without missing a note. I have never heard such a thing in Germany. . . . I thought at once of Herr Wenzel; if these two poor people sang across his grave, he would certainly rise from the dead.

Milan,
December 8, 1770.

Today . . . is the second Recitative rehearsal. The first went so well that one only had to take the pen in hand occasionally to make some literal corrections and alter *della* into *dalla*. This is greatly to the credit of the copyist. . . .

As far as I can judge without fatherly partiality I find the opera good and written with much spirit.

Milan,
December 15, 1770.

On the 12th was the first rehearsal with instruments, but only sixteen, in order to see if everything was correctly written. On the 17th is the first rehearsal with full orchestra consisting of fourteen first and the same number of second violins, two claviers, six contrabasses, two violoncellos, two bassoons, six violas, two oboes, two flutes which, if there are no small flutes, play together with four oboes, four French horns and two trumpets, amounting to sixty persons.[1]

Before the first rehearsal . . . there were not wanting people who with satiric tongues condemned the music beforehand, as youthful and poor and prophesied, as it were, declaring it impossible that such a young boy, and above all a German, could write an Italian opera; they acknowledged him to be a great performer but denied that he could understand and achieve the *chiaro oscuro* needed for the theatre. Since the first rehearsal all these people are dumbfounded and have not a syllable to say. The copyist is delighted, which in Italy is a good omen since, if the music pleases, the copyist often gets more money by distributing and selling the arias than the *Kapellmeister* for composing them. The singers are delighted.

[1] The idea that Mozart's music should be played on small orchestras is one of those bogus antiquarian notions so dear to half-informed dilettantes! [It is only fair to mention that Mozart's Vienna Operas were played by, and presumably composed for, a string section of six first, six second violins, four violas, three violoncellos and four contrabasses. *C.R.*]

... *Basta!* Now it comes before the caprice of the public. For us, except for the little empty honour, it is not of much importance. We have already attempted much in this strange world and God has always stood by us. Now we are on the edge of a no small – under the circumstances – achievement and God will be with us also this time.

Milan,

December 22, 1770.

The greatest and most eminent composers of this town, Fioroni and Sammartino, are our true friends as also are Lampugnani, Piazza Colombo, etc.... At least I hope that we do not have the bad fate of Herr Jommelli whose second opera has just failed in Naples. ...

Milan,

December 29, 1770.

God be praised, the first performance of the opera was generally acclaimed on the 26th....

Never in living memory was there such a desire to see the first opera of the season in Milan as on this occasion. Patronage cannot help the success of an opera since everybody who goes in will talk, cry out and judge for himself what he gets for his money. Patronage serves only and necessarily to prevent the composition of the work being hindered and to protect the composer at the rehearsals from any malice on the part of the orchestra... I write this in haste as the third performance is today. You know that everybody in Italy gets another name: Hasse is called Sassone, Galuppi is called Buranello and our son is known as Il Sgr. Cavaliere Filarmonico....

Milan,

January 5, 1771.

I can scarcely find time to write to you for we go daily to the opera and consequently at half-past one or even two o'clock get to sleep as we want something to eat afterwards; in the morning, therefore, we are up late and the already short day is thus made shorter....

Our son's opera continues its success and as the Italians say is *alle stelle!* Since the third performance we go in the pit, the boxes, etc.... for the *maestro* is only obliged to conduct the opera three evenings. Lampugnani accompanied on the second clavier and now that Wolfgang doesn't play he takes the first and Maestro Melchior Chiesa plays the second. If anyone had told me fifteen or eighteen years ago when I heard so much of the opera songs and symphonies of Lampugnani in England and Melchior Chiesa in Italy that these two men would perform the music of your son and when he left the clavier take his place to accompany his music, I should probably have directed such a person to the madhouse. We see by this how the power of God works in us men when we do not bury the talents he has graciously imparted to us.

Wolfgang's opera *Mitridate, Re di Ponto*, was given twenty times with unfailing success. Father and son then took a short trip to Turin, saw a good opera there and returned to Milan on January 31st, proceeding soon afterwards, for the carnival season, to Venice where Wolfgang gave a successful concert and enjoyed the usual festivities of a Venetian carnival. A few brief notes from Wolfgang, written in Milan to his sister, refer to his fingers aching from writing and from Venice he writes that Venice pleases him very much.

On March 12th they left Venice and stayed at Padua where Wolfgang received a commission to write an oratorio. They were in Vicenza on March 14th, Verona on March 18th, in Innsbruck on March 25th, arriving home in Salzburg on March 28th with a commission to write an opera for Milan for the Carnival of 1773 with an increased fee of one hundred and thirty *gigliati*. They had been away from Salzburg from December 13, 1769, until March 28, 1771, a little less than two years. Wolfgang had spent his fourteenth and fifteenth birthdays in Italy and had now definitely left his childhood and all its triumphs behind him.

Of the opera *Mitridate, Re di Ponto* (K.87)[1] not much needs to be said. It was an opera seria in three acts for four sopranos, one contralto, two tenors, with accompaniment of two violins, alto, two flutes, two oboes, four horns, two trombones, two bassoons and bass. The book, as may be imagined, since it is an adaptation of Racine's tragedy, is an unusually good one: so much so, indeed, that Wyzewa and Saint-Foix express a regret that Mozart did not have such a libretto to compose in his maturity instead of a *Clemenza de Tito* or even *Idomeneo*. The opera consists of twenty-four numbers, exclusive of the overture; they are all solo arias with the exception of one duet and a concluding quintet. Wolfgang conformed to the rather strict rules of the Italian opera seria of the time which were directed towards giving the principal

[1] Only fragments of the original manuscript score survive.

singers opportunities to display their vocal talent and powers of
expression in elaborate arias of a rather grave and formal beauty.
In fact the music of such operas had much the same function as
the verse in French tragedies. It was the beauty of Racine's verse
in its superb and rhetorical justness and inventiveness which supplied the artistic element to these dramas and it was just this
element which the composer had to supply *in music* instead of
poetry when using the same plots.

That Wolfgang before his fifteenth birthday had succeeded in
Mitridate in composing an opera at least as good as those of the
majority of contemporary mature Italian masters is abundantly
clear from the unquestionable success of the work with the public;
but in many details of purity and refinement it also shows his real
superiority as a natural musician without disclosing, however, the
genius of his maturity.

But on the whole Wolfgang reached a higher level in the fault-
less declamatory recitatives of this opera than in the arias.

CHAPTER SEVEN

Salzburg and Italy

Age 15–17 (1771–3)

WE MAY CONVENIENTLY pause here and consider for a few moments the beautiful portrait of Wolfgang painted at Verona by della Rosa in January 1770, the month of Wolfgang's fourteenth birthday (January 27th). It is true that in this picture he looks older than his age and there is not much sign – except perhaps in the fine curves of the well-cut mouth – of his bubbling spirits and exceptional sense of humour. But the fullness above the eyes, the fine development of the forehead round about the eyebrows, with a hint of voluptuousness in the mouth and chin, have an un-mistakable reality which makes this in some ways one of the best portraits of Mozart we possess.

Most of the biographers of Mozart amuse themselves in psychological speculation for which they show themselves quite unfitted. This is true even of the good ones like Jahn, Schurig, etc. who once they leave the secure ground of facts occasionally utter the most preposterous nonsense proving that they have little conception of the real nature of Mozart's genius but owe most of their appreciation to the renown of his name or the enjoyment of his music on its lower levels. It must be a matter for everlasting regret that no great painter – a Rembrandt or even an Ingres, a Cézanne or a Seurat – had the opportunity to portray with fidelity to nature and to art what must have been one of the most remark-able of all human heads. Instead of a portrait of the real man we have only a number of superficial semi-likenesses against all of which the observer must be to some extent warned. The sublety

and complexity of Mozart's personality were unquestionably mir-
rored in his face. His was no physiognomical façade of plain, inherited features on which the average painter may be let loose
without going astray. Rather did his features call for an extraordinary blend of sensuous and intellectual perception in the artist
who observed them, for it is an extraordinary and ever-disregarded
truth that he who looks sees only what exists in himself and what
is not within him, if only in germ, he cannot behold though it be
staring him in the face.

Hence it is that every critic and every performer of Mozart's
music gives us an image not of Mozart but of himself. That it is
not ludicrously apparent how minified[1] or contracted this image is
in nine thousand out of nine thousand and one cases is only due
to the restraining influences on mediocrities of the great men who
have seen Mozart as he really was. 'Ah! we shall never be able to
do anything like that,' remarked Beethoven once to Cramer at an
Augarten concert in Vienna after hearing a performance of
Mozart's Concerto in C minor (K.491). I once quoted this remark
to a hero-worshipper of Beethoven, a very clever man, and he
said: 'Beethoven must have been speaking ironically.' To such
ridiculous lengths does blind and stupid partisanship take those
who are clever but have no instinct! If Beethoven had not been
able to make that remark with complete and passionate seriousness he would not have been Beethoven. For no element of
rivalry enters into the work of the greatest masters since it is the
distinctive mark of a great master that nobody else can do what
he does. It does not diminish Mozart one jot to say that he could
not have written Beethoven's G major pianoforte concerto. And
it is also true – and Beethoven knew it – that even he, Beethoven,
was incapable of composing the C minor concerto of Mozart.
Such works are not only unsurpassable – they are unique.

So Jahn tells us that Wolfgang returned to Salzburg at the end
of March 1771, aged fifteen and two months, with his nature as
'simple, modest and childlike as when he had set out'. Two things
that seem to be the same may be vastly different and let me say
that the word 'simple' as applied to Mozart is not only profoundly

---

[1] I have coined this useful opposite of 'magnified'.

true but is also so utterly different from 'simple' as generally understood that it is highly misleading to all but those few who can truly understand it. '*Consider the lilies how they grow, they toil not neither do they spin.*' That is a simple, a Mozartian remark; but it is profounder than all the wisdom of Solomon, the aphorisms of Lord Bacon and the wisecracks of a *simple* American. Modest! Yes, Mozart was – with the possible exception of Shakespeare – the most modest of all the great artists of history. But what was this modesty? It was the natural expression of the certainty of what he was, a God-given genius. An artist of Mozart's rank cannot be proud; he may show pride in certain unfavourable circumstances which put an unbearable strain upon some element of his nature, and this is the root of the pride which Beethoven and Berlioz occasionally showed. But they were not proud or vain men, they simply failed occasionally in compassion. It is one of the most remarkable facts about Mozart that one may truthfully say that he never failed in compassion. This unfailing, universal sympathy – in whose possession he resembles such a Russian character as Tchekov – was combined with an astounding vitality, so that in Mozart we may find that rarest of all human beings, a saint who is not a bore; a nature so sound, sweet and passionate that I, personally, have for many years felt that among all the great artists of history Mozart and Shakespeare were the only ones whose moral superiority strikes to the core of one's being.

As for the third of Jahn's epithets, 'childlike', which is used by Mozart's own sister and nearly all who knew him personally, it is quite clear to any perceptive and adult person what that means. It means the possession of an eternal freshness of heart. 'Suffer the little children to come unto me, for of such is the Kingdom of Heaven' was the remark of someone who knew the roots of life. Every great creative artist must possess this freshness and purity of heart, for without it there can be no creation, only impotent cerebration.

So we can imagine Wolfgang settling down again in the little town of Salzburg quite as unspoiled by his Italian successes as he was by his earlier triumphant career as a child prodigy. Through

Count Firmian he received a commission in the name of the
Empress Maria Theresia to compose a theatrical cantata for the
celebration at Milan, in October 1771, of the marriage of the
Archduke Ferdinand with Princess Maria, daughter of Prince
Ercole of Modena. In the meantime at Salzburg during the next
five months he composed the Italian oratorio commissioned in
Padua, *La Betulia Liberata* (K.118),[1] a Litany (K.109), a *Regina
Coeli* (K.108), several symphonies, perhaps also the remarkable
Psalm *De Profundis* (K.93), of which the manuscript is in the
British Museum, and a beautiful *Offertorium* (K.72) founded on
the famous chorale of St John the Baptist which Wagner bor-
rowed for *Die Meistersinger*.

On August 13, 1771, Leopold and Wolfgang again left Salzburg, arriving in Milan on August 21st. At the beginning of September he received the libretto for the commissioned theatrical
cantata or serenata and immediately began composing the music.
At Milan they were in the midst of famous musicians, including
the great soprano Catarina Gabrielli[2], the tenor Manzuoli and the
composer Hasse who was busy working at an opera on a text by
Metastasio entitled *Ruggiero* which had been commissioned for
the same festival occasion. Wolfgang's libretto was by a well-
known Milanese poet, the Abbé Parini, who held the chair of
Rhetoric in the University. It was an allegorical pastoral play in
two acts with choruses and dances (these by Favier).

The marriage was to take place in Milan Cathedral on October
15th; on the 16th a public banquet was to be given to more than
four hundred bridal couples to whom the Empress had given
dowries; in the evening Hasse's opera *Ruggerio* was to have its

---

[1] *La Betulia Liberata* is an oratorio on the subject of Judith, in two parts for four
sopranos, one contralto, one tenor, one bass and chorus, with accompaniment of two
violins, alto, two oboes, two bassoons, four horns, two trumpets and bass. In 1786
Mozart, hoping to get it performed in Vienna, added a chorus and a quintet, but
unfortunately these two pieces are lost. This is a remarkable composition worth
reviving on account of its superb choruses. See Wyzewa and Saint-Foix, Vol. I,
pp. 362–6.
[2] Of Gabrielli Mozart writes to his father from Mannheim on February 19, 1778,
with reference to the young Aloysia Weber: 'It is all true what they have written
about the Weberin except one thing that she sings like Gabrielli; for that would
not please me at all. . . . Whoever has heard Gabrielli can only say that she is nothing
but a passage and roulade machine.'

first performance in the newly-decorated theatre with two ballets
in the entr'acte by Pick and Favier, and on the next day, the
17th, after a magnificent procession on the Corso, Wolfgang's
Ascanio in Alba was to be produced. Wolfgang, therefore, had
very little more than a month in which to compose the work.
Some ideas of the conditions of opera-composing is given by
Hasse's statement that six months were needed for a good opera,
while Naumann[1] declared that in Venice it was expected that an
opera should be written, learnt and a produced all within a month.
From Leopold's and Wolfgang's letters written home during this
trip I take the following:

[From Leopold]

Verona,
August 18, 1771.

The first day of our journey was a pleasant medley. In Kalterl
we ate standing . . . while the postilion gave our horses a little hay
and drank . . . a quart of quite good March beer. In Waidring we
had soup and drank a not at all bad Johanser-bier. At St Johann we
stayed and dined, and on the 14th we ate at the Post at Kundl and
stayed the night at Innsbruck. On the 15th at midday in Steinach,
the night in Brixen, midday on the 16th in Botzen, the night in
Trent. On the 17th we arrived in Roberto . . . and today left at about
seven for Verona where at 12.30 we got out at Sgr Lugiati's and
went at one o'clock to lunch. Now, after eating, everyone has gone
to sleep and I have taken the opportunity with a bad pen in a by no
means middling heat to scrawl this letter. Wolfgang, very tired, has
also gone to sleep. . . .

Now I must tell you that in my haste I forgot to bring several
clavier sonatas and a trio for a good friend in Milan who has done
much for us. . . . Nannerl can also get out the two trios, one by
Joseph Haydn in F with violin and 'cello and one in C by Wagenseil
with variations. . . .

[Postscript by Wolfgang]

Dearest Sister,
I have not slept more than half-an-hour for I don't enjoy sleeping
after eating. You can hope, believe, suppose, be of the opinion,
have confidence, find it certain, imagine, conceive and live in assurance that we are well but I can also let you know it. I must hurry,

[1] *Naumann*, J. G. (1741–1801), a renowned operatic and church composer.

farewell. My compliments to all good friends. Ask Herr von Hefner
if he has seen the Anna girl?[1] *Addio*, . . . my hand-kiss to Mama.
Lovely writing.

                                        (*Sgd.*) WOLFGANG.

[From Leopold]

                                        Milan,
                                        August 24, 1771.

. . . I must tell you that the poetry[2] is not yet come. It is ardently
awaited since without it they cannot get on with the preparation of
dresses, etc. . . . On the 15th October the Archduke enters Milan
and arrives at the Cathedral and they are married straightway, then
there is the kissing of hands, afterwards a great Supper-party and
then Good-night! The next day festivities begin . . . meanwhile I
have seen twenty thousand wax candles which are ready for the
lighting of the Cathedral, the Court, etc.

[Postscript by Wolfgang]

My dearest Sister!

We have had to endure great heat on the journey and the dust has
parched us with such persistent impertinence that we should have
suffocated and perished had we not been cleverer. Here it has not
rained for a month. . . .

What you have promised (you know well what . . . O my dear one!)
don't forget. I shall be most grateful. . . .[3]

Above us there is a violinist, beneath us, another, close by a
singing-master is giving a lesson, in the room opposite is an oboist.
That is fine for composing!

Now I melt with heat! Now I have got rid of my vest. *Addio*. My
hand-kiss to Mama.

                                        (*Sgd.*)   WOLFGANG.

                                        Milan,
                                        August 22, 1771.

My dearest Sister,

We are well, God be praised and thanked. I have eaten for you
many good pears, peaches and melons. My only amusement is to
use the deaf and dumb language for I can do it to perfection. Herr

---

[1] An affair of the heart? See also the following letter.
[2] The book of the cantata had to be sent to Vienna for approval.
[3] Again a reference to some affair of the heart; perhaps the daughter of Dr
Barisani, see p. 123.

Hasse[1] came here yesterday; today we visit him. The book of the serenata arrived last Thursday. I don't know what to write.

About that quite other matter of which there can be no more, you understand me. . . .[2]

[From Leopold]

Milan,
September 13, 1771.

The Serenata, which actually is more like a play in two parts, will be finished by Wolfgang, with God's help, in twelve days. The recitatives with and without instrumentation are all ready, as well as the choruses of which there are eight, five of which have dancing. We saw the dance rehearsal today and were astonished at the industry of the two ballet-masters Pick and Favier. . . .

[P.S. from Wolfgang]

I write only . . . in order to write, it is not at all to my mind as I have a bad cold. . . .

[From Leopold]

Milan,
September 21, 1771.

. . . By Monday or Tuesday at latest Wolfgang will have seen everything finished. Sgr. Manzuoli often comes to us we have been over to him. Sgr. Tibaldi [tenor] comes almost daily about eleven and remains . . . till about one o'clock while Wolfgang is composing. Everyone is uncommonly polite and has the greatest regard for Wolfgang: yes, we have not had the slightest trouble because they are all good and famous singers and sensible people. This Serenata is actually a small opera and the opera [of Hasse] is itself no longer, apart from the two big ballets after the first and second acts each of which lasts three-quarters of an hour.[3]

. . . All Milan is in upheaval . . . everyone is working, partly for the reception . . . for the lodgings and rooms . . . for the preparation and lighting of the Cathedral . . . for costumes, liveries of the re-

[1] It is interesting to note that Hasse wrote on March 23, 1771, to the Abbé Ortes: 'The young Mozart is certainly a marvel for his age and truly I love him boundlessly. The father, as far as I can see, is eternally discontented with everything . . . he idolizes his son a little too much and so does all he can to spoil him, but I have such a high opinion of the natural sense of the boy that in spite of his father's flattery I expect him not to let himself be spoilt but to grow into a proper man.'

[2] Nissen mentions that a young lady, of whom Mozart was fond, was about to get married.

[3] Abert in his edition of Jahn does not seem to have understood this reference and thinks it refers to ballets by Mozart.

tainers . . . carriages . . . horses . . . balls . . . renovation and decora-
tion of the whole theatre . . . in short for hundreds of things which
don't just occur to me . . . everything, everything is astir! . . . In
some previous letter you mentioned that many persons had become
crazy and now you write that many are dying of dysentery. That is
very bad. If people go wrong both at the top and bottom they are
indeed in a bad way.

[P.S. from Wolfgang to his sister]

Thank God I am well. I cannot write much; firstly, because I
know nothing, secondly, my finger is so sore from writing. Farewell,
my hand-kiss to Mama. I pipe on my pipe and nobody answers.
Only two arias are now needed for the serenata then I am finished.
My compliments to all good friends . . . I have no more desire to be
in Salzburg. I fear I also might become crazy.

[From Leopold]

Milan,
October 5, 1771.

Herr Caplan tells me . . . that you and Nannerl would have liked
to have taken this trip with us. If you were really serious about this
you ought to have told me so frankly, although the extra cost merely
to travel here and back would have been at least sixty ducats. Do
not have too many regrets about it. You would have had to endure
incredible heat and although many things are happening here yet
they are partly things such as you have already seen – and finer even
– or things which on account of the crowds one sees in great discomfort, even in danger of one's life if one is bent on seeing every
blessed thing. . . .

[P.S. from Wolfgang to his sister]

I am, God be praised and thanked, well but always sleepy. . . .

[From Leopold]

Milan,
October 19, 1771.

Marcobruni presents his compliments, he is with me at this
moment and we are now going to the theatre, for one the 16th was
the opera and on the 17th the serenata which pleased so greatly that
it is to be repeated today. The Archduke has ordered two copies;
all Cavaliers and other people come up and speak to us in the street to
congratulate Wolfgang. In short, I am sorry that Wolfgang's serenata
has so eclipsed Hasse's opera. I shall answer your last letter and

Nannerl's postscript when I write next. You will be able to see Italy with much more enjoyment than at present in the midst of this uproar. Farewell, we both kiss you ten thousand times, your old

(*Sgd.*) MZT.

[From Leopold]

Milan,
October 26, 1771.

... Perhaps news will reach Salzburg of the great success of Wolfgang's serenata since the young Herr Kerschbaumer, who was here some days, was an eye- and ear-witness the day before yesterday, the 24th, how the Archduke and Archduchess not only clapped and had two arias repeated but ... both bowed from their balcony to Wolfgang and showed him their pleasure by calling: '*Bravissimo, Maestro!* ...

On the 24th there was a terrible mishap ... a stand collapsed and fifty people were not only severely hurt but many lost an arm, leg, hand or foot ... while two women were killed ... luckily we were late ... and went on to the Court stand but had we been earlier we should have been on the same stand that collapsed. Let us thank God; we go on no more stands. You see that it is true what I wrote in my previous letter and you may believe that on such occasions there is little to be seen without running risks. ...

... The Archduke and his wife are well and very happy which has greatly pleased Her Majesty the Empress because one was apprehensive lest he might be little pleased with his bride since she is not beautiful: but she is very amiable, pleasing and virtuous and is consequently liked by everybody and has greatly charmed the Archduke ...

[P.S. from Wolfgang]

Dearest Sister,

I am, God be praised and thanked, well; now my work is finished I have time to write, only I don't know what, for papa has already said everything. I know of nothing new, except that numbers 35, 59, 60, 61 and 62 have been drawn in the lottery and if we had had these numbers we should have won but since we have not entered we have neither lost nor won but have the laugh on others. The two arias encored in the serenata were sung by Manzuoli and Girelli.

I hope you will enjoy yourself in Triebenbach with shooting and if the weather permits with walking ... my hand-kiss to mama! Farewell. I am always your faithful brother,

(*Sgd.*) WOLFGANG.

Forgive the wild writing but I am in a hurry.

[From Wolfgang: P.S. to his mother and sister]

Milan,
November 2, 1771.

. . . Herr Kerschbaumer . . . certainly can give a better account of his journey than others of our friends, one of whom said he could not see Paris because the houses were too high. Today is Hasse's opera but as papa does not go out I cannot go. Luckily I know all the arias thoroughly by heart and so can see and hear it in my mind at home.[1]

[P.S. from Wolfgang to his mother and sister]

Milan,
November 30, 1771.

So that you shall not think I am ill I write these two lines. Farewell. My hand-kiss to mama, my regards to all good friends. I have seen on the Domplatz here four fellows swing. They swing here *wie zu lion*.[2]

A few words are necessary about the Pastoral Serenade *Ascanio in Alba* (K.111). It is described as a *Festa teatrale* in two parts and is written for four sopranos, one tenor and choruses with accompaniment of two violins, alto, two oboes, two bassoons, two flutes, two horns, two serpents, bass, two trombones and kettle-drums. The original score, which is now in Berlin, has four hundred and eighty pages in two volumes. The Serenata has thirty-three numbers, consisting of recitatives, arias and choruses and one Trio (No. 31). The choruses are divided into two kinds, those with and those without dancing. Wyzewa and Saint-Foix state that the choral part 'seems to have been written by Mozart with much more pleasure and participation than the dramatic part' and they praise very highly the series of small choruses for shepherds and shepherdesses accompanied often only by wind instruments as being full of grace, beauty and rhythmic variety.

It is possible that the long sketch for a ballet entitled *Le Gelosie del Seraglio* (K. *Anhang* 109)[3] which is of the same date was in-

---

[1] This is truly a remarkable statement because it means that Mozart could have written Hasse's entire score down from memory as he did Allegri's *Miserere*.

[2] I take *wie zu lion* to mean 'as at Lyons'.

[3] Dr Einstein, in his 1937 edition of Köchel, is of the opinion that *Le Gelosie del Seraglio* is the first of three ballets composed by Mozart for the later opera in Milan *Lucio Silla*.

5. Mozart with his Father and Sister in 1763

6 The Mozart Family, 1780-1

tended for performance between the two acts of *Ascanio in Alba*, especially as it bears the names of some of the dancers, e.g. Pick, Binetti, etc. The plot of *Ascanio in Alba* is as follows:

> Venus descends from Heaven with her grandson, Ascanio, promising to give him for wife the beautiful Sylvia descended from Hercules. Sylvia relates to the priest, Aceste, that in a dream she has seen a beautiful young man destined to be her husband. Ascanio disguises himself on the instruction of Venus to test Sylvia who hesitates to recognize in him her destined hero. After certain trials, reconciliation takes place and Venus pronounces to the lovers the duties of their future life.[1]

Leopold and Wolfgang returned to Salzburg from Milan on December 15, 1771. On December 16th the Archbishop Sigismund died and his successor was elected on March 14, 1772. The new Archbishop, Hieronymus Joseph Franz v. Paula, Count of Colloredo, Bishop of Gurk, was extremely unpopular and was elected, according to Koch-Sternfeld, 'to the general surprise and grief of the populace'.

Wolfgang was commissioned to write an opera for the installation of the new Archbishop and the subject chosen was also of the classical, allegorical variety: *Il Sogno di Scipione* (Scipio's Dream) by Metastasio. But before he set to work on this he had a severe illness during January 1772. We know this from a letter written after his death by his sister to Sonnleithner dated July 2, 1819, about a portrait of Mozart's, an unsigned water colour dated 1771-2, now in the Mozarteum in Salzburg,[2] of which she says:

> It was painted when he had returned from the Italian tour, at sixteen years of age; but as he was just recovering from a severe illness, the picture is sickly and yellow.

Previous to this, on December 30th, Wolfgang had composed a Symphony in A (K.114) for two violins, alto, two flutes (two oboes in the andante), two horns, violoncello and bass, consisting of an allegro moderato, andante (in D), minuet and trio (in A

---

[1] *Ascanio in Alba* is worth the attention of the musical director of such theatres as Sadler's Wells, London. A delightful choral ballet might be made of it.
[2] Schurig puts this illness back to the autumn of 1769 on the ground that Sonnleithner was corresponding about the della Rosa picture which, however, was in oils.

E

minor) and allegro molto. But this was only the first of a long series of compositions which were composed during the first part of this year – namely, from February 1772 until October 24, 1772, when father and son left Salzburg again to go to Milan for the production of the new opera which had been commissioned. I shall merely enumerate the works which are known to have been composed during this period without much comment:

Mass in C minor (K.139).
Symphony in G (K.124).
Sonata for four hands in D for Clavier (K.381).
Sonata d'église in D for two violins, bass and organ (K.144).
Sonata d'église in F for two violins, bass and organ (K.145).
Litaniæ de Venerabile Altaris Sacramento in B flat (K.125).
Divertimento in D for two violins, alto and bass (K.136).
Divertimento in B flat for two violins, alto and bass (K.137).
Divertimento in F for two violins, alto and bass (K.138).
Six Dance Minuets with trios for two violins, two oboes, one flute, two trumpets (or horns) and bass (K.164).
Symphony in C for two violins, alto, two oboes, two horns, and bass (K.128).
Symphony in G for two violins, alto, two oboes, two horns, and bass (K.129).
Regina coeli in B flat for four voices, two violins, alto, two oboes (or flutes), two horns, bass and organ (K.127).
Symphony in F[1] for two violins, two altos, bass, two flutes, two horns in F and two horns in C (K.130).
Divertimento in D[2] for two violins, two altos, flute, oboe, bassoon, four horns in D and bass (K.131).
Symphony in E flat for two violins, two altos, two oboes, four horns, violoncello and bass (K.132).
Symphony in D[3] for two violins, alto, two oboes, two horns, two trumpets, violoncello and bass (K.133).
Symphony in A[4] for two violins, alto, two flutes, two horns, violoncello and bass (K.134).
Tantum ergo in D for four voices, two violins, alto, two trumpets, bass and organ (K.197).

[1] This symphony marks a great progress; it is dated May 1772, and shows the influence of Joseph Haydn.
[2] This divertimento in six movements is a wonderful piece testifying to the maturing genius of Mozart at sixteen. It is often performed in the concert-hall today.
[3] One of the finest of Mozart's early symphonies.
[4] Another remarkable work in which J. Haydn's influence is less strong.

Two German songs on the poems of J. C. Günther (K.149 and
150).
Die grossmüthige Gelassenheit (K.149).
Geheime Liebe (K.150).
Song for soprano in F. *Die Zufriedenheit* (K.151).

In addition to this considerable quantity of work there was the
one-act opera, composed for inauguration of the new Archbishop
of Salzburg, entitled *Il Sogno di Scipione* (K.126),[1] composed for
two sopranos, three tenors, choruses, with accompaniment of two
violins, alto, two flutes, two oboes, two trombones, kettle-drums
and bass. This work consists of ten arias, two choruses, overture
and recitative. It was performed at Salzburg during April 1772.

It is worth noting that just during this period when Wolfgang
was developing so fast a correspondent of Burney[2] visited Salzburg in the summer of 1772 and heard Wolfgang and his sister
play duets together; he informs Burney that although Wolfgang
is an undoubted master of his instrument yet he appears to have
reached his climax and, judging from his orchestral music, 'he
affords another example that premature fruits are more rare than
excellent'. One wonders if this visitor could possibly have heard
the Divertimento in D (K.131) composed in June of that year,
with its wealth of melodic beauty and wonderful skill in the varied
use of the wind instruments, or either of the two Symphonies
(K.133 or K.134)? It seems hardly possible that after hearing such
works – so far beyond the capacity of any living composer except
perhaps Joseph Haydn – that anyone could have come to any other
conclusion than that the young Wolfgang was at sixteen a more
wonderful phenomenon than ever.

Leopold and Wolfgang left Salzburg for Milan on October
24th without Wolfgang having written any part of his commissioned opera other than a few recitatives, which he had to
scrap as he found on his arrival that the poet's text had been
revised by Metastasio. The best account of this third Italian

[1] The plot, based on Cicero's *Somnium Scipionis*, is simple: The young Scipio,
asleep in the palace of Massinissa, is visited in dream by the Goddess of Fortune
and the Goddess of Constancy, who call on him to decide between them as his guide
through life. Then his ancestors come, among them Scipio Africanus and Æm-
milius Paulus, and warn him. Finally Scipio chooses Constancy.
[2] Burney's *Travels*, III, p. 263.

journey is to be got from the letters of Leopold and Wolfgang, from which I take the following brief extracts:

[From Leopold]

Botzen,
October 28, 1772.

Have we not travelled astonishingly fast to be in Botzen? . . . One always forgets something. I bought and brought along a new Calendar but we have left this year's somewhere so I must buy a new one, which is a joke. That I should have left my little seal at home is however no joke and annoys me excessively.

My health this time, praise God, has been brought, as it seems, into good order by disorder. If travelling is necessary for my health I shall seek a Courier's job or to become the Conductor of a mail-coach. Wolfgang is well; he kills time by writing a Quartet. . . .[1]

[P.S. to his sister by Wolfgang]

Now we are already at Botzen. Already? Only! I am hungry, thirsty, sleepy, I am lazy but well. At Hall we saw the convent and played on the organ . . . I hope you have kept your word and gone last Sunday to D.N. Farewell, write to me the news! Botzen deep Swinepool!

A poem by one who was devilish ferocious and furious over Botzen:

'I'd rather stick my groats in
My guts than go to Botzen.'

[From Wolfgang to his mother][2]

Milan,
November 7, 1772.

Do not be frightened at seeing my writing instead of papa's; the reason is (1) that we are with Herr von Aste and Baron Christani and they have so much to discuss that it is impossible for him to find time to write and (2) he is too – lazy. We arrived here safely on the fourth at midday and are well. . . . All the talk in Germany about the Italian war and the fortification of castles is untrue. Forgive my bad writing. When you write write direct to us for it is not the custom here as in Germany to carry the letters round, one must fetch them from the post. . . . There is no news here, we await news from Salzburg. We hope you will have had our letter from Botzen. I have

[1] Quartet in D (K.155).
[2] Note the imaginative care Wolfang shows for his mother in beginning this letter.

nothing more to say so I shall stop. We kiss mama 100,000 (I haven't brought any more noughts) times. I kiss mama's hand and my dear sister I embrace *in persona* as in imagination.

[From Leopold]

Milan,
November 21, 1772.

Thank God we are well and active like fish in water for it has rained incessantly for eight days. Today is the anniversary of our wedding. It is, I think, twenty-five years since we had the good idea to get married. We had this idea in truth many years before. Good things take time! The *primo uomo*, Sgr. Rauzzini, has now arrived, so there will be more to do and it will be livelier. There will also be no lack of the usual little comedies customary in the theatre. But these are trivialities. The figs which Wolfgang brought with him from Salzburg were as miraculous as the loaves and fishes in the Gospel; they have lasted till now. . . .

[P.S. from Wolfgang to his sister]

I thank you, you know what for – I cannot possibly write to Hrn. von Heffner. When you see him let him read this. I beg him meanwhile to be satisfied. . . .

[From Leopold]

November 28, 1772.

You ask me to write at length but what shall I write? That we both, thank God, are well is the most important and best news; there is nothing new here, most people are still in the country. . . . As regards my headaches these come only occasionally, at night . . . otherwise my appetite is good and when I can eat I am the healthiest of men. However, we eat only once a day, at about two o'clock. At night we have an apple, a piece of bread and a glass of wine. . . . Wolfgang has written nothing more for the *primo uomo* as yet than the first aria; it is, however, incomparable and he sings it like an angel. . . .

[P.S. to his sister from Wolfgang]

We both congratulate Herr von Amann and tell him from me that I am vexed that he made a secret of it when I have spoken to him of his bride. I took him to be more candid . . . tell him that if he wants a proper wedding he should wait till our return so that what he promised me may come true, namely, that I should dance at his wedding. Farewell! I kiss Mama's hand. . . .

[From Leopold]

Milan,
December 5, 1772.

We are, thank God, well although I am writing with a bad pen; for at Mm. D'Aste – who sends her compliments – the pens are always bad . . . as the *Prima Donna* only arrived yesterday and the tenor is not yet known it is easy to guess that the main and most important part of the opera is not yet composed. . . .

[P.S. to his sister from Wolfgang]

I have still fourteen pieces to do, then I shall be ready, for one can reckon the terzet and duet as four pieces. I cannot write much for I know nothing and secondly I don't know what I write while my thoughts are always on my opera and there is a danger that instead of words I shall write you a whole aria. . . .

I have learnt here in Milan a new game called: *Mercante in fiera*; as soon as I come home we shall play it. I have also learnt a new language from Fr. von Taste, it is easy to talk, troublesome but useful to write, though it is a little . . . childish, but good for Salzburg. *Addio*, farewell! My compliments to all good friends, my regards to our lovely 'Nandl and to the Canary bird for these two and you are the most innocent in our house. Fischietti[1] will soon begin on an opera buffa (in German) and start working on his idiotic opera. *Addio*, my hand-kiss to Mama.

[From Leopold]

Milan,
December 12, 1772.

. . . The tenor from Turin is out of the Royal Chapel and is expected on the 14th or 15th. Then, first of all, four arias must be composed for him. Sgra. de Amicis sends her regards to both of you; she is extremely well contented with the three arias she has up till now. Wolfgang has written her principal aria with passages which are novel and quite especially and astoundingly difficult; she sings these astonishingly and we are the best and most trusted friends. I write with a bad pen and ink. Wolfgang has the good ink, he is writing at another table. . . .

We have had rain here for some time but the last three days have been fine and not cold. We have not yet had a fire lit. It was wrong of Wolfgang not to give Frl. Waberl[2] the Minuet but she will for-

[1] *Fischietti*, Domenico, a Neapolitan opera composer made Church *Kapell-meister* at Salzburg in 1772.
[2] Daughter of Eberlin.

give him when she reflects that he is a fickle fellow who readily forgets. Why he thought of Frl. Barisani,[1] however, is natural enough and needs no explanation. . . .

How is Mlle. Zezi, is she learning? Is Nannerl industrious with her? My love to Nannerl and tell her to practise assiduously and teach patiently the little Zezi. I know it is to her own advantage if she accustoms herself to teach another patiently and thoroughly. I don't write this aimlessly.

[From Leopold]

Milan,
December 18, 1772.

Today three recitatives were rehearsed. Last night the tenor arrived and today Wolfgang wrote two arias for him and still has two to do. Sunday, the 20th, is the second rehearsal, Tuesday, the 22nd, the third rehearsal. Wednesday, the 23rd, the dress rehearsal. Thursday and Friday nothing and on Saturday, the 26th, the first performance of the opera. . . . I write this at eleven o'clock at night just as Wolfgang has finished the second aria. . . .

[P.S. from Wolfgang to his sister]

I hope you are well, my dear sister. When you get this letter, my dear sister, that very evening, my dear sister, my opera is staged. Think of me, my dear sister, and imagine vividly, my dear sister, that you, my dear sister, are seeing and hearing it also. . . .

. . . My dear sister, tomorrow we dine with H. V. Mayer and why, do you think? Guess! Because we are invited. The next rehearsal is in the theatre. The Impresario, Sig. Castiglioni, has implored me to tell nobody, otherwise everybody will rush there and that we don't want so, my child, I beg you to tell it to nobody otherwise too many people will rush there, my child. *Approposito* do you know the story that is going about here? Now I shall tell it to you. We left Count Firmian to go home and when we came to our street we opened our door and what do you think then happened? We entered. Farewell, my *lungel*. I kiss my liver for you and remain like my stomach always your unworthy

frater (*Sgd.*) WOLFGANG
bruder

Please please my dear sister bite me, scratch me.[2]

[1] Daughter of the Archbishop's physician, Dr Sylvester von Barisani, whom Wolfgang then admired.

[2] Every other line of this letter is written by Wolfgang upside down, which was a favourite trick of his. The whole letter is utterly characteristic.

[From Leopold]

Milan,

December 26, 1772.

Since lunch we have remained at Mme. D'Aste's where I am now writing . . . in about two or three hours the opera will begin.[1] God favour us. The dress rehearsal went so well the day before yesterday that we hope for a good success. The music alone without ballets lasts four hours. We received your letter and all its news. Joseph Hagenauer's misfortune has gone to our hearts. Today we both earnestly prayed to God in the church for his recovery. The ghost story of the Barisani household is nothing but an hysterical delusion . . . on the 21st, 22nd and 23rd there was every evening a great gathering of the whole nobility in Count Firmian's house; there was continuous music from five o'clock until eleven. We were invited and Wolfgang played. . . . On these three evenings the best houses of the town were lit with great torches; near Count Firmian's house in the church towers were peals of bells like the Carillons in the Netherlands and in the street there was music with trumpets and kettle-drums. . . .

[From Leopold]

Milan,

January 16, 1773.

. . . We are, praise God, well and my head remains better[2] . . . Wolfgang's opera has now been played seventeen times and will be given twenty times in all. The second opera was to have been begun on the 23rd but as it goes so well the second will not be staged until the 30th. . . .

[P.S. from Wolfgang to his sister]

I am busy writing a motet[3] for the *primo uomo*[4] which must be ready by tomorrow. Farewell. . . .

Leopold was hopeful of obtaining for Wolfgang a post with the Grand Duke Leopold of Tuscany. He had the powerful support of Count Firmian and at first the prospects seemed favourable. It was for this reason that he stayed on in Milan giving as an

[1] It was the custom to begin an hour after *Ave Maria*. At 5.30 p.m. the theatre was full. The Archduke had retired before *Ave Maria* to despatch five New Year messages to Vienna which caused a delay until the arrival of the Court at about eight o'clock. The singers were then irritable and nervous and the first performance finished at two o'clock and did not go well. The next performance was good and twenty performances to crowded houses followed.

[2] Leopold complains often of dizziness and remarks that he suffers from giddiness and overheating of the head after playing, just as in Salzburg every night after music.

[3] *Exsultate, jubilate* (K.165).

[4] *Venanzio Rauzzini.*

excuse – for he was no doubt fearful of the new Archbishop of
Salzburg and of exceeding his leave of absence – that he was confined to his bed with an attack of rheumatism. On January 30th
he writes a long letter to his wife describing his illness and his
inability to travel, to which he adds in cipher the following postscript:

> From Florence no answer has come yet from the Grand Duke.
> What I have written about my illness is all untrue. I was in bed a
> few days but am well and am going today to the opera. You can
> destroy this slip so that it gets into nobody's hands.

Unfortunately, Wolfgang was not to have the good luck of
Beethoven or of Haydn, both of whom found permanent patrons
who provided for their livelihood until they died. The negotiations with the Grand Duke came to nothing; as they had done in
1771 with the Archduke Ferdinand of Austria, who actually contemplated taking Wolfgang into his service and wrote to his
mother, the Empress Maria Theresia, on the subject, who, however, replied on December 12, 1771:

> You ask me about taking into your service the young Salzburger.
> I don't think so, for I do not believe you have any need of a com-
> poser or of useless persons. If, however, it would please you I don't
> want to prevent you. What I say is not to burden yourself with useless
> people. . . .

The failure of his negotiations with the Grand Duke of Tuscany
led to Leopold's and Wolfgang's return to Salzburg at the beginning of March. Leopold now falls back upon the idea of another
great European tour for which, however, money must be saved:
'I grudge,' he writes to his wife, 'every *kreutzer* spent in Salzburg.'
They arrived in Salzburg on March 13th in order to be present at
the anniversary of the Archbishop's election, March 14th.

Something must now be said about the opera seria *Lucio Silla*
(K.135) produced in Milan in January 1773. The text was by
Giovanni da Gammera, partly revised by Metastasio.[1] It is a

---

[1] The plot is as follows: Silla (the Roman Sulla) loves Giunia, promised bride of
the Senator Cecilio, and determines to kill Cecilio after vainly having represented
him as dead in order to win over Giunia. The lovers decide to die together. Silla
then pardons them and gives his sister Celia in marriage to Cecilio's friend, Cinna,
renounces the dictatorship, and gives Rome back her freedom.

rather stiff and dry libretto, making a *Dramma per musica* in three
acts composed by Wolfgang for four sopranos, two tenors with
chorus and two violins, alto, two oboes, two flutes, two bassoons,
two horns, two trombones, kettle-drums and bass. It consists
of an Overture and the following:

Act I:

    I   Aria of Cinna (soprano) in B flat, *allegro*.
    II   Recitative and Aria of Cecilio (soprano), Aria in F, *allegro
        aperto.*
    III Aria of Celia (soprano) in C, *grazioso*.
    IV Aria of Giunia (soprano) in E flat, *andante ma adagio et
        allegro.*
    V   Recitative and Aria of Silla (tenor), Aria in D.
    VI Recitative of Cecilio and scene with Giunia and chorus,
        scene in E flat.
    VII Recitative and duet Giunia and Cecilio, duet in A.

Act II:

    VIII Aria of Aufidio (tenor in C).
    IX Recitative and Aria of Cecilio, Aria in D, *allegro assai*.
    X   Aria of Celia in G, *tempo grazioso*.
    XI Recitative and Aria of Giunia, Aria in B flat, *allegro*.
    XII Recitative and Aria of Cinna, Aria in F, *molto allegro*.
    XIII Aria of Silla in C, *allegro assai.*
    XIV Recitative and Aria of Cecilio, Aria in E flat, *adagio et
        allegro.*
    XV Aria of Celia in A, *allegro*.
    XVI Recitative and Aria of Giunia, Aria in C, *allegro assai*.
    XVII Chorus in F.
    XVIII Trio of Giunia, Cecilio and Silla in B flat, *allegro*.

Act III:

    XIX Aria of Celia in B flat, *allegro*.
    XX Aria of Cinna in D, *allegro*.
    XXI Aria of Cecilio in A, *tempo di minuetto*.
    XXII Recitative and Aria of Giunia, Aria in C minor.
    XXIII Finale for solos and choruses in D.

This opera, written in November and December 1772, about
one month before Wolfgang's seventeenth birthday (January
27, 1773), ought to have been a masterpiece, because at this age
Mozart was capable of such, as his instrumental and church compositions during that year – not to speak of his earlier opera

Mitridate and other dramatic works – abundantly show. *Lucio Silla* is decidedly a remarkable opera seria with some marvellous things in it but the reason that it is not more than this is best explained, I think, by Wyzewa and Saint-Foix in the following words:

> Never, perhaps, during his whole career was he further from the ideal state of mind for a composer of Italian opera than at this moment with a whole world of personal emotions in his heart[1] and in his head a world of new ideas not one of which belonged to the kind of music he had now to deal with. Nevertheless, with his native suppleness perhaps he could have freed himself from these preoccupations and given himself entirely to his opera had he had this time, as before, a good libretto such as the tragedy of Racine: but it so happened that the new libretto was quite incapable of interesting him, containing neither moving situations nor sentiments human and profound enough to cause him to feel them reawaken in his soul. The fact is that one could not imagine more mediocre material than that of *Lucio Silla* as a subject for the dramatic genius of a musician so serious and reflective as Mozart.

Nevertheless, quite apart from one magnificent scene, which I shall mention presently, some of the arias in this opera would be well worth hearing if we possessed singers capable of singing them. And by 'capable' I don't mean singers who can merely sing the notes and think it wonderful to have done so; but singers to whom the difficulties would be a delight since they would transcend them with audacious and breath-taking (in more senses than one) ease. The aria of Giunia (No. 11) is in Wyzewa's and Saint-Foix's opinion 'the most brilliant and most difficult Mozart ever wrote'. This was sung by the Anna de Amicis often mentioned in the Mozart letters. As I shall have occasion to say again, later, the art of singing as it existed at its perfection during the latter part of the eighteenth century is scarcely imaginable today. Firstly we have lost the *castrati* – apparently for ever, although I, personally, should not be surprised if centuries hence they returned – and, secondly, there is no demand, opportunity or suitable environment for the development of the art of singing nowadays to any high degree of perfection. What passes for singing at our

[1] Wolfgang had this year fallen in love – for the first time – with the daughter of Barisani.

concerts and – with very rare exceptions – in our opera-houses either in Europe or America today is relatively the merest amateurish, undeveloped note-scraping and, quite apart from the toneless barking in Wagnerian operas (where singing anyhow is unimaginable), has about as much resemblance to real singing as has yodelling. Therefore such an opera as *Lucio Silla* must remain at present a sealed book since it depends primarily upon that highly-developed singer's art which has vanished. Should, however, a good and capable soprano – such as Toti dal Monte was at her best – read this book I recommend to her the Recitative and Aria No. 22, in C minor, of Giunia: *Sposo mia vita* and *Fra i pensier*.

The instrumentation of *Lucio Silla* is richer than any previous known Italian opera and here for the first time in operatic history, as Wyzewa and Saint-Foix point out, 'the vocal and the instrumental parts are treated symphonically like two members of one body, united for the same life'.

But the gem of *Lucio Silla* is the scene of the encounter of Cecilio and Giunia in a gallery of tombs where Giunia, accompanied by a choir of attendants, has come to invoke the spirit of her father. This scene was apparently written by the librettist in imitation of the invocation scene in Gluck's *Orfeo*. When the day comes that civilized countries possess properly equipped and endowed Schools of Music it will be a delight to an enlightened *Conservatoire* director to have his students produce this scene from *Lucio Silla* in the same programme as the scene from *Orfeo* to show the students and connoisseurs the difference in musical character between Gluck and Mozart. Of this scene which comprises Nos. 6 and 7 Wyzewa and Saint-Foix write: 'It is one of the grandest and most poetic *ensembles* he has ever composed,' and Hermann Abert says: 'In this scene of *Lucio Silla* appears for the first time not only the dramatic Mozart but also the great master of the demoniacal.'

In addition to this opera Wolfgang composed before his return to Salzburg the following:

Quartet in D (K.155), October 1772.
Quartet in G (K.156), November/December 1772.

Finale in D (K.163) for two violins, alto, two flutes, two oboes, two horns, trumpets, kettle-drums and bass; a symphonic version of the overture to *Sogno di Scipione*.

Motet[1] in F (K.165) for soprano, *Exsultate, jubilate*.

Symphony in C (K.96) for two violins, alto, two oboes, two horns, trumpet and kettle-drums.

Quartet in C (K.157).

Quartet in F (K.158).

Sonata in F (K.55) for violin and clavier.

Sonata in C Minor (K.59) for violin and clavier.

Sonata in F (K.57) for violin and clavier.

Quartet in B flat (K.159).

Sonata[2] in E minor (K.60) for violin and clavier.

Sonata[3] in E flat (K.58) for violin and clavier.

Adagio in E minor for string quartet written to replace the *adagio* in the Quartet in G (K.156).

Divertimento in B flat (K.168)[4] for two oboes, two clarinets, two cors anglais, two horns and two bassoons.

Thus concluded the last visit Mozart was destined to make to Italy. The compositions which he wrote during this third sojourn in Italy have a character entirely their own and his return to the less joyous environment of Salzburg affected him profoundly. Even his father wrote to his wife from Milan on February 27, 1773:

It is very hard for me to leave Italy.

Wolfgang is now seventeen years of age and from this time on we shall find developing in him an ever-increasing dislike of Salzburg and its conditions.

[1] See p. 124.

[2] In this remarkable work, supposedly composed in Milan in February 1773, Wyzewa and Saint-Foix see the same wave of romanticism which gave rise to the publication of Goethe's *Werther* the following year (1774). Dr Einstein, however, finds all six Sonatas (K.55-60) of doubtful authenticity and suggests they are the work of Schuster, whose compositions made a great impression on Mozart in 1777.

[3] Another exquisite work but of a more tranquil character. These beautiful Italian sonatas have been undeservedly neglected. Their Italian character makes it unlikely that Dr Einstein's suggestion that they were composed not by Mozart but by Schuster is correct.

[4] A work of unique grace and serenity, a poetic masterpiece.

CHAPTER EIGHT

Four Years at Home

Age 17–21 (1773–7)

THE CONDITIONS IN Salzburg on the return of Wolfgang and Leopold were not too favourable. Leopold, though vice-*Kapellmeister*, had two *Kapellmeisters* over him, Lolli and Fischietti, and he was not destined ever to improve his own position in Salzburg with the new Archbishop, for Leopold was not an easy servant. He was, both in character and general culture, much too superior and although, as Hasse remarked, he was an experienced man of the world, it seems likely that the extraordinary genius of his son was clearer to him than to any other person and it was natural that he should be more anxiously concerned about Wolfgang's future than about anything else.

The four years from Wolfgang's seventeenth to twenty-first birthdays were spent by Wolfgang at Salzburg, broken by two short visits, one to Vienna in the summer and autumn of 1773 and one to Munich for the Carnival season of 1774–5. We know less of this period of Mozart's life than of any other, since all the family being most of the time at home – with the exception of the two journeys mentioned – there are few letters, so that the chief and most reliable source of all biographical information is temporarily dried up. But we have the record of Wolfgang's musical compositions during these four years as a guide to his development and before mentioning the chief of these I shall say something about the general direction which his musical activity took during this period.

It was during these four years that the influence of the Ger-

man school of musicians – especially those of Austria – on Wolfgang became predominant and Wyzewa and Saint-Foix (to whom
everyone must turn for an exhaustive study of the early works of
Mozart) divide this period into six sections which they classify as
follows:

(1) The influence of Vienna and the decisive return to the German
     spirit (1773).
(2) The great creative effort (1773–4).
(3) The transition from the Grand Style to the Polite Style (*Galan-
     terie*).
(4) The triumph of *La Galanterie*.
(5) The Twentieth Year.
(6) A Period of Religious Music.

As Wyzewa and Saint-Foix devote the whole of one very large
volume to the consideration of the compositions of these four
years, as classified above, it is obvious that they must be dealt
with very briefly here. I shall not attempt an analysis of the works;
I shall merely give an idea of the influences acting on Mozart
during this period.

The first influence was that of the Viennese musicians. The
Archbishop Hieronymus visited Vienna in July 1773, and Leopold took the opportunity of following him there with Wolfgang
and received permission to stay in Vienna until the end of September, as the Archbishop was going into the mountains and to
Gmünd.

[From Leopold]

Vienna,
July 21, 1773.

When we arrived in Vienna old Frau Fischer was at her evening
meal for they have it at six o'clock: her daughter and son-in-law
were at Baden and only arrived home on Monday, 19th. They knew
nothing of our coming, since the letter addressed to the daughter lay
unopened as there had been no opportunity to send it on. The old
lady was overjoyed to see us and only regretted you were not with us,
too . . . we have splendid rooms and all we need at the Fischer's. . . .

On Sunday we ate at young Mesmer's with Herr von Heufeld.
Nobody recognized Wolfgang . . . Herr von Mesmer with whom we
are on Monday played to us on the Harmonica, or glass-instrument
of Miss Davis, and very well! It cost him fifty ducats for it is beauti-

fully made. The garden is incomparable, with views, statues, theatre, aviary, dove-cots and on the hill at Belvedere looking on the Prater. We dined there on Sunday, also on Monday evening. . . .

This afternoon we were most cordially received at Herr von Mayer's. . . .

[From Leopold]

Vienna,
August 12, 1773.

. . . Her Majesty the Empress was very amiable to us. . . . At the feast of St Cajetan the Theatin monks invited us to the service and a banquet and as the organ was not in use Wolfgang took a violin from Herr Teiber and played a concerto . . . The Jesuits at Court performed a Mass of Wolfgang's, namely, the *P. Dominicus Mass*.[1] I conducted and the Mass pleased enormously. . . .

[From Leopold]

Vienna,
August 14, 1773.

. . . When are we returning? Not yet, for His Highness [the Archbishop] has kindly given us leave to stay here a while. . . .

[P.S. from Wolfgang to his sister]

My Queen, I hope you are enjoying the best possible health and yet now and then or rather at times or, better, sometimes or still better *qualche volta*, as the Italians say, out of your weighty and urgent thoughts (which at all times spring from the finest and soundest sense) that you, in possession of your beauty – although of such tender years and not required as a lady to have any of the aforesaid sense – that you, O Queen, are possessed of such virtue as to offer some to this man-person so as quite to abash the old fellow. Farewell.

[From Leopold]

Vienna,
August 21, 1773.

A good friend of Herr Fischer's has invited all of us to Baden and as we have never seen the surrounding country we are eating today with Herr Fischer and set out after lunch to Baden and tomorrow Sunday evening we return. We have two carriages, in one are Herr Fischer, his wife and we two; in the other Herr Teiber and his family. . . .

Herr von Mesmer is building two new rooms below to live in in

---

[1] *P. Dominicus Mass* (K.66), composed in 1769.

the winter because above they burn an astonishing quantity of wood and yet the rooms are never warm. . . .

If we had any expectations or were earning any money I should certainly have written to you to come. There are many things one cannot write. . . . We don't know when we shall leave. . . . It depends on things I cannot mention. By the end of September we are certain to be, God willing, at home. Things must and will alter. Take courage! God will help us!

[P.S. from Wolfgang to his sister]

When one considers the favours of the weather and does not forget the consideration of the sun, so it is certain that I am, God be praised and thanked, well. The second part is, however, quite different; instead of sun we should put moon and instead of weather, art,[1] then anyone gifted with a little natural sense will conclude that I am a fool because you are my sister. How is Miss Bimbes?[2] Deliver to her everything imaginable for me. My compliments to all good friends from Herr and Frau von Mesmer. . . .

'oidda. gnagflow Trazom.'[3]

[From Leopold]

Vienna,
August 25, 1773.

. . . My purse is getting very empty, as my body gets fatter so my purse gets thinner . . . Wolfgang is now playing the clavier so I cannot write. . . .

[From Leopold]

Vienna,
September 4, 1773.

Now it is all over with the poor Jesuits.[4] I call them poor only because they were at the top of the tree, for the Rabbis and the whole *Corpus Religionis* might be called rich. The individual members, however, had nothing. On the 16th of this month all Jesuit monasteries must be turned over to the Court. Their Church treasuries, the wine-cellars and wine, in short, all their possessions are already sealed; the Order is suppressed, they may dress like secular priests

[1] Much of Wolfgang's play on words is scarcely translatable; here, for example, his *Gunst* (favour) and *Kunst* (art) cannot be given English equivalents.

[2] Their dog 'Bimberl'.

[3] *Addio*, Wolfgang Mozart.

[4] The Society of Jesus founded by Ignatius Loyola in 1534 was suppressed by a Bull dated July 21, 1773, of Pope Clement XIV. It was, however, re-established on August 7, 1814, by Pope Pius VII. It was still forbidden in 1936 in Germany, Switzerland, Portugal, etc.

and, it is said every one will get three hundred florins annually. That is not so bad! If one adds Masses to that a young fellow may provide himself with a pretty room and a nice housekeeper; for he won't have much else to do as preaching and begging will not be allowed. . . .

Many good Catholics . . . are of the opinion that . . . the Jesuits would have been left in peace had they been as poor as the poor Capucines. . . .

Herr Gassmann[1] was ill but is now better. I do not know what this has to do with our stay in Vienna. But fools are fools all the world over! Wolfgang has no time to add anything as we may lose the post.

[From Leopold]

Vienna,
September 8, 1773.

. . . I am much obliged to the Salzburgers that they are looking forward so to my return. That means that I shall enter Salzburg with more pleasure and will take a walk all night through the illuminated or lighted streets so that the lights do not burn in vain. . . .[2]

I shall, God willing, leave at the end of next week. But as I have . . . never been to Mariazell it may be that I shall return via Mariazell and St Wolfgang in order to take Wolfgang over the way of his name saint where he has never been and to show him the celebrated birthplace of his mother, St Gilgen. . . .

That the money I had with me is now all gone to the D—— you can well imagine and Herr Hagenauer will soon have news that I have drawn a trifle of twenty ducats from Herr Peiffer. That means nothing except that I need money but no Doctor. . . .

Wolfgangerl has nothing to write as he has nothing to do so is going round the room like a dog with fleas. . . .

[From Leopold]

Vienna,
September 11, 1773.

I hope that the departure of Dr Niderl prepared you for a sad event so that the news of his death will not be so painful. . . . On Thursday the 7th between ten and eleven in the morning he was operated on . . . and in one-and-a-half minutes or less it was done and I had the stone in my hands which was larger than a large walnut. I left him the same afternoon as well as such a patient could

---

[1] *Gassmann*, Florian Leopold, the Court *Kapellmeister* at Vienna. It was thought that Leopold was seeking this position for Wolfgang in the event of Gassmann's death. He died in 1774 and was succeeded by Giuseppe Bonno.

[2] A good example of Leopold's sarcasm, which made him feared and unpopular.

be and there was no anxiety then. On Friday the 10th we went between ten and eleven in the morning . . . after midnight there had been a complete change. . . . *Requiescat in pace!* I am quite overcome. For the two nights I have had only a little restless sleep for I woke on Thursday at four o'clock as if I had myself to undergo the operation that morning. . . .

I have reason with the whole of Salzburg to be sad at the second loss of our Salzburg doctor; the newcomer is bound to send many to eternity before he learns the nature of our climate and people. . . .

[P.S. from Wolfgang to his sister]

We are well, God be praised and thanked; this time we are writing to you in spite of being very busy. We hope you, also, are well. The death of Dr Niderl has grieved us greatly, we assure you we have wept and mourned much. . . .

Vienna at our Residence,
September 15, 1773.
(*Sgd.*) WOLFGANG.

[From Leopold]

September 18, 1773.

. . . Write by the first post to Augsburg to Jacob Lottner, printer and music publisher, that your husband asked you to write and tell him that . . . on his return from Vienna he expects the account of the copies of the Violin School in hand. . . .

Wolfgang is very engrossed composing something. . . .

By the end of September Leopold and Wolfgang were back in Salzburg. Leopold says nothing in his letter of the musical life in Vienna during this visit which took place in the off-season; but the Burgtheater was still open and Wolfgang may have heard there the following buffa operas: the *Puntiglioso amoroso* of Galuppi and the *Matilde ritrovata* of Anfossi, both of which were performed during his stay; in the houses of his friends where Mozart played he probably met with the sonatas and quartets of the contemporary masters such as Hoffmann, Vanhall, Ditters, Joseph Haydn, Gassmann, etc.

According to Burney, as well as from the information available from other sources, Vienna in 1773 was the most musical – both in quantity and quality – of all German cities. The Viennese composers of the day were learned musicians with a strong contrapuntal bias. Gassmann, for example, had just completed six

quartets each with two fugues and Joseph Haydn was writing
quartets with fugal movements. The influence of this Viennese
school was, in the opinion of Wyzewa and Saint-Foix, the prevailing influence on Mozart until, at the end of 1777, he visited
Mannheim on the way to Paris. While in Vienna Wolfgang composed the following:

> Serenade in D (K.185) for two violins, alto, two oboes (two flutes
>   in the andante), two horns, two trombones and bass.
> Little Concerto for Violin in F.
> March in D (K.189).
> Quartet in F (K.168).[1]
> Quartet in A (K.169).
> Quartet in C (K.170).
> Quartet in E flat (K.171).
> Quartet in B flat (K.172).
> Quartet in D minor (K.173).[2]
> Divertimento in D (K.205).
> March in D (K.290) (written probably for the Divertimento K.205).
> Six Variations in G for piano on the air *Moi caro Adone* from Salieri's
>   opera *La Fiera di Venezia* (K.180).[3]

The influence of Joseph Haydn was not only a direct one
through those works of his which Mozart had the opportunity of
meeting with in Vienna but it also operated through Haydn's
younger brother, Michael[4] (a musician not so very much less gifted
as a composer than his more famous brother), who since 1762 was
official composer at the Salzburg Court. Although Michael Haydn
had been at Salzburg since 1762 it is probable that Wolfgang had
not been much influenced by him until these four years at home
in Salzburg from 1773 to 1777. This would partly be due to
Wolfgang's frequent and long absences from home and partly

---

[1] This work especially shows the new German influence.

[2] Written, according to Wyzewa and Saint-Foix, under the influence of the
Quartets Op. 20 of Joseph Haydn; this quartet consists of four movements of which
the last is a fugue. It is a particularly interesting work for the study of Mozart's
development.

[3] On this work Wyzewa and Saint-Foix make some interesting remarks on the
difference between Haydn and Mozart's treatment of variations. They find that
Beethoven's Diabelli variations are more in Mozart's character of using the form
with freedom and fantasy rather than with the ingenuity which sticks closer to the
original material.

[4] *Haydn*, Michael (b. 1737; d. 1806), director of the Salzburg orchestra. Composer
of opera and of much fine church music. Weber and Reicha were pupils of his.

to the rather unfriendly relations existing between the families of the two Salzburg musicians. The strict Leopold did not approve of the conduct of the more Bohemian Haydn. He writes to Wolfgang on December 29, 1777:

Who do you think is appointed organist at the Holy Trinity? Herr Haydn! Everyone laughs. He is an expensive organist; after every litany he drinks a quartern of wine and to the extra services he sends Lipp who drinks too ...

On June 29, 1778, he writes:

This afternoon Haydn played the organ for the litany, and the *Te Deum* (at which the Archbishop was present), but so badly that we were all horrified. . . . Haydn will drink himself to death soon; or, at least, being lazy enough already, he will become still lazier the older he gets. . . .

However, Michael Haydn outlived Leopold Mozart and became more industrious as he grew older. Leopold, in spite of the jealousy which he may have felt for a fellow-musician who was not personally sympathetic to him, preserved his usual solid and objective judgment on musical matters. He thought that Michael Haydn's opera, *Andromeda e Perseo*, composed in 1776, showed that he had no dramatic talent and that the principal arias might have been written for a choirboy; but in 1777 he writes to Wolfgang praising Haydn's entr'acte music for *Zaire*, telling him that at table the Archbishop had said to him that he could not have believed Haydn capable of composing such music and that he should henceforth drink nothing but Burgundy instead of beer. He also wrote to Wolfgang on September 24, 1778: 'Herr Haydn is a man whose musical merits you will not deny.'

Wolfgang copied out in his own handwriting many of Michael Haydn's scores.[1] Wyzewa and Saint-Foix consider that it is doubtful whether Mozart ever encountered during his whole life a composer whose genius was so akin to his own as Michael Haydn's, or one whose work exercised so great an influence on him, an influence which they perceive even in the *Ave Verum* and *Die Zauberflöte*. What then was the quality in Michael Haydn

[1] And a great number of Eberlin's as well.

which made him so influential? It was – according to Wyzewa and Saint-Foix – that, like Mozart, he had, essentially, 'the nature of a poet'. He also, they write:

. . . conceived things under the sole aspect of pure beauty. Even in his most careless compositions the melodic line reveals at his hands a grace and delicious sweetness which is found again in his treatment and lends, for example, to his quartets and quintets the singular appearance of works of Mozart from which only the soul of Mozart is absent. Just as in the elder brother of Michael Haydn exactness of expression was always superior to invention of melody rhythm and modulation of striking beauty; so in the younger brother it seems as if poetic beauty always flowed effortlessly, a beauty often a little monotonous, shut within narrow limits, but as adorably fresh, limpid and 'galante' as could be imagined.

It is impossible to give any idea of Wolfgang's musical activity during the period at Salzburg, from October 1773 to December 1774, without mentioning the remarkable works he produced then. As we know practically nothing of his life during this year I shall set these down here with a few comments:

Symphony in G (K.199).
Symphony in C (K.200).
Concerto in D (K.175), for piano and orchestra.
Revision of Quintet for Strings (K.174).
Two Choruses for four voices and five Entr'actes for a heroic German drama by Gebler entitled *Thamos König in Agypten* (K.345).[1]
Sixteen Dance Minuets (K.176).
Symphony in G minor (K.183).
Symphony in A (K.201).
Rondo Finale in G added to his first quartet in G (K.80).
Symphony in D (K.202).
Sonata in B flat for clavier, four hands (K.358).
Litaniae Lauretaniae in D for four voices, orchestra and organ (K.195) (Kyrie, Sancta Maria, Salus Informorum, Regina Angelorum, Angus Dei).
Concerto in B flat for bassoon and orchestra (K.191).[2]

[1] This score was revised by Mozart in 1779. This work was a forerunner of *Die Zauberflöte*, see p. 237.
[2] This fine work, which is well known in the concert halls of today, was succeeded by two other Concertos for Bassoon composed a few months later (Spring, 1775) for a rich amateur, Baron Durnitz, which are, unfortunately, lost.

Missa Brevis in F for four voices, two violins, bass and organ
(K.192) (Kyrie, Gloria, Credo, Sanctus, Benedictus, Agnus Dei).
Dixit et Magnificat in C for four voices, two violins, two trumpets,
kettle-drums, bass and organ (K.193).
Missa Brevis in D for four voices, two violins, bass and organ (K.194).
Serenade in D for two violins, alto, two oboes (or flutes) two bassoons
two horns, two trumpets and bass (K.203).[1]
Little Concerto for Violin in B flat (interpolated in the preceding
Serenade) (K.203).
March in D for the preceding Serenade (K.237).
Sonata in C for clavier (K.279).[2]
Twelve Variations in C for clavier on a minuet of Fischer (K.179).
Sonata in F for clavier (K.280).
Sonata in B flat for clavier (K.281).
Sonata in G for clavier (K.283).
Allegro in G minor for clavier (K.312).
Sonata in E flat for clavier (K.282).

These Sonatas for the clavier were probably directly inspired
by a collection of clavier sonatas published by Joseph Haydn in
1774, and like most of Mozart's compositions for this instrument
were chiefly composed for performance by himself. The Church
music in the above list was officially composed for the Church
services in Salzburg. The Archbishop maintained a school of
fifteen choristers who passed into the Court Chapel choir, or if
they showed special talent were sent to finish their training in
Italy. Archbishop Sigismund allowed the male sopranos (*castrati*)
to die out and in their place had women sopranos; for example, he
sent the daughter of the Cathedral organist, Maria Magdalena
Lipp, to be trained in Italy; and when she returned she married
Michael Haydn. Perhaps it was this tendency of women sopranos
to marry which caused Archbishop Hieronymus, in 1778, to take
another male soprano, Francesco Ceccarelli, into his service.

---

[1] Wyzewa and Saint-Foix remark that the Andante of this Serenade compensates
in its poetic inspiration (henceforward more and more marked in Mozart's music)
for the abandonment of the beautiful learned and elaborated style of his preceding
period. In short, this work is one showing the transition from the Grand Style to
Galanterie, see page 142. The bassoon concerto (K.191) is a good example of the
former style.
[2] This is one of the first sonatas conceived for clavier without violin accompaniment. From this separation was born the later combination of sonata for violin and
pianoforte.

The Cathedral organist at this time was Anton Cajetan Adlgasser, a pupil of Eberlin; the assistant organist was Franz Lipp,
the father-in-law of Michael Haydn, who was Konzertmeister
and director of the orchestra. As vice-Kapellmeister Leopold
Mozart had plenty of opportunities of performing Wolfgang's
instrumental compositions because there was a constant succession of festivals and fête-days on which symphonies and cantatas,
etc. were performed by the Court orchestra. Leopold also had
charge of the music at the metropolitan church and a letter from
Wolfgang to Padre Martini in Bologna dated September 4, 1776,
may be quoted here for the information it gives about the conditions under which Mozart produced practically all his Church
music, Masses, etc:

Much Revered Father and Master,[1]
The veneration, esteem and respect that I bear towards your
revered person stimulates me to trouble you with the present letter
and to send you herewith a feeble example of my music,[2] submitting
it to your sovereign judgment. Last year I wrote for the Carnival at
Munich in Bavaria an opera buffa (*La Finta Giardiniera*). A few
days before leaving there His Highness the Elector desired to hear
some of my contrapuntal music: hence I was obliged to write this
motet in great haste so as to allow time to copy this score for His
Highness and to transcribe the parts so as to be able to perform it the
following Sunday in the offertory of the Full Mass.
Dearest and most esteemed Master, I beg you sincerely to tell
me frankly and unreservedly your opinion of it. We live in this
world to compel ourselves industriously to enlighten one another
by means of reasoning and to apply ourselves always to carrying
forward the sciences and the arts. How many times, oh, how many
times I have wished to live nearer you in order to be able to discuss
things with you, my reverend father. I live in a country where music
meets with little good fortune although, not to speak of those who

[1] This letter is written in Italian. A portrait of Mozart sent to Padre Martini,
now in the possession of the Liceo Musicale in Bologna, is reproduced in Plate
2. This portrait was sent by L. Mozart with his letter to Martini dated Salzburg,
December 22, 1777. Martini had asked for the portrait and Leopold says they had
delayed in the hope of coming across a good painter but had decided to get it painted
in Salzburg before Wolfgang's departure. He says of it: 'It has not much value as a
work of art but the resemblance, which I attest is extreme, gives it value as it is.'
[2] The motet *Misericordias Domini* in D minor (K.222) composed in 1775, at
Munich.

have left us, we still possess excellent artists and particularly composers of great science, depth and taste.

For the theatre we are ill-situated through lack of singers. We have
no *castrati* and will not find them easily since these folk wish to be
well-paid and liberality is not a vice of ours. For my part I write
Chamber and Church music. There are two other contrapuntists here,
Haydn and Adlgasser. My father is Kapellmeister at the Cathedral
which gives me opportunity to write for the Church as much as I
like. However, my father having been already thirty-six years in
the service of this Court and knowing that this Archbishop does not
like to see people of advanced years about him does not take much
part in musical services but devotes himself to the literature of his
art, always his favourite study.

Our Church music is very different to that of Italy and the more
so that a Mass including Kyrie, Gloria, Credo, the Sonata after the
epistle, the Offertory or Motet, Sanctus and Agnus Dei even on the
most solemn occasions when the Prince in person officiates must not
last longer than three-quarters of an hour.

This sort of composition requires a special study all the more that,
notwithstanding, it must be a full Mass with all instruments – including military trumpets and kettle-drums!

Oh, how many things I should have to say to you were you not so
far off, dearest Master! I salute devotedly all the members of the
Philharmonic Society and commend myself always to their good
graces. I do not cease to deplore that I have to live so far from the
person in the world I most love, reverence and esteem and whose
most devoted and humble servant I remain.

(*Sgd.*) WOLFGANG AMADEO MOZART.
Salisburgo, 4 Settembre, 1776.

Before commenting on this letter I may mention that we have a
description of the contemporary arrangements for musical services in the Salzburg Cathedral which reads as follows:[1]

The Cathedral contains a large organ at the back by the entrance,
four side organs in front of the choir and a little choir organ below
the choir where the choristers sit. The large organ is only used on
grand occasions and for preludes; during the performance one of the
four side organs is played, generally that next to the altar or on the
right side where the solo-singers and basses are. Opposite, by the
left side organ, are the violinists, etc. and on the two other sides are
two bands of trumpets and drums. The lower choir organ and double
bass join in when required.

[1] Marpurg, *Hist.-Krit. Beitr*, III, p. 195.

The Archbishop Hieronymus was a worldly man who seems to have liked the more superficial of musical qualities, but it would be too much to impute solely to him the tendency of Mozart during the year 1775 – a year before he wrote the letter (see p. 141) to Martini – to write a more facile Church music than he wrote earlier. This is the period aptly described by Wyzewa and Saint-Foix as *le triomphe de la galanterie* and it includes a number of compositions which I shall not enumerate here but which are listed in an appendix.[1] There are, however, two works among them about which I shall have a little more to say presently, after dealing with the significance of Mozart's letter to Padre Martini.

It would appear from the tone of this letter, and from the change in character of the music Mozart wrote towards the latter half of 1776, that something like a psychological crisis occurred in Wolfgang about his twentieth year. This is interestingly and ingeniously argued by Wyzewa and Saint-Foix and their analysis of his compositions from the years 1773 to 1777 seems to bear it out. After a period of, at times, a slightly superficial fluency, he seems to have turned away dissatisfied and it was here probably that he crossed the artist's Rubicon – inevitable to him, given his creative nature – and instead of pursuing the path of the successful professional purveyor of accomplished music passed into the solitary track of his own genius.

Mozart's nature was so optimistic owing to his prodigious vitality and to the well-balanced harmony of his many-sidedness and his musical gifts also were so extraordinary that it is not to be wondered at that he should have thought he could do anything. Worldly failure was inconceivable to him, as a young man, and for this reason we find him behaving in a way that seemed reckless to his cautious and more disillusioned father. Consequently, there were several periods in his adult career – like the period (1774–6) described by Wyzewa and Saint-Foix as *Le triomphe de la Galanterie* – when Mozart appears to have been hopeful of worldly success and all the financial benefits which would flow from it. Nobody ever set out better equipped with natural gifts for opening the world's oyster and extracting its pearl. When we look

[1] See Appendix I.

back upon these incessant tours of father and son in search of El Dorado (or simply *Gold*), beginning when Wolfgang was six years old, from our present point of observation and with our present knowledge and see how every intention was frustrated, how not one single position at any Court in Europe was ever obtained in spite of the utmost persistence and the most adroit strategy of Leopold, we cannot avoid a strong conviction of fatality.

This constant pruning of Mozart's worldly hopes seems as if absolutely intended by a higher power in order to bring to light a finer bloom and more perfect fruit. It is impossible, I maintain, for any perceptive person to read through this sober and truthful account of Mozart's life, which I am here setting down with a deliberate fullness and with as much accuracy as I can command, not to have the feeling as he reads it of witnessing the action of something like a Greek tragedy, the working out of an inescapable destiny, the destiny of Mozart's genius.

Did Mozart himself ever realize this sacrificial nature of his destiny? I am certain he did; but it seems as if it came only in occasional flashes of insight. His extraordinary ebullience, what one might almost describe as the ferocity of his high spirits (the source of that demoniacal quality in his music Abert and other writers have noticed), prevented him from a fuller realization of his destiny for a long time; but we shall see it slowly penetrating his consciousness and reissuing forth in those strange and enigmatic compositions of his maturity until at last this awareness of his destiny and of himself floods his mind completely and results in the astounding works of the crowning and most bitter years at the end of his life.

The tours of Leopold and Wolfgang in search of a haven for the genius of the young Wolfgang put in my mind the travels of Don Quixote and Sancho Panza. Nothing turned out to be what they first thought it was. Don Quixote is Wolfgang and Sancho Panza is his father and at the end of this story we shall find Wolfgang returning like Don Quixote to his own mind in which alone all the riches of this journey have lain. The giants were windmills, the armies were sheep, the princes were lackeys, the Dulcinea was a commonplace wench and the Flying Horse was merely his

musical science. What gave the colour, life, virtue and existence
to all these things was his own creative soul, his unalienable and
indestructable genius.

One of these early flashes of insight was at work in this letter
to Padre Martini, in spite of any more immediate cause. An immediate cause then was, namely, his father's desire that he should
set forth again to seek a remuneration and stable position worthy
of his talents. In this search a certificate of his ability from the
celebrated and well-respected Martini would be useful – so Leopold may have thought; but whether or not this was the immediate motive of writing the letter, its heartfelt and spontaneous
expression of Wolfgang's musical solitude has its unmistakable
origin in his purely artistic ambition.

From Martini's reply I shall quote the following passage about
the motet:

> I have found in it everything which distinguishes modern music,
> that is to say good harmony, rich modulations, excellent flowing
> violin parts, a natural use of the voices and a remarkable elabora-
> tion. . . .

Only in Martini's phrase 'remarkable elaboration' may we read
any expression of surprised admiration; but this elaboration is
even more surprising nowadays to ears unaccustomed to such
musical science. The Church music of Mozart is one part of his
work which has not as yet had the full recognition in praise and in
performance which it deserves; it still awaits the more careful and
thorough attention of first-class choral societies and singers. The
very great demands it makes, however, on their vocal and musical
capacities, though they ought to be a stimulus, are likely to keep
it unknown until a more favourable age for singing. I shall have
more to say on this subject when I come to his last (C minor)
Mass.[1]

We now return to the one event about which we have some
biographical information during this period of 1773–7, namely,
the excursion from Salzburg to Munich made by Wolfgang. He
received a commission (which he refers to in his letter to Martini)

[1] See pp. 261–2.

to write an opera buffa for the Carnival season of 1775 at Munich. As this came from the Elector of Bavaria, Maximilian III, the Archbishop of Salzburg was unable to refuse leave of absence, so Leopold and Wolfgang set out for what was to be their last journey together on December 6, 1774. Leopold writes:

Munich,
December 9, 1774.

. . . Our lodging is indeed small but comfortable enough and H. v. Pernat shows us, indeed, more politeness and honour than we merit and I am certain that he sacrifices his comfort in many respects to us. About the opera I have nothing to write yet. Today we met our colleagues who were all very amiable and especially His Excellency Count Seeau. . . .[1]

[From Leopold]

Munich,
December 14, 1774.

. . . As for Nannerl I have as yet no suitable lodging for her as in this respect great care is necessary here in Munich. There is another thing. Here as in Salzburg an opera to which one pays to go cannot be given more than twice running, otherwise there would be too few people in the theatre, so in two or three weeks another opera has to be produced and then the former revived as is done with the comedies and the ballets. . . . The opera of Wolfgang's will . . . I believe, be first performed on the 29th. It can so happen that Nannerl will not see it. Once the Carnival has properly begun there will only be light little operettas played in a small theatre that is prepared in the Redoutensaal where there is a crowd of masqueraders and many gaming tables and nothing but noise, talking, etc. . . .

[From Leopold]

Munich,
December 16, 1774.

Now I have a lodging for Nannerl and where do you think? At Madam, or rather the widowed Frau von Durst. . . . Nannerl will have her own bedroom. True, it is rather dark but the rest of the time she will use Frau von Durst's room which looks on the Market Square and in which a harpsichord will be put. . . . Nannerl must practise, especially the Sonatas of Paradies and Bach and the Concerto of Lucchesi. . . .

[1] Count Seeau was the Intendant or director of the Music and Opera in Munich.

[P.S. from Wolfgang to his sister]

I have toothache.

Johannes chrisostomus Wolfgangus Amadeus Sigismundus Mozartus Maria annae Mozartae matri et sorori, ac amicis omnibus, praesertimque pulchris virginibus, ac freillibus, gratiososque freillibus.[1] S.P.D.

[From Leopold]

Munich,
December 21, 1774.

... Nannerl must have a man's fur coat on the journey, otherwise she will not be able to endure it in a half-covered chaise [coach]. She must take care to keep her head warm and her feet must be looked after apart from the felt shoes which in the long run do not help much. So she must put on the fur boots which are in the chest under the roof and H. Geschwendner will be good enough to put a little hay on the floor of the chaise.

You know that we were well provided for; just think what we had to cover us. I had fur boots over the shoes and then we had foot-muffs and yet even so we could not have held out if at the third post-stage at Febertsheim I had not obtained a large bundle of hay and had it put in the chaise and covered our foot-muffs completely with it. ...

Besides the Bach[2] and Paradies Sonatas Nannerl can also bring Wolfgang's Sonata and Variations and other sonatas, whatever she likes, for sonatas don't take up much room. But not many Concertos! Wolfgang's Concerto we already have here[3] and if she brings another couple it is enough. ...

[From Leopold]

Munich,
December 28, 1774.

... the first rehearsal of Wolfgang's opera has pleased so much that it is postponed until January 5, 1775, so that the singers may know it better. ... Wolfgang has been kept indoors for six days with a swollen face. The cheek was swollen inside and out, also his right eye, and for two days he could only take soup. So one must well protect the face and ears for in a half-open chaise the snow flies constantly in one's face. ... Nannerl must take some money with

---

[1] 'Johann Chrisostom Wolfgang Amadeus Sigismund Mozart to Maria Anna mother and sister, and to all friends, especially beautiful virgins, and easy-going and pleasing ones.' I have taken the liberty of assuming that by *freillibus* Mozart intended *facilibus*.

[2] Johann Christian Bach.

[3] Concerto in D (K.175).

her in case of need. Now Nannerl must know where to go. The following must be written out on a slip and given to Hr. Geschwendner or kept by her [here follow precise instructions as to the address in Munich].

[P.S. from Wolfgang]

My dear Sister,

I beg of you not to forget before you leave to have your talk, that is to make the visit you know of – for I have my reasons. I beg you to give my greetings – but most expressive and tenderly – and – oh – I need not be so concerned about it, I know my sister, tenderness is so natural to her I am certain she will do her very best to give me pleasure . . . we will bicker about it all in Munich. Farewell.

[From Leopold]

Munich,
December 30, 1774.

When you get this Nannerl will have already packed but . . . nevertheless I want her to bring five or six copies of our Paris engraving.[1] Herr von Pernat insists on having one. . . . I also forgot to say that Nannerl should bring a Masquerade costume even if it is only a Salzburg one. . . . Nannerl will arrive on Wednesday and on Thursday it will be performed. If Herr von Mölk[2] comes with her he will also see it but if he comes later he will not see it before Easter. . . .

You must know that Maestro Tozzi who this year is writing the opera seria wrote this time last year an opera buffa and exerted himself so as to surpass the opera seria of Sales; he succeeded in quite eclipsing Maestro Sales' opera.[3] Now it so turns out that Wolfgang's opera is ready before Tozzi's and all those who have heard the first rehearsal are now saying that Tozzi is paid back in his own coin since Wolfgang's opera will put his quite in the shade. I do not like this sort of thing and do all I can to stop such talk and protest endlessly but the whole orchestra and all who have heard the rehearsal say they have never heard more beautiful music in which every aria is fine . . . *Basta!* God will put everything right. Farewell. . . .

[P.S. from Wolfgang to his sister]

Please give my regards to Roxelana. . . . To miss Mizerl say

[1] The picture by Carmontelle, see pp. 32, 35.
[2] Herr von Mölk came and embarrassed Wolfgang and his father by his excessive enthusiasm: 'Anyone could see,' writes Wolfgang on January 11th, 'that he had never in his life been further than Salzburg or Innsbruck.'
[3] The respective operas were *Orfeo ed Euridice*, opera seria by Antonio Tozzi, *Kapellmeister* at the Munich Court (1775), and *Achille in Sciro* by P. Sales. Einstein believes that it was Tozzi's *La serva astuta* which eclipsed Sales' opera seria.

everything imaginable, she is not to doubt my love, she is constantly before my eyes in her bewitching *négligée;* I have seen many pretty girls here but none to compare with her. My sister is not to forget to bring the Variations on the *Minuet d'exaude* of Ecart and my Variations on the minuet of Fischer. . . .

Keep very warm on the journey, I beg of you, otherwise you may have to sit in the house for fourteen days sweating by the stove and who will look after you? I'll not get hot, now I talk rot. I am ever

Thy Munich

brother 1774 30 *Anno Decembre.*

Wolfgang's sister arrived in Munich on January 4, 1775.[1] The first performance of Wolfgang's opera *La Finta Giardiniera* took place on January 13th with brilliant success as described by Wolfgang in a letter to his mother dated January 14th:

God be praised! my opera was produced yesterday and succeeded so well that I cannot possibly describe to Mama the reception. Firstly the theatre was so full that many were turned away. After every aria there was a terrific uproar with clapping and cries of *viva Maestro.* . . .

Afterwards Papa and I went into a room where the Elector and Electress[2] and the whole Court were and kissed their hands and they were very agreeable . . . and congratulated me that the opera had so exceptionally pleased everybody. As for our return it will not be so soon. . . . One good reason is that next Friday the opera will be given again and it is essential that I should be at the performance, otherwise one would not recognize it – that is very strange here.[3]

We have two interesting contemporary notices of the performance of *La Finta Giardiniera* in Munich. One is by the Secretary of the Legation, Unger, who writes in his journal of January 15, 1775, as follows:

Friday L.A.R.E. assisted at the first representation of the opera buffa *La Finta Giardiniera;* the music was much applauded; it is by the young Mozart of Salzburg who is at the moment here. This is the same Mozart who was in England and elsewhere at the age of eight to play the clavier which he does surpassingly well.

[1] According to a letter from Leopold to his wife dated Munich, January 5, 1775.

[2] No doubt the Elector's sister, Maria Antonia Walpurga of Saxony; both were good amateur musicians.

[3] In Leopold's letter of February 21st to his wife he remarks: 'Wolfgang's opera has been performed again, but, owing to the singer who was ill, had to be cut. . . .' This refers to the second woman singer who in any case was, so Leopold writes, 'miserable'. The principal role of Sandrina was written for an excellent singer, Rosa Manservisi.

7. Mozart in 1770

8. Constanze Mozart, 1782–3

Schubart in his *Teutsche Chronik* (1775, p. 267) wrote:

> I also heard an opera buffa by the amazing genius Mozart; it is called *La Finta Giardiniera*. Sparks of genius flash here and there; but it is not yet the calm fire from the altar rising to heaven in clouds of incense – a perfume for the Gods. If Mozart is not a forced hot-house plant then he must become one of the greatest composers that has ever lived.[1]

In addition to the opera, Wolfgang's Litany in B flat major (K.125) and his two small Masses (*Missa Brevis* in F (K.192) and *Missa Brevis* in D (K.194)) were performed in the Court Chapel conducted by Leopold on successive Sundays.[2] It was at this time, also, that he composed for the Elector the *Misericordias Domini* (K.222) which he sent to Padre Martini.[3] Wolfgang and his sister Nannerl played in public and there is an interesting account by Schubart of Wolfgang's pianoforte playing. He writes in his *Teutsche Chronik* (1776, p. 276):

> Last winter in Munich I heard two of the greatest clavier players, Herr Mozart and H. v. Beecke.[4] My host, Herr Albert, has an excellent pianoforte in his house. There I heard these two giants compete. Mozart plays the most difficult things and whatever is laid before him at sight. But nevertheless Beecke far surpasses him – winged speed, grace, melting sweetness and a marvellous taste are weapons which none can wrest from the hands of this Hercules.[5]

In spite of these successes Wolfgang did not receive any appointment from the Elector of Bavaria nor the commission for the opera seria for the following year. A few words are now necessary on Wolfgang's opera.

La Finta Giardiniera (K.196), opera buffa in three acts for three sopranos, one castrato, two tenors and one bass with orchestra, on a

[1] Even if we heard *La Finta Giardiniera* for the first time today, after all the musical developments since Beethoven and Wagner, it would strike any perceptive musician as a work of genius.
[2] A Litany by Leopold was also performed.
[3] See page 140.
[4] *Beecke*, Ignaz von (1733–1803), a famous pianist who, with Schobert, inaugurated the modern technique; composer of numerous songs, operas, etc.
[5] An experienced and perceptive connoisseur of pianoforte playing will understand readily from these epithets why Schubart preferred what I have no doubt was the inferior but more superficially striking playing of Beecke. It is always the same story.

F

libretto written in Rome in 1774 for an opera buffa by Pasquale Anfossi consisting of an overture and twenty-eight numbers, all but seven of which are arias.

This opera is thoroughly delightful in performance and, speaking as one who has seen it on the stage, I demur to the remarks of certain critics who point out that the music is not as appropriate to the text as Anfossi's, being far too elaborate and intense. Wyzewa and Saint-Foix though they also make this comparison in the course of so doing give such a just and perceptive description of the character of this most entrancing lyrical work that I shall quote it here. After saying that his music is often more powerful and passionate than the situations demand and that his comic arias are too subtle, elaborate, ingenious and clever for the words, they go on to say that it is still worse when the situation or words permit the musician to express tender or melancholy sentiment. Then, they add, Mozart entirely abandons the conventions of opera buffa:

> The least trace of sadness or love inflames the imagination of the young artist . . . so that he treats the arias like the ariosos or cavatinas of opera seria with a continued use of minor keys and an intensity of lyrical passion which would touch us more profoundly if we could forget that our concern was with carnival weathercocks quite incapable of experiencing the profound emotions which the musician of genius lends them. Thus, to give one example, the ensemble which makes up with their recitatives the two arias of Sandrina, Nos. 21 and 22, will have its counterpart, altogether similar, in one of Mozart's most tragic scenes, a scene from the opera *Andromeda* composed in 1777 for Mme Duschek; and perhaps even this scene does not express grief as profound and pathetic as the two arias in *La Finta Giardiniera* sung by a young girl whom we have just seen and are about to see again humming trifles—to say nothing of the fact that this access of grief arises out of an imbroglio only invented to make us laugh and which, in addition, is so stupid as to be almost incomprehensible.

Though from the purely artistic point of view such divergences between text and music are a defect in a work of art, yet in a work such as *La Finta Giardiniera* we may be free to let ourselves enjoy the entrancing music without reserve; for it has an inimitable charm and gaiety, tenderness and fertility of invention allied to such musical science that I personally prefer it even to the later *Die Entführung aus dem Serail*. Unfortunately the secco recitatives of the first act are lost and mere spoken dialogue can never replace them. Nevertheless *La Finta Giardiniera* will always deserve performance on account of the superior quality, so pure and exquisite, of the music. This question of quality is one to which insufficient attention is paid by scholars and historians, and it is this lack of proportion which blinds critics to the fact that an imperfect work of Mozart's such as *La Finta Giardiniera*, may be superior to the most perfect of the works of a Wagner or a Richard Strauss.

Leopold, Wolfgang and Nannerl returned to Salzburg on March 7, 1775. In April the Archduke Maximilian, youngest son of Maria Theresia, and afterwards Archbishop of Cologne, paid a visit to Salzburg. He had been paying a visit to his sister, Marie Antoinette, in Paris and in his honour the usual musical festivities were arranged in Salzburg. On April 22nd a serenata by Fischietti was performed and on the following day a festival opera hurriedly composed by Mozart, *Il Re Pastore*, was given. We have a brief account by one of the suite of the Archduke Maximilian, written on April 24th, which reads as follows:

Music was the entertainment provided as on the preceding days; at its close the famous young Mozart was heard on the piano; he played various pieces from his head with equal skill and grace.

Only a few words are necessary on this festival opera of Wolfgang's:

Il Re Pastore (K.208), *Dramma per musica* in two acts, for three sopranos and two tenors with orchestra of first and second violins, alto, two flutes, two oboes, two bassoons, two cors anglais, four horns and bass. The text is by Metastasio and this work is rather a pastoral serenade than an opera, thus resembling *Ascanio in Alba* but without the dances and choruses. It consists of an overture and fourteen numbers, all of which are recitatives and arias except No. 7, a recitative and duet, and No. 14, a finale ensemble.

This work is a good example of Mozart's exquisite craftsmanship at this period without having any greater significance.

The character of the opera is well summed up by Wyzewa and
Saint-Foix who point out that all the arias are very well written
for the voice and that the instrumentation is clear, easy and evidently improvised but always rich and exquisite. They add:

> There is little counterpoint and none of those great dramatic
> ventures that are to be found in *Lucio Silla*: but an extreme purity of
> melodic line, a very free and happy use of wind instruments and
> invariably a poetic colour ravishing in its simplicity.

During the period after the production of *Il Re Pastore* (April
1775) up to the date of Wolfgang's departure from Salzburg on
September 23, 1777, Wolfgang passed his twentieth year. Within
these two years and five months he composed more than thirty
works, the list of which will be found in the Appendix. It includes violin concertos, pianoforte concertos and a quantity of
ecclesiastical music,[1] to say nothing of many sonatas and numerous instrumental works such as the famous Haffner Serenade in D
(K.250) and March (K.249) written for the marriage of Elise
Haffner, the daughter of a wealthy Salzburg merchant and *Bürger-
meister*, in July 1776; the delightful Serenata Notturna in D
(K.239) for two small orchestras placed apart; the superb Divertimento or Notturno in F (K.247) composed for Countess Lodron
in June 1776,[2] and the fascinating Divertimento in D (K.251)
written for his sister's twenty-fifth birthday, July 30, 1776.

It must be added that during the last two years of this stay in
his home-town Wolfgang became intimately acquainted with the
members of the higher nobility such as Countess Lodron, for
whom he composed much music. This change of *milieu* is reflected in the character of many of his compositions of the
period in which elegance, taste and brilliance are chiefly aimed at.
It is what Wyzewa and Saint-Foix describe as the style of '*la
galanterie*'.

[1] Two remarkable pieces must be mentioned here, the beautiful *Sancta Maria*
for four voices, two violins, alto, bass and organ (K.273), and the marvellous *Litaniae
de Venerabili Altaris Sacramento* (K.243), a large-scale work in eight sections, which
is a masterpiece of the highest quality.
[2] This work may be taken as one of the finest examples of the flowering of the
genius of Mozart in his twentieth year.

CHAPTER NINE

Father and Son

Age 21 (1777)

ON SEPTEMBER 23, 1777, Wolfgang left Salzburg with his mother on a tour which was to keep him away from home until January 1779, and take him for the last time to Paris where he was to bury his mother. The reasons for his departure are as follows:

The Mozart family were not popular with their lord and master, the Archbishop Hieronymus, whose tyrannical disposition[1] was combined with a sufficiently acute intelligence for him to see the stark independence underlying the formal correctness and subservience of Leopold. When the old *Kapellmeister* Lolli required a joint *Kapellmeister* in 1772 the post instead of being given to Leopold, who had a well-founded claim to it, was given to Fischietti, so that Leopold never advanced further than his vice-Kapellmeistership. Also, as we know from Wolfgang's letter to Martini, the Archbishop did not like to see elderly people about him and Leopold was in 1777 fifty-eight years old. This is not old but Leopold was not the sort of pliant, accommodating nature to please a despot. Biographers of his son have often taken a superficial view of him and have tried to make out that he was as servile as Wolfgang was independent. This is quite false. Leopold had an iron nature

---

[1] One of the favourites of Hieronymus, the singer Meissner, when suffering from a severe cold, was told that he must sing and attend to the service or he would be dismissed. The character of Hieronymus was well known. On the day of his induction, according to Koch-Sternfeld, a dead silence reigned as the procession went by. 'It was a fair day. An urchin in the midst of the gazing throng gave a "Huzza!" and received a box on the ears from a merchant standing by with the words: "Boy, dost thou shout when all the people weep?" '

and in recognizing a hard necessity he protected himself and his family by a punctilious observance of all the formalities customary between an eighteenth-century servant and the man who was not only his employer but also the ruler of his country and the local head of his Church.

It would be superficial not to realize that these obsequious forms – so alien to our present-day taste – admit, by their very nature, of a larger degree of independence than is often obtainable under the looser and supposedly more equalitarian relationships between the powerful and the weak of our present day. The weapons of and the defences against tyranny change from age to age. Nowadays tyranny takes an anonymous form and hides itself behind a bureaucratic machine. The oppressed can never get face to face with his oppressor. It would be a satisfaction to many a harassed individual today if he were able to confront his oppressor (who is a deaf, dumb and blind machine or a system or an institution run by ungetatable committees or councils) as Leopold was able to confront Archbishop Hieronymus and looking him full in the eye make him the prescribed obsequious bow and address him, stating his grievances in the most Chinese of adulatory language.

As every English writer knows from his practice, under the present law of libel it is possible to get in some very hard and unpalatable truths in perfect good taste and under the guise even of flattery. Hieronymus was too intelligent a man not to be aware of the sarcastic and superior nature of Leopold who, it must always be remembered, was a much-travelled man and had mixed with the best society in all the principal European courts. I advise the reader to study carefully the portrait of Leopold Mozart[1] now in the Mozarteum at Salzburg and he will see there, as he will perceive from his letters, the proud stern character of the man conscious of his own strength acquired by enduring self-discipline and the strictest devotion to every duty as a servant, a musician, a husband and a father. Leopold Mozart was built on a Miltonic scale and as is the case with all men who are truly strong he was capable of the utmost tenderness, as his relationship with

[1] Reproduced in Plate 10.

his wife and children abundantly reveals. We may well understand, once we have become closely familiar with Leopold
Mozart, the often-quoted saying of Wolfgang as a child:

After God, Papa.

It may have sometimes occurred to reflective minds that life is
very little worth living for a man if he does not possess genius.
The answer to this implicit enquiry is a man like Leopold
Mozart. Leopold had every virtue (in the Roman sense) a man
can have, but he was denied genius in his own chosen and
beloved art. It must have been a bitter pill for such an ambitious
man – a man, too, of quite exceptional intellectual power – to
see in the course of his life many men inferior in character and
even in musical science to himself more successful and even
gifted with more natural talent. Well, that hard, tough Spartan
had his reward. God, as he fully recognized in his own heart,
gave him Wolfgang. He in return protected, guided and aided
Wolfgang to achieve, what he might otherwise never have
achieved, the *adequate* expression in a mass of completed marvellous musical works of what was probably the greatest natural
musical genius that has ever been born into this world.

The Archbishop Hieronymus was one of those intelligent men
of mean nature who have no instinct whatsoever but are impressed always by externals. Jahn, on information from Koch-
Sternfeld, says:

> Mozart [Wolfgang] with his slender figure and boyish counten-
> ance made a poor personal impression on Hieronymus who was
> singularly apt to be imposed upon by men of commanding height
> and appearance.

He refused any recognition of Wolfgang's musical accomplish-
ments and was unsparing in his criticism of them,[1] telling him – as
Leopold wrote to Padre Martini [December 22, 1777] – that he
knew nothing of his art and should go and study at the Naples
Conservatoire that he might learn something; a sufficiently un-
reasonable proposal to an academician of Bologna and Verona –
to a young man who had traversed Italy in triumph as a composer

---

[1] 'I did not venture to contradict,' writes Wolfgang to his father (February 19,
1778), 'because I had come straight from Salzburg where one gets out of the habit of
contradicting.'

and virtuoso. True, Mozart had no great respect for the Archbishop's critical judgment[1] but in the mouth of his Prince such an expression of opinion was of very unpleasant significance; for in point of fact Hieronymus was well aware of Mozart's genius[2] and never failed to honour him[3] with commissions when any new composition was required, for which he never paid him a penny. . . . He imagined that contemptuous expressions of opinion . . . would be the most effectual means of preventing the younger *Konzertmeister* from preferring his claim to a higher salary than a hundred and fifty gulden a year.

Leopold early recognized the hopelessness of Wolfgang's future in Salzburg and spared no effort, as we have already seen, to get him a position at some other Court. But all these efforts had been in vain and all Wolfgang's successes in Italy, Vienna and finally in Munich had led to nothing. No secure position had been offered to him and if he were to live and compose, some security had to be found. The only thing left was to try another great tour on which Wolfgang could exhibit his prowess as an executant and his powers as a composer in the hope of their acquiring him the offer of some good position. He had not left Salzburg since the visit to Munich in 1775; he was now twenty-one and something had to be done without delay. Accordingly Leopold made the necessary preparations for a tour and then applied to the Archbishop for leave of absence and permission to travel. This, as well as a petition for an increase in salary, was refused, the Archbishop giving as his reason that he would not have his subjects 'going on begging expeditions'.

On August 1, 1777, Wolfgang made a written application to Archbishop Hieronymus referring to his father's applications of March 14th and of June, both of which had been refused by the Archbishop:

---

[1] Wolfgang writes ironically to his father from Mannheim on November 4, 1777: 'I played my concerto . . . and although it was known to be mine it pleased very much. Nobody said it was not well arranged . . . they should ask the Archbishop – he could set them right at once.'

[2] This is more than questionable. Jahn merely means that he could not fail to be aware of his exceptional talents. None of Mozart's contemporaries realized his full stature.

[3] 'Honour' is good!

Your Grace observed that, at most, I (who moreover was only half in service) could travel alone. Our need is urgent: my father took the decision that I must go alone. But even then your Gracious Excellency made some most gracious objections. Gracious Lord and Master! The elders go to great pains to enable the children to earn their own bread: and for that are they responsible to themselves, to the State. The more talent the children have received from God the more are they bound to make use of it in order to improve the conditions of themselves and their parents, to succour their parents and to provide for their own development and for the future. This we are taught in the Gospel.

I am therefore before God responsible in my conscience to my father for all the exhausting hours spent on my upbringing, to be grateful, to lighten his burdens and to take care of myself and also of my sister, for it would be a sad thing to me if she should have spent so many hours at the piano without being able to make practical use of her labour.

I beg your gracious Excellency therefore graciously to allow me to request my discharge as I am compelled to make use of the forth-coming autumn month in order not to have to travel during the following cold months in bad weather. Your gracious Excellency will not take this most humble request ungraciously since more than three years ago when I asked for permission to go to Vienna you graciously informed me that I had nothing to hope for and would do better to seek fortune elsewhere. I thank your gracious Excellency most humbly for all gracious favours received and with the flattering hope that I shall be able to serve you in my mature years with more success I am,

Your gracious Excellency's,
my gracious Prince and Master's
most humble and obedient servant
(*Sgd.*) WOLFGANG AMADÉ MOZART.

The Archbishop, enraged at having the tables turned upon him in this way, accepted Wolfgang's resignation most ungraciously. It was feared that Leopold would suffer but the Archbishop expressed his displeasure only verbally and Leopold was allowed to keep his position. Indeed, anything else would have been too outrageous and, as it was, in the general opinion Wolfgang had been badly treated. Wolfgang's friend, Count Firmian, on his return to Salzburg from a journey in October 1777, was met by the Archbishop with the remark: 'We have one musician less since you left.' Firmian replied: 'Your Grace has lost a great performer.' 'How so?' 'He is the greatest clavier player that I ever heard in my life; he has done Your Grace good service on the violin and he is a first-rate composer.' Whereupon the Archbishop was silent.[1]

After his departure Wolfgang writes to his father:

I hope that you are less annoyed than when I was in Salzburg for I must acknowledge that I was the cause of it. I was badly treated; I did not deserve it. You naturally took my part but too strongly; I assure you that was the chief reason that I hurried out of Salzburg.

To this his father replied on November 17, 1777:

You are quite right as to my extreme annoyance at the tyrannical treatment you received; it gnawed at my heart, and prevented my sleeping; it was always in my thoughts, and would in the end have destroyed me. My dear son, when you are happy, I am happy; and your mother and sister – we are all happy; and this happiness I hope for by the grace of God and my confidence in your own good sense.[2]

It was doubtless with considerable anxiety that Leopold reconciled himself to Wolfgang's departure for the first time without him on a long tour. The presence of his mother would not make up for Leopold's absence and the nature of Wolfgang, in its frankness, excitability and careless good-nature, was such as to make him an easy victim to ill-nature and unscrupulous enmity. One of the most interesting passages in all Leopold's letters, part of which I have already quoted,[3] must be given fully here. It is dated Salzburg, February 16, 1778, and addressed to Wolfgang and his mother in Mannheim:

. . . My son! you are too hasty and hot in all your affairs. Your character has entirely changed since your childhood and boyhood. As a child and a boy you were more serious than childish and when occupied with music at the piano or otherwise nobody might venture the least jesting with you. Even your countenance was so grave that many people in different countries feared that your precocious talent and constantly serious and reflecting expression betokened an early

[1] Letter from Leopold Mozart dated October 4, 1777.
[2] This remarkable letter shows the real nature of Leopold Mozart under his iron exterior.
[3] See page 16.

death. Now, however, it seems to me that you are far too ready to answer jestingly on every occasion—and that is already the first step to familiarity which one must avoid in this world if one wishes to preserve its respect. . . . It is your good heart which causes you to see no fault in a man, to give him your full confidence if he praises you to the skies: whereas, as a boy, your excessive modesty made you weep when you were praised too much. The greatest art is to learn to know oneself and then, my son, do as I do and study other people so as to understand them well. You know that has always been my study and it is truly a good, useful, indeed invaluable study. . . .

The tour was arranged so that Wolfgang should visit the principal German towns and Paris. Leopold carefully impressed upon Wolfgang that his sole aim must be to extend his fame, make money and obtain a sound position. It was indeed putting a strain on a young man of twenty-one to be instructed so categorically that personal gratification and mere amusement were to be kept altogether in the background, but Leopold, with his knowledge of the world, was emphatic. He writes in a letter dated Salzburg, October 15, 1777:

. . . To earn money and to be economical must be your constant care; otherwise one cannot travel honourably; indeed one comes to a standstill and gets into debt –

Leopold's long letters are full of the minutest instructions as to how to take the fullest advantage of every possible opportunity. He thinks of everything, of the music to be taken, of the difficulties with copyists, of the necessary introductions, of the routes, the expenses, etc. etc. He foresees that Wolfgang and his mother will probably need more money than Wolfgang can earn, and as he has no private means and has long ago spent the profits of the first and most successful tour, he is compelled to borrow from his friends Hagenauer and Bullinger, which, as Jahn remarks, must have been 'abhorrent to so conscientious a man'. He cut down his own household expenses to the barest minimum, took up again the drudgery of giving lessons, he and Nannerl sacrificing together all they could to make the tour possible. An outfit for Wolfgang and his mother had to be provided and also a carriage in which the two should travel with their luggage, clothes, music and instruments in a respectable style; for Leopold knew well the importance of cutting a good figure in the world, especially when one is on the brink of beggary. Nevertheless, in spite of all the circumspection, commonsense, foresight and hard labour of Leopold the tour failed, as we shall see, to achieve its object.

CHAPTER TEN

The Last Grand Tour Begins

Age 21 (September 23, 1777 – October 30, 1777)
Munich, Augsburg, Wallerstein

ON SEPTEMBER 23, 1777, early in the morning Wolfgang and his mother left Salzburg. I intend to allow this extraordinary journey with all its adventures to speak mainly for itself; it is so vividly narrated in the letters exchanged between Wolfgang and his father that no description from a third pen could ever have the freshness and vitality of that first-hand account. But these letters are frequently so long and so full of detail that I shall have to select and cut them pretty drastically. Also, I shall interpolate a commentary where I think it necessary.

[From Wolfgang]

Wasserburg,
September 23, 1777,
11 o'clock at night.

Mon très cher Père,
    God be praised and thanked, we have passed safely Wagin, Stain, Ferbertsheim and arrived at Wasserburg; now for a brief description: . . . before Schinn we met with a number of cows among which was a remarkable one – for it was one-sided, which we had never seen before. . . .
    At Schinn . . . we had to change . . . Mama and I were talking when a stout man came up whose 'symphony' was immediately known to me – he was a merchant from Memmingen, he looked at me a long while and said at last: 'Are you Herr Mozart?' . . . I have seen you at the musical performances in the Mirabell.[1] Thereupon

---

[1] The grounds of this palace, once belonging to the Archbishop, are now laid out as a beautiful public park in the centre of Salzburg. The palace possesses an exceptionally fine rococo marble staircase which is little known.

he disclosed his name which I have forgotten, thank God. . . . From Stain we had a postillion who was so phlegmatic, we thought we should never arrive. From Ferbertsheim to Wasserburg all went well. We live like Princes and lack nothing but papa, but God will have it so, all will yet be well . . . I am the other papa, I look after everything. . . . At the 'Star' at Wasserburg one is looked after marvellously. I sat there like a Prince. Half-an-hour ago the servant knocked and asked for instructions and I answered him with my most grave demeanour such as I have in my portrait;[1] I must finish, Mama is ready dressed. We both beg Papa to take care of his health; not to go out too early; not to let himself be vexed; to laugh heartily; be merry and always joyful, remember, as we do, that the Archbishop[2] is a rat but that God is compassionate, charitable and loving. I kiss Papa's hand a thousand times and embrace my brute of a sister as many times as I today already have – taken snuff. I believe I have left at home my *Dekreter*[3] – I beg you to send them soon. In the early morning at half-past six.

Your obedient son,

(*Sgd.*) WOLFGANG AMADÉ MOZART.

[From Leopold]

Salzburg,
September 25, 1777.

My two Loved Ones,

I received dear Wolfgang's letter this morning with the greatest pleasure; Bullinger has just now read it; he laughed heartily and sends his compliments. Am delighted that you are well: I am now, thank God, much better. After your departure I climbed the stairs wearily and threw myself in an armchair.[4] I had taken the greatest care . . . not to make our parting painful and in so doing I forgot to give my son a father's blessing. I ran to the window and sent it after you both, but I could not see you pass out of the gate[5] and no doubt you had already gone by for I had been sitting there for some time incapable of thought. Nannerl wept bitterly and I had great difficulty in consoling her. She complained of headache and pains in the stomach, finally she was sick . . . went to bed . . . the sorrowful Pimps[6] lay beside her.

[1] I think this must refer to the portrait recently made for Martini, reproduced in Plate 1.
[2] In cipher.
[3] Diplomas of the Musical Academies of Bologna and Verona and the testimonial from Padre Martini.
[4] Leopold might well have felt sad. Wolfgang was to be absent nearly two years and he was never to see his wife again.
[5] The town gate.
[6] Their dog.

I went to my room, said my morning prayers, lay on my bed until eight-thirty, read in a book, composed myself and dozed. The dog came, I was awake, he made signs that I should go with him and I understood from this that it was nearly twelve o'clock. I got up, took my fur coat, found Nannerl sound asleep and saw by the clock that it was twelve-thirty. When I came back with the dog I woke Nannerl and had the meal brought in. Nannerl had no appetite; she ate nothing and afterwards went to bed and I spent the time after Bullinger had gone in praying and reading and lay on my bed.

In the evening Nannerl was quite well and hungry, we played picquet, then we had our meal in my room and afterwards had a couple more games, then we went in God's name to sleep. Thus passed a sadder day than I ever expected to live through in my whole life. . . .

Wolfgang and his mother arrived in Munich at four-thirty on the evening of September 24th. They went to the inn of Herr Albert, an old friend, who was known as the 'learned landlord', in the Kaufingerstrasse. Wolfgang immediately set about paying the necessary visits and called upon Count Seeau, the superintendent of the Playhouse, who advised him to approach the Elector at once as there was no doubt a good composer was needed in Munich. In his letter to his father dated September 26, 1777, he gives full details of his visits, tells him he has seen a comedy: 'Henriette, *or* Is She Married Already?' and relates a story of Johannes von Grönner who had just been appointed Konzertmeister 'through an impudent speech'. He had produced two symphonies.

The Elector asked him: 'Did you really compose this?' – 'Yes, your Excellency.' 'From whom did you learn it!' 'From a schoolmaster in Switzerland . . . this schoolmaster has taught me more than all our composers here were capable of.'

Today Count Schönborn and his wife, sister of the Archbishop, arrived. I was at the Playhouse. Herr Albert told them I was here and that I had left the service. They were astonished. They would hardly believe him when he said I received twelve florins and thirty kreutzer of blessed memory! Mama and I hope you are both well. I am in a continuous good humour. My heart is as light as a feather since I have left all this chicanery – I am also fatter. . . .

Wolfgang also visited the Prince Bishop of Chiemsee, Count

Zeil, who was in Munich on a diplomatic mission and promised to help him; but a few days later he said to Wolfgang:

'I do not think you will do much here. I spoke privately to the Elector at Nymphenburg and he said to me: "It is too soon. Let him travel in Italy and make a name. I do not refuse anything but it is too soon yet." '

'There it is,' writes Wolfgang to his father on September 29–30, 1777:

> Most of these great lords have a frightful Foreign-Obsession. Nevertheless he advised me to see the Elector. . . . I have spoken today privately with Herr Woschitka[1] and he . . . will obtain me an audience without fail. . . .
>
> I like it here and am of the opinion, as are many good friends of mine, that if I stayed here a year or two I could earn respect through my work and would likelier be sought after by the Court than have to apply to it. Herr Albert has an idea which seems to be not impossible; namely, he will collect ten good friends each of whom need only spare one ducat for me to have monthly ten ducats, fifty gulden, or annually six hundred florins; if in addition I had two hundred yearly from Count Seeau that would be eight hundred florins – what does Papa think of this idea? – Is it not most friendly – would it not be nice if it were really serious? – I am perfectly satisfied with it; I should be near Salzburg and if the desire came to you, my dearest Papa (as I from my heart should wish) to leave Salzburg and to make your life in Munich it would be quite easy and jolly to do. For if we have to live in Salzburg on five hundred and four florins we could manage well in Munich on six hundred to eight hundred florins.

Wolfgang had his interview with the Elector which he describes to his father in his letter of September 30th:

> Today after a talk with Mr Woschitka at nine o'clock I went to the Court. Baron Kern was the gentleman-in-attendance. All were in hunting uniform. . . .
>
> At ten o'clock I was taken to the small room through which His Highness would pass to hear Mass before the hunt. Count Seeau passed through and greeted me most friendlily: 'My best wishes dearest Mozart!' When the Elector approached me I said: 'I trust Your Highness will allow me to lay myself and my services at Your

[1] *Woschitka*, Frz. Xav., violoncellist in the Munich Court Chapel.

Highness's feet.' 'Indeed, have you left Salzburg altogether?' 'Altogether, Your Highness.' 'Indeed – why? Were you kept too close?' 'May it please Your Highness, I asked only permission to travel which was refused, whereupon I was compelled to take this step although I long had realized Salzburg was no place for me, that is certain.' 'My God, young man! But your father is still at Salzburg?' 'Yes, Your Highness, he humbly commends himself, etc. I have been in Italy three times, have written three operas, am a Member of the Academy of Bologna after a trial accomplished in one hour which has taken many *maestri* four or five hours of hard labour: this may serve as witness that I am qualified to serve any Court. My only wish is to serve Your Highness, who himself is a great ——. 'Yes, my dear young fellow, but there is no vacancy! I am sorry, if only there were a vacancy——.' 'I assure your Highness I should be an honour to Munich.' 'No doubt, no doubt, but there is no vacancy.'[1] . . .

P.S. – My dear sister, I shall write you next time a letter all for you . . . remember me to A.B.C., M.R. and other similar letters. *Addio*. I beg you to take great care of your health. I kiss Papa's hand a hundred thousand times and am and remain

his most obedient son.

Someone here built a house and wrote on it:

> To build is truly a great pleasure
> But its great cost I did not measure.

During the night another added:

> And that it cost so much to do,
> You ought to have known you idiot, you!

[From Leopold]

Salzburg,
September 27, 1777.

. . . I beg of you, my dear son, do not write again to me such things about the Archbishop: remember that I am here and that such a letter might be lost or get into other hands. . . . It does the Prince (Archbishop) no honour that he gave you such a wretched

---

[1] Few people in authority today realize the social importance of a plentiful supply of 'vacancies'. Since Mozart's days artists have exchanged the patronage and official employment of Heads of States, Churches and people in authority for the 'freedom' of selling their work competitively in the market. For a time this worked tolerably well, but with the twentieth century and universal education the artist found that he was now at the mercy of the lowest common taste of the multitude. Mozart's situation today would even be worse than in 1777.

salary and does you no honour that you served him so long for such a trifle. If anyone asks you what your salary was you had better reply straightway that you only remained there out of love for your father until you were a little older, since the salary in Salzburg was only three or four hundred florins apart from the foreigners to whom the Prince pays more . . . Mitzerl, Trefel and all Salzburg greet you. Nannerl has put everything straight, she sends her greeting and kisses Mama and you a million times and I – you know well that my whole heart is with you, God keep you well! On your life depends mine.

I am,

the forlorn Father and husband.

[From Leopold]

Salzburg,

September 28, 1777.

Today I went out for the first time and actually to the Mirabell to the last Mass . . . I am very well today, thank God, and have coughed very little, often scarcely three times in a couple of hours. But I am still taking medicine to make me perspire and I shall have to speak to Dr Barisani for I have become very thin. I hope it will pass away: for my mind is quieter now and I shall take great care of myself.

Only I beg of you, my dear Wolfgang, to indulge in no excess. You have been accustomed to good discipline from your youth and to avoid heating liquor, for you know that you get quickly over-heated and you prefer cold to warmth: a clear proof that your blood is inclined to a high temperature and is easily excited. Strong wines and much drinking are thus harmful to you. . . .

[Leopold]

Salzburg,

October 4, 1777.

Mon très cher fils,

I had no great expectations of Munich. The Elector is bound to take nobody unless there is a vacancy, and one has always secret enemies to hinder one. The Albert project shows indeed the greatest friendliness but likely as it seems to you to find ten persons who will pay you a ducat monthly it seems unlikely to me. And who could these friends of man or of music be? – And what sort of security *is* there or what service in return? That Count Seeau should give something seems more promising but that without the other is useless. . . . In short I cannot see where these ten charming friends are to come from . . . you can continue your journey and await letters from Albert.

The craze for Italians does not prevail everywhere, but is almost confined to Munich. I mean the excessive craze! In Mannheim all are German except a pair of *castrati*. In Trier with . . . Prince Clemens of Saxony there is only Maestro Sales, the rest are German. In Mainz all are Germans; in Warzburg only Sgr. Fracassini[1] a violinist. . . . At all small Protestant Courts there are no foreigners.

[From Wolfgang]

Munich,
October 3, 1777.

. . . At Count Salern's for three days I played many things out of my head, including the two *Cassationen* for the Countess[2] and the final music with the Rondeau,[3] these latter by heart. You cannot imagine what pleasure they gave Count Salern:[4] he understands music for he cries 'Bravo!' when other gentlemen take a pinch of snuff, cough or begin a conversation. I said to him I wished the Elector were there to hear what I could do, of which he knows nothing. . . . All these great people believe whatever is told them and refuse to judge for themselves. That is always the way.

I offered him a trial; he was to get all the composers in Munich and any he chose from Italy, France, Germany, England and Spain; I dare compete with them all.[5] I told him what had happened in Italy and begged him if there were any talk of me to mention all this. He said: 'I have very little influence but will do what I can with all my heart.'

He is firmly of the opinion that if I could remain here the thing would come of itself. For me alone this would not be impossible for I should get at least three hundred florins from Count Seeau; for food I should not have to trouble for I should be invited everywhere and, if not, Albert would be delighted to have me at meals. I eat very little, drink water and at the end with fruit a small glass of wine.[6]

I would make a contract with Count Seeau (only with the advice of my good friends) thus: I deliver yearly four German operas, some seria and some buffa, with one evening's takings of each for

[1] A pupil of Tartini's.
[2] Probably the Divertimenti in F and B (K.247–8) composed in Salzburg for Countess Lodron in 1776.
[3] Perhaps the Serenade in D (K.250) or one of the two Divertimenti in D and B (K.251 and K.254).
[4] Count Jos. von Salern, chief director of music and the opera.
[5] Wonderful, charming and incomparable Mozart, aged twenty-one!
[6] What is the food of genius? Air, fire and water!

myself, which is the usual custom. That alone would bring me at
least five hundred florins which with my salary would make eight
hundred florins; but certainly more, for Reiner the actor and singer
gets two hundred in an evening; and I am very popular here and
how popular I should become if I should help to raise the National
German Opera high in the musical world? And that certainly would
be done by me; for I was at once full of desire to compose as soon as
I heard the German singspiel.

The prima donna is named Kaiser, she is the daughter of the
cook of a nobleman here, a charming girl and pretty on the stage. I
have not seen her nearer yet . . . when I heard her it was the third
time she played. She has a beautiful voice neither strong nor weak
but very pure and with good intonation. Valesi is her teacher and
her style shows that her master understands singing as well as
teaching. When she had to sustain a note for a couple of bars I was
surprised at the beauty of her crescendo and decrescendo. She has a
slow shake and that delights me for it will be all the more clear and
true when she wants to make it quicker. She is a great favourite with
the people here and I agree with them. Mama was in the parterre,
she went at four-thirty to secure a seat. I did not go till six-thirty
for I am well enough known to have the entry to the boxes. . . . I
watched Kaiser through my glasses and she drew more than one tear
from me. I cried: 'Brava, bravissima!' many times. . . . The piece
was called *The Fishermaiden* with a good translation.[1] They want to
have a German opera seria soon and would like me to compose it. . . .

[From Leopold]

Salzburg,
October 6, 1777.

. . . That you would live alone in Munich is true but what honour
would it be to you [without an official position]? How the Archbishop would sneer! You can do this much in any place, not only in
Munich. You must not make so little of yourself and throw yourself
away; there is certainly no need for that. Mama may console herself,
I am much better . . . what troubles me occasionally is that I no
longer hear you play the clavier or violin and whenever I return
home I feel a little melancholy, for as I near our home I think I shall
hear you playing the violin. . . . You must now, with the help of
God, continue your journey and go to Augsburg and stay at 'The
Lamb', in the Heil. Kreutzergasse.[2]

[1] *La Pescatrice* by Piccinni, composed 1766.
[2] '. . . where you pay thirty kreutzers for dinner, get nice rooms and good society,
English, French, etc.'

The composer Mysliwecek, whom Wolfgang had met in Bologna in 1770, turned up in Munich, where his opera *Ezio* was produced, and was kept there by illness. This illness had been brought on by excess and Leopold had forbidden Wolfgang to visit him, but he was so insistent that Wolfgang saw him in the garden of the Ducal Hospital.[1] He suggested that Wolfgang might get a libretto to compose for Naples and wrote on his behalf to the impressario Santorio. To his father on October 10th-11th after describing this meeting he writes:

> I have an inexpressible desire to write an opera again . . . composition is my one and only passion and joy. . . . I only have to hear of an opera or go into a theatre and hear singing to be almost beside myself. . . .

Nothing, however, came of this or of an attempt by Leopold to get him a commission to write an opera for the Feast of the Ascension in Venice. On October 11th Wolfgang and his mother left Munich and arrived the same evening in Augsburg. Following the instructions of Leopold, Wolfgang called upon the town councillor Von Langenmantel whom Leopold had been well acquainted with, and gave his father the following ironical account of his visit to this ridiculous dignitary of Leopold's native town:

> Augsburg,
> October 14, 1777.
>
> . . . My first visit was to Herr Town-councillor Longotabarro;[2] my cousin, a dear good man and an honest citizen, accompanied me and had the honour of waiting in the ante-room like a lackey until I came out from the arch-town-councillor. I did not fail to begin by presenting my father's humblest respects. He was pleased to remember all about it and asked me: 'How has the gentleman been all this time?' To which I replied: 'God be praised, quite well and I hope that your health has also been good?' He then became still more polite and said: 'Sir,' and I said: 'Your Grace,' as I had done from the first. Nothing would satisfy him but I must mount to his son-in-law on the second floor and with my cousin waiting on the steps all

---

[1] His illness seems to have been syphilis, which explains Leopold's attitude. Nevertheless Leopold writes on October 12th, after receipt of Wolfgang's description of his meeting: 'Your horror, your anguish when you saw him is more than understandable to me. I should have felt the same. You know my heart. He is indeed to be pitied.'

[2] This is Wolfgang's cypher for von Langenmantel.

the while! It was with difficulty that I refrained from saying something, with all my politeness. Upstairs I had the honour of playing
for three-quarters of an hour upon a good clavichord by Stein[1] in
the presence of the stiff and starched son, his long-necked, gracious
lady-wife and her silly old mother. I played fantasies and then
everything he had *prima vista*; among others some very pretty pieces
by a certain Edelmann.[2] They were all exceedingly polite and I was
exceedingly polite, for it is my custom to be to people as I find
them; it is the best way.

Wolfgang next visited Stein, incognito at the suggestion of
Leopold, and he was accompanied by the young Langenmantel
who nearly let the cat out of the bag by blurting out: 'I have the
honour to introduce to you a virtuoso on the clavier.' 'I protested,'
Wolfgang tells his father in the letter from which I have already
quoted:

and said I was an unworthy pupil of Herr Sigl in Munich.
. . . He shook his head and said, at last: 'Have I the honour of seeing
Herr Mozart?' 'Oh, no!' said I, 'my name is Trazom and I have a
letter to you.' He took the letter and was going to open it. I did not
give him time and said: 'Why read the letter now? Let us go into the
hall, I am most curious to see your pianofortes.' 'With all my heart;
but I do not think I am deceived.'
   He opened the door. I ran to one of the three claviers and played.
He could scarcely take time to open the letter, his curiosity was so
excited, he only read the signature. 'Oh!' he cried and embraced me.
He crossed himself, made grimaces and was absolutely delighted.
. . . He took me to a coffee-house where, as I entered, I thought I
should succumb to the thick air and smell of tobacco. I had to
endure it for a whole hour.

The main object in going to Augsburg, Leopold's native town,
where there was no Court, was to give a concert and earn some
money. The son of the town-councillor promised to arrange this
with the local 'aristocrats', but later told Wolfgang that the 'aristocrats' had no money; this was after a supper to which he had invited Wolfgang when he had played 'as long as the company

[1] *Stein*, J. A. (1728–82), famous organ and clavier maker.
[2] Probably the composer Johann Friedrich Edelmann, b. Strasbourg, 1749; he
was beheaded in Paris on July 17, 1794, with his pupil, Baron Dietrich.

pleased'.[1] In addition they thought fit to make fun of him. On his father's advice Wolfgang had worn the cross of the Order given him by the Pope.[2] Although he had explained exactly what it was and how he had received it to young Langenmantel this petty *bourgeois* and his friends thought it a great joke in the true style of the *bourgeoisie* all the world over, who always believe that the hereditary nobility are born out of sealed test-tubes sent down from heaven by God while they themselves and all others are merely the descendants of monkeys. It was impossible for town-councillor Langenmantel and his *entourage* to conceive of Mozart as the equal of a baron and it is this servile ignorance of the middle-class which really has justified in the past the attitude to it of the aristocracy so tersely expressed in the famous remark of a German nobleman that below the rank of a baron nobody exists. The infuriated Wolfgang lost his temper with them and wrote to his father a full account:[3]

> Augsburg,
> October 17, 1777.
>
> I shall be truly delighted when I am again in a place where there is a Court . . .[4] I must say that if I had not found such good cousins[5] and such a dear little cousin (Bäsle)[6] there I should regret as many times as I have hairs on my head that I ever came to Augsburg. Now I must tell you something about my dear young Bäsle, but I shall wait until tomorrow for one must be in thorough good spirits to praise her as she deserves. . . .
>
> Early on the 17th I write and assure you that our little cousin is beautiful, sensible, charming, clever, gay, and knows something of the world. She was also for some time in Munich. We suit each other well for she also is a little bit wicked. We hoax people and have great fun. . . .
>
> I beg you write soon to the poor Mysliwecek as I know it would

[1] He played two concertos, something out of his head and a trio by Haseneder on the violin: 'I would have gladly played the violin more but I was so badly accompanied that I got colic.'

[2] See page 94.

[3] After this Augsburg experience Mozart seems never to have worn his Papal Order again.

[4] Mozart found (as many others have found) that responsibility and dignity, culture, amiability, simplicity of manners and respect for individuals are occasionally prevalent among those who are at the top and at the bottom but hardly ever among those who are in between.

[5] Really his uncle and aunt.

[6] More will be heard of this young woman.

give him great pleasure. In my next I shall tell you all about the pianofortes and organs of Stein and about the chamber concert. A crowd of the nobility were there – Duchess Arsefountain, Countess Firejoy and Princess Stinkdirt with her two daughters who are, however, already married to the two Princes Papbelly of Swinetail. . . . I kiss Papa's hands a hundred thousand times, embrace my brute of a sister with a bear's tenderness and am your most obedient son. . . .

Mama, I and our little cousin went after lunch to Herr Stein. At four o'clock came the Herr *Kapellmeister* and Herr Schmittbauer, organist at St Ulrich, a splendid old man. I played at sight a Sonata of Beecke which was rather difficult. How the *Kapellmeister* and the organist crossed themselves in astonishment is indescribable. Here as in Munich I have played by heart and all my Six Sonatas. . . .

Now I must begin about the Stein pianos. Before I had seen something of Stein's work I liked Späth's[1] best, but now the preference must be given to Stein; they mute much better. If I strike hard whether I raise my finger or not the sound passes the instant I have heard it. I may come upon the keys as I like, the tone is always the same; it does not waver, it neither becomes stronger nor weaker, nor does it cease altogether; in a word it is all equal. It is true such a piano is not to be had under three hundred florins but the trouble and labour bestowed upon it is inestimable . . . his hammers fall back the instant they strike the strings whether the keys are held down or not. . . . He often says: 'If I were not such a passionate music-lover myself and were not able to play a little on the clavier I should have long ago lost patience, but I am a lover of instruments which do not tax the player and wear well.' His pianos truly are durable . . . the pedal which is pressed by the knee is also better contrived by him than by others. I need only touch it and it works and when the knee is removed one does not bear the least vibration. . . .

When I told Herr Stein I should like to play upon his organ (in the Barfüsserkirche), for I had a passion for the organ, he was greatly astonished and said: 'What, such a man as you, so great a clavier player, wish to play on an instrument in which there is no place for *douceur*, expression and has no piano, and no forte, but goes on always the same?'[2] 'That means nothing at all. The organ is to my eyes and ears the King of Instruments.' So we went together. I could see from his remarks that he did not expect much; he thought

[1] *Späth*, famous organ and pianoforte maker of Regensburg.
[2] Very strange of Stein! This was the great beauty and artistic merit of the old organs; of course it has now gone altogether. The modern organ has no *douceur* and is nothing but 'expression' – the trumpetings of elephants, the howls of cats, the squeak of rats and the *vox humana*, all tremolo!

I would play clavier-fashion. He told me how he had taken Schubart, also at his request, to his organ and said: 'I feared for him for Schubart had told everybody and the church was rather full. I thought that the fellow would be full of spirit, fire and pace and that would tell on the organ, but when he began I changed my opinion.

I only said: 'What do you think, Herr Stein? Do you imagine I shall come to grief on the organ?' 'Ah, you! That is another matter.' We went into the choir. I began the prelude, he laughed with delight, then followed a fugue. 'I can well believe you like playing the organ when you play like that——.'

At first I did not quite understand the pedal because it is not divided. It begins C then D E in a row. With us D and E are above, as E flat and F sharp are here, but I soon got accustomed to it. . . .

[From Leopold]

Salzburg,
October 15, 1777.

You must know that one must call the Lutherans 'Evangelicals' for they do not wish to be called Lutherans; one also says the Evangelical, not the Lutheran, Church, in the same way as the Calvinists wish to be known as 'Protestants', not Calvinists . . . one may often put a fussy person into a temper with one inappropriate word. . . .

You stayed too long in Munich and must give one or two concerts in Augsburg to make something, however little. Fine words, flattering speeches and *bravissimos* will not pay the postmaster or the inn-keeper and as soon as one can get nothing more one must move on. . . .

I ought to have told you that as soon as you got to Munich you should seek out a good copyist and do the same everywhere where you are staying for some time. For you must also endeavour to make something by composing and that can happen when one has symphonies and divertimenti copied in readiness to present them to a Prince or music-lover. The copying must be arranged so that at least the first violin or another principal part is written in your presence; the rest can be taken away. Now you must absolutely have something ready for Prince Taxis. You can quickly give the oboe, horn and viola parts of six good symphonies to one or more (so as to get it done quicker) copyists . . . the divertimenti are quickly copied though in truth yours have many parts and are long. *Basta!* In every place you must immediately seek out a copyist, otherwise you will lose much. . . .

There are all kinds of copyists. You must get a sample of the work first and also see to the paper that is used. . . . In short you must look after everything so that no mistakes are made, which can only be done by having one's head in the right place. . . .

In my opinion you need not bother about the opera in Mannheim which you can see during the Carnival, but you must not neglect to visit Prince Taxis on his estate. . . .

We are well and I should be better still if I were one of those careless fathers who in three weeks can forget wife and child. That I could not do in a hundred years . . . Nannerl and I kiss you both a million times. . . .

[From Leopold]

Salzburg,
October 18, 1777.

. . . I am not surprised that they made eyes at your playing of your last Cassation. You yourself do not know how well you play the violin and if you did yourself the honour and wished to play with distinction, courage and spirit you would be the first violinist in Europe. . . .

What you have written about your visit to town-councillor Longotabarro . . . made us all, including Herr Bullinger, laugh immoderately. . . . This gentleman does not readily know how to talk to others as he is accustomed only to the servants of the magistracy or to speak down to the burghers from the height of his dirty throne. . . . As for young Longotabarro . . . you have made yourself too cheap with this boob . . . you were not reserved enough and too trusting. In short, you were too natural for such a nitwit and so he thought he could make fun of you. . . .

When you get to Mannheim the principal person you can trust must be Sgr. Raaff[1] who is a God-fearing, honourable man who loves Germans and can help to bring about your being retained by the Elector during the winter. . . .

[From Wolfgang]

Augsburg,
October 24, 1777.

. . . Badly as they fiddle yet the music at the monastery is preferable to that of the Augsburg orchestra. I gave a symphony and played the Violin Concerto in B by Vanhal with universal applause. The Dean is a good, jolly fellow, a cousin of Eberlin's named Zerchinger, and remembers Papa very well. In the evening at supper I played the Strasbourg Concerto. It went as smooth as oil. Everyone praised the beautiful pure tone. Afterwards they brought a clavier. I preluded and played a sonata and the Fischer variations. Then

---

[1] *Raaff*, Anton (1714–97), a famous tenor at the Mannheim Court, for whom Mozart expressly wrote the role of Idomeneo. See page 190.

someone whispered to the Dean that he should hear me play organ-fashion. I said he might give me a theme; he would not, but one of the monks did. I began andante and in the middle (the fugue was in G minor) I began in the major quite playfully but in the same tempo and then returned to the theme but backwards; at last it occurred to me that I might try the playful style for the theme of the fugue? Without more ado I tried it and it went as accurately as if it had been measured for by Daser (the Salzburg tailor). The Dean was beside himself. . . . 'I could never have believed what I have heard,' he said; 'you are a wonderful man. My Abbot told me that never in his life had he heard such solemn and convincing organ playing.' The Abbot had heard me some days before when the Dean was not there.

Finally, someone brought me a sonata, which was fugued, to play. I said: 'Gentlemen, this is too much; I must acknowledge I shall not be able to play the sonata straightaway.' 'I think so, too,' said the Dean eagerly, as he was all on my side, 'that is too much, it would be impossible for anyone.' 'Nevertheless,' I said, 'I shall try.' And as I played I heard the Dean calling out behind me: 'Oh, you rascal! Oh, you young scamp!' I played until eleven o'clock and was bombarded with themes for fugues. . . .

Apropos of Stein's daughter:[1] whoever sees and hears her play without laughing must be as much of a stone as her father himself. . . . Herr Stein is quite infatuated with his daughter; she is eight and a half years old and learns everything by heart. She may become something, she has genius; but if she goes on as at present nothing will come of it. . . . She will never learn the most difficult, most necessary and principal thing in music, namely, *time*, because she has been accustomed since youth to play out of time. Herr Stein and I have certainly talked for two hours on this point. I think I nearly converted him. He now asks my advice on everything. He was quite infatuated with Beecke[2] but now he sees and hears that I play better, that I make no grimaces and yet play so expressively that I show off his pianofortes better than anyone. The correctness of my time astonishes them all. The tempo rubato in an adagio with the left hand keeping strict time was quite beyond their comprehension. They always follow with the left hand.[3]

[1] *Stein*, Maria Anna (1769–1833). She grew up a good pianist and married J. Andreas Streicher, the famous pianoforte maker. She later became a friend of Beethoven.

[2] *Beecke*, see page 179 and Footnote page 149.

[3] This is the hallmark of true musicianship. The ordinary amateur has no idea of how rare it is. One hears it only from a few of the greatest instrumentalists. In the performance of Mozart's works, whether operatic or instrumental, accurate and steady time is of the first importance; in the case of inferior composers it matters less – except that such playing makes their music sound better than it is, as is the case when Toscanini conducts Wagner and Strauss.

Count Wolfegg[1] and others who were very enthusiastic for Beecke, said lately openly at the concert that I had thrown Beecke quite in the shade. Count Wolfegg kept running about the hall saying: 'Have never heard such playing in my life. . . .'

In the Concerto for three claviers[2] Herr Demmler[3] played the first, I the second and Herr Stein the third. Then I played alone the last Sonata in D for Dürnitz,[4] then my Concerto in B,[5] then again alone organ-fashion a fugue in C minor and suddenly a brilliant Sonata in C major[6] out of my head with a Rondeau. . . . There was a fine din and uproar. Herr Stein could do nothing but make faces in astonishment and Herr Demmler laughed incessantly. He is a strange man, if anything pleases him exceedingly he bursts into laughter, with me he began to swear also. *Addio*, I kiss Papa's hands and embrace my sister with all my heart.

[From Leopold to his wife]

Salzburg,
October 23, 1777.

. . . Tell Wolfgang that the big-eyed Royal baker's daughter who danced with him at the Stern and so often made him friendly compliments and then finally went into the Loretto convent has returned to her father's house. She had heard that he was leaving Salzburg and thought to see him and prevent him; he will therefore be so kind as to compensate the father for all the expense, the ceremony, etc. which her entering the convent cost. . . .
P.S.
Mon très cher fils!
I must wish you happiness on your saint-day's anniversary! But what can I wish that I do not always wish for you? I wish you the grace of God that will everywhere accompany you and never leave you if you sedulously carry out the obligations of a true Christian and Catholic.

You know me. I am no pedant, no *bettbruder*, still less a hypocrite; you will not refuse your father's request which is that you will take heed of your soul, that you will occasion your father no anxiety in his last hour so that in that dark moment he may not reproach himself that he had been neglectful in his care for your soul. Farewell! Be happy! Live reasonably. Honour and protect your mother who now

---

[1] *Wolfegg*, Count Anton Willibald, canon of Salzburg cathedral.
[2] (K.242) composed in February 1776.
[3] *Demmler*, Joh. Mich., organist at Augsburg.
[4] (K.284) (one of set of Six Sonatas, K.279–84).
[5] Perhaps the Concerto in B flat (K.238).
[6] Perhaps K.309.

in her age has many cares. Love me as I do you and as your true and anxious father.

[From Wolfgang]

Augsburg,
October 25, 1777.

The concert brought in ninety florins without deduction of the expenses. So we have, with the two ducats from the chamber concert, made one hundred florins. The expenses were not more than sixteen florins thirty kreutzers. . . .

As for the Royal baker's daughter I have nothing to object to. I foresaw it long ago. That was actually the reason why I delayed so long in starting and why I found it so difficult. I hope that this story will not be known throughout all Salzburg? I beg papa urgently to keep it quiet as long as possible and in God's name to repay on my account the expenses which the entry into the convent caused her father until I return and make the poor young girl . . . who naturally is ill . . . well again.

I kiss papa's hands and thank him for his anniversary wishes. Do not be worried. I have God always before my eyes. I recognize His power, I fear His anger; but I also know His love, His compassion and His charity towards His creation. He will never abandon His servant – what happens according to His will happens also according to mine. . . .

Papa writes in his first letter that I had made myself cheap with the boy von Langenmantel – not in the least! I was quite natural, that is all. . . . I must stop, Mama insists on eating and then packing. Tomorrow we go to Wallerstein direct. . . . My dear little cousin . . . to please me yesterday dressed in the French style and looked five per cent prettier. . . .

Wolfgang gave his cousin his portrait in medallion and asked his father to send her something out of the souvenirs accumulated from their tours. They parted very sadly and Leopold tells Wolfgang in a letter dated November 1st when describing their last Salzburg shooting-party, at which Nannerl won, that on the following Sunday the parting of Wolfgang and his cousin, both dissolved in tears, will be represented on the target. Bolt-shooting was the favourite pastime of the Mozart family and their friends in Salzburg. Leopold's letters frequently contains reference to it and during Wolfgang's absence on this tour his sister, Nannerl, would shoot regularly for him and occasionally win a few kreutzers. In a letter dated November 17th Leopold describes the promised Sunday shooting-party:

> Yesterday at the shooting the best was Herr Wolfgang Mozart. The target was charming. An Augsburg maiden stood on the right and presented to a young man in top-boots dressed for travelling, *einen Reise-buschen*; in the other hand she held an immense linen cloth trailing to the ground on which she had dried her weeping eyes. The gentleman had a similar cloth which he used likewise, and in his other hand he held his hat on which was the bull's-eye as it was easier to see there than on the *Reise-busch*. Above was written:

> 'Adieu, my young cousin – Adieu, my cousin dear,
>   Good fortune on your journey, good health and weather clear.
>   We both for fourteen days have been right gaily mad
>   And this it is which on both sides doth make our parting sad.
>   O, cursèd fate! Alas! to come and then to go
>   Now you are far away and sadly my tears flow.'

In the earlier letter of November 1st Leopold gives an account of a Mass by Michael Haydn performed at the Salzburg Cathedral with the composer conducting and Count Lodron officiating, which is interesting for the musical details it gives:

> It pleased me exceedingly because six oboes, three contrabasses, two bassoons and the Castrato[1] who has been engaged for six months at a hundred florins monthly were present. Ferlendis and Sandmayr were the solo-oboists. The oboist with Lodron was a student, the chief watchman and Oberkirchner were the second oboists. Cassel and the Prebendary Knozenbry were the contra-basses next to the organ and close to the trombones. Estlinger was with the bassoon, Hotner and Perwein next to the oboes close to the violins. What pleased me particularly was that as the oboes and bassoons were so like the human voice, the Tutti seemed to be richly scored vocal music, while the soprano and alto voices, strengthened by the six oboes and the alto trombones, balanced the tenors and basses, and the first full choir was so majestic that I would gladly have dispensed with the oboe solos. The whole lasted one and a quarter hours and for me it was too short for it was really excellently composed. . . .

On October 26th Wolfgang and his mother left Augsburg and proceeded via Donauwörth and Nördlingen to Hohenaltheim,

[1] Ceccarelli.

residence of Prince von Œttingen-Wallerstein who was a lover of music and had a good orchestra, notable for the delicacy of its playing under the conductor, Anton. Rossetti. Ignaz von Beecke, the pianist of whom we have heard so often, was a Captain in the Württemberg dragoons and Kapellmeister at Wallerstein (where he died in 1803) to the Prince. The Prince, a young man who had formerly invited Wolfgang to visit him in Naples, was on this occasion suffering from melancholia and could bear no music. Wolfgang and his mother, who was suffering from a severe cold, stayed a few days at Wallerstein, dined with Beecke and his fellow-officers and discussed the Emperor Joseph with him, agreeing that he was 'a fair executant but not a true lover of music'.[1]

---

[1] In his letter dated Mannheim, November 13, 1777, Wolfgang gives his father full particulars of his meeting with Beecke. Wolfgang confesses that bad music gives him a headache but Beecke replies that he is never thus affected by bad music but can be by good, whereupon Wolfgang comments to his father: 'Such a shallow head might well get a headache when it hears something it can't understand.'

CHAPTER ELEVEN

Mannheim

Age 21–22 (October 30, 1777 – March 14, 1778)

ON OCTOBER 30, 1777, Wolfgang and his mother arrived in
Mannheim, which was at that time a town of about twenty-five
thousand inhabitants, the seat of the Court of the Elector Palatine, Karl Theodor (1724–99), who later, on the death of the
Elector of Bavaria, Maximilian, on December 30th of this year,
1777, became Elector of Bavaria.

Mannheim under Karl Theodor, who was a good example of an
eighteenth-century German Prince with a genuine taste for
science, art, literature and music – he was educated by the Jesuits
and had been a friend of Voltaire – was a real centre of German
artistic activity. It housed the Palatinate Academy of Science
founded in 1763, which encouraged historical and scientific research and possessed the best collection of pictures, engravings
and antiquities of the time in all Germany. A national theatre had
been built and the Elector had endeavoured to retain Lessing as
dramatist and Eckhoff as actor and in 1775 had founded a German Society which was the fruit of the literary renaissance then
taking place in Germany under the lead of Klopstock and others.[1]
At his palace of Schwetzingen, which was the Versailles of the
Palatinate, Karl Theodor had produced Schweitzer's *Alcestis* on
August 13, 1775, and commissioned from Professor Anton Klein
a national patriotic libretto *Günther von Schwarzburg*[2] composed
by Holzbauer and performed on January 5, 1777, in the splendid

---

[1] Lessing produced *Laokoon* in 1766, and *Minna von Barnhelm* in 1767. He became director of the National Theatre in Hamburg in the same year.

[2] Some authorities find reminiscences of Holzbauer's *Günther von Schwarzburg* in
Die Zauberflöte (see *Denkmäler Deutsch, Tonkunst,* Vols. VIII and IX).

new opera-house. Between 1749 and 1792 the Elector Karl is reckoned to have spent about thirty-five million gulden on art and science. Karl Theodor has been described as a weak, pleasure-loving man and in a book entitled *Letters of a French Traveller on Germany*, published in Zurich in 1783, we may read:

> Everything that has ever distinguished a rein in the way of priests, mistresses, natural sons of the Prince, parvenus, speculators, castrati, bankrupts and the like are to be found gathered together in the Palatinate.

Well, it all depends upon the point of view; but even if most of Karl Theodor's expenditure on art and music was to provide pleasure and amusements for himself and his mistresses, all that it becomes anybody to say is that his pleasures and amusements were of a more engaging and fruitful character than those of the majority of people who have the power to gratify their tastes freely.

Although its theatre was one of the glories of Mannheim[1] its music was even more so; Mannheim at that time being described as the 'paradise of musicians'. It was here that German opera made one of its earliest appearances. Schweitzer's above-mentioned *Alcestis*, first produced in Weimar on May 28, 1773, and given in Mannheim in 1775, was considered by the poet Wieland to be superior to Gluck's and to approach the musical dramatic ideal. It was a German opera, written by a German poet, composed by a German musician and sung by Germans. This was considered a great step forward in German culture which had been hitherto so dependent on Italy for opera and on France for drama.

The national character of such a movement is apt to be exaggerated for purposes of political propaganda at all times of international struggle and most biographers of Mozart, as also critics writing about his music, have been at pains to emphasize Mozart's interest in trying to found a national German opera. That Mozart expressed the desire to compose German opera is true; but this only meant that he wanted to be allowed to compose operas and

[1] Schiller's star rose there in 1782 with *Die Räuber*.

G

to be considered as capable of so doing as any Italian. It was not
that he had a new conception of opera, a *German* or *Austrian* or
Salzburgian conception which he was anxious to introduce into
the world as the contribution of the German-speaking race to
operatic music. Not at all! No great musician could have such an
absurd idea. But he rightly resented, as every man of talent must,
the snobbish notion that nationality or birthplace was a deciding
factor in the determination of musical values. Actually this is an
anti-national attitude. It amounts to the assertion that nationality
plays no part whatever in the valuation of music. And this is absolutely true of music on the highest level. Whatever differences
nationality may introduce into the character of music are on the
lower levels only. The higher an artist goes the farther does he
depart from local, national and perhaps even personal or individual values.

When we speak of a national renaissance[1] what we really mean
is that the peoples of a country are becoming more active and are
taking a livelier part in the general cultural life of the civilization to which they belong. In music as in painting and, I would
even maintain, also in literature, the whole of Europe has belonged
to one culture ever since the rise of Christianity. What was happening in Germany in the middle of the eighteenth century was a
livelier participation in the more advanced culture of Italy and of
France. It was not at all – as is often misinterpreted, especially by
writers of music – a national reaction *against* Italian and French
culture but a new, more vigorous national participation in the
general European culture to which Italy and France had temporarily been making the greatest contribution.

One among many proofs of this is that though hailed by Wieland in his 'Letters on the German Opera of "Alcestis" '[2] as an
important step in the direction of German opera and superior to
Gluck's, Schwietzer's *Alcestis* was just like any Italian opera of the
time; as for Holzbauer's *Günther von Schwarzburg*, Schubart
might refer to its mixture of 'German feeling and foreign grace'

---

[1] Such as that which was taking place in Germany during Mozart's childhood and
boyhood.
[2] Burlesqued by Goethe, especially on account of Wieland's comparison of himself
with Euripides.

and to the 'glorious revolution in taste'; but even Jahn – who like a true nineteenth-century German frequently indulges in such vague and idiotic phrases as 'a German heart' and 'a German artist'–admits that Holzbauer 'never deviates from the customary Italian form'. In Mozart's criticisms of contemporary operas we never meet with any such nationalistic criticism. Music is always music to him, no matter where it comes from it is criticized from a purely artistic point of view as music. There is a sense in which it is true to say that Mozart is the most eclectic of all the great European composers. Everything was grist which came to his musical mill and he acquired and made use of every sort of material – whether it came from Italy, France or Germany – consuming it, transforming it, and by the strength of his genius making it his very own completely. All other seventeenth- and eighteenth-century music – whether Italian, French or German – now sounds to us like inferior Mozart, with the exception of the great personalities of Handel, Bach and Haydn, who succeeded in the best of their work in reaching as high a plan as Mozart and yet contributing something of their own.[1]

Finally, what needs to be remembered in considering Mozart's environment is that the German artistic renaissance and the new Romantic movement were already in full flood at the time when Wolfgang arrived in Mannheim in 1777 at the age of twenty-one. Goethe's *Sorrows of Werther* had already been published (1774), *Götz von Berlichingen* had appeared in 1773 and the first part of *Faust* was written in 1775 (the peak of the *Sturm und Drang* period), although it was not actually published until 1790. Wolfgang was seven years younger than Goethe and the conception of Mozart as belonging to the earlier artificial and imitation French salon period of German artistic life is historically false and is the source of much of the misunderstanding of Mozart's music throughout the nineteenth century, a misunderstanding which is

[1] This is only partly true of Handel who, though he occasionally rose to great heights, did not live as a composer on the same level as Mozart and Bach. The difference is analogous to that between the amateur of genius and the professional of genius in billiards. An amateur may make the most brilliant of strokes *occasionally*, but the professional is habitually on that level. Handel had not got the universality of Mozart. Mozart might have composed the *Messiah* (only it would have been still better) but Handel could never have composed *Don Giovanni*.

still largely current today. It is necessary to bear always in mind that Mozart was only twenty-one years old at the height of the great *Sturm und Drang* movement in German history and that, as I have said before, historically he belongs to the age of revolution in Europe, not to the earlier Augustan age.

Even the revolution in orchestral playing made by Stamitz (1717–75) was by this time over. The Mannheim orchestra under his successor, Christian Cannabich,[1] was unanimously considered to be the finest in Europe. It was strong in numbers and in quality – Mozart writes to his father on November 4, 1777:

> The orchestra is very good and strong; on either side ten or eleven violins, four violas, two oboes, two flutes and two clarinets, two horns, four violoncellos, four bassoons, four contra-basses, trumpets and drums.

Its standard of playing was extremely high, with delicate gradations of tone unknown hitherto. *Crescendo* and *diminuendo* are supposed to have been invented at Mannheim and Reichardt,[2] referring to a Berlin orchestra, writes:

> I must not speak in this place of the masterly effect produced in the Mannheim orchestra by the swelling and diminution of a long note, or of several successive notes which gives, if I may so speak, to the whole colouring a darker or lighter shade. This would be considered too great an innovation by Hasse and Graun.

He also relates that:

> The first time Jommelli made use of the *crescendo* the audience gradually rose from their seats and at the *diminuendo* they began to breathe freely, and became conscious of having stopped their breath.

He declares that the same effect was produced upon himself at Mannheim. Schubart[3] gave a celebrated description of the Mannheim orchestra's playing which deserves quoting since it presents a model which all orchestras should strive to follow in the execution of certain effects:

[1] *Cannabich*, Christian (1731–98), pupil of Johann Stamitz. Sent by the Elector to Italy where he studied under Jommelli. Appointed leader under Stamitz in 1759 and succeeded him as conductor in 1775.
[2] *Briefe eines aufmerksamen Reisenden* (I, p. 11).
[3] In his *Aesthetik* (p. 130).

No orchestra in the world has ever surpassed that of Mannheim in execution. Their *forte* is a thunder, their *crescendo* a cataract, their *diminuendo* a crystal streamlet babbling away into the far distance, their *piano* the soft breath of early spring.

The Mannheim was the first of the succession of outstanding orchestras whose performances have made them famous throughout the world. During the nineteenth century, as even the German patriot Jahn admits, the Paris orchestra under Habeneck (1781–1849)[1] achieved this pre-eminence. Later, Hans von Bülow (1830–94) made the Meiningen orchestra the best in Europe. The Meiningen orchestra had retained its pre-eminence even so late as 1913–14 when I heard it in Munich under its then conductor, Max Reger, who had revived its glories. Its playing made a tremendous impression upon me at the time. Since then I suppose Furtwängler and the Berlin Philharmonic and Toscanini with the New York and the Vienna Philharmonic orchestras have provided the outstanding examples of orchestral playing.

In Mannheim Mozart first met with the clarinet as an orchestral instrument. He writes to his father after his return to Mannheim from Paris, on December 3, 1778, about a newly-engaged oboist at Salzburg:

Can Feiner play the cor anglais? Ah! if we only had clarinets also! You cannot imagine what a wonderful effect a symphony with flutes, oboes, and clarinets makes.[2]

Wolfgang soon made friends with the Kapellmeister Cannabich and other members of the Mannheim orchestra such as Wendling (the flautist), Le Brun and Ramm (oboists), Ritter (bassoonist) and Lang (horn). He writes to his father:

[1] Habeneck was merciless to singers who did not keep strict time. He introduced Beethoven's symphonies to Paris and Berlioz no doubt learned as much of orchestral possibilities from his orchestra as Mozart did from the Mannheim orchestra. Sibelius has recently declared his opinion [1938] that Mozart is one of the greatest masters of orchestration; this is a sign of the new understanding of Mozart.
[2] The clarinet was described as an innovation by Hiller in Agricola's opera *L'Amore di Psiche* in 1769; but it was already known in the 1740s. Its general use as an orchestral instrument, however, dates from Mozart's 'Paris' symphony. It is said to have been invented in 1690 by Johann Denner of Nüremberg.

Mannheim,
October 31, 1777.

. . . Today I have been with Herr Denner at Cannabich's. He was very cordial. I played on his pianoforte (which is very good) and we went together to the rehearsal. I thought I should burst out laughing when I was introduced to everybody. Some who had heard of me were very polite and full of respect. Others, however, who knew nothing about me stared at me contemptuously. They think just because I am small and young there can be nothing important and mature behind my appearance. They will soon be undeceived. To-morrow Herr Cannabich will himself take me to Count Savioli, the Intendant of Music. . . . The oratorio which they are rehearsing is by Handel[1] but I did not stay, for before that they rehearsed a Psalm and Magnificat by the vice-Kapellmeister here, Vogler[2] which lasted quite an hour. Now I must close as I must write to my little cousin. . . .

[To Leopold]
Mannheim,
November 4, 1777.

. . . This is my second letter from Mannheim. I am with Cannabich every day. Today Mama also went with me. He is quite different to what he used to be; the whole orchestra says so. He is much prejudiced in my favour. He has a daughter who plays the clavier well and so as to make him a good friend I am working now on a sonata for his daughter which is already complete up to the Rondo.[3] When I had finished the first allegro and andante I brought it and played it. Papa cannot imagine what a success it was. There were present young Denner, a French-horn player called Lang, and the principal oboist whose name I can't remember but who plays very well and has a nice clean tone.

[1] Actually the *Messiah*. Mozart does not mention the performance on November 1st but in the *Mannheim Tonsch*. (I, p. 119) it is observed that the audience yawned during the *Messiah* but were delighted with Vogler's *Magnificat*. The second part of the *Messiah* was omitted because it was thought too dry.

[2] *Vogler*, Georg Joseph (1749–1814), famous composer, theorist and teacher; studied with (but was not approved of by) Martini; also studied with Vallotti and Mysliwecek. C. M. von Weber and Meyerbeer were his pupils.

[3] Authorities differ as to the sonata referred to. Wyzewa and Saint-Foix place both (K.309) and (K.311) in the Mannheim period and are for (K.311). The question is of interest because Mozart told Denner that he meant to make the andante 'exactly like Mlle. Rose herself'. His further remark (November 14/16) that 'the andante will give us most trouble; for it is full of expression and must be played accurately with forte and piano as it is marked' seems to suggest (K.309). After playing over the two andantes I am left with no doubt whatever in my own mind that the andante of (K.309) can be a conception of a young girl while that of (K.311) certainly is not. [The modern view concurs with Turner's conclusion. *C. R.*]

I made him a present of the oboe concerto.[1] It was written out in Cannabich's room. The man is mad with joy; today I played him the concerto on the pianoforte at Cannabich's and although they knew it was mine it pleased greatly. Nobody said it was not well-written, because here they don't understand things – they should ask the Archbishop, he would put them right.

Today I played all my six sonatas for Cannabich.[2] The Kappellmeister Holzbauer today took me himself to Count Savioli and told him in Italian that I should like to have the honour to have His Highness the Elector hear me, that I had been here fifteen years ago when I was seven years old but was now older and bigger, also musically. . . .

Wolfgang had not the same high opinion of the Church music as of the orchestral music in Mannheim and writes to his father in the same letter that he would not care to have one of his own Masses produced there:

Why? – Because of their brevity? No, here everything must be short. On account of the style? Not in the least. But because here one must write under present conditions for instruments since one cannot imagine anything worse than the vocal department. Six sopranos, six tenors and six basses to twenty violins and twelve basses stand in the proportion of 0 : 1. Is that not so, Herr Bullinger? . . . They have only two castrati who are already old. They are letting them die off. The soprano prefers to sing alto because his upper notes are gone. The few boys they have are wretched. The tenors and basses are like our funeral singers.

The Herr vice-Kapellmeister Vogler who is new in office is a musical clown, a man who has a very good idea of himself but has not much capacity. The whole orchestra dislike him. Today, however . . . I heard a Mass by Holzbauer which is already twenty-six years old, but good. He writes very well, in a good church style, with good passages for voices and instruments.

They have two organists here for whose sake alone it would be worth a trip to Mannheim. I had a good chance of hearing them for it is the custom to omit the Benedictus and let the organist play instead. The first time I heard the second organist and the next time the first. I have a higher opinion of the second than of the first. When I heard him I asked: 'Who is at the organ?' 'Our second

---

[1] Unfortunately this work, presented to Ramm, is lost, although he played it five times with great success in Mannheim during that winter.

[2] (K.279–284.)

organist.' 'He plays wretchedly.' When I heard the other: 'Who is this?' 'Our first.' 'He plays more wretchedly still.' . . .

It is enough to make one laugh to death to see these gentlemen. The second at the organ is like a child with mud; one sees his trade in his face. The first wears spectacles. I stood at the organ and watched him with the intention of learning something. He lifts his head high at every note. His *tour de force* is to play in six parts, but mostly in five and eight parts. He often playfully lets fall the right hand and plays with the left alone – in one word he does as he likes, he is in this sense complete master of the instrument.

Mama informs Nannerl that the lining for the dress is in the large chest on the right-hand side and at the bottom. . . .

Mama and I beg Papa earnestly to have the kindness to send our dear little cousin a memento. For we both regretted that we had nothing with us. . . .

[To his cousin in Augsburg][1]

My dearest Bäsle Häsle!

I have duly truly received your letter and from it get net that the Herr Father Lather, the Madam Mother, Brother and you are right quite in health. We, thank God, are very merry well. Today I have a tall scrawl from Papa, haha. I hope you also had my scribble dribble from Mannheim.

. . . I beg you, why not, I beg you, dearest idiot, why not, if you write to Mlle. Tavernier in Munich to give my compliments to the Madselles Freysinger, why not? Curious, why not? And from the younger, namely, Fräulein Josepha, I ask for forgiveness, why not – why should I not ask for forgiveness? Curious – I don't know why not? – I ask for her forgiveness that I have not yet sent her the promised Sonata but I shall send it as soon as possible. Why not? What? Why not? Why should I not send it? Why should I not forward it? Why not? Curious! I don't know why not? . . .

Now farewell. I kiss you ten thousand times and am as always the old-young.

(*Sgd.*) SOWTAIL WOLFGANG.

On November 6th at a State concert Wolfgang played a concerto, a sonata and also improvised. He writes to his father:

Mannheim,
November 8, 1777.

. . . The Elector and the whole court are very pleased with me.

[1] It is impossible to translate this letter, but I wished to give English readers who know no German a specimen of Mozart's style of writing to his cousin. It is so extraordinarily individual that a brief attempt must be made to convey the spirit of it.

Every time I played the Elector came quite near my clavier. After the concert Cannabich intimated that I might speak to the Elector. After kissing hands he said: 'I believe it is fifteen years since you were here . . . you play incomparably well.' The Princess when I kissed her hand said: '*Monsieur, je vous assure on ne peut pas jouer mieux.*' . . .

This morning I wrote the Rondeau at Cannabich's for his daughter and afterwards they would not let me go. Yesterday I went with Cannabich to the place Mama has already described.[1] I talked to the Elector quite familiarly. He is both gracious and good. He said: 'I hear that you wrote an opera at Munich.' 'Yes, Your Highness . . . My greatest desire is to write an opera here. I beg Your Highness not to forget me. I can write German, too, thank God!' 'Well, that may happen.'[2] He has a son and three daughters. The eldest and the young Count play the clavier. The Elector consulted me quite confidentially about his children. I spoke quite openly but without blaming their master. Cannabich shared my opinion. When the Elector left he thanked me very politely.

Today, after lunch at two o'clock I went with Cannabich to the flautist Wendling . . . His daughter Augusta, a former mistress of the Elector, played the clavier well and I played afterwards. I was in such wonderful spirits – not to be described! I did nothing but improvise and also played three duets for violin which I had never seen by a composer I had never heard of. Everybody was delighted. . . . I had to kiss the ladies which was no task as regards the daughter who is far from ugly. . . .

Now follow the congratulations:[3]

Dear Papa,

I can write nothing poetical; I am no poet. I cannot distribute phrases with light and shadow; I am no painter. I cannot even indicate through signs and pantomime my feeling and thoughts; I am not a dancer. I am a musician. Tomorrow at Cannabich's I shall play all my congratulations for your name – and birthday on the clavier. Today I can only wish you, my dear father, from my heart what I wish for you every day, morning and evening, good health, a long life and a joyful heart . . . I wish you as many years' life as are needed in order to have nothing more left to do in music.[4] Now farewell. . . .

[1] The residence of the Elector's mistress. The Elector took Mozart to see his natural children by the actress Seuffert (Countess Haydeck) and to advise about their musical studies.

[2] We shall see that it did happen. The opera was *Idomeneo* and was written for the Elector at Munich – after he had become Elector of Bavaria – in 1780.

[3] On his father's birthday.

[4] A wish that we could have desired for Mozart himself.

Wolfgang was much liked by the musicians in Mannheim. His mother[1] describes his success as a clavier-player in a letter to Leopold dated December 28, 1777:

> Wolfgang is made much of everywhere but he plays quite differently from what he does at Salzburg for there are pianofortes everywhere here and he manages them in a way that has never been heard of. In short everyone says who hears him that his equal is not to be found. Although Beecke and Schubart have been here everyone agrees that he far surpasses them both in beauty, taste and delicacy; and what they most admire is that he plays whatever is put before him and out of his head.

These 'successes' did not bring him in much money. In the letter to his father dated November 13th he tells how he had to go with Cannabich to get a present from Count Savioli which turned out to be a gold watch 'worth twenty carolines':

> . . . I would rather had had ten carolines, one needs money travelling. I have now five watches. I have a good mind . . . to have a pocket made . . . and to wear two watches (which is indeed the fashion now) so that it may not occur to anyone to give me another.

In Mannheim Wolfgang heard in *Günther von Schwarzburg* the celebrated tenor Raaff, for whom he was to write the part of Idomeneo, then sixty-three years old. He was one of the great singers of the age, a friend of Farinelli with whom he sang in Madrid from 1755 to 1759; he is said to have made such an impression by his singing in Naples in 1759 on the Princess Belmonte-Pignatelli as to cure her of a deep melancholy into which her husband's death had thrown her. Wolfgang's first impression was not at all favourable:

> Whoever hears him begin an aria and does not at the same moment remind himself that it is Raaff the old and once so famous tenor who is singing could not help laughing.

[1] Wolfgang's mother writes to her husband in a letter dated December 6th complaining of the cost of fires, that a small one which is soon burnt out and leaves the room as cold as before costs twelve kreutzer and that during the day she is so cold that 'I can now, as I write, scarcely hold the pen I am so frozen'. In the same letter she mentions the salaries of the Elector's musicians and adds: 'It makes one's mouth water.'

In Paris, the following year, Wolfgang heard him again and wrote on June 12, 1778, to his father:

> Now I must write something about our Raaff. You will doubtless remember that I did not write very favourably of him from Mannheim . . . that was because in Mannheim I had not heard him, so to speak. I heard him at the rehearsal of Holzbauer's *Günther*. He was in his own clothes, with his hat on his head and a cane in his hand . . . he began the first recitative quite well but when he made a dramatic exclamation it was not pleasing. He sang the arias lazily and often some notes with too much intensity . . . it is a habit he has always had which comes perhaps from the Bernacchi School for he is a pupil of Bernacchi. . . .[1]
>
> Here at his début in *Concert Spirituel* he sang the Bach[2] scena *Non so d'onde viene*, which is my favourite song . . . he pleased me . . . but the style of this Bernacchi School does not please me. There is too much *cantabile*. I admit that when he was younger and in his prime the effect would be fine and surprising. I like it too but there is too much of it . . . what most pleases me in him is when he sings certain little things *andantino* which he does in a style of his own. Everything in its place. I imagine that his forte was bravura singing . . . a good chest and long breath and then this andantino. His voice is fine and very pleasing. When I shut my eyes as I listen I find much resemblance to Meissner, only Raaff's voice is pleasanter . . . Meissner, as you know, has the bad habit of trying to make a tremolo . . . and I have never been able to bear that. It is truly horrible . . . Raaff does not do it . . . he sang four German songs wonderfully. He is very fond of me and we are good friends together. . . .

Another musical celebrity, already mentioned, whom Wolfgang met in Mannheim, was the famous Abbé Vogler. Whether because Wolfgang's friends among the Mannheim musicians belonged to the anti-Vogler party or because the mixture of pious cleverness and learned pretentiousness (Vogler seems almost to have been a sort of earlier Liszt) was antipathetic to Mozart, he certainly gives a very unfavourable portrait of this remarkable man. In his letter to his father dated November 13, 1777, he writes of Vogler:

> . . . he is a fool who imagines that there is nothing better or more

---

[1] *Bernacchi*, Antonio (1690–1756), founder of the Bologna school of singing.
[2] *Bach*, Joh. Christian.

perfect than himself. . . . His book[1] is of more use for learning to count than to compose. He says he can make a composer in three weeks and a singer in six months but one has not seen it yet. He despises the greatest masters. To me he has spoken contemptuously of Bach. . . .

On January 17, 1778, he writes to his father that he is going to pay a brief visit to Kirchheim-Poland to the Princess of Orange who was musical and had an orchestra and that he is taking with him to sing some arias the fifteen-year-old daughter[2] of a certain Herr Weber[3] who is copying them out. He then goes on to describe his meeting with Vogler at a party:

Herr Vogler has strongly wished to make my acquaintance; he already has often plagued me to come to him and now he has subdued his pride and paid me the first visit. . . . After dinner he had two claviers brought which were tuned together and also his boring printed sonatas. I had to play them and he accompanied me on the other clavier. At his insistent request I had to send for my sonatas also. (*N.B.* Before dinner he had stumbled through at sight my concerto, the Lützow[4] one [K.246].) The first movement went prestissimo, the andante allegro and the rondo really prestissimo. He played the bass mostly other than it was written and at times the harmonies and even the melodies were altered. This is indeed inevitable at such a speed; the eyes cannot see and the hands cannot grasp it. But what kind of playing at sight is that? The hearers (I mean those worthy to be so-named) can only say they have *seen* music and clavier-playing. They hear, think and feel just as little as the performer. You can imagine that the worst was my not being able to say: '*Much too quick.*' Moreover it is also much easier to play a piece fast than slow; notes can be dropped out of passages without being noticed; but is that right? . . .

In what does the art of playing at sight consist? In playing the piece in the correct time with all the notes, appoggiaturas, etc., exactly as they are written, and with the appropriate expression and

---

[1] *Tonwissenschaft und Tonsetzkunst*, Mannheim, 1776.

[2] *Weber*, Aloysia, later Aloysia Lange (1750–1839), a famous singer. Mozart's first love. He wrote for her the part of Madame Herz in *Der Schauspiel direktor*, six airs (K.294, 316, 383, 418, 419, 538) and a rondo (K.416). She married the actor Lange in 1780.

[3] *Weber*, Fridolin (1733–79), an uncle of Carl Maria von Weber, and father of Aloysia and Constanze (later, Mozart's wife). He was singer, prompter and copyist at the Mannheim Theatre.

[4] Composed for Countess von Lützow, wife of the Commandant of Hohensalzburg.

taste so that one believes the player has himself composed it.[1]
Vogler's fingering is also wretched: his left thumb is like Adlgasser's
and he makes all the runs with the first finger and thumb.

Wolfgang wrote constantly from Mannheim to his 'little cousin'
in Augsburg. It is almost impossible, as I have already said, ade-
quately to translate these letters but here is a specimen, for those
who can read German, with Mozart's spelling and punctuation
preserved:

Mannehim,
le 13 novembre, 1777.

jezt schreib ihr einmahl einen gescheiden brief, Du kannst dessent-
wegen doch Spass darein schreiben, aber so, dass du alle die briefe
richtig erhalten hast; so darf sie sich nicht mehr sorgen, und küm-
mern.

Ma trés chére Niéce! Cousine! Fille! mére, sœur, et Epouse!

Potz himmel tausend sakristey, Croaten schwere noth, Teüfel,
hexen, truden, kreüz-Battalion und kein End, Potz Element, luft,
wasser, erd und feüer, Europa, asia, affrica und America, jesuiter,
Augustiner, Benedictiner, Capuciner, minoriten, franziscaner,
Dominicaner, Chartheüser, und heil: kreüzer herrn, Canonici
Regulares und irregulares, und bärnhäüter, spizbuben, hunds-
fütter, Cujonen und schwänz übereinander, Eseln, büffeln, ochsen,
Narrn, Dalcken und fuxen! was ist das für eine Manier, 4 soldaten,
und 3 Bandalier? – – so ein Paquet und kein Portrait? – – ich war
schon voll begierde – – ich glaubte gewis – – denn sie schrieben mir
ja unlängst selbst, dass ich es gar bald, recht gar bald bekommen
werde. Zweifeln sie vielleicht ob ich auch mein Wort halten werde
– – Das will ich doch nicht hoffen, dass sie daran zweifeln! Nu, ich
bitte sie, schicken sie mir es, je ehender, je lieber. es wird wohl
hoffentlich so seyn, wie ich es mir ausgebeten habe, nemlich in
französischen aufzuge.

wie mir Mannheim gefällt? – – so gut immer ein ort ohne bääsle
gefallen kann. Verzeihen sie mir meine schlechte schrift, die feder
ist, schon alt, ich scheisse. . . .

Ich hoffe auch sie werden im gegentheil, wie es auch so ist, meine
briefe richtig erhalten haben, nemlich einen von hohenaltheim und
2 von Mannheim, und dieser, wie es auch so ist, ist der dritte von
Mannheim, aber in allen der 4te, wis es auch so ist. Nun muss ich
schliessen, wie es auch so ist, denn ich bin noch nicht angezogen,

[1] Here indeed is the true touchstone for all pianoforte playing! But it also shows
what Mozart's sight playing was and it is no wonder that good musicians were
astonished at it.

und wir essen iezt gleich, damit wir hernach wieder scheissen wie es
auch so ist; haben sie mich noch immer so lieb, wie ich sie, so werden
wir niemahlen aufhören uns zu lieben, wenn auch der Löwe rings-
herum in Mauern schwebt, wenn schon des Zweifels harter Sieg
nicht wohl bedacht gewesen, und die Tiranney der wütterer in
abweg ist geschliechen, so frist doch Codrus der weis Philosophus
oft roz für haber Muss, und die Römer, die stüzen meines arsches,
sind immer, sind stehts gewesen, und werden immer bleiben – –
kastenfrey. Adieu, j'espére que vous aurés deja pris quelque lection
dans la langue française, et je ne doute point, que – – Ecoutés: que
vous saurés bientôt mieux le français, que moi; car il y a certaine-
ment deux ans, que je n'ai pas ecrit un môt dans cette langue.
a dieu cependant. je vous baise vos mains, votre visage, vos
genoux et votre – – afin, tout ce que vous me permettés de baiser.
je suis de tout mon cœur votre

trés affectionné Neveu et Cousin

Wolfg: Amadé Mozart.

Two members of the orchestra, the flautist Wendling and the
oboist Ramm, contemplated making a visit to Paris during Lent
and Wolfgang thought of going with them; but Leopold was
against it at first, as he thought it was useless for Wolfgang to stay
any longer in Mannheim and suggested his going to Mayence and
Coblenz. He was beginning to be not at all pleased at the light-
hearted way Wolfgang was enjoying himself in Mannheim. He
had urged him to get some appointment to enable him to stay the
winter in Mannheim but as nothing of this sort materialized
Leopold began to get impatient. It is clear that Wolfgang in his
letters does all he can to cheer his father, being aware – as his
father more than once declares – that the eagerly-awaited post-
days when letters arrived from Mannheim were his chief entertainment in Salzburg, and not only of Leopold and Nannerl but
probably also of Bullinger. Wolfgang's letters are full of lively
touches and comic endings such as his signature to his letter of
November 22, 1777:

Wolfgang Amadé Mozart, Cavalier des Goldenen Sporns and, as
soon as I marry, of the Double Horns, Member of the great Academy
of Verona, Bologna.

Leopold and Bullinger laughed, as Leopold often says, 'immoderately' at Wolfgang's letters except when the material side

of things became too pressing. Then Leopold has to remind
Wolfgang of the need for him to earn some money. In his letter of
November 20, 1777, Leopold writes:

> . . . Where do you want to go next? To Paris? Which way will
> you go? Do you want to go to Paris without any letters of intro-
> duction? And what route will you take in order to be able to earn
> something on the way? Without this supposition you know well
> what a lot of money will be needed for this tremendous journey?
> And if it is forthcoming to whom shall you go? Must there not be
> enough money in your pocket to be able to live until you have made
> the necessary acquaintances in order to be able to earn something?
>
> By giving lessons one can make a good deal in Paris. This is cer-
> tain; but can one get pupils immediately and will people dismiss
> their teachers immediately in order to get the first newcomer?
>
> One can earn much by getting compositions engraved, that is
> true! But all this requires patronage, one or more friends, a sub-
> scription, and necessitates, does it not, a previous acquaintanceship?
> . . . It is quite clear that the journey and the first part of your stay
> will demand a long purse.
>
> You know that we owe Herr Bullinger three hundred gulden,
> Herr Weiser over a hundred gulden. I don't know how much we
> owe Kerschbaumer but it will run to forty gulden.[1] In the new year
> the men and the women's tailors will send in their accounts and
> there are other liabilities besides our daily indispensable living.
> Eating costs little but there are other extras, now in winter there is
> wood and lighting, etc. . . .

Leopold was indefatigable with good advice and must have
spent an immense amount of time studying maps and routes and
in recollecting acquaintances, notabilities, princely music-lovers
throughout the country so as to select a route to Paris which
offered most favourable opportunities for earning money. His
letter of November 24th covers more than six printed pages and
Wolfgang received such letters every few days. In this letter of
November 24th Leopold writes:

> . . . Such a journey is no joke and you have not yet realized this.
> You must have something more serious in your head than non-
> sense; you must take the trouble to think beforehand of a hundred

[1] In every city there should be a statue erected to the unknown men who have lent
money to artists. A statue to the UNKNOWN LENDER who was responsible for the
country's art!

things, otherwise you will find yourself in a mess, without money –
and where there is no money there is no friend left even if you give a
hundred fruitless lessons, compose sonatas and instead of doing more
sensible things play the fool from ten to twelve nightly. Ask one of
these friends of yours for money! All jokes will come to an end and
the most jocular face will suddenly turn grave. . . .

All this you will, I hope, take reasonably, for on whom will everything fall in the end but on your poor old father. . . .

Wolfgang, in his letter of November 26th, admonishes his
father not to lose time in superfluous speculations. 'What will
happen,' he says, 'we don't know and yet we do – what God wills,'[1]
and on November 29, 1777, he writes:

. . . You reproach us both without our deserving it. We spend
nothing that is not necessary. . . . Can you believe that I should
remain anywhere without reason? . . . Good! you shall know the
reason, yes, the whole course of events. But, by God, I did not want
to write a word because I could not do so in detail and a vague
account would, as I know, have perturbed you which is what I
always try to avoid. But if you ascribe my inaction to carelessness
and laziness I can do nothing but thank you for your good opinion
and lament from my heart that you do not know your son better.

I am not careless. I am only prepared for everything and so can
wait with patience and endure all – provided my honour and good
name of Mozart do not suffer. Well, if it must be it must. But I beg
you beforehand not to rejoice or to be vexed before it is time; for
whatever happens it is all right if only one is healthy; for happiness
consists – entirely in the imagination.

To this Leopold replied on December 4, 1777, saying that what
is past is past and not to be altered:

. . . But that you, my son, should write to me *that all speculations*[2]
are useless and do not help, that we don't know what may happen, that
is indeed utterly without reflection and certainly senselessly written.
That all will and must go according as God wills no reasonable man,

---

[1] One cannot avoid the suspicion that occasionally Wolfgang uses his father's
devout expressions against him slightly maliciously; but I am convinced that although Wolfgang's enormous sense of humour made this possible the expressions
are nevertheless sincere on his part. If there is one thing that Wolfgang is not, it is
cynical. He is realistic but not cynical.
[2] Leopold uses the word *Speculationen*, which is not a German word and, of
course, does not mean speculating with money but taking into account future possible
events.

I will not say, Christian, will deny. But does it follow that we are to act blindly and live without forethought, make no preparations and only wait until something from above falls of its own accord under the roof? . . .

Is it indeed enough that you have taken the step to remain by the Elector during the winter?

Your dear good Mama writes to me that she will make a careful account of your expenditure. Good! I do not ask for an exact account and never thought of such a thing. . . . From Mannheim you should at least in your second letter have written: 'The journey has cost us so much, we have now so much' – then I would have had time to make arrangements . . . was my preparation to provide a letter of credit at Augsburg an unnecessary speculation? . . . Good God! I am not to speculate when I am already in debt on your account four hundred and fifty florins and you think you can put me in a good humour by writing all sorts of absurd nonsense. . . .

To have something in hand and to form two or three plans and to make the necessary preparations so that if one fails one may pursue the other are not useless speculations. Whoever acts differently is a silly or frivolous person who, especially in the world as it is today, will in spite of the greatest cleverness always remain in the rear and be continually unhappy; especially if, in addition, he is deceived by flatterers, lip-friends and those envious of him.

Mark well, my son, that *one man in a thousand* who is not your true friend merely out of self-interest *is one of the greatest wonders of this world*.

Examine all who call or show themselves as friends and you will find the reason why they are so; if they have no self-interest in it they are concerned for others.

Meanwhile Wolfgang had kept his father informed about his prospects with the Elector. On November 29, 1777, he writes that he discussed with Cannabich his interview with Count Savioli who said:

'I should be very glad if you remained with us the whole winter but I should be still more pleased if you were taken into service here altogether.' I replied: 'I could wish for nothing better . . . but I do not see how that is possible. You already have two Kapellmeisters and I do not see what I could be. I could not consent to come after Vogler.' 'Nor need you,' he said, 'no musician here is under the Kapellmeister, not even under the Intendant. The Elector could appoint you his chamber composer. Just wait a while. I shall speak to the Count about it.'

The following Thursday was the State concert; when the Count saw me he apologised for not having spoken yet . . . he would speak [to the Elector] on Monday. I let three days pass and as I had heard nothing I visited him to enquire. He said: 'My dear Mozart (this was Friday, i.e. yesterday), today the Elector went hunting and it was impossible to speak to him, but tomorrow I shall certainly have an answer.' I begged him not to forget. In truth I was a little annoyed . . . and I determined to take my easiest six variations on the Fischer Minuet (K.179) to the young Count so as to get an opportunity to speak myself with the Elector.

When I brought them the governess could not contain her delight. I was very politely received and when I produced the variations and said they were for the young Count she said: 'O, you are very kind! But have you nothing for the Countess?' 'Not yet,' I said, 'but if I remain here long enough to have time to write I shall – – ' '*Apropos*!' she said, 'I am glad that you are staying here for the winter.' 'Indeed! I did not know!' 'That surprises me, that is strange, for the Elector told me so himself.' . . .

I then told her the whole story. We agreed that I should come the next day at four o'clock and bring something for the Countess. She would speak to the Elector before I came, and I should meet him there. I went today but he was not there. Tomorrow I shall go again. I have written a Rondeau for the Countess. Now have I not reason enough to remain here and await the issue? . . . The Elector likes me, thinks much of me and knows what I can do. I hope to be able to give you good news in my next letter. I beg you once more not to rejoice nor to worry about it too soon and to say nothing to anyone but Herr Bullinger and my sister. . . .

But for some reason the affair hung fire,[1] as his next letter shows:

Mannheim,
December 3, 1777.

Monsieur mon très cher Père,

I can still tell you nothing certain. . . . Last Monday I had the good fortune after having gone for three days, morning and afternoon, to see his natural children, to meet the Elector. We all thought our trouble was again in vain . . . when we saw him coming. The governess at once placed the Countess at the clavier and I sat near her giving her a lesson: the Elector saw us so when he entered. We stood up but he told us to continue. When she had finished playing

---

[1] Those who think a Mozart would come off any better today applying to a Government committee in a Fascist, Communist, Socialist, Capitalist or any other kind of State are incurable optimists.

the governess remarked that I had written a charming Rondeau. I played it and he was highly pleased. Then he asked: 'But will she be able to learn it?' 'O, yes!' I said, 'I only wish that I had the happiness of teaching it to her myself.' He took some snuff and said: 'I should also like it but would it not harm her to have two masters?' 'O, no, Your Highness! It only matters whether she has a good or a bad master; I hope Your Highness has confidence in me.' 'O, certainly!' he said. Then the governess said: 'M. Mozart has also written variations on the Fischer Minuet for the young Count.' I played them and he was again very pleased.

Then he began to play with the Countess. Then I thanked him for the presentation watch. He said: 'Well, I shall think it over. How long will you remain here?' 'As long as Your Highness commands. I have no engagement elsewhere.' And that was all. This morning I was there again and was told that the Elector had said several times last night that Mozart was remaining all the winter. Now it has gone so far I must wait.

Today for the fourth time I dined at Wendling's. Before dinner Count Savioli came with the Kapellmeister Schweitzer who arrived yesterday evening. Savioli said to me: 'I have spoken several times yesterday with the Elector but he has not yet made up his mind.' I said I should like to have a word with him and we went to the window. I told him my doubts of the Elector, complained of being kept waiting, that I had spent so much here, and begged him to induce the Elector to engage me. I feared that there would be so little work for me that I should not be able to stay the winter. Let him give me work. I wanted work. He promised to propose it . . . Now let happen what will. If he does not keep me I shall ask for a parting gift for I do not intend to make the Elector a present of the Rondeau and variations. I assure you that I take the matter quite calmly since I know for certain that only good can come, happen what may. I have resigned myself to the will of God . . . the Kapellmeister Schweitzer is a good, decent, honest man, dry and smooth like our Haydn [Michael] only with a more cultivated speech. In his coming opera there are very good things and I don't doubt it will succeed. His *Alceste* pleased greatly and it is not half so good as *Rosemunde*. No doubt it has helped it considerably that it is the first German singspeil. . . .

Finally the Elector was compelled to make up his mind and the result was communicated by Wolfgang to his father on December 10, 1777:

There is nothing to be done here at present with the Elector.

The day before yesterday I went to the concert at Court to get my answer. Count Savioli avoided me but I went up to him and when he saw me he shrugged his shoulders. 'What!' I said, 'still no answer?' 'A thousand pardons,' said he, 'but unfortunately there is nothing to be done.' '*Eh bien!*' I answered, 'the Elector might have told me that before.' 'Yes,' he said, 'he would not have made up his mind now if I had not driven him and represented to him how long you have been waiting here and spending your money in the hotel.'

'That vexes me most of all,' I said, 'it is not at all good behaviour. But I am exceedingly obliged to you, Count (he is not called "Excellency"), that you have taken such trouble on my account and I shall be obliged if you will thank the Elector for his gracious though somewhat tardy intelligence and assure him that he would never have regretted it if he had engaged me.' 'O!' he said, 'I am more sure of that than you believe.'

I told the outcome to Wendling who went red and said hotly: 'We must find some means of keeping you here for the two months before we go together to Paris.' . . .

Wolfgang went to the Cannabichs and told what had happened to his wife, as Cannabich was away hunting:

When Mlle. Rose who was busy . . . three rooms away . . . came in and said to me: 'Is it your pleasure that we begin?' – for it was time for a lesson – I said: 'I am at your service.' 'Today we shall have a good lesson,' said she. 'Yes, indeed,' I replied, 'for it will not last much longer.' 'How so? Why is that?' She went to her mother who told her. 'What!' she said, 'is it really true? I do not believe it.' 'Yes, yes, quite true,' I replied. Then she played my sonata through quite seriously: believe me I could not refrain from weeping . . .

Wolfgang then tells his father that when he dined the following day with the flautist Wendling he made him a proposal. A Dutch nabob of independent means named De Jean, or Dechamps, an admirer of Wolfgang's, offered to give him two hundred florins for three small, easy concertos and two flute quartets; Cannabich would guarantee him at least two pupils who paid well. Wendling also offered him free board and quarters at the house of the Chamberlain Serrarius. Then, he tells his father, he must find quarters for his mother who will return home when he departs with Wendling for Paris. He continues:

Mama is quite content with this plan, it now depends on your consent, of which I am so certain that if it were the right time for travelling I should set off for Paris without waiting for an answer; for from a father who up to now has been so reasonable and considerate for his children one could not expect a refusal. Herr Wendling, who sends his compliments, is a great friend of our great friend Grimm . . .

I would also ask you to obtain for me, if possible, as we shall not leave before March 6th, either through Herr Mesmer in Vienna, or someone else, a letter to the Queen of France – it is of no great importance but it is better to have it, no doubt. This has been suggested by Wendling.

I imagine that what I have written appears strange to you for you are in a town where one is used to stupid, hostile, silly and faint friends who because the sorrowful bread of Salzburg is indispensable to you are always flattering. . . . You see the reason I am always writing jokes and childish stuff to you and little that is sensible is because having to wait the outcome here I wanted to spare you vexation and to exempt my good friends who guiltlessly would have taken the blame as though they had secretly worked against me, which is certainly not true. . . .

I am obliged by your letter to tell you the whole story. I beg you, above everything, don't make yourself ill about this. God has willed it. Only reflect on this too-certain truth . . . one often thinks this would be very good and that would be very bad and then after the event one finds the contrary is true. Now I must go to sleep. I shall have plenty to do in the two months to write three concertos, two quartets, four or six clavier duets and I also have in mind a Grand Mass. . . . I beg you to let me have your answer quickly. I kiss your hand a hundred thousand times and embrace my sister from my heart and am your obedient son.

(*Sgd.*) WOLFGANG AMADÉ MOZART.

Baron Durnitz was not in Munich when I was there. I shall write next post to Count Zeil about the Munich business. If you would write also to him it would be good, but short and to the point. Only don't crawl, for I can't bear that.[1]

In his letter of December 8th Leopold explains to Wolfgang that all his anxiety was due to his fear that he was leaving Mannheim without adequate preparation. If he had told him he was staying on then neither he nor Nannerl nor Bullinger would have been worried. He impresses on him again the necessity of always

[1] Little did Wolfgang dream of the humiliations he would have to endure later in his life!

having letters of credit properly provided for travelling in case of misfortune and reminds him how lucky it was that he had not been without resources when he himself was dangerously ill in England and the two children were so ill in Holland. Then he adds:

> You think that I cannot accommodate myself to good or ill fortune. Do you know when I can do so? When I can think without care of all preparations carefully made and cannot reproach myself; then I can rest perfectly happy because there is nothing I can reproach myself for. . . . Enough! nothing can oppress my heart and cause me such deadly anxiety as uncertainty and doubt. . . . Remain the winter in Mannheim, a winter journey was causing me anxiety on account of your Mama. . . .
>
> Now I must reply to your saying that happiness is only in the imagination. I agree completely. I only ask you whether this is to be understood so generally that a traveller who sits in an inn or a post-house and has no more money . . . can then convince himself that happiness is in the imagination?
>
> My dear Wolfgang, this saying is a moral for men who are content with nothing. And as most men, in fact almost all, are discontented and each considers his neighbour more fortunate than himself so one may learn from this – and rightly – that every man should be content with his position and circumstances in which he is placed according to his capacities and not envy his neighbour whom it is most probable he would not find enviable if he knew his secrets, for we judge always by outward appearances and everyone keeps the darker side carefully hidden.
>
> Yesterday Nannerl was the best. I won and for Mama shot ten kreutzers' worth. . . .

Leopold adds a note to his wife that he is sufficiently informed about their expenses and tells her to be careful of the cold and buy a man's fur-coat. In a letter of December 15th he writes to his wife:

> May I ask whether Wolfgang has not forgotten to go to Confession lately? God before everything! From Him alone must we expect earthly happiness and have care for Eternity. Young people don't like to hear such things, I know. I have been young myself. But, God be praised, I never failed to come to myself after youthful follies, to flee from all danger to my soul and always kept before my eyes God and my honour and the dangerous consequences of my actions.

In the same letter he asks whether Wolfgang's beard is cut, burnt or shaved off. His wife replies that up till now his beard had been cut by scissors but that in future it would have to be shaved. She also informs Leopold that Wolfgang had confessed at the Feast of the Immaculate Conception and that they went to Mass regularly on Sundays. Wolfgang himself wrote on December 20th, after wishing his father happiness for the New Year:

> By your last letter of December 15th I was made very happy since I learned that you were – God be praised – in good health. We are also, thank God, both well. . . . I am writing this at eleven o'clock at night as I have no other time. We cannot get up before eight as it is not light in our room (which is on the ground floor) until eight-thirty. Then I dress quickly. At ten I sit down to compose until twelve or twelve-thirty, then I go to Wendling and write there a little more until one-thirty. Then we eat. At three I have to go to the Mainzischer Hof to give lessons to a Dutch officer in gallantry and thorough-bass, for which if I am not mistaken I get four ducats for twelve lessons. At four I return home to give a lesson to the daughter of the house but we never begin before four-thirty waiting for lights. At six I go to Cannabich and teach Mlle. Rose. I remain there to dinner and then we talk and play a little or I take a book from my pocket and read – as I used to do at Salzburg.
>
> I have written that your last letter gave me great pleasure; that is true; but one thing vexed me a little, the question: whether I had forgotten to confess – I have nothing to reply to this except to make one request, which is, not to think so badly of me. I am fond of fun, but be assured that nevertheless I can be serious. Since I left Salzburg (and also in Salzburg itself) I have met people whose speech and behaviour I should be ashamed to copy although they were ten, twenty and thirty years older. So I beg you earnestly to have a better opinion of me.[1]

On December 18th Leopold replied in full to Wolfgang's letter of December 10th, agreeing to the proposal that Wolfgang should remain in Mannheim for the winter and go to Paris in the spring. He tells him to be patient and adds that a young man 'even if he has fallen from heaven and overlooks all masters' will have to wait until he is older before he obtains due recognition. He also tells him that he is not to leave his mother and that he will not allow

---

[1] The letter concludes with twenty lines of rhymed couplets addressed by Wolfgang to Nannerl.

him to let his mother live alone: 'So long as Mama remains there you must stay with her.'

So far all seemed well and both Leopold and Wolfgang were contented; but a situation was developing which was to alter everything. An attempt by Leopold to get Wolfgang a commission from the Emperor to write a German opera for Vienna failed and he was informed by Herr von Henfeld in Vienna that the Emperor already had Gluck and Salieri in his service and would not take on anyone else at present. Adlgasser, the organist at Salzburg, died on December 21, 1777, and the authorities began to hint to Leopold that the post might be given to Wolfgang if he applied, which, however, was the last thing Wolfgang wanted.

In the meantime the friendship between Wolfgang and the young Aloysia Weber had been steadily deepening. Wolfgang had taken her on his visit to the Princess of Orange at Kirchheim-Poland, where she sang the aria he wrote for De Amicis (K.135) as well as the bravura arias *Parto*, *m'affretto* and *Dalla sponda tenebrosa*[1] 'superbly'. On January 17, 1778, he had written to his father about Herr Weber:

> He has a daughter who sings superbly, has a beautiful pure voice and is fifteen years old . . .

On February 4, 1778, he writes about their visit, on which she sang the above-mentioned three arias, and tells his father how well she plays the clavier and that he would rather hear her play his sonatas than Vogler. He adds that his sister would find her a true friend and comrade and that the whole Weber family is truly 'Mozartisch'. He has the idea of touring Switzerland and Holland with her and her family and then goes on to say:

> *Apropos*, you must not be surprised that out of seventy-seven florins not more than forty-two remain. That has happened in the pure enjoyment of being once again with honest and sympathetic friends. . . . I have paid half but that won't happen on our other journeys; I have already made that clear that I shall only pay for myself. Afterwards we stayed five days at Worms where we were very jolly. . . .

[1] Both these arias are out of Mozart's opera *Lucio Silla*.

In this same letter he calmly tells his father:

Now comes something important about which I beg an immediate answer. Mama and I have discussed the matter and agreed that the Wendling manner of living does not suit us.

Wendling is a thoroughly honest and good man but unfortunately is totally lacking in religion. It is quite sufficient that his daughter was [the Elector's] mistress. Ramm is a food gellow but a libertine. I know myself. I know that I have so much religion that I certainly could never do anything which I would not do in the face of the whole world; but the mere thought of travelling alone with people whose way of thinking is so remote from mine (and from that of all honest people) shocks me. They can do what they please but I have not the heart to accompany them; I should not have one pleasant hour. I should not know what to say for in one word I do not trust them. Friends who have no religion do not last long. I have already prepared them. I have said that while I was away three letters arrived of which I can say no more than that it is doubtful whether I can go with them to Paris. Perhaps I shall follow, perhaps I shall go elsewhere. . . .

The astonishment of Leopold on receiving this letter may easily be imagined. Wolfgang was in love and his extraordinarily impressionable nature is perfectly displayed in this letter which for flexibility, naïvety, ingenious but transparent humbug is precisely what many men of character would deplore in a young man unless they were unusually clear-sighted and understanding. But I would claim that this letter is another example of the absolutely sincere but Protean character of a man whose genius is rooted in his extreme sensibility. His father, however, was shocked. He had already (February 5th) given Wolfgang a long list of their Paris acquaintances on whom to call and on February 12th he answers:

Your letter of the fourth has been read by me with astonishment and alarm.

In this letter Leopold good-humouredly but, nevertheless, ironically refers to his changeability and recalls how in Munich he was full of enthusiasm for the young soprano Mlle. Kaiser; then in Augsburg spent his time gaily with his pretty young cousin; played the fool in Wallerstein; then in Mannheim wrote a sonata for Rosa Cannabich; and could not speak highly enough of Wend-

ling, Ramm, etc. until he met the Webers; and now all the others
are forgotten. The Webers are the most Christian family and the
daughter is the favourite and is to be made at once a *prima donna*
in Italy. He goes on to beg Wolfgang to reflect more, telling him
he is responsible to God for the extraordinary talent he has been
given:

It depends now on your good sense and way of living whether you
become an ordinary musician, forgotten by the whole world, or a
celebrated Kapellmeister of whom posterity will read in books –
whether you are herded with a woman in a garret full of beggarly
children on straw-bedding or live a Christian life in honour, pleasure
and renown with your family provided for and respected by the
world. . . .

On February 16th Leopold adds:

That you should not travel in such company is right enough but
you have been familiar with the bad side of these men for a long time,
but you had so little trust during this period in your attentive father
that you did not write and ask his advice; and (shocking) neither did
your mother. . . .

In his letter dated February 7, 1778, Wolfgang added another
reason for not going to Paris – namely, that he does not see what
he could do there except give lessons, which is distasteful to him,
except in the case of a pupil who has some genius, gaiety and a
desire to learn, but

to be compelled to go at a fixed hour to a house or wait at home is
impossible for me even if profitable. I leave that to those who are
incapable of anything more than playing the clavier. I am a composer and am a born Kapellmeister, I cannot thus bury my talent for
composition which a gracious God has so richly given me (I can
say this without arrogance for I feel it now more than ever) and that
would be the result of having many pupils for it is a distracting occupation. I would rather neglect the clavier than composition, for the
clavier is secondary for me but, God be praised, a useful second
string.
    To write opera is my firm intention; French rather than German;
Italian rather than French or German. Wendling and his friends have
the opinion that my compositions would please exceptionally in
Paris. I certainly have no fear about it for, as you know, I can adapt
myself to every kind and style of composition. . . .

He also criticizes adversely a Salzburg friend, Schidenhofen, for marrying for money and adds:

> I could not make such a marriage. I hope to make my wife happy, not make my fortune through her. Therefore I shall wait and enjoy my golden freedom until I am in a position to provide for a wife and children. . . .

In the same letter he speaks again of Aloysia Weber (who sings a 'superb cantabile'), to whom he has given the De Amicis aria, the scene composed for Duschek (*Ah lo previdi*, K.272, composed in Salzburg in August 1777, for the Prague singer Josepha Duschek) and four arias from *Il Re Pastore*. In his letter of February 14, 1778, he describes how charmingly Mlle. Weber sang two of his arias at a Cannabich concert. On February 4th he tells his father how like him Herr Weber is and that travelling with Weber is just like travelling with Leopold: 'Mama would say the same if she were not so averse from letter-writing';[1] he suggests that he and the Webers should go to Italy. He asks his father to make inquiries as to what pay a *prima donna* gets in Verona and that he vouches with his life for Aloysia's singing. On the journey to Italy, he adds, they would all have the pleasure of visiting Leopold for a fortnight. On the fourteenth he informs his father that Herr De Jean is leaving for Paris and has only paid him ninety-six florins because he had only written two concertos and three quartets:[2]

> That I have not done more is quite simply explained. I have no peace. I can write nothing except at night and so cannot get up early. One is not always in the right mood for working. Of course I can scribble the whole day long; but such pieces go out into the world and I am determined not to be ashamed of them if my name is on them. Besides, as you know, I become bored and dull if I have to write always for one instrument (which I can't bear). . . . Don't forget about Italy. . . .

[1] This was all so transparent that it could not have annoyed Leopold to be told that a mere ordinary Herr Weber was almost exactly the same as Leopold Mozart!
[2] Quartets for flute, violin, viola and 'cello in D (K.285) and A (K.298 and C (K.Anh.171); Flute Concerto in D (K.314); Andante for Flute and Orchestra in C (K.315); Flute Concerto in G (K.313); Quartet in G for flute, violin, viola, and 'cello not in original Köchel but in Peter's Edition. See No. 293, Wyzewa and Saint-Foix, Vol. II, p. 404.

But Wolfgang's mother had taken a hand in spite of her aversion from writing, and on February 4th wrote to her husband as follows:

> From this letter you will have seen how when Wolfgang makes a new friendship he will give his blood and substance for such people.
>
> It is true that she[1] sings incomparably but one must never put one's own interest quite aside; I have never approved of the company of Wendling and Ramm but dared not make any objection and am never listened to.
>
> As soon as he knew the Webers he altered his mind; in one word, he prefers being with other people to being with me. I tell him what I do not approve of and that displeases him. You must reflect what is to be done. . . . I write this in the greatest secrecy while he is eating. . . .

On February 23rd Leopold replied to Wolfgang:

> As if to convince me that you are distracted and unobservant you say at the beginning of your letter of the fourteenth that you see from my letter of the ninth that I have not received your last two letters. So I should have answered your visionary letter of the fifth, which almost killed me, on the ninth although by our long exchange of letters from Mannheim you must know that every letter takes six days. . . .
>
> I know quite well when you can get my letters and have taken trouble that they should always reach you in time. But what is the use of all my exactitude, care, reflection and fatherly trouble about such a weighty and vital undertaking if you . . . have no proper trust in your father. . . .
>
> So you have got only ninety-six instead of two hundred florins – and why? – Because you have only completed for him two concertos and three quartets. How much had you to write for him that he has only paid you the half? – Why do you write me a lie, that you had only to write three easy concertos and a pair of quartets? And why did you not follow my advice when I expressly told you to deliver to this man as quickly as possible? Why? So as to make sure of the two hundred florins, because I know mankind better than you. Did I not guess what would happen? I have to see further ahead . . . than you. . . .
>
> You will only give lessons as a favour! And you will leave your old father stranded. To give lessons is too much trouble for you, a young man, even though well-paid. It is more fitting for your fifty-eight-year-old father to run round for a miserable pittance to sup-

[1] Aloysia Weber.

port himself and his daughter and to send what little is left to support you instead of paying his debts – and merely that you may amuse yourself giving superfluous lessons to a young girl!

My son, reflect and listen to your reason! Consider whether you are not dealing more hardly with me than our Prince himself. . . . You can be the death of me, he can only make me ill . . . My dear Wolfgang, you convince me in all your letters that you go by the first wild idea that enters your head or is brought before you, without proper consideration. For example you write: 'I am a composer and I must not bury my talent for composition.' Who said you should do this? – Is vagabondage a way to exercise your talent? To make yourself known in the world as a composer you must go to Paris, Vienna or Italy. Paris is nearest. . . . In Naples alone there are three hundred *maestri* and through the whole of Italy these composers have libretti in hand for two years, but in Paris only two or three write for the theatre and one can count on one's fingers other kinds of composers. . . .

In short, could I bring about in you a more stable frame of mind and induce more reflection into your excitable impressions I would make you the most fortunate man in the world. But I see you are not ripe in this respect. And yet in respect of your talent you are wholly ripe. Also you grasp every kind of knowledge with the greatest ease. Why can't you learn to know men – to guess their intentions – to hide your heart before the world. . . .

My dear son, God has given you a wonderful understanding . . . try to understand yourself, my dear Wolfgang; you will find a little too much arrogance and self-love and then that you make yourself too quickly familiar and open your heart to everybody. . . . Your pride and self-love are only hurt when one does not immediately show you the appropriate esteem; so that people who do not know you must read on your forehead that you are a man of genius. If, however, they flatter you with the intention of drawing you according to their own plans and laud you to the skies then you open your heart with the greatest readiness and believe in them as in the Gospel. . . .

Reflect in cold blood with sound impartial reason and you will realize that I speak not only as your father but as your true friend, since, agreeable and dear as is the name of son, very often the name of father is hated by children. That is not so with you . . . I beg you do not think I mistrust your filial love; all I say is said only with the object of making a thorough man of you. Millions of men lack the great favour you have received from God. What a responsibility! Would it not be an everlasting pity if such great genius were to go astray! And that can happen in a moment. . . .

Mama must go with you to Paris. . . . By the next post I shall give you all particulars.

In his letters of February 19th and February 22nd Wolfgang again speaks of Mlle. Weber and expresses his feelings still more clearly when he says there are people who believe it is impossible to love a young girl without 'bad intentions' and that he is no Brunetti or Mysliwecek, but

a Mozart, a young and well-meaning Mozart, and so you will, I hope, forgive me if at times I express myself hastily and heatedly. . . . I had a great deal to say on this matter but I cannot, it is impossible. I have among many faults also this one, that I always believe that my friends who know me do know me! Words then are superfluous; if they don't know me what is the use of words?

That does not refer to you, dear Papa; no, you understand me well. . . .

I fully expected that you would disapprove of the journey with the Webers, for I myself was unable to conceive it under our present circumstances. But I had given my word to write to you about it. Herr Weber does not know how we stand. I have told no one and so, as I wanted not to have to think about anyone and for us all to be happy together, I forgot its impossibility at present. . . .

What you write about Mlle. Weber is all true and as I have written I knew as well as you that she is too young and needs acting experience. . . . The good Webers are as tired of being here as others you know of. They think everything is possible. I promised them I would write to my father but even before my letter reached Salzburg I was telling them they must be patient and that she was still a little too young, etc. They take everything well from me for they have a high opinion of me. Now her father has taken my advice and talked to Mme. Toscani (an actress) about giving his daughter lessons in acting.

All you have written about Mlle. Weber is true except that she sings like Gabrielli,[1] which I should be very sorry for. Those who have heard Gabrielli know that she is nothing but a scales and roulade machine and while she does it in a way to excite astonishment, which, however, does not last longer than the fourth time one hears her . . . in a word she sings with technique but without understanding. Mlle. Weber sings from her heart and by preference *cantabile*.

[1] In his letter of February 12th from Salzburg, Leopold writes: 'I will grant that Mlle. Weber sings like a Gabrielli, etc. etc.'

Wolfgang resigned himself to the sheer impracticability of his scheme to go to Italy with the Webers and began to make preparations for his departure with his mother to Paris. In his letter of February 28th he tells his father of an aria, *Se al labbro mio non credi* (K.295), which he has written for the singer Raaff which pleased him greatly; also, of an aria for Aloysia Weber, *Non so d'onde viene* (K.294), with a second aria, *Ah non lasciarmi*,[1] which he composed for Mlle. Wendling. The words *Non so d'onde viene* come from Metastasio's *Olimpiade* and their setting by J. C. Bach was described by Wolfgang as his favourite aria. He describes to his father how he has tried to set it quite differently from Bach and that in two days Aloysia Weber knew it and sang it accompanying herself with perfect accuracy.[2]

Into the aria *Non so d'onde viene* Wolfgang put much of the tenderness with which the fifteen-year-old Aloysia then inspired him. The Italian text is as follows:

> Non so d'onde viene
> Quel tenero affetto.
> Quel moto, che ignoto
> Mi nasce nel petto,
> Qual gel, che le vene
> Scorrendo mi và.
> Nel seno a destarmi
> Si fieri contrasti
> Non parmi
> Che basti
> La sola pietà,

which may be translated thus:

> I do not know whence comes
> This tenderness of feeling;
> What is this new emotion
> That in my breast is stealing,

---

[1] (K.486a)=(K.294a) in Dr Einstein's edition of Köchel.

[2] Wolfgang was not blinded by love in his admiration of Aloysia Weber's singing. As Aloysia Lange she became one of the best singers of the time. Schubart in his *Aesthetik* (p. 135) attributes her *portamento*, accuracy, delicacy, excellent *piena-vot* and *mezza-voce* and wonderful cadenzas to 'her great master', Vogler; but Vogler only gave her lessons later and her earlier association with Mozart was not then well known.

> This ice which so benumbs
> Burning thro' my veins?
> Can pity in me waken
> This strife by which I'm shaken?
> No, I fear
> Pity ne'er
> Such dominions gains.

In this same letter of February 28, 1778, Wolfgang tells his father:

> I put my trust in three friends, namely, God, your head and my head. Our heads are naturally different but each very good of its kind, serviceable and useful and with time I hope that my head will approach nearer to yours in the things in which yours is best. Now farewell! Be jolly and in high spirits. . . .

Wolfgang was always chiefly concerned that his father should not worry and his letters are always written with this intention. On the same day as his letter of February 28th to his father from which I have quoted, he writes to his cousin (*das Bäsle*) in Augsburg. As usual it is written with frequent rhyming and play on words and in Wolfgang's own particular and lively vein of foolery. He begins by telling her that she must have thought him dead as it is so long since he has written, but he has had time only to think of her, not to write to her. He asks how she is getting on with her French and asks if he shall write her a letter in French from Paris, where he is going in fourteen days. Then he adds that as he has nothing to do at the moment he will relate to her a short story, which happened recently in the neighbourhood and caused a great stir, 'though one doesn't yet know the outcome of the story'. Then he continues (and I shall leave his first sentences in the original, for they are hardly translatable):

> *Also kurz zu sagen, es war etwa 4 Stunden von hier, das Ort weis ich nicht mehr, es war halt ein Dorf oder so etwas; Nu das ist endlich ein Ding ob es Tribsterill wo der Drek ins Meer rinnt oder Burmesquik wo man die krummen Arschlöcher dräht war; mit einen Wort, es war halt ein ort.*

There was once a shepherd or herdsman who was already rather old but who still looked strong and robust; he was single and comfortably off and lived happily and – this I must tell you beforehand

9. Mozart's two sons, Wolfgang and Karl, in 1802

10. Leopold Mozart, *c.* 1765

ere I begin to tell the story – he had a frightful voice when he spoke
so that one was always terrified when one heard him speak. Now, to
be brief, you must know that he had a dog whom he called 'Bellot',
a very fine and large dog, white with black spots. Now, one day he
was going along with his sheep, of which he had eleven thousand;
he had a stick with a fine red-coloured ribbon in his hand. For he
never went without his stick. That was his custom. Now, to continue: when he had been walking for a good hour he was tired and
sat down by a river. There he fell asleep and dreamed that he had
lost his sheep and in his fright he awoke and to his great joy saw all
his sheep again. At last he got up and went on but not far, since
before half-an-hour had gone by he came to a bridge which was
very long but was protected on both sides so that one could not fall
off. There he observed his flock and as they had to cross he began to
drive over his eleven thousand sheep. Now, please have the kindness
to wait until the eleven thousand sheep are across then I will tell
you the whole story. I told you at the beginning that the result is
not yet known. . . .

Adieu, Bäsle. I am, I was, I were, I have been, I had been, I
might have been, O, if I were that I were, would God I were; I
should be, I will be, if I should be, O, that I would be, I would have
been, I might have been, O, if I had been, O, that I had been,
would to God I had been, what? – A dried cod. *Adieu, ma chère
Cousine* . . .

On March 14, 1778, Wolfgang and his mother left Mannheim
and arrived in Paris at four o'clock on March 23rd. The next day
(March 24th) Wolfgang wrote to his father describing his departure:

Mlle. Weber kindly knitted me two purses as a remembrance and
a slight acknowledgment of my services. Her father copied for me
what I needed and gave me some music-paper and presented me with
the comedies of Moliére (because he knew that I had never read
them) with the inscription *Ricevi, Amico, le opere del Molière in
segno di gratitudine e qualche volta ricordati di me* and when he was
alone with Mama he said: 'Our best friend and benefactor is leaving
us. Yes, it is certain . . . your son has done much for my daughter and
has interested himself in her so that she cannot be grateful enough
to him.' The day before I left they invited me to supper but I
could not go as I had to be at home. Nevertheless I spent two
hours beforehand with them. They never ceased thanking me. . . .
When I left they all wept. I am sorry but the tears come into my
eyes when I think of it. . . .

H

We have been nine-and-a-half days on the journey. We thought we should never last out. I have never been so bored in my life. . . .

There can be no doubt that Wolfgang was in love with Aloysia Weber and he probably consoled himself with the thought of her age and the possibilities that Paris might offer to him.

CHAPTER TWELVE

Paris

Age 22 (March 23, 1778 – September 26, 1778)

WHEN MOZART ARRIVED in Paris in March 1778, there existed a highly developed school of French opera, and to Joseph Frank, who later found him engaged in the study of French scores and asked him if it were not better to study Italian composers, he is reported to have said:[1]

> As far as melody is concerned, yes; but as far as dramatic effect is concerned, no; besides, the scores which you see here are by Gluck, Piccinni, Salieri, as well as Grétry, and have nothing French but the words.

The development of French opera may be best stated diagrammatically, showing the chief operatic composers and their principal works and dates of production in Paris, in historical perspective, thus:

THE DEVELOPMENT OF FRENCH OPERA

LULLY (1632–87)
Les Fêtes de l'Amour et de Bacchus (1672)

RAMEAU (1683–1764)
Castor et Pollux (1737)

GLUCK (1714–87)
*Iphigénie en Aulide (1774)
*Orphée et Eurydice (1774)
*Alceste (1776)
*Armide (1777)
Iphigénie en Tauride (1779)

PICCINNI (1728–1800)
*Roland (1778)
Atys (1780)
Iphigénie en Tauride (1781)

[1] Jahn, from Prutz (Deutsches Museum II, p. 28).

PHILIDOR (1726–95)
Ernelinde (1767)

MONSIGNY (1729–1817)
Le Déserteur (1769)
Félix ou l'enfant trouvé (1777)

GRÉTRY (1741–1813)
Le Huron (1768)
Le Tableau Parlant (1769)
Zémire et Azor (1771)
*Le Jugement de Midas (1778)
L'Amant Jaloux (1778)
*Matroco (1778)
*Les Trois Âges de l'Opéra (1778)

GOSSEC (1734–1829)
*La Fête de Village (1778)

The operas in the above schedule marked with an asterisk are those which are known to have been performed during Mozart's stay in Paris in 1778;[1] but it is likely that, in addition, he heard excerpts from many others sung and played in private houses and also that he saw the scores of all the important works of the century. The names of Gluck and Piccinni are included in this table for the reason that Gluck revised his earlier works specially for Paris where they received their first performance, while *Armide* and *Iphigénie en Tauride* were actually composed for Paris and of course all of them were written in French. Piccinni, though then a famous Italian composer, was brought to Paris as a rival to Gluck and was coached in French by Marmontel, who helped him with the libretto of Piccinni's first French opera *Roland*.

What chiefly distinguished French opera, as founded by Lully and Rameau and developed by Gluck and others, was its bias towards the poetical and dramatic rather than the purely melodic and vocal bravura of the Italian school and that is why Gluck's work found more favour in Paris than in Vienna, where Italian opera was paramount. Truthful and forceful dramatic declamation was a feature of French opera and Gluck's famous preface to *Alceste* setting forth his creed that the music should be subordinate to the words (though it was only the expression of that ever-recurrent need to return to nature in the history of art when an art has become too conventional and is in danger of being lost in mere virtuosity) was attuned to the French taste of the time.

[1] Also, Rousseau's *Le Devin du Village*, Piccinni's *Le Finte Gemelli*, Paisiello's *Le due Contesse* and *La Frascatana*, Pergolesi's *La Serva Padrona* and Anfossi's *Il Curioso Indiscreto*.

The Italian opera buffa is a similar reaction – i.e. a break away from the too stiffened conventions of the opera seria in an attempt to get back to nature. One brand of French opera, the comic opera, however, developed a feature of its own in the substitution of spoken dialogue for recitative which must be considered as a musical loss, though it is certainly suitable for special texts. One other feature must be mentioned, since it was to find its fullest development in Mozart, and that was the mixture of serious and comic together. This was a French contribution to opera and may be described as an example of the French genius for realism.

Gluck had left Paris when Mozart arrived and Grétry is never mentioned by Wolfgang, nor does the French composer mention Mozart in his *Mémoires*. Grimm, who was the chief hope of Wolfgang and his father in Paris, was a supporter of the Piccinni faction in the fierce rivalry existing at the time between the Gluckists and the Piccinnists and Wolfgang met Piccinni at one of the *Concerts Spirituels* which were held at the Louvre. He writes to Leopold on July 9, 1778:

> I met Piccinni at the *Concert Spirituel* – he is very polite to me and and I to him – when we meet without danger – otherwise I do not make the acquaintance of other composers – I understand my affairs and they theirs and that is enough . . . that my symphony[1] at the *Concert Spirituel* pleased enormously I have already told you. If I get an opera to compose I shall have trouble enough. That does not worry me much as I am used to it, but if only this cursed French language were not so deadly to music! That is the worst, German is divine by comparison – and then the singers, male and female! One can scarcely call them such for they do not sing, they shriek and howl and all from the nose and throat. . . .

Wolfgang had arrived in Paris with his mother in no good mood and their circumstances were not pleasant, since they found everything very dear and had a dark lodging in the Hôtel des Quatres Fils Amyon in the Rue du Gros-Chenet. Leopold had not been able to obtain a letter to the Queen, Marie Antoinette,[2] so that

[1] 'Paris' Symphony in D (K.297).
[2] Her husband, Louis XVI, had become King in 1774 in succession to his grandfather, Louis XV. She was the daughter of Maria Theresia of Austria. It was through her influence that Gluck obtained the first performance of *Iphigénie en Aulide* in Paris in 1774.

their chief hope lay in Grimm whom Wolfgang at once visited. Grimm gave him a letter to the Duchesse de Chabot recommending him to the Duchesse de Bourbon. 'There,' he tells his father in a letter dated May 1, 1778:

I waited half-an-hour in an unheated, ice-cold, large room without a stove. At last the Duchess came and very politely begged me to excuse the clavier since she had none in proper condition; would I try it? I said I would willingly play something but it was impossible as I could not feel my fingers for the cold and requested that she might at least let me be taken to a room in which there was a stove. '*O, oui, Monsieur, vous avez raison,*' was her only answer. Then she sat down and began to draw for a whole hour in company with other gentlemen who all sat in a circle round a large table. Then I had the honour of waiting for a whole hour. Doors and windows were open. Not only my hands but my feet and my whole body was cold and my head began to ache. Nobody spoke and I did not know what to do for cold, headache and weariness. If it had not been for Mr Grimm I should have left.

At last to cut it short I played on the wretched pianoforte. What was most irritating was that Madam and the gentlemen never for a moment stopped drawing so that I played to the walls, table and chairs. In these circumstances I lost patience. I began the Fischer variation, played half and then stopped. Then followed no end of praise but I said what had to be said, namely, that I could not do myself justice with this clavier and should like to play another time on a better one. But she did not comment and I had to wait another half-hour until her husband came. He, however, sat down beside me and listened attentively and I – I forgot then my headache and the cold and played, disregarding the wretched clavier, as I can play when in a good mood. Give me the best clavier in Europe but with an audience who do not or will not understand and have no sympathy I lose all pleasure in it. I told the whole affair to Mr Grimm.

You write to me that I must pay visits, make acquaintances and renew old ones. But that is not possible. The distances are too far to go on foot or it is too filthy, for the dirt in Paris is indescribable. To drive is to waste four to five livres in vain, for people pay you compliments and then it is finished. They ask me for such and such a day: I play and then: '*O, c'est un prodige, c'est inconcevable, c'est étonnant,*' and then: '*Adieu.*' . . .

Nevertheless he was offered through Rudolph, a French horn-player in the royal service, a post as organist at Versailles for two thousand livres a year, but refused it as this pay was small and

Grimm and other friends were against it. A renewed acquaintance with Noverre[1] led to his being commissioned by him to compose a ballet *Les Petits Riens*[2] which was produced on June 11, 1778. A suggested commission for an opera on the subject *Alexandre et Roxane* came to nothing. It was very hard to find a good poem: 'The old, which are the best,' he tells his father, 'are not suited to modern style and the new are worthless.' 'Nevertheless,' he writes in a very long and interesting letter dated Paris, July 31, 1778:

> I must write a great opera, not a little one; if I write a little one I get little (for here everything is taxed) and if it has the bad luck not to please the stupid French all is lost – I get no more to write, have little profit and my reputation suffers. . . . I assure you that I shall be only too pleased if I get an opera to compose. The language is the invention of the devil, it is true, and I see all the difficulties . . . but nevertheless feel as well able to overcome them as any other composer – when I imagine all goes well I feel a fire in my body and my hands and feet tingle with the desire to make the French learn to know, honour and fear the Germans more. . . .

In the meantime Wolfgang's mother, who had been ill for three weeks in May, fell ill again in June and wrote to Leopold on June 12th that she was still weak but better. She then became worse again, a physician was sent in by Grimm, but after a fortnight's anxiety she died on July 3rd. Wolfgang, in order to soften the blow, wrote a letter to his father informing him that his mother was very ill, but to Bullinger he wrote the truth and asked him to break the news personally to his father. Some extracts from these letters must be given, as they show the sensitiveness to other people's feelings typical of imaginative minds and specially characteristic of Mozart. On July 3rd he wrote to Bullinger as follows:

> Best of friends, for you absolutely alone,
>   Grieve with me, my friend! This has been the saddest day of my life – I write this at two o'clock in the morning – I have to tell you that my mother, my dear mother, is no more! God has called her.

---

[1] *Noverre*, Jean Georges (1727–1810), famous ballet-master, director at Vienna 1770–5; appointed *maître des ballets en chef* at the Paris Opera in 1775.
[2] (K. Anh 10=K–Einstein 299[b].) The score was discovered in 1872 in the library of the Paris Opera by Victor Wilder. Vestris danced in the original production of this ballet.

He wished to have her, I saw that clearly, and I have accepted the will of God. He gave her to me and He could take her away. Imagine the unquiet, the anxiety and care which I have endured during the past fourteen days. She died unconscious, went out like a light. She had confessed three days before, taken Communion and received the Blessing. The last three days, however, she was constantly delirious, but today at twenty-one minutes past five o'clock her death-agony began, she lost all sensibility – I pressed her hand, talked to her but she did not see me or hear me and understood nothing – so she lay until she died five hours later, at 10.21 in the evening. Nobody was present except myself and a good friend of ours, Herr Haina, and the nurse – I cannot tell all about her illness today. I am of the opinion that she had to die. God would have it so.

I beg you out of pure friendship to prepare my poor father for this sad news. I have written to him by the same post but only that she is very ill. . . . God give him strength and courage. My friend, I am not only now but have been for a long time consoled. I have been able by the special grace of God to bear all with firmness and resigna-tion. When her condition became dangerous I prayed God only for two things, namely, a happy last hour for my mother and then strength and courage for myself and the good God heard me and has granted me my desires completely.

I beg you, best of friends, to support my father, lend him courage so that he does not take it too hardly when he first hears the worst. I commend my sister to you with all my heart. Go straightway to them, I beg you; do not say that she is dead yet but prepare them for it. Do what you think best . . . act so that I may be reassured and have not to suffer a further misfortune. Sustain my dear father and my dear sister and write to me at once, I beg you.

                                        (*Sgd.*) WOLFGANG AMADÉ MOZART.

'*Rue de gros chenet*
vis à vis celle du croissant
a l'hôtel des quatres fils aimont.'

To his father he wrote first of all a letter on the same day in-forming him of his mother's illness, from which I shall take the following:

   . . . I believe (and this I am not to be dissuaded from) that no doctor, no man, no misfortune, no accident can give or take away a man's life but only God – those others are only the instruments which He for the most part uses . . . we see how people collapse and die – when once their time is come, then nothing avails. . . .

In this same letter he goes on to speak of other things and then continues:

> Now I give you a piece of news which perhaps you know already, namely, that the godless, arch-scoundrel Voltaire is dead, like a dog, like a beast – that is his reward.[1]

We need not be surprised at the tone of Wolfgang's reference to Voltaire. He probably had not read a word of Voltaire's works; he was also writing to his father to whom – except on personal matters about which he felt strongly – he always adapted his language, and he only later in life freed himself from the conventional form of his strong and genuine religious feeling. It is, however, fitting to refer here to the fact that Wolfgang himself was, also, thirteen years later, to die unconfessed, 'like a dog', unblessed by the Church to which he nominally belonged. I shall deal with the general intellectual development of Mozart when I come to give the account of his later association with Freemasonry in Vienna. It is enough to say here that although at twenty-one Wolfgang may not have been ripe for the appreciation of a mind such as Voltaire's – even if he had come in contact with it – we can only take this reference to him as the mere instinctive ignorant attitude of a deeply-religious nature to someone whom he only knew by hearsay as an 'atheist'.

On July 9, 1778, Wolfgang writes again to his father, this time saying that he will know by now of the death of his wife:

> You can only imagine what I have suffered, what need I had for courage and steadfastness so as to endure patiently everything becoming harder and worse and yet God lent me this grace – I have had grief enough, have wept enough – but what is the use of this? I had to console myself. Do you likewise, my dear father and dear sister – weep, weep you hearts out – but at last be consoled – consider that Almighty God would have it so and what can we do against Him? . . .
>
> Dearest father, take care of yourself – and you, dearest sister – you have as yet had no enjoyment of your brother's good heart for there was not yet occasion for it – Both my dearest, take care of your health – remember that you have a son and a brother who directs all his powers towards making you happy. . . .

---

[1] Voltaire died at Ferney at the age of eighty-four on May 30, 1778.

O, then we shall live so peacefully, so honourably, so happily (as far as is possible in this world) – and finally when God wills we shall come together again – for the purpose for which we have been destined and created. . . .[1]

On hearing that his father and sister were now aware of the death of Wolfgang's mother he wrote on July 31st:

. . . I have received your letters of 13th and 20th. The first forced painful tears from me because it reminded me of the sad dying of my dear, blessed mother and it all came before me vividly again. I will not forget it all my life – you know that never (although I had wished to) had I seen anyone die – and the first time it must be my mother. . . .

Sad as your letter made me I was nevertheless quite beside myself with joy when I realized that you had taken it all as it had to be taken and that I need not be worried about my best of fathers and my dearest sister. As soon as I had finished your letter I fell on my knees and thanked my dear[2] God from a full heart for His mercy. . . . Now I am quite at rest for I know that I have nothing to fear for the two persons dearest to me in this world. . . .

In the same letter he informs his father that Herr Grimm had told him he did not push his affairs enough, to which he replied that the long illness of his mother had not allowed him much time for going about. Two of his pupils, he adds, are in the country and the third, the daughter of the Duc de Guines, is not going on with her lessons, 'which is certainly on my honour no great loss, for the Duke does not pay more than anybody else'.[3] Even this he got with difficulty and by dint of constant asking. 'Monsieur le Duc,' he says, 'has no particle of honour in his body . . . he has had already for four months a Concerto for Flute and Harp[4] from me, for which he has not yet paid.'

Grimm, although he took Wolfgang into his house after the

[1] This sentence of Mozart's is worth noting.

[2] I have taken care to translate Wolfgang's letter faithfully. This is an interesting example of what I consider a chief element in his genius, his extreme sensibility, that in his affectionate nature he includes God among his loved ones.

[3] I am surprised at this. I should have thought that he would have paid less. It is notorious that the richer and more powerful you are the less you pay; some of the French nobility, however, may still have had a sufficient sense of dignity and responsibility to pay *as much* as less important people; and a few in every age have always put their honour before their convenience.

[4] Concerto for flute and harp in C major (K.299).

death of his mother and lent him small sums of money from time to time, was an experienced and adroit man of the world and began to doubt of the possibility of Mozart becoming successful in Paris. He recognized his talents up to a point but we must remember that he could not see Wolfgang with our eyes. He wrote to Leopold the following letter on August 13, 1778, about Wolfgang:

He is too sincere (*treu-herzig*), too little concerned with the means by which one may become successful. Here, to make your way, you must be shrewd, enterprising, bold.[1] I should prefer, from the point of view of making his fortune, that he had half his talent and twice as much tact; then I should not be troubled about him.

For the rest, there are only two ways of getting on here. The first is to give clavier-lessons; but apart from the fact that one does not get pupils without much effort and even charlatanry I doubt if he is strong enough for this occupation, since it is extremely fatiguing to run about Paris and wear oneself out talking for effect. And then this occupation does not please him as it prevents him composing, which he prefers to everything.[2] He could give himself up to that altogether but the public in this country is not a judge of music. Consequently names are everything and the merit of a work can only be judged by a few. At the present moment the public is so ridiculously divided between Piccinni and Gluck that all the arguments one hears about music are ludicrous. It is thus very difficult for your son to succeed in the midst of this rivalry. You see, *mon cher maître*, that in a country where so many mediocre and inferior musicians have made fortunes I much fear that your son will not come off very well.

It ought to be remarked here that just as Wolfgang was little fitted for getting on in the world, having none of the arts of the careerist,[3] he was also little suited to the life and ways of the Bohemian artist and did not therefore get the support of that

[1] He really means 'impudent'. Impudence is the key that unlocks the golden gates of fortune in the every-day world.

[2] On July 31st Wolfgang wrote to his father: 'To give lessons here is no joke. . . . You must not think it is laziness. No! But it is quite contrary to my genius, to my way of life. You know that I am, so to speak, immersed in music, that I am haunted by it all day long, that I speculate, study, reflect. Now I am hindered from this by giving lessons.'

[3] The reader will have understood by now that this is quite a different matter from being unable to see through people. At the latter Wolfgang was very good indeed – e.g. he writes to his father on July 9th to be careful when he is talking with the sister of the Archbishop: 'She has sugar and honey on her lips but pepper in her head and heart.'

world either. He was too sober, self-disciplined, and, above all,
too fastidious, especially as a young man, for Bohemia. His remarks to his father about the sons of Stamitz in reply to a question
by his father are significant on this point. Leopold in a letter dated
Salzburg, June 29, 1778, writes:

> Not a word whether Wendling is still in Paris? Whether Wolfgang
> has seen the Baron Bach?[1] Whether Piccinni is still in Paris?
> Whether he knows the two Stamitzs?[2] Whether he has seen Grétry?

To which Wolfgang replies on July 9th:

> To see Baron Bach I should need very good eyes as he is not here
> but in London. . . . Kapellmeister Bach is said to be coming here
> soon. . . . Of the two Stamitzs, only the younger is here, the elder . . .
> is in London. They are two wretched music-dabblers – gamblers,
> soakers and lechers – they are not my sort . . . the one that is here
> dresses like a ragamuffin.

In addition to the symphony for Le Gros Wolfgang composed
a *Sinfonia Concertante* in E major (Köchel, supplement 9) for
flute (Wendling), oboe (Ramm), horn (Punto), bassoon (Ritter)
and orchestra, as well as a number of smaller works; but he
obtained no important commissions and, above all, no suggestion
of an opera. He would have had to remain years in Paris in order
to achieve any real position. His father, after receiving Grimm's
letter must have had very little hope of Paris; but as it happened
there was a prospect of getting Wolfgang a position at Salzburg
and Leopold set himself warily to work to try to get a definite
offer from the Court for a position good enough and well-paid
enough to induce Wolfgang to return. He knew how Wolfgang
hated Salzburg[3] and that he would need no small inducement to
return, so he had to play his cards carefully.

In the meantime, Wolfgang had quite different ideas in his
head. He corresponded from Paris with Aloysia and her father,
Fridolin Weber, but of his letters to Aloysia only one has survived. It is written in Italian and dated July 30, 1778. It begins:

---

[1] *Bach=Bagge*, Baron Karl Ernst Bagge.
[2] *Stamitz*, Karl (1746–1801) and Anton (1753–1820).
[3] Wolfgang constantly expresses his hatred of Salzburg in his letters. He writes to
Bullinger on August 7th: 'You know, best of friends, how I hate Salzburg.'

'*Carissima amica*', and has a warmth and seriousness of tone markedly different from the style in which he writes to his Augsburg cousin; it is the letter of a man in love who is avid of every scrap of news. 'You know,' he says, 'how everything that concerns you interests me'; and to her father he writes on July 29th:

> If I had no father and no sister for whom I must live more than for myself, for whose support I must care – I should with the greatest joy neglect my own fate and only be concerned with hers – for her wellbeing, her pleasure, her happiness makes up (if I think of myself alone) the whole of mine – farewell.

One of the reasons Wolfgang detested Salzburg was the small respect paid to music there: 'If only music were appreciated as it is in Mannheim,' he writes to his father on July 9th, and continues:

> The discipline that rules in this orchestra! The authority that Cannabich wields . . . and he is respected by the whole town and also his soldiers[1] – they behave themselves quite differently, have good manners, are well-dressed and don't soak themselves in pubs. . . .[2]

After the Mannheim orchestra he was not to be unduly impressed by the Paris orchestra and he still considers Cannabich 'the best director I have seen'. As for the famous *premier coup d'archet* (first attack of the bow) on which the strings of the Paris orchestra prided themselves, he writes to his father (June 12, 1778):

> What the devil is it? They begin together – as in other places. It is ludicrous. Raaff told me a story of Abaco[3] that is *apropos*: he was asked by a Frenchman in Munich or somewhere: '*Monsieur, vous avez été à Paris?*' '*Oui,*' '*Est-ce-que vous êtiez au Concert Spirituel?*' '*Oui.*' '*Que dîtes-vous du Premier Coup d'archet? Avez-vous entendu le premier coup d'archet?*' '*Oui, j'ai entendu le premier et le dernier.*' '*Comment le dernier? Que veut dire cela?*' '*Mais oui, le premier et le dernier et le dernier même m'a donné plus de plaisir.*'

---

[1] Members of the orchestra.

[2] Like every great artist Wolfgang in his youth detested dissipation and squalor—the refuge of the minor artist in every age.

[3] E. F. dall'Abaco (1675–1742), composer.

Meanwhile Leopold with great diplomatic skill had manoeuvred matters in Salzburg after the death of Adlgasser so that the suggestion that Wolfgang should return came from the Archbishop's side. On June 29th he writes to Wolfgang:

... After the litany Count Starhemberg asked me to see him the next day as he wanted to speak to me. I went, there was nobody there but his brother, the Major ... who is here recovering from the fright Prussian powder and lead has given him. He told me that an organist had been recommended but he would not have him unless he were sure that he was good ... his name was Mandl or something like it; he himself did not know exactly – 'O, you idiot!' I thought, 'is it likely ... that a recommendation from Vienna should not mention the candidate's name. As if I should not guess this was by way of inducing me to mention my son!' But I? Not a word! I said I had not the honour of knowing the name and that I should never venture to recommend anyone to the Archbishop, as it would always be difficult to find anyone exactly to suit him. 'Yes,' he replied, 'I also will not recommend anyone, it is too difficult – Your son should be here now!' ('Bravo! the bait has taken,' thought I. 'What a pity this man is not a great minister of State or ambassador!') I then said: 'We shall speak plainly – is it not the case that everything possible was done to drive him out of Salzburg?' I began at the beginning and enumerated every circumstance, so that his brother was astounded....

He wanted to persuade me to write to my son. I said I could not do so, that it would be useless, that my son would laugh unless I could tell him what salary he could expect, for Adlgasser's salary would be quite unacceptable....

There's the rub! I do not write, my dear Wolfgang, to persuade you to return to Salzburg for I place no reliance on the words of the Archbishop and I have not yet spoken with the Countess.[1] I have rather avoided meeting her as she would take the least word as consent and petition....

More manoeuvring took place and Bullinger was induced to write to Wolfgang hinting that the Archbishop would engage a fresh singer who might be Aloysia Weber, to which Wolfgang sarcastically replied that the Archbishop was always talking about engaging people and as for himself nothing would please him more than to be able to embrace again his dear father and sister but that his joy would be doubled if it were to happen anywhere

[1] Countess Franziska von Wallis, sister of the Archbishop.

else but in Salzburg, where there was no opera, and where music was not properly respected.[1]

However, Leopold, in the meantime, had spoken his mind to the Countess and the result was that he was asked whether Wolfgang would return if Leopold were given Lolli's place[2] and Wolfgang Adlgasser's,[3] which would bring in about a thousand florins a year, with permission to Wolfgang to travel to Italy every second year. 'The Countess and old Arco,' writes Leopold on August 27th:

are afraid that I shall leave. They have nobody to undertake the teaching of the clavier. I have the reputation of being a good teacher and the proofs indeed are there. They know of no one and should a teacher come from Vienna is it likely he would give twelve lessons for four florins and one ducat when one pays elsewhere two or three ducats?

. . . if this happens [the offer to Leopold and Wolfgang of the positions of Lolli and Adlgasser] you could safely reckon on our having one hundred and fifteen florins a month at least . . . without reckoning on the sale of my *Violin School* which brings in annually fifty florins at the lowest and without the earnings of your sister which are now ten florins monthly and with which she dresses herself . . . in this way we shall be better off than anywhere else where it is twice as dear . . . only the principal point is that I don't place any reliance on the latter because I know how hard it will be for our Prince to come to such a decision. . . .

You are always writing about the hard circumstances of the Weber family. But tell me how can it enter your sound head that you are the one who is in a position to make the fortune of these people? You realize more and more (I hope) how much money a single person needs to maintain himself decently. You are now in the position – and have been since September 23rd of last year with your mother of blessed memory – of calculating for two persons and I have been obliged to support you for the journey and travelling expenses first with three hundred florins and then with two hundred florins more. Now you are alone have you not to be very careful about your daily expenditure? And have you enough? . . . Supposing – which God forbid – you were ill and had saved no money? . . .

[1] This letter to Bullinger, dated August 7th, goes into great detail on these points.
[2] *Lolli*, Jos. Franz., succeeded Eberlin as *Kapellmeister* in 1763 at Salzburg and died in August, 1778. Leopold had been his *vice-Kapellmeister* during that period.
[3] *Adlgasser*, Anton Cajetan (1728–77), Court composer and organist.

You write that you have many good friends who, however, are not in a position to help you. Such friends . . . exist in plenty . . . I beg you to have some regard for yourself and for your poor father. . . .

One can take pains to help Mlle. Weber as much as possible . . . but have we means to aid one out of the six children in this family? Who can do this? I? You? who can scarcely maintain ourselves! How can you help others before you have helped yourself? You write: 'dearest father, I commend them to you from the bottom of my heart. If only they had a thousand florins a year!' My dearest son! when I read this how can I help fearing that you are not in your right mind? . . .

In his next letter, dated August 31st, Leopold was able to announce that owing to his clever tactics in hiding from people in Salzburg their true position and making them think that Wolfgang was very successful in Paris he had got the definite offer from the Archbishop of the appointments indicated in his previous letter:

You are to have five hundred florins and he has excused himself for not being able to make you a Kapellmeister straightaway. You are, however, to be allowed to act as my deputy . . . further he has given five florins more to Paris[1] so that he can take the heaviest duties. . . . The Archbishop has declared that he will allow you to travel if you want to write an opera. . . . Mlle. Weber has made a great impression on the Prince and everybody . . . she must stay with us . . . her father seems to have no head. I shall manage the affair better for them if they take my advice. You must speak a word for her for there is another singer required for opera besides the castrato. . . .

But I do not wish you to leave Paris until I have the decree in my hands. . . .

Wolfgang was ready under these circumstances to please his father and return to Salzburg; meanwhile, however, Aloysia Weber obtained an operatic engagement at Munich at a salary of a thousand florins, her father getting four hundred florins with an additional two hundred as prompter. This made Wolfgang wish to try to get a position with the Elector of Bavaria which he determined to try to do on his return journey before definitely accepting the Archbishop's offer. His father did not object to this and wrote to him on September 3, 1778:

[1] *Paris*, Anton, assistant organist.

As the Elector with his Court is expected in Munich on September 15th you can, on your journey through, speak with Count Seeau and perhaps the Elector himself. You can say that your father writes you to return to Salzburg, that the Prince has offered you seven to eight hundred florins (add on two or three hundred florins) as Konzertmeister, that you, out of filial respect to you father, have accepted although you knew he wished to see you in the Elector's service. But, note well, no more than that! Then you may want to write an opera in Munich and that you can and must manage from here; that cannot fail to happen as there is a lack of German opera composers. Schweitzer and Holzbauer will not write every year. . . .

. . . My heart laughs when I think of the happy day when I shall again have the pleasure of seeing and embracing you . . . now the day is approaching I hope, my dear son, God will let me live to see it. You will scarcely know your poor father; the Archbishop whom I had to see twice was so startled that he told everybody. When you left I was ill and that is a year ago – and what I have had to endure this year! My nature is of iron, otherwise I should be dead, and if you with your presence do not lift the heavy stone from my heart everything is in vain. . . . Nobody can save me from death except you. . . .

During the end of Wolfgang's stay in Paris J. C. Bach came over from London and both were delighted to renew this acquaintance. On August 27th Wolfgang writes to his father from St Germain:

You can imagine our joy – perhaps his is less than mine yet one must admit that he is an honourable man and does people justice. I love him, as you know, from my heart and esteem him and he, it is certain, praises me to others as well as to myself – not exaggeratedly as some do but seriously. . . .

On September 11th Wolfgang writes from Paris to his father that his friends are surprised at his intention to leave Paris; he repeats that it is only his desire to see his father and sister again and the promise that he can make a journey every two years which influence him:

I assure you that without travelling (at any rate for people belonging to the arts and sciences) one is a paltry creature – and furthermore if the Archbishop did not allow me to make a journey every two years I could not possibly accept the engagement; a man of mediocre talent remains always mediocre, let him travel or not, but a man of superior talent (which I cannot deny myself to be, without blasphemy[1]) deteriorates when he has to remain always in the same place.

If the Archbishop would trust me I should soon make his music famous, that is certainly true. I assure you my journey has not been useless – for composition, that goes without saying; as for the clavier, I play as well as I can.[2] One thing I must insist on in Salzburg and that is that I do not play the violin as formerly – I am not going to be a violinist again . . . it would be well if I had a written assurance about the position of Kapellmeister for otherwise I shall have the honour to render double services for the pay of one and then find a stranger put in front of me.

Dearest father, I must say that truly if it were not for the pleasure of seeing you both again I could not decide to leave Paris just as my affairs are beginning to improve and I don't doubt that if I could resolve to hold out here a few years my affairs would go well. . . .

Chi va piano va sano; with my good nature I have gained friendship and protection; my fingers would ache were I to write you everything – this I shall tell you by word of mouth and make you see clearly that Mr Grimm is in a position to help children but not grown-up people and – but no, I shall write nothing – yet, I must; don't imagine that he is as he once was; if Mme. d'Epinay were not here I should not stay in his house; he need not plume himself on his hospitality for there were four other houses offering me the same. . . .

This was Wolfgang's last letter from Paris, which he left on September 26, 1778, in an ordinary conveyance which took seven days to get to Nancy where he arrived on October 3rd. From there he wrote to his father for the first time since September 11th complaining how Grimm had deceived him, saving himself money by sending Wolfgang by a slow conveyance which, however, cost Wolfgang more in food and lodging. In this letter he mentions that Le Gros thinks he has the only copy of the *Sinfonia Concertante* (K.*An*.9) but

it is not so; I have it fresh in my memory and as soon as I am home will write it out again.

In Strasbourg, where he arrived about the middle of October,

---

[1] Every great man knows exactly what he is. This fact is to be recognized in the famous remark: 'He spoke as one having authority.'
[2] He means: 'I could not play better.'

he gave a small concert on October 17th and made three louis d'or, the principal takings consisting of '*Bravo!*' and '*Bravissimo!*', and another on October 31st which brought in one louis d'or. On November 6th he arrived at Mannheim which he had left in company with his mother on March 14th of the same year.

CHAPTER THIRTEEN

Munich and Salzburg

Age 22–25 (December 1778 – June 1781)

IN MANNHEIM WOLFGANG stayed from November 6th to December 9th enjoying the society of his old friends, especially that of Mme. Cannabich, who seems to have been an understanding admirer of his genius. His dislike of Salzburg kept him in Mannheim in spite of his father's reproaches. The Webers were in Munich where the Elector had moved with his Court. The Mannheim National Theatre, soon to become associated with Schiller, had, however, started on its renowned career under Dalberg, who wanted Mozart to compose a Duodrama[1], a sort of composition which he describes to his father after seeing several examples – 'a *Medea* and *Ariadne auf Naxos* by Benda, my favourite among Lutheran Kapellmeisters' – performed by the Seyler troupe. He writes on November 12th:

> I have always wished to write a Drama of this kind . . . you know that it is not sung but declaimed and the music is like an obbligato recitative. Speaking is sometimes introduced with striking effect. . . . Imagine my joy at having just what I have so wanted to do. Do you know what my idea is? One should have mostly recitatives of this kind in opera and only occasionally when the words are suitable for musical expression have the recitatives sung. . . .

In this same letter he expresses his pleasure at the good fortune of the Webers in Munich:

> The daughter [Aloysia] gets a thousand florins herself and the father four hundred and another two hundred as prompter.

[1] This was *Semiramis*, text by von Gemmingen.

To Baron Dalberg, who suggested he should compose music to a libretto *Cora*, having already applied to Gluck and Schweitzer, he writes on November 24th asking for twenty-five louis d'or as a remuneration in return for which he undertakes

> to write a monodrama, to remain here two months and attend rehearsals. . . . As for your opera . . . I could not undertake such a work for twenty-five louis d'or since, reckoned at the smallest, it means twice as much work as a monodrama and what would make me hesitate most is that, as you yourself told me, Gluck and Schweitzer are working at it. Even if you were willing to give me fifty louis d'or nevertheless as an honest man I would advise you against it . . . an opera without male or female singers! What can one make of that? . . .

In the meantime his father was pouring cold water on Wolfgang's idea of getting a position at Mannheim. On November 19th Leopold writes:

> Indeed I do not know what to write. I shall go out of my senses or just waste away. It is quite impossible to recollect all the projects which you have had in your mind and written to me about since you left Salzburg without going off one's head. . . .

He reminds Wolfgang of the time he has wasted getting to Mannheim from Paris and the money he has spent and tells him finally that the Mannheimers are crazy to think that the Elector will leave Munich and return to live in Mannheim. On November 23rd he writes again that he is tired of hearing of Wolfgang's projects and tells him that he, Wolfgang, is incapable of thinking about anything in cold blood and without prejudice and knows nothing of the world:

> Two things fill your head and prevent all reasonable judgment. The first and principal is your love for Mlle. Weber. I am not altogether against it. I was not when her father was poor so why should I be now when she might make your fortune instead of you hers? I suppose her father is aware of your love since all Mannheim knows it, since Herr Fiala has heard of it since Herr Bullinger, who is instructor at Count Lodron's, tells how travelling with Mannheim musicians . . . they spoke of nothing but your ability, compositions and love for Mlle. Weber.

Leopold then goes on to say that by accepting the Salzburg position Wolfgang will be nearer Munich (eighteen hours) where he can see the Webers, and that he will be able to invite the Cannabichs and other Mannheim friends to Salzburg and have the chance of visiting Italy:

> The acceptance is absolutely indispensable unless you have the most abominable and damnable idea to bring your considerate father into scorn and derision . . . I am not in a position to repay the thousand florins I owe unless my burden is lightened by you. . . .

The desperate Leopold then describes the preparations he has made for Wolfgang's comfort: 'I have had a useful cupboard made in your room where you can put your clothes . . . the little clavichord is by the writing table,' and ends, finally:

> I should like, God willing, to live a few years longer, pay my debts – and then you can if you like run your head against the wall – but no, you have too good a heart! You have no wickedness, you are only thoughtless – it will all come right!

Wolfgang was not at all pleased with these letters. He writes on December 3, 1778, asking his father's pardon for not having written before and for the shortness of his present letter. He says:

> That I have not replied sooner is your fault alone through your first letter [dated November 19th]; I had truly never imagined that – but silence! I will say no more for it is now past! Next Wednesday, the 9th, I am leaving . . . I must be short because . . . I am writing now to please Herr von Gemmingen and myself the first act of the declamatory opera gratis; I am taking it with me to finish at home, so great is my desire for this kind of composition . . . this duodrama is called *Semiramis. . . .*

Nevertheless Wolfgang did not go direct to Munich but accepted an invitation from the Bishop of Kaisersheim to make a visit there on the way to Munich, which he reached on December 25th. On the 23rd he wrote to his Augsburg cousin asking her to come to Munich where she might 'have to play an important rôle' – thus referring to his anticipated suit for Aloysia Weber.

In Munich came a terrible disillusionment.[1] He went to stay

---

[1] Wolfgang must have been to some degree prepared for it through correspondence, or lack of correspondence, with Aloysia. This might explain his delay in Mannheim, for one would have expected him to rush as fast as possible from Paris to Munich where Aloysia was.

with the Webers, who invited him. What exactly happened is clear in effect although lacking in detail; every biographer has to rely on Nissen's bald statement that Aloysia – now further developed as a singer, with an excellent engagement at the Munich opera – was not prepared to return Wolfgang's love. Wolfgang, wearing a red suit, with black buttons in mourning for his mother, found Aloysia altered.

> It seemed as if she no longer recognized him for whom she had wept. So Mozart sat down at the clavier and sang aloud: 'I leave that maiden gladly who does not want me.' From now on her sister Constanze who had perhaps more feeling for his talent than his person and was sorry for the deceived one sought to entertain him. He taught her – a pupil eager for learning – the pianoforte with pleasure. Later, they met again in Vienna and it happened that Constanze made more impression on Mozart than Aloysia once had done.

I have translated Nissen's statement literally from the edition published in Leipzig in 1828, as it was sponsored by Mozart's widow, Constanze, after the death of her second husband, Georg Nikolaus von Nissen. Nissen may have written the sentence about Constanze's feeling for Mozart out of mere male vanity but this book was edited by Constanze *after Nissen's death* in 1826. One cannot believe that Constanze, if she had really ever loved Mozart, would have allowed that sentence to stand. I think, therefore, we may take it that it accurately represents her true attitude, which was one of admiration for his talent rather than of love for the man. This accords with her general nature which was clearly not profound.

On December 29th Wolfgang wrote to his father:

> ... I arrived here, God be praised and thanked, safely on December 25th but it was impossible to write until now. I keep all until I shall have the pleasure to talk with you again for today I can do nothing but weep – my heart is much too sensitive. . . . I have naturally a bad writing I know, for I have never learned to write, yet I have never written so badly as now; for I cannot write – my heart is too disposed to weep!

The profound realism of Wolfgang and the depth of his nature

could not be better indicated than in a few sentences of his letter
of December 31st to his father:

> ... What does this mean, 'rosy dreams'? As for dreaming I shall
> not stop, for there is nobody living on this earth who does not often
> dream! But 'rosy dreams'! – serene dreams, refreshing, sweet dreams
> – that is the thing – dreams which, were they true, would make me
> more sorrowful than happy life bearable. ...

On January 8, 1779, Wolfgang completed for Aloysia the fine
recitative and aria, *Popoli di Tessaglia* (K.316), on the words of
Alceste used by Gluck in his opera.[1] About two years later, May
16, 1781, Wolfgang wrote to his father:

> I was a fool about Lange's wife,[2] that is true, but who is not when
> he is in love. But I did indeed love her and feel that I am not yet
> indifferent to her[3] and it is well for me that her husband is a jealous
> fool who never lets her out of his sight so that I seldom see her. ...

In 1788 Aloysia Lange added to the voice part of the aria *Ah se
in ciel* (K.538) written out in Mozart's hand the following words of
her own: '*Nei giorni tuoi felici pensa qualche volta al Popoli di
Tessaglia.*' That is all we know about Aloysia and Wolfgang.

On January 8th Wolfgang also wrote to his father expressing
his pleasure at their approaching meeting but adding:

> I swear on my honour that I cannot bear Salzburg and its in-
> habitants ... to me their speech and their manner of living are quite
> unendurable. ...

However, it had to be borne and he arrived in Salzburg on
January 15th or 16th accompanied by his Augsburg cousin who
had come to Munich as he had asked. One very natural result of
his youthful disillusionment with Aloysia must be remarked upon
and that is the freedom and sensuality of his letters to his cousin,
which now breaks out afresh. These letters are almost impossible
to translate, not so much owing to their outspokenness but owing
to Mozart's use of dialect, of idiom and of puns, rhymes and

---

[1] Schweitzer's *Alceste* was performed in Munich on January 11, 1779, and was
heard by Mozart before his departure for Salzburg.
[2] Aloysia Weber married the actor, Joseph Lange, on October 31, 1780.
[3] This has appeared in some translations into English as: 'She is not yet indifferent
to me.'

allusions. It is sufficient to say that they would shock all ignorant people who are unaware that an extreme degree of vitality is bound to take such forms when it is thwarted or disturbed in its full development into a profound and harmonious love-union such as Wolfgang had hoped for with Aloysia but was doomed never to experience.[1]

It is not necessary to go into much detail about the year 1779 spent in Salzburg. It is sufficient to say that he felt miserable there and unappreciated at his true value. In spite of this he composed many instrumental works and several Masses and other Church music. One work should be mentioned here, *Thamos, König in Ägypten* (Thamos, King of Egypt) (K.345), a music drama with text by Baron Tob. Phil. von Gebler, which had been produced at the Vienna Burgtheater in 1774. Wolfgang had met Gebler in Vienna during his visit there between July and October 1773, and had then composed part of the music for *Thamos*, namely, the choruses *Schon weichet dir, Sonne!* and *Gottheit, über alle mächtig!*; he now added instrumentation, also composed a third chorus (words by Schachtner) and incidental music in the hope of performance in the Salzburg theatre which was visited by theatrical and operatic troupes. One troupe under Böhm was playing there in 1779 and another under Schikaneder[2] in 1780. On this occasion Schikaneder made the acquaintance of the Mozart family and used to join their bolt-shooting parties, but Wolfgang's revised *Thamos* was not performed.[3] It is of interest to students as a precursor to *Die Zauberflöte*. It is also worth noting for the confusion of those academic minds who love strict categories that Mozart, who is commonly considered the most abstract of composers (whatever that means!), actually wrote above the themes denoting the characters in this play such

[1] On July 25, 1781, Wolfgang writes to his father: 'If I had been compelled to marry all with whom I have enjoyed a joke I should have had easily two hundred wives.'

[2] *Schikaneder*, Emanuel (b. Regensburg, 1751), actor, singer and impresario and librettist of *Die Zauberflöte*.

[3] Wolfgang wrote from Vienna to his father on February 15, 1783: 'I am extremely sorry that I cannot make use of the music of *Thamos*. The piece has failed here and won't be revived. It would have to be done solely for the music and that's not likely. It is a pity.'

expressions as 'Pheron's Hypocrisy', 'Thamos' Noble Nature', 'Pheron's despair, blasphemy and death' in purely instrumental movements where there were no words but where the dramatic situation was to be musically depicted. The revised choruses of *Thamos* are superb and are worth reviving by choral societies. Latin words were later, in Vienna, fitted to the first and third choruses.[1]

Another unperformed work of this Salzburg period must be mentioned, *Zaide* (K.344), a German singspiel in two acts, words by Schachtner.[2] The full score was found complete, all but overture and conclusion, after Mozart's death and was first published by André. It is a delightful work and has many resemblances to and foreshadows the later *Die Entführung aus dem Serail*. An opportunity for a production that did materialize was, however, soon to present itself. Wolfgang received a commission to compose an opera for the Munich Carnival of 1781. This was the chief fruit of his stay in Mannheim and Munich and of his and his friend's attempts to interest the Elector Karl Theodor in him and to obtain for him a post in his service. The libretto chosen, *Idomeneo, Re di Creta* (K.366), was written by the Salzburg Court Chaplain Varesco and was based on a French opera by Danchet composed by Campra and produced in Paris in 1712 and revived in 1731. Varesco turned the old five-act tragedy into an Italian opera seria but with choruses in the French manner. Mozart began the music about October 1780, and went to Munich to continue it, arriving there about November 8th.

At the end of November the first act was rehearsed and there were many difficulties with the singers. On December 16th the first and second acts were rehearsed with orchestra. At the end of December these acts were again rehearsed in a large room in the palace instead of as previously in Count Seeau's small room. In January Mozart was writing the third act and the dances for the divertissement and the end was reached on January 18, 1781. The last rehearsal was on Wolfgang's twenty-fifth birthday, January 27, 1781, and the first performance took place on January 29,

[1] [*Thamos* is occasionally performed, usually in a concert version. *C.R.*]
[2] [In recent years *Zaide* has been revived in more or less its original form. *C.R.*]

1781. It now remains to say something of this opera which was highly thought of by Mozart himself and is one of the greatest and most ambitious of his works.

IDOMENEO

The full score in Breitkopf and Härtel's edition of *Idomeneo* (K.366) runs to three hundred and thirty-three pages without the appendix of twenty-seven pages – which, however, contains among other things a marvellous recitative of Elettra (No. 10). This compares with other scores in the same edition thus: *Don Giovanni* three hundred and fifty-three pages, *Così fan Tutte* three hundred and fifty-eight pages. *Idomeneo* is thus one of Mozart's largest as well as one of his best works. The original cast was as follows:

IDOMENEO, *re di Creta*	Il Sign. Raaff, virtuoso di camera.
IDAMANTE, *suo figlio*	Il Sign. Dal Prato
ILIA, *principessa Trojana, figlia di Priamo*	La Sigr. Dorothea Wendling, virtuosa di camera.
ELETTRA, *principessa, figlia d'Agamemnon*	La Sign. Elisabeth Wendling, virtuosa di camera.
ARBACE, *confidente del re*	Il Sign. Domenico de' Panzacchi, virtuoso di camera.
GRAN SACERDOTE *di Nettuno*	Il Sign. Giovanni Valesi, virtuoso di camera.

This is the plot:

Act I: Idamante, son of Idomeneo, King of Crete, awaits his father's return from the Trojan war. Elettra, daughter of Agamemnon, has taken refuge and is in love with Idamante. But Ilia, daughter of Priamo, sent as a captive with their women to Crete by Idomeneo, also loves Idamante and is loved by him. A storm threatens the returning fleet of Idomeneo but is calmed by Neptune to whom in gratitude Idomeneo vows to sacrifice the first person he meets on shore. Idamante, his son, enters and offers shelter to Idomeneo, whom he does not recognize, but in course of conversation makes known that he is mourning for his father, Idomeneo. Idomeneo then reveals who he is, but overcome with horror of his situation departs, forbidding Idamante to follow him. The returned soldiers of Idomeneo disembark and join their wives and children amid scenes of rejoicing.

Act II: Idomeneo informs Arbace of his vow and decides to send Idamante to Argos with Elettra. Ilia comes to express her delight at Idomeneo's safe arrival and in extolling Idamante reveals her love. Elettra and her followers prepare to depart with Idamante, who does not understand the reason of his father's displeasure. As they prepare to sail a storm arises and a sea-monster appears. This convinces Idomeneo of Neptune's anger at his broken vow and he decides to die himself.

Act III: The High Priest, with the multitude, demands deliverance from the monster and to know the name of Idomeneo's promised victim. Idomeneo names his son and in their horror the people offer prayers to the god. Arbace enters announcing that Idamante has slain the monster. Idamante arrives and is prepared to be sacrificed, but Ilia demands to take his place. As Ilia kneels before the altar there is a subterranean disturbance, the statue of Neptune totters, the High Priest stands spellbound and a voice announces the will of the gods: Idomeneo shall renounce the throne and Idamante is to ascend in his place and marry Ilia. Idamante is crowned amid rejoicings with ballet and chorus.

In *Idomeneo* we may see the influences of Gluck and of his *Alceste*; in particular both in the use of the chorus and in the recitatives; but Mozart remained what he was always, not so much an innovator or inventor of new forms but rather a master who used and filled every traditional form that came his way. If ever there were an artist who poured new wine into old bottles (but wine of an incomparable and never-to-be-repeated vintage!), it was Mozart. So in *Idomeneo* we find the tradition of the Italian opera seria in full force and this must be accepted just as we accept the conventions of Giotto's painting and see in his works masterpieces that have never been surpassed, if ever equalled. The musical public of today is totally ignorant of *Idomeneo*. There is a version by Richard Strauss which has been produced in Germany but should not be used; there is another version – better, I am informed, because more conservative than Strauss's – by Wolf-Ferrari. One can only say that the first essential in the stage production of *Idomeneo* is fidelity to Mozart's own text.[1]

---

[1] Some of Mozart's alterations, made in 1786, may be adopted – but not the curtailment of the part of Elettra, which was due to an incompetent singer in the part. [It is no longer true to say that the public is ignorant of *Idomeneo*. Since 1938 there have been frequent revivals in Austria, Germany and elsewhere. Possibly the most important was that at Glyndebourne in 1951 conducted by Fritz Busch and produced by Carl Ebert. The programme contained the following note: 'Glyndebourne

When *Idomeneo* is produced correctly with adequate singers, chorus, orchestra and a first-rate conductor who understands and believes in the work, then all music-lovers will be able to recognize it for what it is – namely, one of Mozart's grandest and most ambitious works and unique among his operas for brilliance of instrumentation, virtuosity and dramatic intensity and in the splendid use of the chorus. It may be mentioned here that Mozart had a large share in the planning of the libretto – making many suggestions and requiring numerous alterations by Varesco – and displayed far more dramatic sense than the librettist. *Idomeneo* is a work written in a white-heat of artistic passion and belongs to the class of works which a great genius can only create in the first flowering of his maturity before too much and too long endured bitter experience has cast a shadow upon the bloom of his imagination.

After the successful production of *Idomeneo* in Munich the Archbishop of Salzburg summoned Wolfgang to accompany him to Vienna in the spring of 1781. It was here that the final rupture between Mozart and the Archbishop took place. Much more has been written about this event than its importance deserves. Given the character of the two men, the fact that Mozart was a great genius and that the Archbishop was not even dimly aware of it – as, for example, in Beethoven's case his patrons, the Archduke Rudolf and Prince Lichnowsky, on the contrary, seem to have been – the result was inevitable. It is not true, however, to say, as some biographers have done, that the Archbishop was not to blame. One might admit that he was not to blame for not being naturally more perceptive than he was; but nevertheless he did not behave like a gentleman and his underling, Count Arco, went even further in the same direction, as all underlings do. I am not proposing to recount here all the grievances Mozart and the Arch-

---

has included "Idomeneo" in this year's Festival in memory of the late W. J. Turner (the distinguished critic of the *New Statesman*) who, before the war, continually besought us to perform this work.'

No production, as far as I know, has used Mozart's original version in its entirety. Turner was justly cautious of the various editions available. In 1956 yet another version appeared arranged by B. Paumgartner; it cannot in any way be regarded as a definitive edition. *C.R.*]

bishop had against one another, I shall merely quote from Wolfgang's letters to his father, acquainting him of the breach:

Vienna,
April 28, 1781.

. . . How and when I am leaving I cannot tell you at present. It is
lamentable how one never knows with this gentleman – suddenly it
will be *allons, weg!* First we are told a carriage is being arranged in
which the Comptroller, Ceccarelli, and I shall travel, then it is going
to be by the diligence, then that everyone will be given the money for
the diligence and can go as he pleases – which would please me best.
First, it is to be in eight days, then fourteen, then three weeks, then
sooner again – God! one doesn't know where one is. . . .

Vienna,
May 9, 1781.

I am still full of gall – and you as my best and dearest father will
certainly sympathise. My patience has been taxed so long – finally
it has given out. I am no longer so unfortunate as to be in the Salzburg service – today was the most fortunate of my life; listen:

Twice already this – I don't know what to call him – has used the
grossest and most impertinent language to my face which I have not
wished to mention out of consideration for you and for which – were
it not that I have always before my eyes – I should have revenged
myself on the spot. He called me a knave and a slovenly fellow, said
he would send me packing, and I – bore it all – allowed not only my
honour but also yours to be attacked and – you would have it so –
was silent. Well, listen:

Eight days ago the courier came unexpectedly and told me I was
to leave at once. All the others were advised beforehand but I was
not. I packed up and old Frau Weber was so kind as to offer me her
house – there I have a nice room, am with obliging people who get
me everything I want at once which I should not be able to get
living alone.

I fixed my journey for Wednesday (that is today, the 9th) with
the stage coach but as I could not get in the money that was owing
to me I deferred my departure until Saturday. Being seen about today, one of the valets said the Archbishop had a parcel for me. I
asked if it were urgent, he said, Yes, it was of the greatest importance;
whereupon I replied: 'I am sorry that I cannot have the honour of
obliging His Grace but I cannot leave before Saturday for the above
reasons: I am out of the house, living on my own means and it is clear
that I cannot leave until I am ready for nobody will collect my debts.'

Kleinmayr, Moll, Bönike and the two valets thought I was right.

When I went in to him (I must tell you that Schlaucher had advised me to excuse myself by saying I had already taken my seat in the coach as that would have more weight with him) as I entered he began:

'Well, fellow, when are you going?' *Mozart*: 'I wanted to go tonight but there was no seat.' Then he broke out – that I was the most careless fellow he knew, that nobody served him so badly; he advised me to be off today, otherwise he would write home to stop my pay. It was impossible to get a word in; he blazed like a fire. I listened quite composed. He lied to my face, saying I had five hundred florins salary, called me objectionable names – oh, I really could not write it all! At last as my blood was boiling I said: 'Is Your Highness not contented with me?' 'What, you threaten me, you villain? There is the door; I will have nothing more to do with such a wretched fellow.' At last I said: 'And I also will have no more to do with you.' 'Then go!' And as I went I said: 'Let it be so – tomorrow you will hear from me in writing.'

Tell me, my dear father, whether I did not say that rather too late than too soon. Now listen: my honour is dearer to me than anything and I know it is to you, also. Don't worry about me. I am so certain of my affairs here that I might have resigned without any cause. As I now have had one and that three times I am not to blame. On the contrary, twice I was a coward; the third time I could not be one any longer.

So long as the Archbishop is here I shall give no concert; your belief that I may suffer in the estimation of the Emperor and the nobility is groundless. The Archbishop is hated here and most of all by the Emperor. I shall send you by the next post a little money and convince you that I shall not starve. Above all, I beg of you to be in good spirits for my good fortune is beginning now and I hope that mine will be yours also. Write to me privately that you are contented – and that you can be, indeed! – and publicly scold me so that no blame can attach to you. Should, however, the Archbishop show you the least impertinence then come with my sister to Vienna at once; we can all three live, I assure you of that, on my honour, though it would be better if you could hold out for a year. Do not write to me any more at the Residence or with the mail – I don't want to have anything more to do with Salzburg. I hate the Archbishop to frenzy....

The worldly side of Leopold's character now showed at its worst. He was far from backing up Wolfgang as he should have done and the many subsequent letters written by Wolfgang to his father justifying his action make melancholy reading. Nothing, however, could alter Wolfgang's determination and from this time onward we see that a certain change has taken place in the relation between father and son. Wolfgang is no longer the son; he is at last completely independent and his father can influence him only as a friend. It was a misfortune for Wolfgang that his father – after having been in many ways the model of what a father should be to a son of genius – when it came to the harder task of relinquishing his special position and taking up that of his son's dearest, wisest and least selfish of friends was not equal to that exacting relationship. He failed Wolfgang at this critical period in his life and also – a little later – on the occasion of Wolfgang's marriage; so that from henceforth Leopold sinks back into a relatively unimportant position in his son's life. Before we leave this subject, however, I must give one example of the sensitive and passionate nature of Wolfgang, since this is truly part of his genius.

On May 12, 1781, he writes to his father:

> All the edifying things which the Archbishop said to me in the three audiences, especially the last, and the language used by this truly worthy man of God, had such a physical effect on me that in the evening at the opera in the middle of the first act I had to go home and lie down, for I was feverish, trembled in every limb and tottered along the street like a drunkard. . . .

What men of genius suffer is commensurate with the joy they are capable of experiencing and giving to others.

The attitude of Mozart to his father after the breach with the Archbishop is best conveyed by quoting a passage from his letter to Leopold of May 19th:

> I also do not know what to write first, my dearest father, for I cannot and never will be able to recover from my astonishment while you continue to think and to write as you do. I must tell you that I don't recognize a single trait of my father in your letter – a father, certainly, but not the best, most loving father, considerate of his own and his children's honour – in a word, not my father. . . .

It is also significant that in this letter for the first time he

11. Anna Maria Mozart, *c.* 1775

12. Mozart in 1788

abandons the cipher in which all references to the Archbishop had hitherto been made and openly refers to him in plain words as if he wanted to make his new independence clear to all the world.

I

CHAPTER FOURTEEN

Manhood and Marriage
in Vienna

Age 25–27 (June 1781 – December 1783)

IN VIENNA MOZART renewed old friendships with the Mesmers, von Auernhammer and the Kapellmeister Bonno, who performed one of his symphonies[1] which went very well, he writes to his father on April 11, 1781, 'played by forty violins, all the wind instruments doubled, ten violas, ten double-basses, eight violoncellos and six bassoons'.

Among new acquaintances were the Hofrat von Braun, Countess Thun and Countess Rumbeck (née Cobenzl). Mozart also played at a concert of the famous Vienna Tonkünstlersozietät in the Kärntnerthortheater, which had been founded by Florian Gassmann in 1771. His chief immediate hope of supporting himself in Vienna was as a pianist giving subscription concerts, obtaining pupils for the clavier and then publishing his compositions by subscription. Countess Thun set about securing subscriptions for a set of sonatas and during the summer succeeded in obtaining seventeen subscribers at three ducats each, with the result that Mozart published, in November 1781, the six sonatas for pianoforte with violin accompaniment (K.296 and K.376–80).[2] At a concert given during Lent he played his Concerto in D (K.175) with a new Rondo (K.382) and selections from *Idomeneo*. He also showed the music of *Zaide* to the younger Stephanie, then In-

[1] Possibly (K.338).
[2] No. 2 in C major was composed in Mannheim and No. 4 in B flat major had also been composed earlier, in 1779, at Salzburg.

spector of the Opera, and through Count Rosenberg, director of the theatre, who had heard portions of *Idomeneo* at Countess Thun's house, he received a libretto to compose for the opera. He writes to his father on August 1, 1781:

> The day before yesterday Stephanie the younger gave me a libretto. . . . It is very good. The subject is Turkish and it is called *Bellmont und konstanze* or *Die Verführung*[1] *aus dem Serail* – the overture (symphony), the chorus in the first act and the final chorus I shall compose in Turkish music. . . . I am so delighted to have the book that, already, I have finished the first aria for Cavalieri and for Adamberger and the terzet which closes the first act. The time given is short, certainly, for it must be produced by the middle of September. . . .

On August 8th he wrote that he had just finished the chorus of the janissaries and on August 22nd that he had finished the first act; but he learned that the Grand Duke Paul of Russia, in whose honour the opera was to have been performed, was not coming until November and on August 29th he writes that this will give him time to write 'my opera with more reflection'. As an example of the attention Mozart always gave to his libretto I shall quote from his letter of September 26, 1781, to his father:

> . . . I had nothing important to write and thought it would give you pleasure to have a short description of my opera.
>
> It begins with a monologue and then I begged Stephanie to write a short arietta and instead of the two chatting after the little song of Osmini's, to have a duet. The rôle of Osmin is intended for Hr. Fischer who has a fine bass boice . . . and one must use such a man, especially as the public likes him. This Osmin, however, in the original book has only one little song and nothing else except his part in the terzet and finale, but he has now got an aria in the first act and will have another in the second. I gave Stephanie the aria – and most of the music of it was composed before Stephanie had written a word of it . . .
>
> The rage of Osmin will be rendered comic in it as the Turkish music is thus brought in. In the execution of the aria I have let his fine deep voice . . . display itself. The *drum beym Barte des Propheten* is actually in the same tempo but with quicker notes and as his rage increases then – when one thinks the aria is at its end – the allegro

---

[1] A mistake of Mozart's; *Verführung* of course means *seduction*, *Entführung* means *abduction*. It would have to be *Die Verführung im Serail*, not *aus dem Serail*.

assai in quite another tempo and in another key must make a splendid
effect; for a man who is in such a rage oversteps all moderation,
measure and bounds; he does not know himself – so the music must
not; although the utmost passion, violent or not, must never be pushed as far as the disgusting and music even in the most awful places
must not offend the ear, but give pleasure, that is, music must always
remain music; so I have chosen no foreign key to the F (the key of the
aria) but a consonant one, not, however, the nearest D minor but the
further A minor.

Then comes the aria of Belmonte in A major, *O wie ängstlich, o
wie feurig* . . . here is indicated the beating, loving heart – two violins
in octaves. This is the favourite aria of all that have been heard,
mine also, and is written wholly for Adamberger's voice. One sees
the trembling, hesitating – one sees the swelling breast heave –
which is expressed by a crescendo – one hears the whispering and
sighing – which is given by the first violins with mutes and a flute in
unison.

The Janissaries' chorus is all that one could ask for a Janissaries'
chorus – short and lively – and written specially for the Viennese.
The aria of Konstanze I have had to sacrifice to some extent to the
flexible throat of Mlle. Cavalieri. . . .

Next the terzet, the close, namely, of the first act . . . as the text
permits I have written it rather well for three voices. Then begins
immediately the major pianissimo which must go very fast and this
close will make a really good row – and that is everything desirable
in the finale of a first act – the more noise the better; the shorter the
better, so that the audience does not cool off in its clapping. . . .

The first act has been ready for three weeks – an aria in the second
act and the drinking duet (for the Viennese gentry) . . . are ready.
I can't do more because the whole thing is turned round, and at my
request. At the beginning of the third act is a charming quintet, or
rather finale, but I should prefer to have this at the end of the second
act. For this a large alteration, even an entirely new intrigue, must
be made and Stephanie is head-over-ears in work. . . .

Frl. v. Auernhammer and I await eagerly the two double concertos[1] – I hope we shall not wait as fruitlessly as the Jews for the
Messiah. . . .

In the meantime the performance of the opera was delayed con-
siderably, partly owing to the production of Gluck's *Iphigénie in
Tauride* and *Alceste*, the latter being presented in honour of the
Grand Duke Paul of Russia at Schönbrunn on November 25,

[1] Two concertos; probably (K.242) for three pianos and (K.365) for two pianos.

1781. About this time there was a prospect of Mozart's becoming the teacher of the Princess Elizabeth, who was the prospective bride of the Archduke Franz. The Emperor's younger brother, the Archduke Maximilian, was a supporter of Mozart, but unfortunately for him the Emperor Joseph II[1] recommended Salieri[2] and Salieri, who had succeeded Gassmann, his master, in the Emperor's favour, was chosen. This was the first occasion out of many on which Salieri proved an obstacle to Mozart's success.

In December 1781, the famous clavier-player Clementi[3] arrived in Vienna and the Emperor Joseph was immediately anxious to have a rival display between Clementi and Mozart and according to Bridi he laid a wager with the Grand Duchess that Mozart would prove the superior, and won it. Clementi's account to his pupil, L. Berger, is as follows:

> I had only been a few days in Vienna when I received an invitation to play before the Emperor on the pianoforte. Entering the music-salon I saw there someone whose elegant attire made me take him to be an Imperial gentleman-in-waiting, but we had scarcely begun to speak when the conversation turned on music and we recognized one another as fellow-artists – as Mozart and Clementi – with the friendliest greetings.

Clementi described Mozart's playing thus:

> I had until then never heard playing so full of spirit and grace. Especially was I delighted with an Adagio and with several of his extemporised variations, the theme of which was chosen by the Emperor, each of us varying it, alternately accompanying one another.

The composer Dittersdorf in his autobiography (p. 236) gives an account of the conversation he had with the Emperor:

> *Emperor:* 'Have you heard Mozart play?' *I:* 'Three times already.' *Emperor:* 'How do you like him?' *I:* 'As every connoisseur must.' *Emperor:* 'Have you heard Clementi also?' *I:* 'Yes, I have also heard him.' *Emperor:* 'Some prefer him to Mozart, Greybig[4] chief among

---

[1] Emperor Joseph II (1741–90), succeeded to the Austrian throne in 1780.
[2] *Salieri*, Antonio (1750–1825), composer, succeeded Gassmann as Court composer at Vienna in 1774 and Bonno as Court Kapellmeister in 1788.
[3] *Clementi*, Muzio (1752–1832), pianist and composer.
[4] Greybig, or Kreibich, first violin among the Emperor's chamber musicians.

them. What do they mean by it?' *I:* 'In Clementi's playing there is only art, in Mozart's art and taste.' *Emperor:* 'That is just what I have said.'

Characteristically, Mozart's account of Clementi's playing is nothing like so favourable as Clementi's is of his. He writes on January 16th to his father:

... Now about Clementi. He is a fine player but that is all. He has great facility with the right hand, his great forte is his thirds – but apart from this he hasn't a particle of taste or feeling – he is a mere machine.

The Emperor, after sufficient compliments had passed, gave the signal to commence, '*La Santa Chiesa Cattolica*,' he said because Clementi is a Roman. He preluded and played a sonata. Then the Emperor said to me: '*Allons drauf los* ('fire away').' I preluded and played variations. Then the Grand Duchess produced some sonatas by Paisiello (miserably written out in her own hand) and I had to play the Allegro and Clementi the Andante and Rondo. Then we took a theme and developed it on two pianofortes. I may say I had borrowed the pianoforte of Countess Thun but only played on it when I played alone, as the Emperor wished it so. The other instrument was out of tune and had three keys sticking – 'It doesn't matter,' said the Emperor. I took it that the Emperor knew already my art and knowledge of music and wished to treat the stranger justly. Moreover I know from a reliable source that he was content with me ... also he has spoken to me about my marriage.

About six months later Mozart wrote to his father (June 7, 1783) as follows:

... Now I must say a few words to my sister about the Clementi sonatas. That they are valueless as Compositions everyone who plays or hears them will recognize.[1] There are no noteworthy or striking passages apart from sixths and octaves and I beg my sister not to be too much taken with these lest she spoil thereby her quick firm hand and ruin its natural lightness, suppleness and rapidity. For what is the object of these passages? They must be executed with the greatest speed (which nobody, not even Clementi, can achieve) and the result is a horrible hash, nothing else in the world!

Clementi is a charlatan like all Italians. He writes *Presto* and even *prestissimo* and *alla breve* on a sonata and plays it allegro in $\frac{4}{4}$ time. I know this for I have heard him do it. What he does well are passages

[1] An example of the isolation of a man of great genius, Mozart never realized that people without his genius did not hear with his ears.

in thirds but he had sweated day and night in London to achieve this; apart from this he has nothing, absolutely nothing, not the slightest enunciation (*vortrag*)[1] or taste and still less feeling.

I wish to draw special attention to these remarks of Mozart's because they reveal the ruthlessness in his character which so many biographers and writers on music have completely missed. Nobody who has a genuine musical understanding could ever have conceived that the composer of *Don Giovanni, Così fan Tutte* and the great Quintets and Symphonies was a merely amiable and agreeable man with an enormous talent for music. Of course inferior characters will impute motives of jealousy to Mozart in such harsh judgments and I have no doubt whatever that Mozart must have appeared as arrogant to people who had not the instinct to recognize the colossal differences between him and his gifted contemporaries such as Clementi and Salieri. The fact is that only an exceptional man of genius like Haydn, among Mozart's contemporaries, could have had the slightest inkling of Mozart's superiority and when one considers Mozart's judgments harsh one has also to remember that time has proved them to be just. A man like Mozart raises the standard in his art to a level so high that for hundreds of years gifted musicians of every generation remain struggling beneath it.[2]

Everywhere Mozart went he made for himself bitter enemies. Every mediocrity who met him immediately hated him; only those who loved music more than themselves admired and loved him; the egoists and careerists immediately recognized him as not one of their kidney and detested his superiority which they called arrogance. Mozart's outspokenness earned their undying enmity. His father had always reproached him for his lack of tact but this unconscious sincerity was a part of his genius. How could he praise rubbish? How could he enjoy, or pretend to enjoy, inferior music? His reaction was instinctive, immediate and intense.

[1] I take it he means sense of phrasing, intelligent expression.
[2] On his return from London Haydn writes (December 20, 1791): 'I am childishly glad to be home and welcomed by my old friends. I only regret to miss the greeting of the great Mozart whose death I deplore. Posterity will not see such a talent for a century to come.' It is now nearly 150 years and posterity has not yet seen such a talent.

He spoke out of his intensity and with mortal offence to everybody who did not share it. But how could they share it? They did
not feel what he felt. His father writes to him that he was making
himself 'detested in Vienna by his arrogant manners' and Mozart
replies on July 31, 1782:

> The whole world declares that through my boasting and criticising
> I have made the professors of music and also other people into
> enemies! What world? I presume the world of Salzburg. . . .

Here is another instance of Mozart's inevitable blindness. In his
hatred of Salzburg he finds an easy explanation for the criticism
his father retails. But what his father told him was true. The
professors of music and many others hated the superiority of this
man who always spoke on musical matters as if he were a god, 'as
one having authority'.

One concrete example of how Mozart inevitably made enemies
on all sides must be given here. One of the most successful
pianists and teachers in Vienna at the time of Mozart's settling
there was Leopold Kozeluch. Niemetschek, Rochlitz, Griesinger
(the biographer of Haydn) and Nissen are the authorities for the
following story:

A new quartet of Haydn's was being performed before a large
company. Kozeluch, who was standing beside Mozart, began
finding fault first with one thing then with another, and at last he
exclaimed with the impudent effrontery of his kind: 'I should
never have done it in that way!' 'Nor should I,' replied Mozart,
'and do you know why? Because neither you nor I would ever
have had such a good idea.'

This is how a great man makes implacable enemies. It always
has been so and it always will be so. On the other hand sincere
and sound natures who truly loved music never failed to recognize Mozart's quality.

Does it surprise the reader that in spite of his extraordinary
virtuosity, Mozart, as Jahn says, 'was never a fashionable and
well-paid music master in Vienna such as Steffan, Kozeluch or
Righini'? There is no doubt, too, that teaching bored him. A
celebrated physician, Jos. Frank, known to his contemporaries as

a great musical amateur, gives an account[1] of going to Mozart in 1790 for twelve lessons. He writes:

> I found Mozart a little man with a large head and plump hand and was somewhat coldly received by him. 'Now,' he said, 'play me something.' I played a fantasia of his own composition. 'Not bad,' he said, to my great astonishment. 'But now listen to me play it.' It was a miracle! The piano became another instrument under his hands. It was strengthened by a second piano which served him as a pedal.[2]

Teaching must always be an intolerable drudgery to a man of genius except when he has pupils of exceptional talent. Even then Mozart was not often inclined to teach, for a mind like his, constantly working at high pressure, needed relaxation when his serious work was over and for him the only serious work was composition. Actually his serious work was never over. We have to try to realize with our utmost effort of the imagination how a mind like Mozart's never rested from music. Music was going on in his head continuously; probably even in his sleep, and the disinclination to teach was due to the fact that this disturbed his natural musical thinking in a way that dancing, playing billiards, bolt-shooting, etc. did not. Most of his pupils were women of talent with whom he could have some genuine personal relationship as, for example:

1. Franziska von Lagusius (née von Jacquin), for whom he wrote the trio for pianoforte, clarinet and viola (K.498) and to whom he sent the Sonata in C major for four hands (K.521) with a message that it was rather difficult.
2. Frau von Trattner, for whom he composed his Fantasia in C minor (K.475).
3. Babette Ployer, for whom he composed the Concerto in E flat (K.449) (February 9th, 1784), the Concerto in G major (K.453).[3]
4. Josepha, or Josephine, Auernhammer to whom he dedicated the Sonatas for pianoforte and violin (K.376–80), published in 1781.

[1] Prutz' *Deutsch. Museum II*, p. 27.

[2] On March 12, 1785, Leopold writes to his daughter from Vienna: 'He has had a great forte piano pedal made which stands under the instrument and is three spans long and tremendously heavy.'

[3] Mozart writes to his father on June 9, 1784: 'Tomorrow Herr Ployer . . . will be at the concert where Frl. Babette plays her new Concerto in G, I the Quintet in E flat [K.452] and both of us the great Sonata for two claviers. I shall take Paisiello in the carriage so that he may hear my compositions and my pupils.'

Mozart played with Josepha Auernhammer at one of his own concerts (May 25, 1782); at a concert of hers on November 24, 1781, he played with her the Concerto *a due* (K.365) and a Sonata (K.381) and also played at her concert in the theatre at Vienna on October 26, 1782. She became well known as a teacher. Mozart, in spite of the assistance he gave her, wrote a very unfavourable account of her, which is so characteristic of him as to deserve quoting. To his father he writes on August 22, 1781:

> . . . As I have observed from your letter that you have confidence in this family I see myself obliged to let you know the bad as well as the good about them.
>
> He [Herr von Auernhammer] is the best of men – too good; as for his wife she is the most stupid and idiotic gossiper in the world – wears the trousers so that when she speaks he has nothing to say. Whenever we have gone for a walk he begs me not to say in his wife's presence that we have taken a cab or drunk some wine. Now I have no confidence in such a man. . . .
>
> I am not in their house for my convenience but for theirs and have met nobody there whose name is worth putting on paper . . . decent people and that's all. . . .
>
> Of the mother I shall say nothing beyond that one has enough to do to keep from laughing at her at table. Enough! . . .
>
> As for the daughter, if a painter wanted to paint the devil from life he could take refuge in such a face. She is fat like a peasant, sweats so as to make one sick . . . to see her is enough to make one blind . . . one is punished enough for the whole day if one's eyes have unluckily fallen upon her, for then one needs cream of tartar – she is so hideous, dirty and horrible – *pfui teufel!*
>
> I have already written to you how she plays the clavier and why they begged me to help her. I am most willing to help people but not people who pester me. She is not content that I should pass two hours daily with her, she would have me sit there the whole day. And then she makes herself agreeable and what is more is seriously in love with me. I thought it was a joke but now I am certain of it. . . .

These extracts are sufficient evidence in themselves of Mozart's natural manner of expressing himself. Like many other passages from his letters they have always been softened down (with the most forcible expressons omitted) by previous translators. This has helped to create the totally false image of the 'sweet' Mozart current among schoolboys and schoolgirls and those who have taught schoolgirls and boys at Colleges of Music for generations past. But it is absolutely essential for our understanding of Mozart and of his failure to obtain in Vienna any of the remunerative posts during his lifetime (which habitually go to those who have a moderate talent in their art but know how to be complaisant, to flatter and make themselves agreeable to everybody) to realize how different his true personality was from this pretty picture.

On December 15, 1781, he wrote to his father that he wanted to marry Constanze Weber:

> . . . Nature speaks as loudly in me as in any other, and perhaps louder than in many a great heavy blockhead. I cannot live like most of the young men nowadays. Firstly, I have too much religion; secondly, too much love of my neighbour and too much feeling to be able to lead astray an innocent girl, and, thirdly, too much fear and disgust and horror of illness and too much regard for my health to go running after whores. I can swear that I have as yet had nothing to do with any woman in this way, for if it had happened I should not conceal it from you, for such errors are natural enough in men and to fail once would be mere weakness – although I could not guarantee that I should not repeat it if I had once given way on this point. . . .
>
> I know that this reason, strong as it is, is not enough for marriage. But my temperament which is more inclined to a quiet domestic life than to rowdiness . . . makes a wife indispensable. . . . I am quite convinced that I could do better on my income with a wife – and with a wife one lives – in a word – an orderly life. In my opinion a single man only half lives. . . . I have thought and reflected enough. I shall not change my opinion. . . .
>
> But who is the object of my love? Don't be alarmed, I beg of you – not a Weber? Yes, a Weber, not Josepha, not Sophie, but Constanze, the middle one. In no family have I seen such variety of character. The eldest is a lazy, clumsy, false person. . . . The Langin [Aloysia, wife of Joseph Lange] is false, unprincipled and a coquette; the youngest is too young to be anything . . . the middle one, however, my good dear Constanze, is the martyr and just on that account, perhaps, the best-hearted, cleverest and in a word the best of all. She does everything in the house and yet can do nothing right.
>
> She is not ugly but is far from being beautiful. Her whole beauty is in her small black eyes and good figure. She is not intellectual but has enough commonsense to fulfil her duties as a wife and mother. She is not used to luxury – that is completely false; on the contrary

she is accustomed to be poorly dressed, since the little her mother can do is done for the two others, never for her. It is true she likes to be clean and neat but not smart, and most of what a woman needs she can make for herself . . . she understands housekeeping, has the best heart in the world. She loves me and I love her truly – could I wish for a better wife?

I must tell you that at the time I left[1] love was not there but was first born through her tender care and attention when I lived in the house.

I now wish for nothing more than that I have something a little more settled to do (of which, God be praised, I have hopes) and I shall then beg your permission to rescue my unfortunate one and be with her and make, as I dare to think, us all happy – for are you not happy when I am? . . . Now have compassion on your son!

This was the second crisis in Mozart's adult life and again his father did not approve of what he was doing. Leopold quite genuinely thought very badly of the Weber family and looked on Wolfgang's proposed marriage with one of the Webers as not only foolish from every point of view but he considered that his un-worldly-wise son had been trapped into this marriage by old Frau Weber. He was not without grounds for so thinking. Frau Weber, by suggesting that Wolfgang was compromising her daughter's honour, obtained his signature to a document drawn up by Johann Thorwarth, who had been left as guardian of his children by Weber, in which he pledged himself to marry Constanze within three years or to pay her three hundred florins a year. Mozart tells his father that as soon as the guardian was gone his dear Con-stanze tore the agreement up; but the affair had developed too far and all Leopold's remonstrances and criticisms were useless. In spite of the fact that there is not the slightest doubt that Mozart was not in love with Constanze as he certainly had been in love with Aloysia and that there is little evidence that Constanze was in love with him, the relationship 'worked'. By July 1782, Mozart is writing to his father:

I must beg of you . . . give me your consent to my marrying my dear Constanze . . . it is essential for my honour, for the honour of my dear girl, and for my health and wellbeing it is unavoidably essential. My heart is disquieted, my head swims – how can one

[1] He means, left the Archbishop's service.

work and think? . . . most people here believe we are married already – the mother is quite upset and the poor girl and myself are tormented to death. . . .

On August 4, 1782, without waiting further for his father's consent, Wolfgang and Constanze were married, but letters from Wolfgang's father and sister with the father's consent arrived the following day.

I shall not attempt a description of Constanze's character.[1] Mozart's own account of her, which I have quoted, must in any case be nearer the truth than any I could possibly give. The marriage turned out a moderate success. That Constanze was not an ideal wife for Mozart is undoubted; that she suited him in many ways is also not to be doubted; but the fact that the relationship lasted, that it 'worked', until Mozart's death is proof that there was some solid substance in it. This is the place to mention that there were six children[2] born of this marriage, of whom two survived to manhood, namely:

1 Karl Thomas, born Vienna, September 21, 1784, died in Milan, October 31, 1858, a gifted pianist who became an official in the Austrian Government service and was unmarried.
2 Franz Xaver Wolfgang, born Vienna, July 26, 1791, died Carlsbad, July 29, 1844. He became a well-known professional musician; his compositions have never been studied thoroughly.

In the meantime the first performance of *Die Entführung aus dem Serail* had taken place on July 13, 1782, at the theatre in Vienna, and had a considerable success. It received sixteen performances in the course of the year. Gluck at his own request heard it on August 6th and complimented Mozart on it and asked

[1] Perhaps her worst failing was her bad health. She played the clavier and was a good singer.
[2] The four children who did not survive their father were:
    (a) Raimund Leopold (b. June 17 and d. August 19, 1783),
    (b) Joh. Thomas Leopold (b. October 18 and d. November 15, 1786)
    (c) Theresia (b. December 27, 1787, and d. June 29, 1788),
    (d) Anna (b. and d. November 16, 1789).

him to dinner on August 8th.[1] But it must not be assumed that its success was unquestioned. Niemetschek relates that the Emperor Joseph declared of it:

> Too fine for our ears and a tremendous number of notes, my dear Mozart.

To which Mozart replied:

> Exactly as many, Your Majesty, as are necessary.

The composer Dittersdorf in his Autobiography was also critical and found that the orchestration overpowered the voices. Nevertheless, the success of the opera greatly strengthened Mozart's position as a new arrival in Vienna, enabled him to take the decisive step of marrying Constanze – he described his marriage jokingly as *Die Entführung aus dem Auge Gottes*, the Auge Gottes being the name of the house where the Webers lived – and gave him and his friends confidence in his future.

Of this opera *Die Entführung aus dem Serail* (K.384) I intend to say little. Many authorities have affected to see in it a great achievement in the history of music, namely, the development of an essentially German opera on the grand scale.[2] This seems to me mere academic categorism. What is German opera? In my opinion there is no such thing; or if there is it is utterly unimportant musically, though it may be of sociological or historical interest for those who lecture or attend lectures, or write or read books on sociology and history. All these things belong to the realm of information, and information as such is of no aesthetic importance.

Die Entführung is well known to musical audiences today. It is one of the most popular of Mozart's operas and is a work of genius. Nevertheless it is not in the highest class of his productions. This is not because it is a beginning of German opera with the faults of a primitive work. We know now that the primitive are usually the best works. Giotto is a primitive Italian painter who painted his pictures before artists properly understood the 'laws of per-

[1] Letter to Leopold dated Vienna, August 7, 1782.
[2] Professor Edward J. Dent: 'The development of an essentially German dramatic style out of the old German chamber style.'

spective'; but Giotto is nevertheless one of the greatest of all painters and the knowledge of the laws of perspective is not worth a damn to a painter and has nothing to do with the creative art of painting. It is a subject for lectures on painting, not for painters. The chief defect of *Die Entführung* is the dullness of Constanze, who is not a woman but a mere singer in the opera; but given a singer of great virtuosity and with a beautiful voice we should not even worry so much about this. The fact that we never hear a really good Constanze is the explanation for most adverse criticism of this opera on the part of music-lovers. As for experts, they are so apt to be misled by irrelevant sociological and historical theories that they rarely have any genuinely direct experiences of works of art to discuss.

Mozart was very busy arranging *Die Entführung* for wind instruments when he received a commission from the Haffner family in Salzburg to compose a new serenade. In a letter dated July 20, 1782, he writes about the score of *Die Entführung*:

> Before I gave it to be copied I first made here and there alterations and cuts . . . here and there parts for the trumpets, kettle-drums, flutes, clarinets and Turkish music are missing because I could get no paper with enough lines . . . they are written on a separate paper. . . .
> Now I have no light task. Sunday week my opera must be arranged for wind, otherwise someone else will forestall me and get my profit[1] and now you ask me for a new symphony! How is that possible? You cannot think how difficult it is to arrange anything for wind, so that it suits the wind-instruments and yet loses nothing . . . well, I must give my nights to it, otherwise it can't be done and to you, my dearest father, they shall be sacrificed. You shall get something by every post and I shall write as quickly as possible and as well as the time allows. . . .

On July 27th he writes that he has only been able to send an allegro as he was called upon to compose a serenade, but only for wind instruments, otherwise it might have served for the Haffner

---

[1] [This is precisely what appears to have happened. If Mozart did complete his arrangement, it has been lost. Eight pieces were arranged by a contemporary for two oboes, cor anglais, horns and bassoons. There was also an arrangement for two flutes and string quartet. *C.R.*]

work. He promises the two minuets, the andante and the last movement; also a march, if possible:

> ... otherwise you must just use the Haffner music [K.249] which is very little known.

I have written it in D because you prefer it.

On July 31st he writes:

> You see that my will is good but if one cannot, one cannot! I cannot slur over anything so I cannot send you the whole symphony before the next post.
>
> I have received today your letter of the 26th, but such an indifferent, cold letter as I could not suppose you to be capable of on receiving the news of the good reception of my opera. . . .
>
> You will in the meantime have received my last letter and I do not doubt that in your next I shall receive your consent to my marriage. . . .
>
> All that you have written or could write can be no more than mere idle advice which, good as it may be, no longer meets the case of a man who has gone as far with a girl as I have. . . .

Under such conditions was the celebrated Haffner music (K.385) and the superb Serenade for Wind Instruments in C minor (K.388)[1] composed.

It was about this time that Mozart came into contact with a prominent official, President of the Education Commission in 1781, Baron van Swieten, who had been for many years in Berlin where he had acquired a taste for Handel and Bach. He was a passionate music-lover and had musical parties every Sunday morning in his house at which Mozart soon became a constant visitor. One of the first results of Mozart's closer acquaintance with the music of Handel and Bach was that he asked his father to send him six fugues by Handel and toccatas and fugues by Eberlin, telling him[2] that he is making a collection of Bach fugues: 'of

---

[1] He later arranged this Serenade for String Quintet (K.406).
[2] April 10, 1782.

Sebastian's as well as Emanuel's and Friedemann Bach's'. Ten days later he writes to his sister sending her a Prelude and a three-part Fugue (K.394), on which he makes the very interesting remark that it was badly written out because he wrote out the fugue, which he had composed first, while he was thinking out the Prelude.[1]

> If Papa has not yet had the Eberlin works transcribed do not bother about them. I have found them here and unfortunately see that they are of little importance and do not deserve a place between Handel and Bach....

The fugue for two pianofortes in C minor (K.426)[2] composed on December 29, 1783, and the great but incomplete Mass in C minor (K.427),[3] were fruits of this study of Bach. Also, Mozart wrote an adaptation for String Quartet of five four-part fugues from J. S. Bach's *Wohltemperirte Klavier* (K.405).[4] What is less known is that Mozart composed four Adagios for String Trio (in F minor, G minor, D minor and F major) as introductions to his adaptations of the fugues of Sebastian and Friedemann Bach (K.404a).

Since it has become known, this Mass has been criticized adversely in some quarters for being 'operatic' rather than 'religious'. As this criticism is likely to be foolishly repeated and levelled also against his other church compositions when they are performed, owing to the flower-like richness of Mozart's style and the high standard of virtuosity he expected from his singers, let me say that it is entirely mistaken. Mozart's church music is intensely serious but the Anglo-Saxon mind, with its puritan cast, invariably associates seriousness with plainness. The extraordinary efforts modern singers have to make to sing this music ought, in the course of time, to dispel this illusion for only when such a high

[1] In this same letter he tells his sister that his wife Constanze has a passion for fugues.

[2] Beethoven wrote out this fugue in score. The autograph was in the possession of Artaria.

[3] Parts of this Mass were used by Mozart in 1785 for his cantata *Davidde Penitente* (K.469). It ranks with the *Missa Solemnis* and the Bach B minor Mass as one of the greatest works in music of its kind.

[4] No. 2 in C minor; No. 5 in D; No. 7 in E flat; No. 9 in E; No. 8 transposed from D sharp to D.

degree of virtuosity has been achieved that its difficulties are no longer apparent is it possible to give its intense seriousness proper expression.

Mozart was one of the supreme masters of counterpoint. His early studies under Martini, his later study of Bach, corresponded to something innate in his musical genius. Every great composer must be a polyphonic writer, but Mozart and Bach shall be considered to be in a class by themselves above all others in their power to combine creatively freedom with form in their polyphonic writing. Much of Mozart's finest polyphony is in his great ecclesiastical works such as the Litaniae (K.243), the Kyrie in D minor (K.341), the Kyrie in C (K.323), the Mass in C major (K.337), the Vesperae de Dominica (K.321), the Vesperae Solennes (K.339), the Graduale (K.273) and the Missa Brevis (K.258).

CHAPTER FIFTEEN

Brief and Incomplete Success

Age 27–51 (1783–7)

THE SUCCESS OF *Die Entführung* was chiefly useful in increasing Mozart's prestige, but it won him no permanent appointment such as he needed. The available musical positions were all occupied. Gluck, Salieri and Bonno were in possession and the Emperor would have had to create a new post – which, of course, he could easily have done – in order to give Mozart the liberty he so much needed. Even as early as August 1782, he writes to his father complaining of the indifference shown by the Emperor to men of talent, and adds:

> Where did they make their fortune and their fame? Certainly not in Germany! Even Gluck – was it Germany that made him the great man he is? Unfortunately not – Countess Thun, Count Zichy, Baron van Swieten, even Prince Kaunitz are very discontented with the Emperor that he no longer prizes men of talent and keeps them in his service. Recently the latter said to the Archduke Maximilian when the conversation turned on me that *such people only come into the world once in a hundred years* and that one must not drive such people out of Germany, especially if one is so lucky as to have them in the capital. . . .

Characteristically, Mozart began to think of leaving Vienna and trying his fortune in Paris or in England and actually took lessons in English for this purpose. It was also characteristic of him to inform his father of these notions, but they only drew from Leopold the habitual animadversions on his son's character; as, for example, the following written on August 23, 1782, to Baroness Waldstätten:

I should be quite reconciled [to the marriage of Wolfgang with Constanze] if I did not see a great fault in my son; he is too indolent and easy-going; at times too proud even and all these qualities make a man inactive; or else he grows impatient and cannot wait. He is ruled absolutely by opposite extremes – too much or too little, never any medium. . . .

Leopold goes on to say very sensibly that the Kapellmeister Bonno was an old man and that at his death Salieri would be promoted and leave a place vacant, and that Gluck also is old. This was all very sensible but it did not help Mozart to earn money at the actual moment when he needed it so badly or obtain for him the commissions to write operas with the certainty of their production for which he was burning.

There was nothing for him to do but to go on giving lessons and concerts – at which the great attraction was his own playing. He played at a concert given by Aloysia Lange on March 11, 1783, and gave a very successful concert of his own, which the Emperor attended, on March 22, 1783, the programme of which he copied out for his father. It was as follows:

1. Haffner Symphony (K.385).
2. Air from *Idomeneo*, *Se il padre perdei*, sung by Aloysia Lange.
3. C major Pianoforte Concerto (K.415).
4. Scena *Misera dove son* (K.369), sung by Adamberger.[1]
5. Sinfonia Concertante in G major from Serenade in D (K.320).
6. Concerto in D for pianoforte and orchestra (K.175). This was composed in Salzburg in December 1773, but Mozart wrote a new final Rondo (K.382) for this concert.
7. Scena *Parto, m'affretto* from *Lucio Silla* (K.135), sung by Mlle. Teyber.
8. Impromptu Fantasia beginning with a fugue, followed by variations on an air by Paisiello, *Salve tu Domine*, and as an encore he chose the air *Unser dummer Pöbel meint* by Gluck as a theme for variations.
9. Scena and Aria in B flat from Mme. Lange, *Mia speranza adorata* (K.416).

For a number of years Mozart gave regular subscription concerts for which he wrote many of his pianoforte concertos, and

---

[1] *Adamberger*, Valentin, tenor was the original Belmonte. The aria was originally written for a soprano, the Countess Baumgarten, who was a favourite of the Elector Karl Theodor.

these concerts were patronized by the Austrian nobility and were in every way successful. This was his main source of income, but for some reason – perhaps through growing loss of interest due to familiarity – these concerts seem to have gradually fallen off. After 1788 there is no record of them and he ceased composing symphonies or concertos until January 1791, when he composed the last pianoforte concerto in B flat major (K.595). As there was no copyright law in those days he made very little by the publication of his music which was frequently pirated. He sold his famous set of six String Quartets dedicated to J. Haydn to Artaria for a hundred ducats;[1] but according to Rochlitz, the publisher Hoffmeister is said to have found that he could not sell Mozart's works owing to their difficulty; a Berlin publisher, whose name does not deserve to be recorded here, boasted that he had refused many works by Mozart, of whom he declared he had a poor opinion. Nevertheless it is clear that Mozart earned a considerable amount of money in Vienna during the period from 1783 to 1786, when he was most in demand. In spite of this he began very soon after his marriage to get into debt and Leopold in his statement in a letter to his daughter, dated March 29, 1785, says:

I believe that my son if he had no debts to pay could now deposit two thousand florins in the Bank; the money is certainly there and the household expenses, as far as food and drink are concerned, are extremely economical.

Leopold overlooked the fact that these earnings were irregular and that there were long periods when Mozart earned comparatively little. It is possible that Leopold could have saved a large sum out of Mozart's earnings but we do not need to ask where this money went. One can say with perfect truth that it went in composing. What most people fail to understand is that creative work takes a great deal of time and during that time the

[1] These are the quartets which, on being sent by the publisher Artaria to Italy, were returned with the complaint, 'the engraving is full of mistakes'. On first hearing them, according to Nissen, the Hungarian Prince Grassalkowitsch declared that his musicians were playing incorrectly and on being handed the parts to convince him that they were playing what was written he tore them up in a rage. There is still occasional controversy over the introduction to the C major quartet, of which Haydn declared that if Mozart wrote it thus he must have had his own reasons for doing so.

artist is earning nothing; nor does he feel in the mood to earn any thing and so Mozart when busy with a big work used to put off pupils regardless of money. If one looks at the list of Mozart's compositions written between 1783 and his death in 1791 one is astounded that any man could have done so much and such work within eight years. To expect him to earn large sums of money in addition by other means is absurd; but this is actually what he had to try to do because the total sum brought in by all these works during eight years would hardly have kept him and his family for a single year.

Mozart and Constanze paid a visit to Leopold in Salzburg at the end of July 1783. Wolfgang took with him the Kyrie, Gloria, Sanctus and Benedictus of his great Mass in C minor (K.427), which was performed at St Peter's Church on August 25th, with Constanze singing the difficult soprano part. While in Salzburg he composed two duets for violin and viola (K.423 and 424) for Michael Haydn who was ill and had been ordered to write them by the Archbishop. In Salzburg he induced Varesco to supply him with another libretto for an opera. This was *L'Oca del Cairo* (K.422) for which Mozart wrote considerable portions of the music, but he eventually abandoned it owing to his dissatis-faction with the libretto. The same fate befell another libretto, *Lo Sposo Deluso* (K.430). It foreshadows *Figaro*; there is a fine quartet for two tenors and two sopranos, but some of the music has been left in a rather sketchy state and it does not make a really successful whole.[1]

On his return from Salzburg to Vienna he went to Linz where he wrote a symphony in a few days for a concert on November 4, 1783; this is the Symphony in C major (K.425). Jahn relates that at Linz Mozart was so much impressed by a painting *Ecce Homo*, that he made a drawing of it for his wife with the in-scription '*dessiné par W. A. Mozart Linz ce 13 novembre 1783; dédié à Madame Mozart son épouse*'. After his death Constanze wrote to Breitkopf and Härtel that this drawing which she had

---

[1] In a letter to his father dated December 6, 1783, Mozart writes of *L'Oca del Cairo*: 'Only three arias are now lacking for the first act. I can say that I am perfectly satisfied with the Buffo Aria, the Quartet and the Finale.'

preserved showed that Mozart had 'some talent for drawing' – which is also shown by the occasional sketches in his letters.

Throughout 1784 he was giving concerts and playing at the private homes of Esterhazy and Gallizin. For these concerts he wrote the Pianoforte Concertos in E flat (K.449) composed in February 1784; in B flat (K.450) and in D (K.451), both composed in March, as well as the Quintet in E flat for pianoforte, oboe, clarinet, horn and bassoon (K.452) of which he writes to his father on April 10th that these works were much appreciated and that the Quintet

> is the best which I have as yet written in my life. I wish you could have heard it.

Another Concerto for the pianoforte (K.453, in G), written for Babette von Ployer, as well as a Sonata in B flat for pianoforte and violin (K.454). were written in the following April. The period between 1784 and 1786 is that of Mozart's greatest popularity in Vienna and his works rather reflect this fact, which is why Wyzewa and Saint-Foix call it *La Grande Période de Virtuosité.* Mozart himself, in a letter to his father dated May 26, 1784, refers to these three Concertos (K.450, 451 and 453) as 'Concertos to make one sweat'.

Early in 1785 Leopold paid a visit to Vienna, staying from February to April. A few extracts from his letters to his daughter, which were not all accessible to Jahn, may be given here:

Vienna,
February 16, 1785.

On Friday at one o'clock we were in the Schulerstrasse, No. 846, on the first floor. You may see what a fine apartment your brother has from the fact that he pays four hundred and sixty florins rent.

The same day we went in the evening to his first subscription concert where there was a large assemblage of persons of rank. Everyone paid for these six Lenten concerts a gold sovereign or three ducats. . . .

The concert was incomparable, the orchestra splendid . . . there was a superb new Concerto by Wolfgang[1] which was still being copied out when we arrived and your brother had not had time to play through the Rondo because he had to supervise the copying. . . .

[1] (K.466) Concerto in D minor.

On Saturday evening Herr Joseph Haydn and the two Barons Tindi came to us and the new Quartets[1] were played, but only the three new ones which he has added to the other three we have – they are actually a little easier but marvellously composed. Herr Haydn said to me:

'*I tell you before God and as an honest man that your son is the greatest composer of whom I have ever heard; he has taste and in addition the most complete knowledge of composition.*' . . .

Salzburg,[2]
May 27, 1785.

I cannot deny that I find time hangs heavily on my hands. . . . Have I anyone with whom I can exchange a sensible word? I don't know whether I am too clever or others are too stupid. Briefly I find too great a drop from the acquaintances I had in Vienna, Linz and Munich.

November 3, 1785.

. . . I have not had a single line from your brother, his last letter was dated September 14th and since then the quartets should have come by any post; were he ill Herr Artaria would have informed me in his letter of October 28th. . . .

November 11, 1785.

. . . At last I have had a letter dated November 2nd from your brother but only twelve lines. He excuses himself because he has been up to the neck in work getting the opera *Le Nozze di Figaro*[3] finished. He thanks me and you for our congratulations and asks me to make you especially his excuses and to tell you he has not had time to answer your letter immediately: that in order to have the mornings free to work he has put all his pupils off until the afternoons, etc., etc.

I know the piece [Figaro], it is a tiresome work and the translation from the French must certainly have been revised to make a possible opera. God grant that it may please in performance; about the music I have no doubts. But it will cost him much running about and discussion before he gets the libretto arranged to his liking. . . .

Mozart had made the acquaintance of Lorenzo da Ponte (1749–

---

[1] B flat (K.458), A major (K.464) and C major (K.465).

[2] Written on his return to Salzburg to his daughter Nannerl, who lived at St Gilgen with her husband, Baron von Berchtold zu Sonnenberg, whom she married in 1784.

[3] It is worth remarking that Beaumarchais' famous play *The Barber of Seville* (1775) was known to Wolfgang in 1782, for on October 19th of that year he writes to his father: 'The Barber of Salzburg (and not of Seville) came to see me. . . .'

1838) at the house of Baron Wetzlar, a musical amateur of Vienna, and Mozart asked da Ponte to adapt, as a libretto Beaumarchais's comedy *Le Mariage de Figaro* which had been first produced in Paris on April 27, 1784. Rautenstrauch's translation, of which Mozart possessed a copy, was well known in Vienna, but a proposed production by Schikaneder was banned by the Court in February 1785. Lorenzo da Ponte had come from Venice, where he was a schoolmaster, with a letter of recommendation from the Italian poet Mazzolà to Salieri and through Salieri's influence he was appointed a Court theatrical poet by the Emperor Joseph II. Fortunately the first libretto written by da Ponte for Salieri and composed by him, *Il Ricco d'un Giorno*, was a failure whereas Paisiello made a great success with an opera *Il Re Teodoro*, the libretto of which was written by a rival poet, Casti. Salieri now abandoned da Ponte for Casti and so da Ponte turned to Mozart, after having also arranged to write a libretto for the composer Martin. According to da Ponte[1] the music was composed by Mozart as the words were written and the whole was finished in six weeks. Like most theatrical writers da Ponte scorns dates; there is scarcely a date to be found in the whole of his *Memorie*. There is no doubt that once committed to Mozart he helped to get the opera produced and was of assistance to Mozart in the midst of the intrigues against him on the part of Count Rosenberg and such musical rivals as Salieri. The composition of *Figaro* was begun in the autumn of 1785. It was finished before April 29, 1786, the overture being written just before the first performance on May 1, 1786.

In spite of the fact of his being busy with the composition of *Figaro* we know that Mozart found time to write during the winter of 1785-6 a number of other works, which were entered by him in the Thematic Catalogue which he had begun to keep in February 1784;[2] these are as follows:

---

[1] *Memorie* (New York, 1823–7).

[2] Mozart also for a short period, from March 1784 to February 1785, kept an account of his receipts and expenses. On May 1st he enters 'flowers 1 kreutzer' and on May 27th 'a starling 34 kreutzers'. Mozart was extremely fond of birds and animals and when the starling died he buried it in his garden and raised a monument to it.

1785	Nov. 5	Quartet ⎱ to *Villanella Rapita*
	Nov. 21	Terzet ⎰ (K.479 and 480)
	Dec. 12	Sonata for pianoforte and violin in E flat (K.481).
	Dec. 16	Pianoforte Concerto in E flat (K.482).
1786	Jan. 10	Pianoforte Rondo in D (K.485).
	Jan. 18	Terzet for *Der Schauspieldirektor*.
	Feb. 3	*Der Schauspieldirektor* (K.486).
	Mar. 2	Pianoforte Concerto in A (K.488).
	Mar. 10	Duet and Aria for the private performance of *Idomeneo* (K.489 and 490).
	Mar. 24	Pianoforte Concerto in C minor (K.491).
	April 29	*Le Nozze di Figaro* (K.492).

The dates entered are the dates on which the works were completed and one may sometimes reckon the time they took from the finished date of the preceding composition.

A few words are needed here on the short opera *Der Schauspieldirektor*, which was the musical part of a dramatic gallimaufry by Stephanie performed in the Orangery at Schönbrunn for the entertainment of the Governor-General of the Netherlands on February 7, 1786. The opera consists of an overture, two arias for two rival sopranos, a terzet for the two sopranos and the tenor and a final quartet. The music is superb in the brilliant virtuoso style of Mozart at this period.

On May 1, 1786, *Le Nozze di Figaro* was first performed at the National Theatre in Vienna. It was a success, but no extraordinary success; certainly nothing to compare with the success, a few months later, of Martin's *Cosa Rara*, which quite overshadowed *Figaro* both in popular estimation and in that of 'connoisseurs' such as the Emperor Joseph II and the composer Dittersdorf. For example, during the whole of the two following years of 1787 and 1788 *Figaro* was not once performed in Vienna. It was first performed in Berlin in 1790; but although praised by the critics the public preferred the operas of Martin and Dittersdorf It was a complete failure in Italy where it was first produced, only after Mozart's death, in 1792, and Mozart has remained incomprehensible to the Italian opera public practically ever since.[1]

---

[1] This is no 'Latin' inferiority. Mozart is even misunderstood by numbers of eminent German and Anglo-Saxon musicians; but I venture to think that a lack of something I shall risk calling 'vulgarity' in Mozart's music has been responsible for its lack of popularity in modern Italy.

On the other hand it was performed in Prague in the winter to 1786-7 with tremendous success, of which I shall have more of say presently.

Something must be said here about *Figaro*, which is the best-known and most popular of Mozart's operas.

LE NOZZE DI FIGARO

The original cast, according to Mozart's own thematic catalogue, was as follows:

IL CONTE ALMAVIVA	Signor Mandini
LA CONTESSA	Signora Laschi
SUSANNA	Signora Storace
FIGARO	Signor Benucci
CHERUBINO	Signor Bussani
MARCELLINA	Signora Mandini
BASILIO / DON CURZIO	Signor Kelly
BARTOLO / ANTONIO	Signor Bussani
BARBARINA	Signora Nannina Gottlieb

Beaumarchais's original French play *Le Mariage de Figaro*, first publicly performed in Paris in April 1784, was a social and political satire, but in constructing the Italian libretto the political sections were entirely omitted by da Ponte, and although this may have been partly out of regard for the Austrian Emperor and the court, it was certainly done at the express wish of Mozart, who had no interest in politics. This is a point on which all his biographers have to agree. Unlike his father, Leopold, he never mentions political affairs in his letters and Abert has rightly pointed out that for him the State 'came even less into consideration as primary experience than society'. He was indifferent to political principles and had only an interest in the men who represented them. This indifference to mere abstractions extended naturally to moral as well as political principles, and if many people advocating certain moral principles have found *Figaro* an immoral work it is because Mozart is never concerned with expounding theories of right and wrong or with mere tendentious caricature but only with life in all the manifestations of its individual reality. It is significant that although he lived in the midst of the French Revolution he never once mentions it. Napoleon, according to Sainte-Beuve, in his *Causeries de Lundi*, declared of Beaumarchais's *Figaro*: '*c'était la révolution déjà en action*'; but there is nothing of this in Mozart's *Figaro* and the famous 'frondeur-monologue' in the fifth act is replaced in Mozart's work by an outburst of rage and jealousy. This remarkable piece, however, is of the most fiery character but it is entirely personal. Mozart understood and had every sympathy with a hatred of injustice, but he was too realistic to express a revolutionary detestation of the strong as such and a glorification of the weak as such with the object of changing their places so that the oppressed might become the oppressors. He was also far too personally humane to be carried away by mechanical theories and in this his resemblance to Shakespeare is most marked.

But little as Mozart's *Figaro* is a political work, it is equally far from being a social document aiming either at glorifying or at decrying the aristocratic society of the age he lived in. To look upon his *Figaro* merely as a sort of rococo memorial to the fashionable brilliance of the great age of Vienna is to misunderstand it completely. That it is also a mirror of its age, as one might almost say all great works of art – including Dante's *Commedia* and Milton's *Paradise Lost* – are, is true; but it is far more than that. It is the expression of a great individual personality with a unique experience of and attitude to life; just as I would say Proust's *A la recherche du temps perdu* is. The characters in *Figaro* are not the characters of Beaumarchais's play at all; they are entirely the creation of Mozart and the expression of his own personality in every single respect. How utterly Mozart has transformed the Countess and Susanna! And what are we to say of that miraculous creation Cherubino, a figure absolutely unique in the world's dramatic literature? Never has the dewy freshness, sensitiveness, sensuousness, and ecstasy of the human heart in the first bloom of its youth had such adequate, let me say perfect, expression! Cherubino's first aria: '*Non so più cosa son, cosa faccio* (I no longer know what I am, what I do),' must always remain one of the loveliest things that genius of an artist has ever conceived in the history of the world. That the artist who could conceive such exquisite things as this and the Countess's '*Dove sono*' and the 'Zephyr' duet, was also capable of the intellectual constructive power of the finale of Act II is in itself sufficient to rank him with Shakespeare as the complete artist, the musician of all musicians who was truly universal.

A final word must be said. It has been suggested that Mozart's apparent unconcern with the world-events about him and even, after he was mature, with the work of musicians who were his contemporaries is a sign of limitation. Surely this is not so, but quite the opposite is true. Mozart took so very much for granted which lesser minds argue about. He was too understanding and too profound (though active) a fatalist to be a partisan. He never turned his works of art into judgments. He merely – like the Creator of nature – gave them individual life, and in his works his music, like the rain and the sunshine, falls alike on the just and the unjust.

I now continue with a few more extracts from Leopold's letters to his daughter:

January 13, 1786.

... At last I have had an answer dated December 28th from your brother to my two letters. He writes that he has given three subscription concerts with a hundred and twenty subscribers[1] and that he has written a new Piano Concerto in E flat for them, of which the Andante was encored, which is rather unusual. ...

March 31, 1786.

I am sorry the letter has been lost ... I wrote that ... seven of the

[1] In a letter to his father dated Vienna, March 20, 1784, Mozart gives a list of his subscribers, numbering 174. He also gives a list of his engagements, which is worth quoting:

'Thurs. Feb. 26, Count Gallizin.	Sat. Mar. 28, Richter.
Mon. Mar. 1, Joh. Esterhazy.	Sun. Mar. 21, 1st S. Concert in Theatre.
Thurs. Mar. 4, Gallizin.	Mon. Mar. 22, Esterhazy.
Fri. Mar. 5, Esterhazy.	Wed. Mar. 24, 2nd S. Concert (private).
Mon. Mar. 8, Esterhazy.	Thurs. Mar. 25, Gallizin.
Thurs. Mar. 11, Gallizin.	Fri. Mar. 26, Esterhazy.
Fri. Mar. 12, Esterhazy.	Sat. Mar. 27, Richter.
Mon. Mar. 15, Esterhazy.	Mon. Mar. 29, Esterhazy.
Wed. Mar. 17, 1st S. Concert.	Wed. Mar. 31, 3 S.C. (private).
Thurs. Mar. 18, Gallizin.	Thurs. Apr. 1, 2 S.C. (theatre).
Fri. Mar. 19, Esterhazy.	Sat. Apr. 3, Richter.'

riddles[1] had been correctly solved, that none of us could solve the eighth and that I have written to your brother about it as he is the philosopher and author of the riddles and the fragment.[2] The riddles are only fun but the fragment is of serious use for the cultivation of morality in every reflecting person. . . .

end of April, 1786.

On the 28th *Le Nozze di Figaro* will have its first performance.[3] It will be a great thing if it succeeds, for I know that he has a tremendously strong clique against him. Salieri and all his followers will again set heaven and earth in motion. Duschek told me recently that your brother has so many cabals against him just because he is so greatly esteemed for his exceptional talent and ability.

November 17, 1786.

. . . To-day I have had to reply to a letter from your brother which has cost me so much writing that after it I can write very little to you. . . .

That I have had to write a very emphatic letter you can easily imagine since he made me no less a proposal than that I should take his children into my care while he during Lent might make a trip through Germany to England. . . .

But I have spoken my mind . . . It would be a nice thing indeed – they could travel in peace, might die – might remain in England and leave me with his children on my hands. . . . Enough! my answer is strong and full of good advice if he will make use of it.

December 8, 1786.

. . . you will see from the enclosed very illegible letter from your brother that my reply has calmed him and that he is giving four Advent concerts at the Casino.

May 10, 1787.

. . . Your brother now lives at 224, Landstrasse. He does not explain why. Not at all! But unfortunately one can guess.

Some time before March 1785, Mozart had entered one of the eight lodges of Freemasonry in Vienna, for we have it on the authority of Nissen that his father Leopold was introduced as a member by him in the spring of that year, when Wolfgang was already a member. Freemasonry was very much in vogue in intellectual circles in Vienna about this time under the leader-

[1] Sent by Mozart to amuse his father.
[2] What this was I do not know.
[3] The *première* was postponed until May 1st.

ship of Ignaz von Born (1742–91) and was favourably regarded by the Emperor. All institutions lend themselves readily to abuses and necessarily sink to the common level of the majority of their members, but there was a serious and highly intellectual section in the Vienna Freemasonry of this period and it was to this that Mozart and his father belonged. Mozart's lodge was the *Zur gekrönten Hoffnung im Orient in Wien*, of which Count Franz von Esterhazy became Grand Master in December 1785.

We may find in their common membership in Freemasonry the explanation of certain phrases written in the following letter by Mozart to his father:

Vienna,
April 4, 1787.

Mon très cher Père,

. . . Just now I have had news which quite overwhelms me – all the more since your last letter led me to suppose that you were, God be praised, well. Now I hear that you are really ill! How earnestly I look forward to reassuring news from yourself I need hardly tell you. And I certainly hope for it although I have accustomed myself to expect the worse in all things.

Since death (properly understood) is the true ultimate purpose of our life I have for several[1] years past made myself acquainted with this truest and best friend of mankind so that he has for me not only nothing terrifying any more but much that is tranquillizing and consoling!

And I thank my God that He has bestowed on me the good fortune to provide the opportunity (you understand me) of recognizing death as the *key* to our true blessedness.

I never lie down in my bed without reflecting that perhaps I (young as I am)[2] shall never see another day; yet none of all who know me can say that I am socially melancholy or morose. For this blessing I daily thank my Creator and wish it from my heart for all my fellow-men.

I wrote to you on this point in the letter which Mlle. Storace mislaid on the occasion of the sad death of my dearest best friend, Count von Hatzfeld – he was thirty-one years old, as I am. I do not mourn for him but for myself and all those who knew him as well as I did.

I hope and pray that even as I am writing this you may be better; but should you, contrary to expectation, not be better I beg you . . .

[1] *ein paar.*
[2] Mozart was thirty-one years old when he wrote this letter.

not to conceal it from me but to write, or have written for me,
the exact truth, so that I may be as quickly as possible in your arms.
Nevertheless I hope to receive soon a reassuring letter from you
and with this hope my wife, Carl[1] and I kiss your hands a thousand
times and am ever,

                                        Your most dutiful son.

Leopold made a slight recovery but died suddenly on May 28,
1787. On May 29th Mozart wrote to his friend Gottfried Freiherr
von Jacquin in Vienna:

I must let you know that today when I returned home I received
the sad news of the death of my dear father. You can imagine the
state I am in.

And on June 16th he wrote to his sister:

My dearest and best of sisters,
    That you yourself did not advise me of the sad and unexpected
death of our dearest father did not offend me as I could easily guess
the reason. . . .
    Be assured, my dear, that when you have need of a good, loving
and protecting brother you will certainly find one in me.
    My dearest and best of sisters, if you were still unprovided for[2]
all this would be unnecessary.[3] I should, as I have a thousand times
said and thought, give up everything to you wholeheartedly; since,
however, it is in a way not needed but is of great assistance to me,
I hold it my duty to think of my wife and child.

From a letter dated August 1, 1787, written to his sister we
learn that Mozart received a thousand florins from his father's
estate.

With the death of his father and the production of *Figaro* a
definite phase of Mozart's life was concluded. The failure of
Figaro to make any material difference to his life in Vienna marked
the beginning of Mozart's realization that worldly success was
not to be his. He was destined for other and higher things. The
success of *Figaro* in Prague was a success due to the purer musical
taste of the Bohemians at that time. Among the musicians of
Prague (where the conductor, Strobach, and the orchestra used

[1] His son Carl, born in 1784.
[2] She had married Freiherr von Berchtold zu Sonnenburg in 1784.
[3] Reference to the inheritance.

13. Emanuel Schikaneder as Papageno

to get so excited in playing *Figaro* that they declared they would willingly have played it all over again) Mozart must have come to the conclusion that henceforth he had to write mainly for himself and for a handful of musicians capable of understanding his music.

Chief among these must be remembered Joseph Haydn, who wrote a justly famous letter which was first published in 1798 by Niemetschek. He obtained it from Chief Administer Roth, to whom it was addressed, and in printing it stated that it was: 'one of the finest flowers that can be strewn upon the grave of the artist so prematurely taken away.' Haydn's letter written in December 1787 is as follows:

> You desire an opera buffa from me; right gladly, if you wish to possess for yourself one of my compositions. But not for presentation in your theatre at Prague because all my operas are intended too particularly for our own company (at Count Esterhazy's in Hungary) and would never have the intended effect outside the prescribed setting. It would be quite different if I were to have the good fortune to get a new libretto to compose for that theatre. Even then, however, it would be a risk since one can hardly compete with the great Mozart.
>
> Could I only impress in the soul of every music lover, and especially the great, the inimitable works of Mozart as deeply and with such musical understanding as I myself feel and comprehend them then the nations would compete to possess such a precious jewel within their walls. Prague must stick to this precious man but also reward him; for otherwise the history of a great genius is a sad one and gives to future times little encouragement for similar striving; on the contrary, unfortunately! How many hopeful spirits have gone under! I am indignant that this unique Mozart has not yet found employment at any Imperial or Royal Court. Pardon me that I digress but I honour the man so dearly.
>
> My compliments to the Prague orchestra and virtuosos.
>
> JOSEPH HAYDN.

At the end of a visit in January 1787, Mozart left Prague with a contract to compose a new opera for the following season at a fee of one hundred ducats.

CHAPTER SIXTEEN

Last Years

Age 31–35 (1787–91)

THE HISTORY OF Mozart during the last four years of his life is the history of a great man of genius who is so completely superior in every respect that he is practically left alone to be consumed in his genius (which in his case is the refining fire of which great religious teachers speak!) and die – unregarded by the world at large.

In the *Magazin der Musik*, 1788, Vol. II, Cramer, a musical connoisseur visiting Vienna, writes:

> Kozeluch's works hold their own and are everywhere acceptable, but Mozart's are not by any means so popular. It is certainly true – and it receives additional support from the quartets he has dedicated to Haydn – that he has a decided leaning to what is difficult and unusual. But on the other hand how great and noble are his ideas, how daring a spirit is displayed in them!

During the greater part of the year 1787, in which occurred his father's death, Mozart was at work on the composition of *Don Giovanni* for which Lorenzo da Ponte again furnished the libretto. Nevertheless he found time for other compositions, the following being entered by him in his own Thematic Catalogue:

1787	Mar. 11	Rondo for Pianoforte, A minor (K.511).
	Mar. 18	Scena for Fischer, *Non so, d'onde* (K.512).
	Mar. 23	Aria for Gottfried von Jacquin, *Mentre ti lascio* (K.513).
	April 6	Rondo for horn for Leutgeb (K.514).
	April 19	Quintet for two violins, two violas and 'cello in C major (K.515).

K

May 16	Quintet in G minor (K.516).
	Four Songs
May 18	*Die Alte* (K.517).
May 20	*Die Verschweigung* (K.518).
May 23	*Das Lied der Trennung* (K.519).
May 26	*Als Luise die Briefe ihres ungetreuen Liebhabers verbrannte* (K.520).
May 30	Pianoforte Sonata, four hands, in C (K.521).
June 11	*Musikalischer Spass* (K.552).
	Two Songs
June 24	*Abendempfindung* (K.523).
June 24	*An Chloe* (K.524).
Aug. 10	Serenade (K.525). 'Eine kleine Nachtmusik'.
Aug. 24	Sonata for Pianoforte and Violin in A (K.526).

Mozart is supposed to have brought his opera *Don Giovanni* (K.527) to Prague in an unfinished state in September 1787, and to have completed it in the summerhouse in the vineyard of his friend Duschek. He is said to have written *La ci darem la mano* five times before being able to satisfy his singers and this duet is written on smaller paper in the autograph score, as is Masetto's aria. On October 14, 1787, *Figaro* was performed in his presence and on October 29th the first performance of *Don Giovanni* took place, the overture, it is said, being only written out on the previous night.[1] The opera was received with enthusiasm in Prague and the following account appeared in the *Wiener Zeitung* No. 91, 1787:

On Monday October 29th Kapellmeister Mozart's long-expected opera *Don Giovanni* ... was performed by the Italian opera company of Prague. Musicians and connoisseurs are agreed in declaring that such a performance has never before been witnessed in Prague. Herr Mozart himself conducted and his appearance in the orchestra was the signal for cheers, which were renewed at his exit. The opera is exceedingly difficult of execution and the excellence of the representation, in spite of the short time allowed for studying the work, was the subject of general remark. The whole powers, both of actors

[1] But in Mozart's Catalogue the whole opera, including the overture, is entered as finished on October 28th. Probably it was written on the night of October 27th, before the second rehearsal.

and orchestra, were put forward to do honour to Mozart. Considerable expense was incurred for additional chorus and scenery – the enormous audience was a sufficient guarantee of the public favour.

The success of *Don Giovanni* in Prague had one minor result which was that after the death of Gluck on November 15, 1787, Mozart was appointed by the Emperor Joseph II his successor as Kammermusikus on December 7, 1787; but not, unfortunately, with Gluck's salary, for he received only eight hundred florins a year instead of several thousands. It is recorded that he attached to one of the receipts of his pay a note stating:

Too much for what I do – too little for what I could do.

Don Giovanni was nevertheless not given in Vienna until May 7, 1788, and then it was only by the command of the Emperor Joseph II. It was a failure although it was not withdrawn but was given fifteen performances during that year. Then it fell out of the repertory and was not revived until after Mozart's death and then in a wretched German adaptation. The Vienna production, however, was responsible for Mozart making two additions, namely, the famous aria for Elvira, *Mi tradì*, and the duet between Leporello and Zerlina, *Per queste due manine*. The aria *Mi tradì* is generally retained but the duet seems to have been an attempt by da Ponte and Mozart to make the opera more acceptable to the Viennese and is generally omitted in present-day performances. The aria for tenor, *Dalla sua pace*, was also added for this production as the tenor found the big aria of Ottavio's, *Il mio tesoro*, beyond his powers.

Don Giovanni both in Prague and Vienna had a *succès d'estime*, that is, a success with the few discriminating music-lovers and musicians, just as *Figaro* had; for even *Figaro* did not have a popular success, being quite eclipsed by Martini's *Una Cosa Rara*; just as Salieri's *Axur* and Dittersdorf's *Der Doktor und Apotheker* were everywhere preferred to *Don Giovanni*. A contemporary writer named Schink in the *Dramaturgische Monate* of 1790 (II, p. 320) put the matter very well:

How can this music so full of force, majesty and grandeur be expected to please the lovers of ordinary opera . . . ? The grand and noble qualities of the music in *Don Giovanni* will appeal only to the small minority of the elect. It is not such as to tickle the ear of the crowd and leave the heart unsatisfied. Mozart is no ordinary composer. . . .

Another contemporary, Schneider, in the *Gesch. d. Berl. Oper.* after the first performance of *Don Giovanni* in Berlin, wrote:

. . . Vanity, eccentricity, fancy have created *Don Giovanni*, not the heart . . .

A writer in the *Chronik v. Berlin* (IX, p. 132) praises the music but adds:

Oh, that he had not so wasted the energies of his mighty mind! that his judgment had been brought to the aid of his imagination and had shown him a less miry path to fame! . . .

Goethe, however, seems to have had a sense of the greatness of *Don Giovanni* for he writes to Schiller on December 30, 1797, after the performance in Weimar:

Your hopes for opera are richly fulfilled in *Don Giovanni* but the work stands absolutely alone and Mozart's death prevents any prospect of its example being followed.

Mozart himself may have had qualms whether he was not giving the musicians and music-lovers of Prague rather more than they were able to digest in *Don Giovanni*; for Niemetschek, after referring to the fact that Mozart, in spite of having had a natural genius like Shakespeare's, had also studied his art profoundly, relates the following story:

Once – it was after the first rehearsal of *Don Juan* – Mozart went for a walk with the then director of the orchestra and Kapellmeister, Herr Kucharz. Among other things they spoke of *Don Juan*. Mozart said: 'What is your opinion of the music of *Don Juan*? Will it please as much as *Figaro*? It is of a different character!

KUCHARZ: How can you doubt it? The music is beautiful, original, profound. What comes from Mozart will certainly please the Bohemians.

MOZART: Your conviction reassures me, it comes from a connoisseur. But I have not spared trouble and labour to accomplish something exceptional for Prague. People err who think that my art has come easily to me. I assure you, dear friend, nobody has devoted so much time and thought to composition as I. There is not a famous master whose music I have not industriously studied through many times.

Here it is worth mentioning some remarks of Niemetschek on Mozart's methods of composing, since Niemetschek's evidence is contemporary evidence. Niemetschek says:

> Mozart wrote everything with such ease and speed as might at first be taken for carelessness or haste; also he never went to the pianoforte while composing. His imagination held before him the whole work clear and lively once it was conceived. His great knowledge of composition made easy for him the general harmonic panorama. One seldom finds in his scores improved or erased passages. But it does not follow that he merely sketched out his works hastily. The composition had long been finished in his head before he sat himself at his writing desk. When he received the text for a vocal work he went about with it for some time, thought himself thoroughly into it, and gave it all the power of his fantasy. Then he worked out his ideas fully on the pianoforte and then for the first time sat down to write. Consequently, the writing was for him an easy task during which he often joked and chattered . . . often he spent half the night at the pianoforte for these actually were the creative hours of his heavenly ideas. In the quiet peacefulness of night, when no object fettered his thought, his imagination flamed to its liveliest and embraced the whole wealth of tones with which nature had endowed his spirit. . . . Whoever heard Mozart in such hours alone knew the depth, the vast extent of his musical genius: free and independent from all other considerations his spirit could then venture on the boldest flights thro' the highest regions of art. In such hours of poetic inspiration Mozart created his inexhaustible store; out of this he ordered and constructed with an easy hand his immortal works.

Mozart was always in his thoughts occupied with music and he had a habit when eating alone or with his family of taking his napkin and folding it very exactly at the corners and drawing it through his mouth, grimacing in his concentration on some musical idea or problem. Niemetschek's remark that Mozart rarely improved or erased passages is generally true but there are quite a number of important exceptions where Mozart has had striking and significant second thoughts. Also, like Beethoven, he was occasionally critical of his own works when he heard them. There is a story of his playing an aria from *Die Entführung* in a private house and remarking afterwards: 'It may do well enough in this form for the salon but on the stage it is too long. At the time I wrote it I was never tired of hearing myself and did not know how to bring my work to a conclusion!'

Don Giovanni only slowly made its way into the European opera-houses and even up to today this masterpiece remains an unpopular work which is constantly revived owing to the passionate admiration of the best musicians and most discriminating musiclovers from generation to generation who cannot rest until they have heard it. Never, however, in the whole hundred years and more since it was written has it achieved the popularity of a *Bohème* or a *Cosa Rara* or a *Pagliacci* or any other of the great successes of a day and an hour. As a contemporary of Mozart wrote: 'Mozart's operas . . . have met with the fate which would befall a sober man introduced to a company of drunkards; the rioters would be sure to treat the sober man as a fool.'[1] E. T. A. Hoffmann, in his *Don Juan, eine fabelhafte Begebenheit*, written in September 1812, which appeared in his *Phantasiestücke in Callot's Manier* in 1813, was one of the first to appreciate the great qualities of *Don Giovanni*. The famous Danish philosopher Kierkegaard's celebrated essay on the opera written in 1842 has also had a certain influence on the Continent, although it is still unknown in England and America.[2]

The production of great works such as *Figaro* and *Don Giovanni* did nothing to provide for Mozart's future financially. He was compelled to continue to try to earn his living by teaching and by obtaining commissions for dance and other music. In 1788, the year of the production of *Don Giovanni* in Vienna, he composed a considerable quantity of miscellaneous music, including the three last symphonies in E flat (June 26th), G minor (July 25th) and C major (August 10th), and numerous country dances and waltzes.

[1] *Berlin. Mus. Zeit.*, 1793, p. 77.
[2] See Chapter XIX.

Having arranged at Baron van Swieten's request Handel's *Acis und Galatea* in November 1788, Mozart did the same for Handel's *Messiah* in March 1789, and in July 1790 for the *Ode for St Cecilia's Day* and *Alexander's Feast*. A great deal has been written about these additions and alterations to Handel's scores by Mozart and it is a matter of taste whether one prefers the originals or Mozart's versions. In my opinion good schools of music would make their students perform both versions and request critical comments from them, regarding such work as an essential part of their studies.

On April 8, 1789, Mozart set out with a pupil-friend, Prince Karl Lichnowsky, on a visit to Berlin. He played at the Court in Dresden in competition with a famous virtuoso named Hässler (1747–1822). Visiting Leipzig he played the organ at the St Thomas Church and the Cantor Doles, a pupil and the successor of Sebastian Bach, was so pleased that he made the choir sing for Mozart the Bach eight-part motet *Singet dem Herrn ein neues Lied*. According to Rochlitz he was so delighted that he exclaimed: 'That is indeed something one can learn from!' and he asked to see other motets by Bach, of which the St Thomas school possessed manuscripts; as there was no full score available he spread the parts out around him and was soon deep in study.

In Berlin he was presented to the King, Frederick William II, by Prince Lichnowsky. The Prussian King was an amateur 'cellist and very fond of music, his taste, according to his Kapellmeister Reichardt, being more catholic than that of his predecessor, Frederick the Great. According to tradition the King made Mozart an offer of a Kapellmeistership at a good salary, which he refused out of loyalty to the Austrian Emperor; a number of letters written by Mozart to his wife during this journey went astray and there is no precise mention of this offer in any we possess. On May 21, 1789, he wrote:

> . . . my dearest little wife, you must rejoice more at my return than at any money I am bringing. . . .

On June 4th he was back in Vienna, having had little pecuniary profit from his tour, but having made acquaintance with un-

known works of J. S. Bach and having left behind him the famous
Gigue (K.574) written in the album of the Leipzig Court organist
Engel on May 17th, which is a little masterpiece of Mozart's con-
trapuntal art.

On July 12, 1789, he wrote a long letter to a friend and fellow-
mason, Michael Puchberg, who was a Viennese business man and
music-lover. From this letter I take the following extract:

> My God! I am in a position such as I should not wish my worst
> enemy to be and if you my best friend and brother forsake me then I,
> together with my poor sick wife and child, am blamelessly and
> lucklessly lost. Even when I saw you last I wanted to pour out my
> heart – but I had not the heart and still would not have it but only
> dare do it tremblingly in writing and could not do it even so if I
> were not sure that you know me and my circumstances and are con-
> vinced of my innocence and my most unfortunate and sad position.
> O, God! instead of coming with gratitude I come to you with fresh
> requests, instead of settlement I bring fresh demands. If you know
> my heart then you must know what pain this gives me; how through
> this unlucky illness[1] I am deprived of my earnings I need not repeat
> to you; only I must tell you that in spite of my unfortunate situation
> I decided to give subscription concerts so as to be able at least to
> provide for my great and increasing expenses – for I was convinced
> of your friendly willingness to wait – but I did not succeed. My fate
> is sad but only in Vienna is it so adverse that I can earn nothing even
> when I want to. I have run around for fourteen days with my list[2]
> and so far there stands the single name of Swieten.[3]
>
> Now since it appears that my dear wife is improving from day to
> day I should be able to work once more were it not for this blow, this
> heavy blow – we have the consolation that at least she is going to im-
> prove, although yesterday evening she upset me and made me doubt-
> ful again; she suffered so much and I with her; but this night she has
> slept so well and is so much easier this morning that I am more hope-
> ful; now I can again begin to think of work but I am unlucky in
> another respect – truly only for the moment – dearest and best friend
> and brother, you know my present circumstances but you also
> know my prospects; these remain as mentioned so and so . . . you
> understand me. Meanwhile I am writing six easy pianoforte sonatas
> for the Princess Frederika [of Prussia] and six quartets for the King,[4]

[1] Of Constanze, his wife.
[2] To obtain subscribers.
[3] Baron van Swieten.
[4] Only three were ever written, namely (K. 575, 589 and 590).

all of which I am having printed by Kozeluch at my expense; the two dedications will bring in something; in a couple of months my fate in the little affair[1] will be decided, consequently you my best friend stand to risk nothing; now it depends on you my only friend whether you can and will lend me a further five hundred florins.

I undertake to pay back until my affair is settled ten florins monthly and then (which must be in a few months) to repay the whole sum with proper interest and also to declare myself for life your debtor which I indeed must yet remain since I shall never be in a position to be able to thank you enough for your friendship and love. Thank God it is finished! Now you know all, only don't take amiss my trust in you and reflect that without your support the honour, the repose and perhaps the very life of your friend and brother would be sacrificed. . . .

July 14, 1789.

God knows I can hardly bring myself to send off this letter – yet it must go – If only this illness had not happened I should not have been compelled to seem so shameless to my one friend and yet I hope for forgiveness since you know the good and evil of my situation. The evil certainly is only for the moment but the good certainly will last, once the momentary evil is removed. *Adieu!* Forgive me, in God's name, just forgive me – and – *adieu!*

Only a sensitive and imaginative person can understand what it must have cost Mozart, the proud and – as his father even used to declare – 'arrogant' Mozart to write this letter. But who was to blame that Mozart during the last years of his life had to endure an ever-increasing pressure of poverty and neglect? Every ardent young spirit reading this book will feel that there is something wrong with a society in which such things can happen. There is. But a society in which such a thing could not happen is not as easy to achieve as most reformers pretend to believe. Of course, one thing may be curable – namely, the mere lack of adequate means of existence which forces men like Mozart into such humiliating positions and exhausts their nervous energy. No society can be considered either satisfactory or stable – that is to say, no society has a proper and firm foundation – which has not secured for every one of its members the means of civilized subsistence

---

[1] This is supposed to be a reference to Mozart's application to the Vienna Court for a position in view of the offer made to him by the King of Prussia.

quite independent of merit or what used to be called 'desert'. It may be true that no man 'deserves' to live; but certainly nobody's livelihood should depend upon popular support. No doubt economic security will in time be established because without it no permanency of civilization is possible; but even then the Mozarts of the future may suffer from the neglect and indifference of the majority of their contemporaries and successors. But that is precisely the index of their value and will not interfere with their work; rather, it will often help it.

When Hoffmeister, the publisher, advised Mozart that he should write in a more popular style Mozart replied with a bitterness which, as his first and excellent English biographer Edward Holmes comments, was 'unusual' for him:

> Then I can make no more by my pen, and I had better starve and go to destruction at once!

There are in existence no less than thirteen letters to Michael Puchberg written during this one year from July 1789 to August 1790, every one of which contains an urgent request for a loan of money. We know that Puchberg sent him, in answer to these letters, the following sums:

July 17, 1789	150 florins
December 1789	300 florins
January 1790	100 florins
February 1790	25 florins
March, April, 1790	150 florins
April 8, 1790	25 florins
May 17, 1790	150 florins
June 12, 1790	25 florins
August 14, 1790	10 florins

None of Mozart's many biographers has given sufficient attention to the harassed situation of their hero during the last years of his life. Most people imagine – no, not 'imagine', assume – that great artists produce great works out of the air. It is perfectly true. They do, since they are produced in the teeth of the indifference or even hostility of the world around them by sheer dint of courage, tenacity, and genius. Even so, their creators need food and drink and a few other necessities and the few generous and understanding persons who provide these in times of necessity are indispensable. If one considers the word 'indispensable' one will soon realize that I am not giving too much attention to that otherwise unknown business man, Michael Puchberg, to whom the world is so much indebted; for without Puchberg the opera *Così fan Tutte* might never have been written and Mozart might have died a year earlier than he did and before the composition of *Die Zauberflöte*.

Così fan Tutte (K.588) was commissioned by the Emperor Joseph II some time in the middle of 1789, the Emperor possibly being reminded of Mozart's existence by the successful revival of *Figaro* in Vienna in August 1789. Mozart entered it in his catalogue as finished in January 1790 – no doubt by the aid of Puchberg's florins – and it was produced on January 26, 1790, and had, like most of Mozart's works, a *succès d'estime* but no popular success. It was performed ten times during 1790 and was then dropped. It could not possibly have had any other fate since even today – nearly a hundred and fifty years later – it is far beyond the comprehension of the average musician and music-lover.

As the reader will probably think this an exaggeration I shall give him an example of what a well-known musical critic has said about this opera in a book on Mozart written as recently as 1935. Mr Eric Blom, who is certainly a genuine admirer and appreciator of Mozart's music, writes:

> The supreme joke is that one cannot possibly help seeing the utter harmlessness of this mildly amusing piece which contains nothing so seriously unpleasant as the Count's pursuit of Susanna in *Figaro*. Nor is it possible to see how anyone could fail to be captivated by its deliberately and delectably artificial music.

Mr Blom – and I once more repeat that I only select Mr Blom because of his superiority in learning and taste to the majority of Mozart idolaters – has in the same book declared that Mozart

> cannot, in fact, be called one of the world's most distinctive melodists, for the plain truth is that he is often, even in his greatest works, content to use tunes that are part of the common stock of the composers of his time . . . others have been much more individual in their inventions including minor masters like Borodin or Grieg or Chab-

rier and composers of far less taste like Tchaikovsky and Puccini, who have written far more personal and more immediately striking music and found compensation for the lack of the most judicious artistry in a much more easily gained and general popularity.

Now, I quote this because Mr Blom has here perfectly expressed what is the considered opinion of a great body of musicians past, present and possibly to come; but which opinion is, I maintain, utterly wrong. Mozart is not superior to the composers named by Mr Blom (and to most others!) because he is 'incapable of the slightest offence against good taste'. Mozart was, on the contrary, a constant offender against what was considered good taste in his day and against what is still considered good taste today. Mr Blom's own contradictory reference to the 'seriously unpleasant' in *Figaro* is in itself a witness to this fact. The truth is that we mediocre men cannot even imagine what it is to be a great man like Mozart or Shakespeare and to be thus free from the domination of the contemporary prejudices, beliefs, morals, artistic rules, scruples (call them what you will!) with which even the most enlightened of us are – often unconsciously – obsessed.

The truth about Mozart is quite the contrary to what Mr Blom and nearly all other critics and musicians maintain. The truth, as I see it and as I have written this book to demonstrate, is that Mozart was a wholly superior man, intensely serious, deeply compassionate, almost all-comprehending, with a profound understanding of life and a universal sympathy with human beings that reminds one of Shakespeare and is in distinct contrast to Beethoven and Tolstoy. This superiority is an essential part of his nature and therefore of his musical genius. The greater includes the less. Mozart as a melodist is the greatest there has ever been; his melodies are purer and more beautiful than any others because they come from a purer source. While Beethoven could be described for the greater part as a flame (to borrow Artur Schnabel's description of Toscanini) Mozart was a spring, a fountain of the creative spirit, which ran more purely, less muddied and yet more variedly because it came from a deeper source than any other in the history of music. To say that the originator of such melodies as *Dove sono*, *Voi che sapete* – to say nothing of hundreds of exquisitely lovely themes throughout his instrumental and ecclesiastical music – was not one of the world's 'most distinctive melodists' can only mean that Mozart's melodies are too beautiful for ordinary ears – which is undoubtedly true.

The death of the Emperor Joseph II and the accession of Leopold II to the Austrian throne on March 13, 1790, did no good to Mozart. Salieri retired from the conductorship of the opera and was succeeded by his pupil, Joseph Weigl. Mozart's candidature for the second Kapellmeistership was unsuccessful. The coronation of Leopold II took place in Frankfurt-am-Main on October 9, 1790. Salieri as Court Kapellmeister, his assistant Umlauf and fifteen musicians were taken to Frankfurt in the retinue of the Emperor but not Mozart, who, however, in view of his desperate financial plight and the possibility of having a large audience among the visitors to the Coronation, pawned his silver plate and decorations to pay his expenses and took along with him his even poorer brother-in-law, the violinist Hofer. They set off on September 23rd. He writes from Frankfurt-am-Main to his wife as follows:

September 28, 1790.

. . . The journey was very pleasant; we had fine weather except for one day. . . . In Regensburg we had a splendid midday meal and had capital music, an English reception and a first-rate Mosel wine. We had breakfast in Nürnberg – a hideous town. At Würzburg we strengthened our poor stomachs with coffee – a fine, beautiful town – the expenses everywhere were moderate.

I await with longing news from you, of your health, of our circumstances, etc.[1] and am quite determined to do the best I can here and return happily to you. What a splendid life we shall lead. I shall work – work so hard – in order that I shall not again through unforeseen circumstances get into such a desperate position. . . .

September 30, 1790.

. . . My love, I shall certainly make something here – but not as much as you and various friends have imagined. . . .

As I do not know whether you are in Vienna or Baden[2] I address

[1] A reference to an attempt to raise a loan of a thousand florins through Hoffmeister.

[2] This Baden is not Baden-Baden but a small place in delightful country outside Vienna.

this letter again to Hofer. I am as gay as a child at the thought of seeing you again. If people could look into my heart I should be almost ashamed it is so cold – ice-cold. If you were with me perhaps I should find more pleasure in people's kind behaviour to me – but my heart is so empty – *adieu.* . . .

October 3, 1790.

. . . I had so determined to write immediately the Adagio for the clockmaker[1] so that my dear wife may have a few ducats in her hand, and I did it but was unluckily – as it is a most hateful work – unable to complete it. . . . I write every day . . . if it were for a great clock and the thing sounded like an organ then I should enjoy it, but the work is for mere tiny piping, which sounds shrill and childish.

I live quite retired here and don't go out the whole morning but stick in my hole of a room and write. . . .

October 8, 1790.

. . . I beg you to fix up the business with Hoffmeister if you want me to return. If you could only see into my heart! There the wish to return and embrace you fights with the desire to bring home plenty of money. I have often the idea of travelling further but when I make myself consider this decision it always occurs to me how I should regret it if I had separated myself from my dear wife for so long on a very uncertain and perhaps fruitless quest . . . and then it is mere idle talk what they say one can make in the German cities – celebrated, admired and loved I certainly am here, but beyond that the people here are even more parsimonious than in Vienna. . . .

It is somewhere about this time that we may date the following postscript which I quote for its characteristic outburst of Mozart's lively and affectionate nature in gloomy circumstances. It is not certain to which of Mozart's letters of this period it belongs, as the original is only a fragment:

P.S. As I wrote the foregoing page many tears fell on the paper. But now let me be merry. Prepare yourself, kisses begin to fly around amazingly . . . what the devil! I see a crowd of them. Ha! ha! I've just caught three – they were delicious! You cannot answer this letter but you can address me poste restante Linz, that is the safest for I do not know whether I go to Regensburg or not . . . adieu dearest and best of little wives, take care of your health and don't go on foot in the town – write to me how you like our new lodging – adieu, I kiss thee a million times.

[1] (K.594).

October 15, 1790.

I am still without any news in reply to my Frankfurt letters which disquiets me not a little. To-day at eleven my concert took place, which as far as reputation is concerned was superb but the result as regards money is meagre....

At this concert Mozart played his own Concertos in F major (K.459) and D (K.537). On his way back to Vienna he heard a performance of *Figaro* at Mannheim; he played at the Elector's Court in Munich at the beginning of November and arrived soon after in Vienna, no better off than he had left it. His sore lack of money would not have been such a burden had it not been for his wife Constanze, who clearly seems to have had no inkling of the real stature of Mozart but saw in him only a musician of talent, but one who had never won popular success and who indeed very likely, in her opinion, was inferior as a composer to such great figures as Dittersdorf,[1] Salieri, etc. who in contemporary opinion and in Court favour were much more important than Mozart. In December 1790, the English impresario Salomon came to Vienna and induced Joseph Haydn to accompany him back and produce a number of compositions for the Philharmonic Society in London. Haydn left Vienna on December 12th and Mozart probably saw him off. Salomon apparently suggested a similar trip to Mozart to be made after Haydn's return; in the meantime Mozart received a letter, dated October 26, 1790, from the director of the Italian opera in London inviting him to stay in London from December 1790 to June 1791, and compose two opera for three hundred pounds sterling.

It may seem strange that Mozart did not accept this offer, but he probably did not want to leave his home again so soon. It is clear that he was crippled with debt at the end of 1790 and he probably could not raise the money for the journey; also, he may have been sceptical about the results. During that winter, however, he was busy composing, as the following entries in his Catalogue show:

1790 December   Quintet for two violins, two violas, 'cello, in D major (K.593).

---

[1] Dittersdorf, for example, was given a patent of nobility and a Government post.

1791 January 5	Pianoforte Concerto in B flat (K.595).
January 14	Three Songs:
	Sehnsucht nach dem Frühlinge (K.596).
	Im Frühlingsanfang (K.597).
	Das Kinderspiel (K.598).
January 23 }	Dances (K.599, 607, 609, 611).
March 6 }	
March 3	Piece for Clock in F minor (K.608).
March 8	Aria for bass with obbligato contrabass, *Per questa bella mano* (K.612).
	Variations for Pianoforte on *Ein Weib ist das herrlichste Ding* (K. 613).
April 12	Quintet for two violins, two violas, one 'cello, in E flat (K.614).
April 20	Chorus for Sarti's opera *Le Gelosie Villane*, *Viviamo felici* (K.615).
May 4	Andante for waltz on a small barrel-organ in F (K.616).
May 23	Adagio and Rondo for harmonica, flute, oboe, viola and 'cello in C minor (K.617).
June 18 (in Baden)	Motet *Ave, Verum Corpus* (K.618).
July	German Cantata for solo voice and pianoforte *Die ihr des unermesslichen Weltalls Schöpfer ehrt* (K.119).

Again, through the spring of 1791, Mozart was compelled to borrow money from Puchberg to keep himself going. In May he wrote a letter to the magistrates asking to be nominated as successor to the Kapellmeister Hoffmann at the Cathedral of St Stephen's as Hoffman was ill and advanced in years.[1]

In the summer of 1791 his wife again went to Baden for her health – she was expecting another child – while Mozart stayed in Vienna working at the opera *Die Zauberflöte* which the actor-manager and writer Schikaneder had asked him to compose, supplying him with a libretto which he himself had made up out of elements taken from Wieland's oriental story *Lulu*, which were combined by Mozart and Schikaneder into a rhapsody on the virtues of Freemasonry. Schikaneder and Mozart were fellow-masons and it is fair to assume that Mozart had as great a hand in

[1] His request was granted; he was nominated as assistant without salary and as successor, but it was too late. Mozart never lived to succeed.

the fashioning of the libretto as his friend, Schikaneder; also, from their respective characters, we may be sure that Mozart was chiefly responsible for giving the fairy-tale a serious symbolical expression. Mozart writes to his wife as follows:

June 11, 1791.

. . . I cannot tell you what I would give to be with you in Baden instead of sitting here. Out of sheer weariness I have composed to-day an aria of my opera. . . .

June 12, 1791.

Why have I had no letter yesterday? . . . It is not good for me to be alone when I have something on my mind. . . .

In order to raise my spirits I went to the new opera *Kaspar der Fagottist*[1] which has made such a stir, but there is nothing in it. . . .

[To Michael Puchberg]

June 25, 1791.

. . . I have a request to make. My wife writes that she notices that they would like to see some money on account of the lodging and also to cover expenses for food and she desires me to send her some. As I expected to settle everything on her departure I am now in a fix. I don't want to disturb my poor wife with these unpleasant explanations but I can't leave myself quite destitute. If you my best friend can help me so that I can send something you will do me a great favour – it is only a matter of a few days before you will receive in my name two thousand florins with which you can immediately settle my debt to you.[2]

[To Constanze]

July 2, 1791.

. . . I beg you to tell that lad Süssmayer he is to send me my copy of the first act from the introduction to the finale so that I can instrument it. . . .[3]

July 6, 1791.

. . . You cannot give me greater pleasure than by being happy and gay for if only I am certain that you are all right then my troubles are light and easy for the fatal and strained position I am in becomes a mere trifle if I only know that you are well and happy. . . .

July 7, 1791.

. . . Now I wish for nothing but that my business were finished so that I could be with you again. You cannot imagine how the time

[1] An opera by Wenzel Müller.
[2] Puchberg sent him twenty-five florins.
[3] *Die Zauberflöte.*

here has gone without you. I can't explain my feeling, it is a certain emptiness which makes me sad, a certain longing which is never satisfied and thus never ceases but is always present, even increases from day to day; when I think how merry and youthful we were together in Baden and what sad, tedious hours I pass here – my work also does not make me happy, accustomed as I am till now to pause and exchange a few words with you which is now unfortunately impossible. If I go to the pianoforte and begin something out of the opera[1] I have to stop immediately as it affects me too much. . . . *Basta!* . . .

It is quite clear from these letters that Mozart was in an abnormal state of sensibility. The persistent ill-luck, hard work and scarcity of money which had now gone on for years with no prospect of improvement was sapping his vitality. There is another cause of strain, too, which is generally overlooked, and that is the inevitable intellectual and spiritual isolation in which a man of such genius is necessarily condemned to live. It is this which was responsible for Mozart's craving for the affectionate companionship of his wife. On July 26th Mozart's youngest son, Wolfgang, was born in Baden and somewhere about this time Lorenzo da Ponte, according to his account in his *Memorie*, tried to induce him to go to London with him; but he says that Mozart 'was occupied with composing his German opera *Die Zauberflöte* and asked for six months' delay', to which da Ponte could not agree.

Another invitation was received about the same time and it was from a Count Franz von Walsegg who commissioned Mozart to write a Requiem in memory of the Count's wife. The Count was a good amateur musician and used to order compositions anonymously and pretend to be the author.[2] He sent his steward, who was 'the mysterious stranger' so often referred to in biographies of Mozart – on this errand and Mozart agreed to compose the Requiem. He had hardly started on this when he received an order to compose a new opera for the approaching coronation of Leopold II as King of Bohemia at Prague. This order came to Mozart through the Bohemians and not through the Emperor; so once again we owe an opera of Mozart's to the people of Prague

[1] *Die Zauberflöte.*
[2] He re-wrote Mozart's score and had the work performed from his duplicate on December 14, 1793.

who were his truest and most consistent admirers during his lifetime.

The subject selected was Metastasio's *La Clemenza di Tito* re-
modelled by the Court poet of Saxony, Caterino Mazzolà. About
the middle of August Mozart set out for Prague, accompanied by
his wife and his pupil, Süssmayer. He had to work at the opera
during the journey, making sketches in the carriage and con-
tinuing his work at night in the inns they stayed at. The opera was
due for performance on September 6th in Prague and was completed in eighteen days. Süssmayer is supposed to have written
the secco recitatives but nothing else. According to Niemetschek,
Mozart was very unwell when he arrived in Prague and was continually taking medicine during his stay. It is not surprising under
the circumstances that *La Clemenza di Tito* (K.621) is not one of
Mozart's greatest operatic works and those who think genius
cannot be frustrated or hampered by circumstances may be confronted with the fact that given other circumstances *La Clemenza
di Tito* might have been another masterpiece.[1] Nevertheless the
opera achieved later a certain measure of popularity. It was the
first of Mozart's operas to be performed in London[2] and it remained in the German operatic repertory throughout most of the
nineteenth century. There is a good deal of fine music in this
opera. Professor Dent has remarked on the beauty of the two
duets, *Deh prendi* and *Ah perdona*, the melody of the latter being
that, he says, which apparently inspired Shelley's 'I arise from
dreams of thee'. Other gems are Vitellia's second aria (22, 23) and
the fine choral finale to the first act, already mentioned.

The new opera was not an immediate success even in Prague
and Mozart returned to Vienna in the middle of September, un-
solaced and in ill-health, to complete *Die Zauberflöte* and the
Requiem. The chorus *O Isis and Osiris* was written after September 12th and the overture and march of the priests was completed on September 28th.

---

[1] Mozart took his opera seriously and thought highly of Mazzolà's adaptation of
Metastasio's text. It is questionable whether this opera has received the estimation
it deserves. It contains a choral scene which is one of the finest achievements of
Mozart.
[2] In 1806.

His wife went again to Baden while Mozart stayed in Vienna. A brief happiness was granted him by the unexpected success of *Die Zauberflöte*, which was produced in Vienna on September 30th. Even so, this was not unalloyed, because the success was due more to Schikaneder's tomfooleries than to Mozart's music, and the profundity of Mozart's conception in handling the raw material of this opera completely escaped nine out of ten opera-goers then as it does to this day.[1] That this is not mere fancy on my part can be proved from Mozart's own correspondence. For example, in a letter to his wife in Baden dated Vienna, October 8th and 9th, he writes about an acquaintance who went to hear *Die Zauberflöte*:

> . . . showed himself such a Philistine that I could not remain or I should have had to call him an ass. . . . Unluckily I was in the theatre when the second act began; in the ceremonial [*feierlichen*] scene he laughed at everything; at first I was patient enough to want to draw his attention to some things but he was always laughing; that was too much for me. I called him Papageno and went out. I do not believe, however, that he understood. . . .

The significance of Mozart calling this dolt Papageno will not be lost on those who understand Mozart and *Die Zauberflöte*. When, towards the end of October, Constanze returned from Baden, Mozart did not conceal his state of mind. One fine autumn day when they were sitting in the beautiful Prater, Mozart spoke of his approaching death and told Constanze that he was composing the Requiem for himself. He also said that he must have taken poison.[2] In November Mozart had a slight recovery and

---

[1] If this is thought an exaggeration I refer the reader to the excellent performances at Glyndebourne since 1935 under Fritz Busch. Even these are spoiled by occasional facetiousness and the introduction of asides in English to tickle the dull ears of the public.

[2] The idea that Mozart was poisoned by Salieri is, of course, ridiculous. Mediocre men do not need to poison geniuses; they have nothing to fear from them. But the idea was very prevalent in Vienna long after Mozart's death and his own statement is only a sign of the obscure nature of his death. [Turner included as an Appendix an article by a French doctor, J. Barraud, written in 1905, entitled *A quelle maladie a succombé Mozart?* His diagnosis was that Mozart had died of Bright's Disease. However, over fifty other articles have been written on the subject; from all the evidence it is clear that Mozart was not poisoned, and that he died of some disease hastened by overwork, worry and malnutrition. *C.R.*]

composed a cantata (K.623) for a Masonic festival, and then continued working at the Requiem. The landlord of the *Silberne Schlange*, Joseph Deiner, has related how in the winter of 1790 he called on Mozart one day and found him and Constanze dancing up and down his workroom; on his asking him whether he was teaching his wife dancing Mozart replied: 'We are making ourselves warm because we are very cold and have no money for fuel.' One day in November 1791, Mozart came to Deiner's inn and ordered a drink, but sat there with his hand on his head and did not touch it and on the next day Deiner called and was informed that Mozart was very ill in bed. He was taken into his room and when Mozart saw him he could be just heard to say: 'Nothing today, Joseph; we have to do with doctors and apothecaries today.'

A Dr Closset attended him and on November 28th he called in Dr Sallaba, the chief physician at the hospital. During the fortnight he was confined to his bed Mozart never lost consciousness. His canary, of which he was very fond and to which he often referred in his letters home, when he was travelling, was removed, to his distress, to another room. He used to follow in imagination the performance of *Die Zauberflöte* every evening with his watch laid beside him. The day before his death he said to his wife: 'I should like to have heard my *Zauberflöte* once more,' and began to hum the birdcatcher's song. Kapellmeister Roser, who was at his bedside, went to the pianoforte and played it to his great pleasure. The Requiem was also constantly in his mind. The afternoon before his death, according to Schack who was present, he had the score brought to his bed and sang the alto part, while Schack took the soprano, Hofer the tenor and Gerl the bass.[1] When they got to the first bars of the Lacrimosa Mozart burst into a fit of weeping and laid the score aside.

Towards evening when his sister-in-law came Mozart said to her: 'I am glad you are here; stay with me tonight and see me die.' She tried to reason him out of this conviction but he replied: 'I

[1] Benedikt Schack, tenor and flautist, was the original Tamino, Franz Xaver Gerl, the first Sarastro, and Franz Hofer, the violinist, was married to Mozart's sister-in-law, Josepha.

have the flavour of death on my tongue – I taste death and who will support my dearest Constanze if you do not stay with her?' She left him at the wish of her sister to induce a priest from St Peter's 'to come as if by chance'; but it was only with difficulty that one could be found to come. This, no doubt, was due to Mozart's connection with Freemasonry. On her return she found Mozart talking to Süssmayer about the Requiem. Later in the evening the physician arrived and ordered cold compresses. Mozart lost consciousness and became delirious and in his delirium was evidently still occupied with the Requiem, or, at any rate, with music, for in his unconsciousness he kept blowing out his cheeks as if imitating trumpets. About midnight he raised himself from his bed, opened his eyes, lay down with his face to the wall and at 12.55 on the morning of December 5, 1791, he died, aged thirty-five.

Constanze became completely prostrate and the wealthy Baron van Swieten made all the funeral arrangements. As if inspired directly by God he arranged for the cheapest burial possible (third-class) at the cost of eight florins thirty-six kreutzer, with three florins for a hearse. A service was held at St Stefan's and the bier was carried through a storm to the churchyard of St Mark's. Van Swieten, Salieri, Süssmayer, Roser and the 'cellist Orsler were present at the service but found the weather too bad to accompany the body to the cemetery. No grave had been bought and nobody was present – not a single one of his friends or acquaintances – when the corpse of Mozart was flung into a common pauper's vault containing fifteen to twenty coffins. When his wife recovered and visited the churchyard there was a fresh gravedigger who could not tell her where Mozart had been buried. All subsequent attempts to discover the spot have been in vain. A more fitting end for this great genius could not be conceived. Shakespeare's 'Do not dig for my bones' was thus made superfluous.

Mozart left books and music to the value of twenty-three florins forty-one kreutzers and some furniture and household effects of the simplest character. Jahn, who saw the list which was printed in the *Deutsche Musik-Zeitung* in 1861, page 284, says:

'It is affecting to see how simple, even poverty-stricken, was the whole *ménage*.' Various people, including Stadler who had borrowed five hundred florins, owed Mozart money and his debts amounted to about three thousand florins. It must not be thought by the reader that the neglect and misunderstanding from which Mozart suffered during his lifetime when he was no longer a child-prodigy and a novelty ceased with his death. On the contrary, Mozart is as much misunderstood and as inadequately appreciated now as ever. The music shops of the world are full of fake pictures of him which are false in every respect; he is the victim of innumerable essays and biographies which reduce him to the size of the writer, while the majority of the performances of his works are painfully inadequate in conception and execution. But:

> The world knows nothing of its greatest men:
> Alive neglected and dishonoured dead,
> Renown on them its hydra-dark shall spread,
> Digging ten thousand graves for every ten;
> Fame on false headstones writes with ironic pen
> The glorious name, in the procrustean bed
> Of each man's mind a Dummy sleeps instead,
> Fitted to match exactly to his ken.

> The priests themselves, who think the god resides
> Within the temple, kneel to dead Desire
> In painted image – Enter! If you would know
> Where that Immortal Spirit now abides,
> Where springs again the every-mysterious Fire,
> Look in your heart whether its cinders glow.

CHAPTER SEVENTEEN

The Genius of Mozart

IT IS MY belief that the essential nature of genius is always the same whatever its sphere of manifestation. Therefore we can truly speak of the nature of genius apart from whether, in its objective materialization, it takes the form of music, poetry, mathematics, painting or any other non-realistic abstraction invented by the human mind. This 'essence' of genius is vividly suggested in the well-known saying of Goethe's:

> That glorious hymn *Veni Creator Spiritus* is really an appeal to genius. That is why it speaks so powerfully to men of intellect and power.

But we must be careful to discriminate between the emotion – however deep – expressed in the prayer: *Veni Creator!* which voices the desire for the coming of the creative spirit and the actual non-emotional functioning of the creative spirit when it has indeed come and *is* actually present.

Within historical times, at all epochs when there has been a pure apprehension of things rather than a mere Philistine interest in things, men and women have naturally regarded all exceptional powers as divine and coming from a spiritual source. Mozart's highly-gifted musical sister referring to her brother speaks of 'the talent given to him by God'. This may be accepted as voicing the instinctive popular recognition that genius is not only born and not made by industry applied to a talent; but also that it rather possesses the person than is possessed by him. A man 'possessed' necessarily acts otherwise than always sensibly and in his own interests; he can never achieve that purely reasonable goal of all self-education because he is controlled by, rather than in control of, a natural force. But this natural force which possesses

him is not without its laws, it is not irresponsible; if it were, then
genius would be the same thing as madness, to which it is ad-
mittedly akin. Is there a fundamental law of genius, and if so
what is it? Goethe has perhaps formulated it in his saying:

> The first and last thing required of genius is the love of truth.

This love of truth is quite a different thing from the love of
truths and must be clearly distinguished from it. The love of
truths is the necessary and useful passion of all unoriginating
minds for rules, formulas, prescriptions and methods which are
of proved utility and can be passed on to others. The 'truth' of
'truths' is purely pragmatic; it is therefore limited to time, place
and occasion which it must fit and it is this fittingness which con-
stitutes its truth. What, then, is this other 'truth' about which
Pilate asked his famous question? Now I would answer very
simply that it can be nothing else but the love of God.

A light on the meaning of this comes from what may be considered as a very odd quarter – namely, Schopenhauer. Schopenhauer has said in *The World as Will and Idea* that the fundamental
condition of genius is an abnormal predominance of sensibility
over the will and reproductive power. I believe that here we have
a clue to that opposition between self-assertion, the will of the
individual ego – which is an uncreative thing reproducing only
itself – and the selflessness of creative genius which is in itself a
pure love of God. In the case of Mozart his most striking characteristic is his abnormal or supernormal sensibility. Mozart as a
boy burst into tears when he was over-praised. Can one imagine
the type which Keats has so well distinguished from men of
genius, but which, I think, he not too happily describes as 'men
of power' – can one think of such a one, an Edison ('Genius is
one per cent inspiration and ninety-nine per cent perspiration'),
a Napoleon or a Stalin bursting into tears at lavish praise?

The modesty of men of genius is not ignorance. This has been
well noted by the observation of Miguel de Unamuno that there
is 'a certain characteristic common to all those whom we call
geniuses. Each of them has a consciousness of being a man apart.'
The modest Mozart calmly informs his father in a letter from

Vienna how the Archduke Maximilian had remarked that such a man as he (Mozart) does not come into the world more than once in a hundred years. I am convinced that this remark made about himself did not in the least surprise Mozart because he knew it already and here we have the key to what might seem – and actually did seem to Mozart's father, Leopold – a baffling change in his nature.

'As a boy you were excessively modest and serious,' complains Leopold in a letter to his son, 'but now you turn everything to joking; your character seems to have entirely changed.' Actually what had happened was that, after puberty and his contact as an adult with the rest of the world and the prolonged practice of his art among other musicians, Mozart had come to a fuller realization of himself and his powers and now knew himself for what he was. Nothing could depress him, nothing seemed serious to him compared with this overwhelming secret of which he had become conscious that he was born to the happiness of praising God in music. A rose bush bursting into blossom does not need advice and Mozart, in whom this hidden joyous creativeness now was fully functioning, could not take anything else seriously at all.

But, even so, this love of God is only the energy, the mainspring of genius. We have more to discover when we examine its functioning. It is here pertinent to recall what Samuel Johnson had to say of genius because of the Doctor's colossal commonsense and uncommon penetration. Johnson said: 'The true genius is a mind of large general powers, accidentally determined to some particular direction.' This, as far as it goes, is certainly true. The word 'genius' ought not to be applied to gifted men of a minor category in whom their particular talent seems to derive from an absence of other possibly inhibiting qualities, i.e. from a minus rather than a plus endowment as human beings. Indeed, this is the deciding factor between talent and genius. The true genius is always a great man in the fullest meaning of the word 'great'. He is a superior man, a man in every respect above the average, a man who includes, comprehends and surpasses the majority. And as he surpasses them in goodness he can surpass them in badness – 'Genius even,' said Emerson, 'as it is the greatest good is the greatest harm.' And why is the man of genius capable of the greatest evil as of the greatest good? Because of the predominance of his sensibility: 'A person of genius should marry a person of character,' once wrote that curious American writer, Oliver Wendell Holmes, and this remark, though its biological inferences are probably not sound, is useful as a perhaps un-conscious testimony to the fundamental principle of genius – which Schopenhauer has enunciated and which Keats discovered for himself – that there is a certain antithesis or repulsion or in-compatibility between genius and what we call 'character'; in that genius is of its very nature unstable and chameleon-like by virtue of its supersensitive universality there we may recall the uncon-scious testimony of Schachtner on Mozart: 'I believe . . . he might have become a profligate – he was so ready to yield to every attraction which offered.'

Actually, the man of genius is kept from subsiding into evil by force of that mysterious attraction which we may find symbolized in the myth of the good and the evil angels – on the one side Michael and his fellows who were faithful, and on the other Satan and his fellows who instead of loving God turned to hating Him, because they loved themselves more. It is significant that no poet has succeeded in portraying the antithesis of Satan as vividly as Milton has portrayed Satan; but to do so it would be necessary to indicate clearly that Michael (taking Michael as the antithesis) contained all the potentialities of Satan. In other words, if a poet is to create a convincing symbol of goodness, he must succeed in making it include evil – comprehending, assimilating and con-suming it.

The man of genius is a man of good and evil and that is the explanation why Mozart, who wrote the Isis and Osiris chorus of *Die Zauberflöte*, the *Ave Verum* and numerous other pieces of the purest single-minded ecstasy, also wrote the Queen of Night music *Don Giovanni*, *Così fan Tutte*, *Figaro* and other, wholly instru-mental, works in which the elements of darkness and light are both present.

But beyond all this the man of genius not only possesses a mind of larger general powers but has, as its foundation, a physical vitality much above the normal. We do not know exactly what is meant by 'vitality', but we can feel it, and we feel it in the work of all men of genius. This extra vitality, it may be, is connected with their double-intellect – which Schopenhauer considered to be a chief characteristic. There is the normal consciousness functioning in life purposively for the usual practical ends of the individual in his environment and as a social animal and there is the extra-consciousness which is dominant and is always dealing with generalities and creating a synthesis which has no practical bearing whatever and is of no use to the genius as a man, but rather a hindrance. And as a man of genius grows older he comes to realize that his genius is nothing but a hindrance and a handicap to his success as an individual man, struggling for the usual aims of the individual – his livelihood and security in the society of his fellows, to say nothing of personal happiness and repose in human relationship.

There is one aspect of genius to which I shall only make the briefest reference and it is, that I believe that *intellectually* all men of genius are hermaphroditic. How this comes about and what the particular nature of this synthesis of masculine and feminine elements is I do not wish to discuss here. Mozart (and, as far as we know, also Shakespeare) was passionately fond of women and had not got either the physical or the psychological traits of either of the two main classes of homosexuals who are unattracted by women. Nevertheless, there is a duality of intellect in Mozart which is very striking indeed, just as there is in Shakespeare, and it is this which gives his work its extraordinary comprehensiveness.

It remains to draw attention to a certain characteristic of Mozart's music which does not obviously apply to all his works but is nevertheless a general quality which pervades all and of which he himself was certainly aware and was referring to when he said that music, whatever the intensity of the passions and thoughts it was expressing, must always remain music. I cannot do better than extract something of what I have said before on this point, with certain emendations that increased experience has suggested to me.

Mr Bernard Shaw once remarked that nothing could be more uncharacteristic of Mozart than the portraits of the beautiful young man exhibited above his name in all the music-shops of the world today. These portraits show Mozart as the most handsome, the most regular-featured of all great composers. Such 'classic' proportions seem at first sight to be peculiarly appropriate to a composer who is universally admired as the classic of classics. Where else in music shall we find those qualities of serenity, limpidity, simplicity, lucidity, which we concentrate in one adjective, 'Mozartian'? It is impossible in music to find a parallel to that flawless perfection. Whether we take a whole opera – such as *Le Nozze de Figaro* – or a mere scrap scribbled impromptu on the page of a visitor's book – such as the Gigue written in 1789 for the Leipzig organist, Engel – we are confronted with a completely finished musical composition in which there is not a superfluous bar, not a redundant or meaningless note. There is no 'waste' in Mozart – no overlapping, no exaggeration, no strain, no vagueness, no distortion, no suggestion. He is so pure that he seems often meaningless. His music *disappears*, like the air we breathe on a transparent day. All those who have really appreciated Mozart will admit that at one time or another they have felt certain Mozart masterpieces as one would feel a still, bright, perfect, cloudless day. Such a day has no meaning, none of the suggestiveness, the 'atmosphere', the character of a day of cloud or storm, or of any day in which there is a mixture of warring elements whose significance has yet to appear. Such a day does not provoke or in the faintest degree suggest one mood rather than another. It is infinitely protean. It means just what you mean. It is intangible, immaterial – fitting your spirit like a glove. Thus, as Sir Charles Stanford has said, when you are a child Mozart speaks to you as a child – no music could be more simple, more childlike – but when you are a man you find to your astonishment that this music which seemed childlike is completely adult and mature. At every age this pure pellucid day, this intangible transparency, awaits you and envelops you in its unruffled light. Then suddenly there will pass through you a tremor of terror. A moment comes when that tranquillity, that perfection will take on a ghastly ambiguity. That music still suggests nothing, nothing at all; it is just infinitely ambiguous. Then you may remember the phrase of a German critic who wrote of the 'demoniacal ring' of Mozart. Then you look at a genuine portrait of Mozart, and instead of that smooth regular young beauty you see a straight jutting profile with a too-prominent nose and an extraordinary salience of the upper lip, and for an instant you feel as if you have had a revelation. But that revelation escapes you as suddenly as it came, and you are left face to face with a mask whose directness and clarity is completely baffling.

One may speak often of a movement of Mozart just as a mathematician might speak of a beautiful proposition. Whereas in the music of most composers it is a case of content *and* structure, it is with Mozart a case of structure only, for there is no perceptible content – *ubi materia ibi geometria*. This is strikingly shown in the overture to *Le Nozze de Figaro*. I would suggest to the reader that he should buy the gramophone records of this overture and of Rossini's overture to *Il Barbiere di Siviglia* and compare them. The difference is astonishing. Rossini was born the year after Mozart's death; he also had the advantage of following instead of preceding Beethoven and he was a composer of striking natural genius. But, after *Figaro*, listen to *Il Barbiere di Siviglia* overture, with its alluring tunefulness over its easy *tum-ti, tum-ti, tum-ti* bass, and you will be struck with its straggling formlessness. Its tunes are very engaging, but you can carry them away with you and hear them mentally on a penny whistle, a cornet, or any instrument you like. They are like bright threads in a commonplace piece of stuff which you can pull out without compunction as there is no design to spoil. But you can do nothing of the sort with the *Figaro* overture. There are no bright threads to pull out. There is no melodic content as such. You cannot even hear the music in your memory apart from the rush of the strings and the accents of the woodwind. It cannot be played upon the piano. Take away a note of it and the whole is completely disintegrated. Nor can anyone put his hand upon his heart and say what feeling that music arouses in his breast. It is completely without expression, as expression is vulgarly understood; but the oftener you hear it the more excited you become, the more passionate grow your asseverations that there was never music like this before or since. Its effect upon the mind is out of all proportion to its impingement on the senses. To hear it is as though one has been present at a miracle and had seen a mountain of matter blown into a transparent bubble and float vanishing into the sky. Your desire to hear that overture again and again and again is the simple but intense desire to see the miracle repeated. It is an astonishing experience, and it is an experience which Mozart is constantly giving us.

It would be useless to attempt to explain this peculiar intellectual gift which was Mozart's to a degree that separates him from all other composers. It must just be stated and left. But there are certain facts known about Mozart which are so relevant to this point that they should be mentioned now. He was exceptionally good at dancing and playing billiards, which were his two chief pleasures. He was small, but his limbs, feet and hands were beautifully proportioned. He composed away from any muscial instrument entirely in his head, and could complete the whole of a work, from the first note to the last, and then write it down – often weeks or more later – from memory. Thus the overture to *Don Giovanni*, which was written on the night of October 28, 1787, for the first performance of the opera in Prague on the next day, while his wife kept him awake by telling him fairy-stories, was not composed on that night but merely copied out from memory. He would often compose at meals, and while composing would take his napkin by two corners and continually fold and re-fold it very neatly and exactly. To me this is all extraordinarily illuminating. Conciseness – even conciseness so unparalleled and amazing as Mozart's – is not surprising in a composer who could work in this way. One also cannot but think that his invariable serenity and good temper – upon which all who knew him have left comment – was yet another sign of perfect physical and mental poise. It is on record that Mozart never used glasses and that his eyesight was perfect at his death in spite of the strain which manuscript music imposes. This, also, is not without significance. Mozart's mental grip never loosens; he never abandons

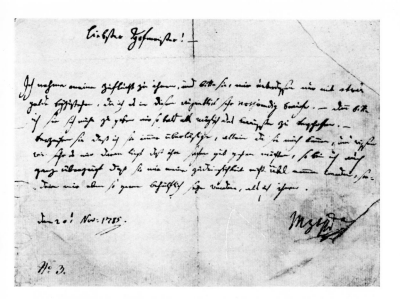

15a. Facsimile of a Letter from Mozart to his Publisher, Hoffmeister

15b. First effort in choral writing

Office of THE NEW STATESMAN AND NATION
10 Great Turnstile, High Holborn, London, W.C. 1

For the New Statesman I am naturally obliged not t' seem too extravagant in my praise, especially as I am not overgiven t' praise; but in this personal way I want t' tell you how deeply I feel about these Mozart productions at Glyndebourne. I doubt if production of this high quality has ever been known before. Certainly nothing of the kind has ever been given in Great Britain. Not t' take this opportunity of hearing Mozart's great works so wonderfully produced without cuts — is t' risk missing one of the finest artistic experiences that it is possible t' have.

W. J. Turner

16. Postcard written by the Author after a pre-war Glyndebourne Festival; the 1951 Glyndebourne production of *Idomeneo* was dedicated to his memory

himself to any one sense; even at his most ecstatic moments his mind is vigorous, alert and on the wing. It is from this astounding elasticity that his conciseness largely derives. Most artists are unable to tear themselves away from the most delightful discoveries; they linger on them and handle them fondly, but not Mozart. He dives unerringly on to his finest ideas like a bird of prey, and once an idea is seized he soars off again with undiminished power.

It is not astonishing that a mind so well-balanced as Mozart's should show so great a sense of humour. In this he surpasses all other composers and, as the sense of humour is essentially intellectual, it is natural that Mozart, the most intellectual of composers, should be the greatest master of comic opera. But what might be altogether unexpected is his power to make one's flesh creep. Nothing has ever been written of such truly diabolical verve as the aria for the Queen of the Night in *Die Zauberflöte*. It is the rarest event to find a light soprano who can sing this at all; it is certain that we shall never have it sung so as to do full justice to its startlingly cold-blooded ferocity. And yet that aria has the smooth, glassy surface of a mere bit of coloratura virtuosity; but it is the surface of ice beneath which is a fathomless black water. This sinister ambiguity is a quality quite apart from the more familiar power of striking the imagination which he shows in the music which announces and accompanies the entrance of the statue at the supper-party in the last act of *Don Giovanni*.[1] Yet I would like to insist that there is another and even more troubling quality in Mozart's music. Linked with the 'demoniacal ring', which is probably the result of that bareness which makes Mozart's music appear a mere rhythmical skeleton beside the work of more sensuous composers such as Brahms and Wagner (but a skeleton of electric vitality!) there is a pro-

[1] This is an example of Gluck's precept of using music to enforce the dramatic situation such as was, possibly, within the power of Gluck himself to achieve. But that complex and subtle musical propriety which consists in writing ensemble music in which a number of characters are differentiated psychologically and yet have their separate musical expression coherently combined in a convincing and harmonious form, absolutely beautiful in its proportions and meaning, was not so highly developed by Gluck as by Mozart, for whom music was not a means of enforcing the expression of the poetry but was the very expression and poetry itself.

L

foundly disturbing melancholy. It is never active in Mozart's
work as it is frequently in the work of Tchaikovsky, in Brahms,
in Chopin, and even in Beethoven. It is a still, unplumbed melancholy underlying even his brightest and most vivacious movements. It is this which gives his music that ambiguity to which I
have drawn attention, an ambiguity which makes one sometimes
find a peculiar, all-pervading, transparent gloom in Mozart's
music. I am not even sure that 'gloom' and 'melancholy' are the
right words to use. Mozart is very mysterious – far more mysterious than Beethoven, because his music *seems* to express much
less of his human character. But the mystery lies also in Mozart
himself and there for the present we will let it remain.

CHAPTER EIGHTEEN

The Comic and Tragic in Mozart's Operas

DON GIOVANNI

MUSICAL HISTORIANS WRITE at length about the genesis of opera and go into great detail on this subject. I prefer to be as brief as possible. The origin of opera is threefold; or we may say that it has a threefold root in Poetry, Dancing and Music. No matter how opera develops in the future its seeming changes of form will depend upon the balance and adjustment of these three primary factors. In every good opera, in every opera that is a work of art by a truly creative composer, these three elements are differently combined. We approve of and enjoy all these different combinations according as we are in the mood for this or that proportion of the primary ingredients. The human need for change in order that each element may be freshly experienced is what promotes the so-called new developments; but these new developments are new only in the sense that each opera composed by a musician of genius is a fresh solution of the problem of combining the three primary elements and of making at the same time a creation which is absolutely his. The creative genius not only solves a problem, but his solution is an individual offspring with a life and character of its own.

Instead, therefore, of giving the reader a lengthy description of the development of opera in Italy during the sixteenth and seventeenth centuries, illustrated by the names of Peri (1561–1633), Caccini (1545–1618), Cavalieri (1550–1602), Monteverdi

(1567–1643), Legrenzi (1626–90), Stradella (*c.* 1645–82), Carissimi (1605–74), Cesti (1620–69), Cavalli (1602–76), Alessandro Scarlatti (1660–1725), etc. I shall just present this history, up to Mozart, abbreviated into the following diagram:

THE GENEALOGY OF OPERA

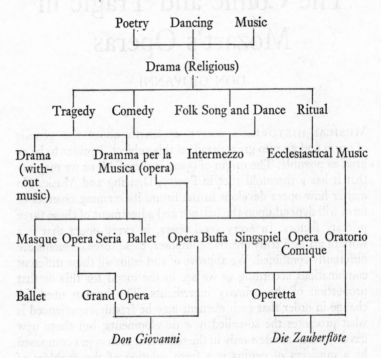

If we take the six best-known operas of Mozart's we shall find that *Idomeneo* is an example of opera seria – i.e. an opera in which there is no comedy – springing as it does in my diagrammatic scheme from the 'Tragedy' division; that *Die Entführung* is an example of singspiel – i.e. a derivation from Comedy and the more popular sort of Italian variety show known as Intermezzo; that *Figaro* is an example of opera buffa; and that in *Die Zauberflöte* we have a unique example of the combination of singspiel and Oratorio or Cantata. This leaves us with the two other master-pieces, *Don Giovanni* and *Così fan Tutte*. In these two great works the two forms: (1) Opera Seria and (2) Opera Buffa – i.e. of Tragedy and Comedy – are for the first time in the history of opera perfectly united into one, and we may take as a sign that Mozart was aware of this new unity the fact that he described each of them as a *dramma giocoso* instead of *opera buffa*.[1] It is also significant that these two works are precisely those which have most puzzled musicians, musicologists and music-lovers during the past hundred years.

What puzzles the average person is just this strange blend of the tragic and the comic. Most people like to have these elements carefully separated into different works of art so that they may feel safe. They are prepared to look upon life either as a comedy or a tragedy, since, in such a presentation, life is made a little less real and provides a form of escape, a convention or refuge. One may thus laugh or weep to the full, knowing in one's heart that life is not quite like this; it is neither so comic nor so tragic. When, however, a major dramatist like Shakespeare (or, on a smaller scale, Ibsen or Tchekov) combines in one piece the tragic and the comic, the average person does not know where he is. Is he meant to laugh or weep? Is the author truly serious or is he laughing up his sleeve? Not only does the auditor feel that his leg is being pulled, but he is not quite sure which leg, and that spoils the whole thing for him. The history of the reception of Shakespeare's plays by the French is an example of a whole nation (with rare exceptions) being outraged by what seemed to its logical genius a frantic illogicality, amounting almost to lunacy. But the French are not the only ones to suspect lunacy. English Shakespearean criticism is tainted with the suspicion that Hamlet is more or less mad, and perhaps Shakespeare, too.

Now in Mozart we have an exact musical parallel to Shake-speare. Critics have been perplexed to exhaustion by the question whether *Don Giovanni* is or is not a comic opera. Can an opera be comic when its chief character ends by being dragged down to Hell in flames to music of awe-inspiring solemnity and

[1] [In his Werkverzeichnis Mozart refers to them both as 'Opera Buffa'. *C.R.*]

terror? Or is this a great joke of Mozart's – his supreme and final joke? Some have actually thought so, and have pointed to the concluding sextet, the tempo of which is marked *Presto* – i.e. very fast – in which the three women and the three men sing with the utmost liveliness the words:

Questo è il fin di chi fa mal (This is the end of one who lived ill).

This lively sextet has so bothered musicians that in five out of six representations of *Don Giovanni* during the nineteenth century it was cut out as introducing a disturbing levity, or even, perhaps, mockery, at the end of an intensely moral tragedy in which Mozart uses trombones for the first time in the score with terrific effect. 'But how can a comic opera have trombones?' groan the musical pedants, enslaved by their knowledge of musical history! In those days, as these scholars are aware, trombones were only used for solemn or religious music; a trombone in a comic opera was unthinkable! Mozart, however, thought of it for Mozart was not writing a conventional comedy or tragedy. His *Don Giovanni* is not to be put into either class, for in this work Mozart transcends not only the academic formal classifications but also the conventional categories of good and evil, and blends the tragic and the comic into a unity which is not to be dissolved.

Even Professor Dent in his admirable book on Mozart's operas seems to me to have a distorted conception of *Don Giovanni*, owing perhaps to a certain moral conventionality of judgment, and a temperamental dislike to intensity of expression. He actually states that Mozart 'has intended to depict Donna Anna as not quite in her right mind', and refers to 'violence of expression' and 'Anna's ravings', commenting that Mozart 'had a tendency to lay his colours on more thickly than was always appropriate to the style'. Elsewhere he says that there is nothing tragic about Donna Anna; as if what he calls her 'ravings' were not completely accounted for by seeing her father murdered by Don Giovanni before her eyes. In fact, he is quite inconsistent in his attempt to make out that *Don Giovanni* is only an opera buffa after all, and actually says: 'a really serious treatment of the whole story would have been too utterly repulsive for stage-presenta-

tion.' This totally disregards the intense realism of Mozart.
But we have the librettist's (da Ponte) own statement, which
Professor Dent even quotes, that Mozart wished to treat the subject seriously and this he has certainly done. But to treat human
experience seriously requires a comprehensive vision that includes both the comic and the tragic. Critics who try to turn *Don
Giovanni* into an opera buffa have a conventionally moral attitude
to, rather than a tragic view of, life; while critics who, like Beethoven, cannot understand how Mozart could write an opera on
what they consider to be so immoral a subject as Don Giovanni
are deficient in the detachment and universality which enables
geniuses such as Shakespeare and Mozart to be serious without
being earnest and to preserve that sense of proportion in which
the essence of comedy lies. *Don Giovanni*, I maintain, is an intensely serious opera in which the tragic and the comic are in-
extricably blended with such mastery and truth that the effect is
unutterably grand.

COSÎ FAN TUTTE (THUS DO ALL WOMEN)

The second great opera to be described by Mozart as a *dramma
giocoso*, is *Così fan Tutte*.[1] It was commissioned by the Emperor
Joseph II of Austria for the Vienna opera in 1789, and the
libretto was written by the Italian poet Lorenzo da Ponte, who
also wrote the books for Mozart's *Figaro* and *Don Giovanni*. The
subject is supposed to have been taken from an actual occur-
rence in Vienna some time previous to the writing of the opera;
nevertheless this groundwork of possible actuality has not been
sufficient to put literary and musical critics on their guard against
dismissing the plot as absurd, ridiculous, etc., etc., because it did
not square with their preconceptions about men and women, love
and sex. The libretto of *Così fan Tutte* has been a constant object
of attack and this attack has been prolonged throughout the nineteenth century until the present day by the seemingly irrecon-
cilable fact that Mozart – in the opinion of all the best musicians
from generation to generation – had put into this opera some of

[1] [See footnote on page 313. *C.R.*]

the finest music he ever wrote and that from a musical point of
view it might even be considered to be the most perfect and flawless of all his operas. Consequently, there have been numerous
attempts during the past hundred years to rewrite the text with
the notion of fitting to this flawless music an equally flawless and
satisfying libretto. Needless to say, all these attempts have failed,
thus showing that fate sets a limit even to the stupidity of men.

The controversy about the text is far from having ceased, even
today; for example, Professor Edward J. Dent in his dissertation
on Mozart's operas calls the foundation of the libretto an idea 'in
itself absurd enough'. For Professor Dent the libretto of *Così fan
Tutte* is an artificial comedy. It may be true that Lorenzo da Ponte
wrote it less seriously than Mozart composed it, but none the less
I think he wrote it as a serious comedy; by which I mean that it
had the ironic truthfulness of deliberately conceived satire, which
is essential to true comedy. To call it an 'artificial' comedy is to
mislead the reader, unless one is very careful to point out that
one is using the word 'artificial' in a very special sense – namely,
in the sense that every work of art must be an artifice; i.e. something made within a convention and not something that has
happened in nature.

This artifice or convention of the theatre which requires that a
drama representing the experience of many years has to be exhibited within the space of three hours consecutively on the stage
is all that is artificial about the libretto of *Così fan Tutte*. We are
given a dramatic fiction by means of which we are to be shown
two pairs of lovers, a maid-servant and an onlooker who is the
mainspring of the action, in a complete and psychologically convincing plot. The action of this plot – which in real life would be
spread over at least many months – is telescoped for the theatre
into the space of a few hours. This is quite ingeniously and art-
fully done and shows the exceptional skill of Lorenzo da Ponte
as a writer for the theatre. We may also assume that Mozart himself had a hand in the devising of the plot, for although we know
no details of the collaboration between poet and composer during
the writing of *Così fan Tutte* as we do in some other cases yet we
know that Mozart was very particular about the texts of his operas

and that in the earlier operas he made many suggestions to his librettist and secured various alterations to meet his requirements. We may presume, therefore, that in the case of a collaborator such as Lorenzo da Ponte, with whom he had twice before worked successfully, Mozart may be given a fair share of responsibility for the libretto of *Così fan Tutte* as it exists.

Now let us see exactly what the plot of *Così fan Tutte* is. First of all I shall set down the list of characters:

Fiordiligi Dorabella	}	sisters from Ferrara living in Naples.
Guglielmo Ferrando	}	lovers of the two sisters, officers in the Neapolitan Army.
Despina		maid to the sisters.
Don Alfonso		an old philosopher.

It will be noticed that this is an ideal cast for a comedy as it consists of only six characters, not one of whom is superfluous to the action, which is managed with extreme economy. The play opens with the young officers sitting in a café drinking with Don Alfonso and bragging about the merits of their respective young women. Don Alfonso maintains that they are like any other two young women and no more or less constant. An absolutely constant woman, he says, is like the phœnix, a bird often talked about but never seen. Each of the lovers, however, declares his prospective bride to be this phœnix. In the end they agree to a wager. The two young men promise on their word of honour to do exactly what Don Alfonso tells them to do for the next twenty-four hours and he in return promises to prove to them the inconstancy of their two mistresses.

In the next scene the two girls are awaiting their lovers, each of whom they declare to be the best and bravest of men. Alfonso enters with the news that the two young men have been ordered to join their regiment on active service. The lovers enter, there is a sad farewell and the two young men go off to the strains of a military march of the regimental band. In the next scene the maid, Despina, brings the two disconsolate young women their chocolate and tries to console them, but their grief seems inconsolable. Then Alfonso, who has bribed Despina and let her into the secret as an accomplice, arrives bringing in the two young men now disguised as foreigners. They pay court to the two sisters but are indignantly repulsed to their own great delight. Don Alfonso, however, tells them that all is not over yet and reminds them of their promise to obey his commands. He now instructs them to persist in their suit and finally to pretend to take poison in the ladies' presence as a sign of their desperate love. All this they do. The terrified sisters send Despina for the doctor and Despina returns disguised as a physician, who restores them to life by waving over their dead bodies a large magnet. This, incidentally, is a skit on a prevailing medical fashion of the time, a fashionable cure no more and no less silly than any of the fashionable medical panaceas before or since.

The young men restored to life now return to their ardent wooing of the sisters, each paying his addresses to his friend's betrothed. But their feigned death has awakened sympathy in the young women and presently Dorabella responds to Guglielmo's endearments much to the consternation of Ferrando who, when he hears of it, wants to break the pact. Don Alfonso reminds him of his bond and Ferrando again pursues Fiordiligi, who being made of sterner stuff than her sister only succumbs when Ferrando is about to kill himself at her feet. A double marriage is now arranged with Despina, as the pretended notary, bringing the marriage contracts. A feast is prepared and as they are about to sign the contracts the military band of the returning regiment is heard. The young men rush out in their disguises and return as their original selves to the consternation of the sisters. Reconciliation is made by Don Alfonso, who says philosophically: 'This is how all women behave,' and the drama ends happily with the marriage festivities of the proper lovers.

Now it is a sign of the extraordinary imbecility and sentimentality of the average critic that this play, which is not only profoundly true in its portraiture of human nature but reveals four young men and women in a most favourable light, has everywhere been attacked for its unreality and cynicism. There is nothing cynical or disagreeable in it from beginning to end. As a woman once declared to me it 'only shows the charming and essentially responsive nature of women' and those who are so dull-witted as not to be able to accept the necessary stage convention of the young women not seeing through the disguises of their lovers and of the telescoping of the action within the space of a few hours are not yet equipped for the understanding and appreciation of dramatic art.

Now, how has Mozart treated this plot? That is the vital question. Has he written for it charming and superficial music such as would justify the interpretation of those who declare it frivolous and artificial – in the sense of being unreal – the sort of music which a Johann or even a Richard Strauss would write? Far from it! He has written for this opera the most tender, poignant, intensely dramatic and powerful music of which he was capable. He has made every character real, pulsing with life and has given to each one all the emotions proper to such experiences as young love, the anguish of separation, the horror of infidelity, the ruth-lessness of nature, the unexpectedness of one's own natural be-haviour, the tortures of jealousy and the differences in human characters even when fundamentally they are subject to the same iron laws of nature. In short, *Così fan Tutte* is a tragi-comedy and the most profound and terrifying work of its kind that has ever been written; for it neither idealizes nor sentimentalizes nor falsi-fies the reality and the depth of human feelings – especially in the sex-relationship between normal young men and women. *Così fan Tutte*, far from being the silly, artificial comedy which it has so often been described as being, is, on the contrary, a work of an iron realism in which Mozart pours out in marvellous music, always just, proper and adequate to every occasion, the delight, anguish and desperation of human hearts, who, finding themselves behaving exactly contrary to their own preconceived notions of what they are and of what they want to be, are bewildered and tortured.

The music given to Guglielmo when he discovers that Fior-diligi is also untrue; the sublime aria given to Fiordiligi when, in despair, she realizes that she too is weak and is about to give way to newly-awakened feelings and sings to her absent lover: 'Forgive the error of this loving heart; the knowledge of it shall at least never be revealed except to the flowers of this garden' – these things alone are sufficient to prove how passionately and seriously Mozart conceived this opera which I personally am inclined to think is his most perfect achievement in opera and a masterpiece of a kind which stands absolutely alone and unequalled in the history of art, even if we think that in some respects *Don Giovanni* is greater and *Die Zauberflöte* more sublime.

We now come to the third of the great operas of Mozart, that in which he has succeeded in attaining to the highest dramatic expression in the comic and in the super-tragic or religious, both united, however, into one work of art so that the two elements of the comic and the serious are inseparable, are indeed made into one great synthesis:

DIE ZAUBERFLÖTE

Grand Opera in Two Acts, words by Schikaneder, based on the story of *Lulu* or *The Magic Flute* from Wieland's *Dschinnistan*; the plot was modified after the production on June 8, 1791, of an opera based on the same story, *Kaspar der Fagottist oder die Zauberzither*, words from *Lulu* by Perinet and music composed by Wenzel Müller.

Mozart was at work on *Die Zauberflöte* as early as June 11th, for, on that date, he writes to his wife in Baden that 'out of sheer tedium I have composed an aria for the opera' and also quotes a line from the text: *Tod und Verzweiflung war sein Lohn*,[1] and on the following day (June 12th) he writes that he went to hear the new opera *Kaspar der Fagottist* 'which has made such a noise, but there is nothing in it'.

The characters and plot of *Die Zauberflöte* are as follows:

Sarastro	a magician who reigns in the Temple of Wisdom
Tamino	a Prince
Orator	
First, second and third Priests	
Queen of Night	
Pamina	daughter of the Queen of Night
First, second and third Ladies	

[1] Death and despair were his reward.

Papageno   a bird-catcher
An Old woman (Papagena)
Monostatos   a Moor
First, second and third Genii

It consists of an Overture, an Introduction, 9 Arias, 1 Aria with chorus, 2 Duets, 3 Terzets, 2 Quintets, 1 Chorus of Priests, 1 March of Priests and 2 Finales.

The plot is, roughly, an account of the trials undergone by Tamino before he is received by Sarastro into the Temple of Wisdom and given Pamina as bride. He is accompanied on his trials by Sancho Panza, Papageno, who lives altogether in a lower world ignorant of all that happens in the spirit of Tamino but experiencing certain trials and vexations on his own plane and being in his place rewarded with his proper mate, Papagena.

I now refer the reader back to the diagram at the beginning of this chapter from which he will see that I have shown *Die Zauberflöte* as a special combination of the whole gamut of opera comprising the threefold root of poetry, dancing and music in its entirety; no longer as a primitive beginning but, on the contrary, as a culmination in which the widest divergences – due to the specialized development extending from, though not including, secular dramatic tragedy to religious ritual – are once again recombined. From my diagram, 'The Genealogy of Opera', it may be seen how *Die Zauberflöte* descends via singspiel through intermezzo from comedy, folk-song and dance and via oratorio and ritual from serious religious drama. From this diagram we may see that *Don Giovanni* and *Die Zauberflöte* are two works which may be described as two poles opposite to one another, since the tragic element which is the counter-balance to the comic in *Don Giovanni* is replaced by the super-tragic or religious element as a counter-balance to the comic in *Die Zauberflöte*. The dualism which is inescapable from all human thought thus returns into *Die Zauberflöte*, which at first sight may seem one-sided through its lack of the tragic element.

Don Giovanni, in including the tragic, excludes the religious element; while, in *Die Zauberflöte*, the religious necessarily excludes the tragic. The comic and the serious are nevertheless combined in both works; but, just as the failure of Papageno to rise to the level of Tamino in *Die Zauberflöte* is accepted not only as no personal tragedy for him but as a delightful comic way of life with its own validity, so the career of *Don Giovanni* in the other opera has no religious significance but is a purely personal experience in which his so-called 'damnation' (the dragging-down into hell) is merely symbolical of his exclusion from certain other and, if you like, higher experiences due to his nature – just as Papageno owing to *his* nature is excluded from certain of the experiences of Tamino.

There is, however, in Mozart's presentation in both operas no confusion of the higher and the lower. What Don Giovanni is excluded from is not the mixed good and evil of a Don Ottavio or a Tamino on a superior plane, or of a Leporello or a Papageno on an inferior plane; he exists on an altogether different plane and his opposite is Sarastro. The extraordinarily universal quality of Mozart's genius enables him to represent all these human characters and the superhuman characters with complete sympathy and without any conventional moral judgment. The dualism of the universe as manifested in human life is accepted by Mozart. Tamino and Papageno are Don Quixote and Sancho Panza over again. They may be said to represent the spiritual and the material in their mixed human manifestations. Mozart shows no desire whatever (any more than Cervantes!) to turn Papageno into Tamino. His extraordinary dramatic instinct is shown by the fact that the real counter-figure to Don Giovanni is not put into the opera *Don Giovanni* at all. It is Sarastro from *Zauberflöte* not Don Ottavio in *Don Giovanni* who is the polar force opposite to Don Giovanni. Mozart has thus heightened the significance of Don Giovanni by giving him full swing, i.e. by giving him his full rights and thus not being afraid to let it be seen plainly what a poor figure the Don Ottavios of the world cut beside a Don Giovanni as conceived by a Mozart. The terrific power of Don Giovanni is a witness to the greatness of Mozart, as the figure of Satan in *Paradise Lost* is to the greatness of Milton; but it is an ironic commentary on the moralizers of the world that the good men, the Ottavios and the Taminos, do not attain to the same grandeur and force as Don Giovanni. This is because they are drawn to a smaller scale, since real goodness is not a quality attainable by normal human beings. Mozart's conception of men was the opposite of Rousseau's who thought all men were born good but became corrupted. For Mozart the good and bad in men was (so it seems, singular as it may appear) necessarily and inevitably mixed; he evidently considers Papageno just as worthwhile as Tamino, and Leporello just as valuable as Ottavio. Neither Don Giovanni nor Sarastro are conceived as real human beings by Mozart but rather as supernatural forces. It is also significant that the women in all his great operas are all neither great nor small but thoroughly real. The one exception to this is the Queen of the Night in *Zauberflöte*. In my opinion she is a sheer incidental ebullience of Mozart's genius; he has created her by virtue of his music but she plays no real rôle in the drama since it would have required a poet of Shakespearean genius to have given her complete significance as a figure on the same super-human scale as Sarastro and opposed to him in a convincing action. It is sufficient that Mozart made her *appear*. She is a witness to the same instinctive creative power in him which went to the making of a Don Giovanni and a Sarastro but he was not given a dramatic action which enabled her to display herself completely and as he was a musician and not a poet he could not by himself have invented such a dramatic action. Having made her appear he had therefore to make her disappear because such a being could not have existed in the plot of *Die Zauberflöte* as it stands. There would have to have been a real conflict between the Queen of the Night and Sarastro, which in itself would be an all-sufficient theme for another drama. We are not given that drama but a totally different one and one from which she must vanish or decline to a mere lay figure in absolute contradiction to her appearance in Mozart's music. That Mozart dropped the Queen of the Night as a serious protagonist to Sarastro is in obedience to the same law which excluded any intrusion of the religious element into the opera *Don Giovanni*, since the inclusion of the Queen of the Night as a real and equal protagonist opposed to Sarastro in a real conflict to be fought out in *Die Zauberflöte* would have introduced into that opera the element of tragedy. By excluding religion from *Don Giovanni* and tragedy from *Die Zauberflöte* Mozart has created two great polar works in each of which the destiny of a group of human beings is worked out under the influence of a dominating supernatural or super-normal power – the power of Don Giovanni and the power of Sarastro respectively. Thus each of these great works is an expression of human life conceived under one of the two poles of Good and Evil and is a sublime demonstration of the fact that human morality is only relative and that above and beyond it are great mysterious forces of the universe working out their own destiny, to whose existence the very music of Mozart is a sufficient testimony.

CHAPTER NINETEEN

Kierkegaard on Mozart
and Music

THE DANISH PHILOSOPHER Sören Kierkegaard[1] in his famous book *Entweder/Oder, ein Lebensfragment*, published in Copenhagen in 1843, wrote a remarkable essay entitled *Die unmittelbar erotischen Stadien oder das Musikalisch-Erotische*. (The Stages of the Directly Erotic or the Musical-Erotic.) This essay covers eighty-two closely printed pages in the German edition of Eugen Diederichs (June 1922) and ninety-four pages in the German edition of C. Ludwig Ungelenk (Dresden and Leipzig, 1927) and has ostensibly as its subject Mozart's opera *Don Giovanni*.

Not being acquainted with the Danish language I have used these two German editions and I have translated literally in my own hand the whole of this essay solely with the purpose of discovering for myself exactly what Kierkegaard has to say on *Don Giovanni*. He is a difficult writer, owing partly to his extreme elaboration, not to say diffuseness, and neither of the two German translations I have used is particularly lucid. There are famous living Continental musicians who think Kierkegaard's long essay to be the finest thing ever written about Mozart, and in view of Kierkegaard's immense reputation it was obviously necessary to study this essay.

It is easy to sneer at philosophers. What they have to say is

---

[1] In justice to Kierkegaard I have to emphasize that his disquisition on *Don Giovanni* is only a part of a book called by him *ein Lebensfragment* and that it is rather a declaration of love than a philosophic essay. If I have appeared to treat it unsympathetically here it is because I have confined myself to the examination of some of the very interesting ideas he throws out in the course of his declaration of love for Mozart. With the declaration itself I am in complete sympathy.

generally obvious when it is true, and unsound when it appears original. Kierkegaard is hardly an exception. He abounds in platitudes – in which he resembles German rather than Greek, French or even Italian thinkers. Also, he is long-winded to a degree that almost drives the reader frantic. What he has to say he says over and over again. Worse than this is a sort of latent sentimentality, that sentimentality which seems to spring from pent-up feelings that have been corrupted by repression; so that he is most frequently indirect and rarely direct. His indirectness is not always the ironic approach of a highly subtle and keen mind but frequently the ingratiating, almost apologetic roundabout-ness of a man who is nursing his emotion as if it were his illegiti-mate baby and his respect for legitimacy were greater than his natural love.

Philosophers, without any exception known to me, are never at their best when writing about any of the arts. I think it is im-possible for a thinker who is not primarily an artist to discuss art in a way that will satisfy artists that he really understands what he is talking about. This is particularly true of music, which is an art that a great many people can enjoy – and even enjoy deeply – without much understanding of its nature. Since the average educated European is taught as a child the reading and writing of the notation of letters, but not that of music, he is familiar with literature in a way in which he never becomes familiar with music. There seems to him no mystery in literature but music seems to him a great mystery. Actually the mystery – I mean by 'mystery' that creative use of literature or music which makes it an art – is equally great in both cases and exactly the same essentially.

What is the function of art? I would say that at bottom it is nothing more or less than the expression of the relationship be-tween an individual and the universe. We do not know what an individual is nor do we know what the universe is. Neither art nor science can answer these questions; but it is the foundation of human life that the individual exists separated in some finite way from a surrounding universe and yet in communication with it. The individual is, as it were, isolated but not cut off – and his communication is art. Therefore the nature of all the arts is essentially the same – the communication or relationship of the individual with the universe.

In men of genius this communication is more than commonly intense and profound. That is why their works, in which this relationship is expressed, are so stimulating to other men and women who find their own living enriched by contact with them just as a piece of steel is magnetized when an electric current passes through it. This 'electric current' is the artist's own life, his experiencing power with which he has magnetized his work. Works of art are therefore, as it were, bodies magnetized by the artist. And this living essence of the artist – which is, as I have said, actually a relationship, an experience between him as an individual and the universe – is what used to be called in religious writings the soul.

The value of a work of art is nothing more or less than the value of the soul of the artist, i.e. the value of the active relationship between him and the universe. It is this which makes great works of art profoundly refreshing and regenerating. In experiencing a great work of art it is as if we were bathing in the ocean of the universe and all its virtue and richness were passing into us and becoming a part of us. In other words, when we truly experience a great work of art we are, as it were, flooded with new life.

Now, this being so, it is clear that all the arts – poetry, drama, literature, painting, sculpture, music – have essentially the same function; it is only their means which seem different. At this point I can quote the first thing Kierkegaard has to say about Mozart's music in his essay on *Don Giovanni*:

> Since the hour when my soul was most deeply seized by Mozart's music and inclined before it in humble admiration it has often been both a delightful and quickening occupation to reflect upon it as that joyful hellenic contemplation of the world (according to which it is named *cosmos* because it appears as a well ordered whole, as a tasteful and transparent veil of the spirit which forms and transforms it), as that gay and serene way of contemplation repeated in a higher order of things, in the world of the ideal; since here also an ordering wisdom prevails which in a marvellous way brings together in due

course all that is related to one another . . . Homer with the Trojan War, Raphael with Catholicism, Mozart with Don Juan.

There is a miserable incredulity which presents itself with a learned air. It says: such mutual approaches are accidental and it finds in them nothing but a fortunate collision of different powers in the game of life. It takes it as accidental that two lovers meet, as accidental that they love one another; there might be a hundred other maidens with whom he could have been just as happy, whom he might have loved just as tenderly. Such incredulity supposes that many a poet has lived who might have become as immortal as Homer if the latter had not just already used up the splendid material, many a composer just as undying as Mozart if only the opportunity had offered itself. Now, for all mediocrities this is a marvellously consoling and soothing idea by means of which they and all like them imagine that it is a pure mistake of Fate, a world-wide error that they have not become as excellent as certain others. Thus there spreads a cheapening optimism.

But to every high-minded person, to every aristocrat to whom it is less important to make something of oneself in this miserable fashion, than to forget oneself in the contemplation of true greatness this is naturally a horror whereas it is a holy bliss and delight to see what belongs together united. Such marriages are fortunate but not by chance; for they require two factors whereas chance belongs to the unarticulated interruptions of Fate. This divine collaboration of forces is the good fortune of history, making the feast and gala days in the course of the years. The accidental has only one factor: it is an accident that Homer found in the Trojan War the most pregnant epic material conceivable. Fortune has two factors: it is a special luck that the most pregnant epic material was given to a Homer. Here the emphasis is as much on Homer as on the material, whence comes the deep harmony which informs every product we call classical. So it is with Mozart. It is a piece of good fortune that this, in the deepest sense, perhaps unique musical subject was given to no other than Mozart.

With his *Don Juan* Mozart enters the small immortal band of men whose names and works time will not forget since eternity remembers them and although it may be unimportant to each one among this band whether he stands high or low – since, in a certain sense, all stand equally high, being infinitely high – although, here, struggles for the highest or lowest place is just as childish as a struggle for the first place at Confirmation before the altar, yet I am childish enough or, rather, like a young girl I am so in love with Mozart that cost what it may I must place him first. . . . And I shall ask Mozart to forgive me if his music instead of inspiring me to great deeds has turned me into a fool who has lost the little sense he had so that I now spend my time in melancholy, humming softly what I don't understand, what hovers round me like spirits day and night. Immortal Mozart, you to whom I owe everything, to whom I owe it that once again my soul has lost itself in wonder, yes, is thrilled to its depths, to whom I owe it that I have not gone through this life without being deeply shaken, that I have not died without having loved even though my love has been unfortunate! What wonder then that I am more jealous of his glory than of the happiest moments of my life, more jealous of his immortality than of my own existence! Yes, should he be taken away, his name erased, then the one pillar would fall which till now has prevented everything collapsing for me into a frightful chaos, a terrible nothingness.

Philosophers have an unfortunate habit of letting an idea run away with them and, instead of checking their idea or theory by a scrupulous observation of the facts, they distort the facts to fit their beloved idea. So Kierkegaard starts with several ideas at the beginning of his essay on *Don Giovanni* and all his observations are made to illustrate these ideas. One of these ideas is that speech, or language, is the most concrete medium and music the most abstract medium. He does not define what he means by a concrete medium, he merely states that the 'most concrete of all mediums is speech'. He further says: 'the medium required by architecture is the most abstract one can think of', and also that music is an abstract medium. I think that Kierkegaard has made a mistake in trying to divide the artist's medium into two classes of concrete and abstract and I am supported by the fact that he nowhere attempts a definition of concrete. We cannot accept his dogmatic statement that speech is the most concrete of mediums and that the medium furthest removed from speech is the most abstract as a satisfactory definition.

Actually Kierkegaard is here making a division between the medium and the content which he elsewhere wisely repudiates. For there is no such thing in art as a material or a medium in itself separated from the idea of which it is the form. The material and the idea are one and inseparable as Kierkegaard himself points this out in an interesting passage:

Should one emphasize Homer's poetical capacity – shown in the working of the material – one might easily forget that the poem would never have become what it is if the Idea which Homer has expressed, the Idea immanent in the poem had not already been the innermost form of the material itself. The poet desires his matter. To desire is no art, one may say, and this is quite true of a mass of weak poetic ideas. Rightly to desire is, on the contrary, a great art, or rather, it is a gift. This is the inexplicable mystery of genius like the divining rod which never has the idea of desiring unless what it desires is there.

There has existed a school of aestheticians who, because they suggested the significance of form, were not guiltless of spreading a misunderstanding to the contrary. I have often wondered how those aestheticians could without further explanation adhere to the Hegelian philosophy when even a general acquaintance with Hegel, especially with his aesthetic, convinces us that he actually emphasizes the importance of the material in respect of aesthetics. Naturally, material and form belong together fundamentally and a single reflection will suffice to prove this, since otherwise such a phenomenon would be inexplicable.

If, however, it is impossible to separate the medium from the idea, what becomes of Kierkegaard's analysis of ideas as such? He never faces this fundamental objection, but it is an objection which goes to the root of philosophy and once we have stated this objection we see that it is destructive of all absolutes and explains why all that philosophy which deals in absolutes is so lifeless and barren. The more real philosophy is that which is itself a work of art and belongs to the art of writing. Nevertheless, absolutes, though they must never be taken for realities, have their use; so the classification of ideas can be used in a way similar to the use of such unrealities as numbers in mathematics and the use of such non-existent things as points and straight lines in the artificial three-dimensional geometry of Euclid.

Therefore let us consider another of Kierkegaard's ideas:

The more abstract the idea the smaller the probability of a repetition. How does the idea become concrete? By being penetrated historically. The concreter the idea the greater the probability of repetition. . . . So the idea appearing in sculpture is thoroughly abstract and stands scarcely in any relation to an historical event. . . .

Whereas, he says, 'history incessantly deposits new epic stuff' and so, although Homer is a classic, we can 'imagine a number of classic works in the class which includes epic poetry'. So he considers *The Trojan War* a concrete idea and *Don Giovanni* an abstract idea and says:

Because the idea is so limitlessly abstract and the medium likewise abstract there is no probability that Mozart should ever have a competitor. It was most lucky for Mozart to find a material which was absolutely musical in itself, and should at any time a composer want to rival Mozart there is nothing else for him but to recompose *Don Giovanni*.

Homer also found a perfect epic material, but one can think of a whole row of epic poems, since history is ever providing epic material. What I mean can be best seen by contrasting with *Don Giovanni* a similar idea. Goethe's *Faust* is certainly a classic work but the idea is historical and therefore every significant epoch will have its *Faust*. *Faust* has speech as its medium and since this is a much more concrete medium so on this account many works can be imagined having the same tendency. *Don Giovanni*, on the contrary, remains the only work of its kind, in the same way as the classic works of Greek sculpture.

But as the idea of *Don Giovanni* is still much more abstract than any in sculpture so one can easily see that in sculpture one has a number of works but in music only one.

Truly it is possible to imagine many classical works in music; but there remains always only one work of which one can say that its idea is absolutely musical, that music does not enter it as an accompaniment but displays its own innermost being while revealing the idea. Therefore Mozart stands with his *Don Giovanni* first among the immortals.

Nonsense as all this may appear and, as it appears, *is* yet, there is some useful meaning to be extracted from it. The idea of *Faust* is surely not any more or less historical than the idea of *Don Juan*? Kierkegaard is led into confusion by his dogmatic statements; but some of these dogmatic statements have virtue in spite of the contradictions into which they lead Kierkegaard and those who can only follow him literally. But let me take this statement by Kierkegaard:

The most abstract imaginable Idea is the sensuous quality of Genius.

Here is something valuable. It cannot even be spoilt by
Kierkegaard's immediately following sentences:

> But through what medium may it be represented? Only and solely
> through music. In sculpture it cannot be represented because it is as
> such something inward. Just as little may it be painted, for it does
> not allow itself to be put in a definite outline, since it is utterly
> lyrical, a gusto, a power, a storm, a passion. . . . It cannot be repre-
> sented in poetry either.

I am afraid it is not only a characteristic of philosophers to
avoid difficulties; but they are as tender with their ideas as mothers
with their children and as reluctant as are some mothers to let
them face hard facts. Surely it is not true that what is inward
cannot be expressed by what is outward? The whole problem of
every art lies precisely in the necessity of expressing the inner by
the outer – i.e. of giving form to idea – which otherwise has no
sensuous existence. Kierkegaard's 'sensuous quality of genius'
is precisely what is given line and colour in great painting and
sculpture – therein is the whole mystery of all creative art, and to
think that music is more inward than painting and sculpture is
to have a false conception of it. As for poetry, Kierkegaard does
not even attempt to produce an argument; he merely states dog-
matically that poetry cannot do it, which is again untrue.

The whole of Kierkegaard's attempt to make out that music is
more inward and more abstract than any other art falls to the
ground. It involves him in an immense amount of vague or contradictory rigmarole. Let me add, also, that 'a gusto, a power, a
storm, a passion' are not limited to music but can even be expressed in architecture. And with this collapse of his theory
about music callapses also his attempt to make out that *Don Giovanni* is Mozart's one classical work; because it is based on the
assumption that the idea of *Don Juan* is the most abstract of all
possible ideas and that music is the most abstract of all possible
arts, and that since these two super-abstracts are united together
in the one work, and only in that work, therefore it follows that
Don Giovanni is the unique classical work of art in existence. A
philosopher might accept this idea but no musician would.

I myself have something to say on the meaning of classical, but before dealing with this subject I wish to refer to another notion of Kierkegaard's. I shall not deal here with his acute and interesting remarks about the Greek and Christian attitudes to the erotic because it is much too big a subject and would take us too far afield; but one of his ideas is that Christianity introduced into the world the idea of the Sensual-Erotic as a principle or power that could be represented and that if this is to be expressed directly it can only be done in its directness in music; for if it is expressed in language it must of necessity be given indirect or reflective expression and ranged under ethical rules. Here again we see the philosopher with his limited conception of the nature and power of literature and equally limited – though in the opposite direction – conception of music. It is possible to be as indirect in music as in literature. Poetry and drama can be direct or indirect; so can music. Music can also be as descriptive and imitative as literature. It is an inadequate knowledge of music that has led Kierkegaard to make this unreal division just as it is a too-great acquaintance with the rationalizing and categorizing branch of literature which makes him overlook its tremendous power to express feelings.

Actually, but quite unconsciously, he has been compelled to make his highly elaborate argument and demonstration of the special character of the art of music by his sufferings due to the one-sided development of literature. Even today, when literature is at last escaping from its enslavement to the propaganda of moral though not yet of ethical, political and formal criticism, so that its creative function may begin to be enjoyed, the very fact that it lies ready at hand for every man to use and that even educated men do not yet perceive that so-called moral laws, ethical principles and political, sociological and economic theories have no more importance than the rules of counterpoint and harmony, and that the true values lie wholly and solely in the realm of the aesthetic are obstacles which prevent us from realizing that the creative function of literature as an art is the same as that of music or any of the other arts – namely, the expression of the relationship between the individual and the universe. What real differences there may be between the arts are not touched upon by Kierkegaard and I shall not deal with them here.

It is amusing to find Kierkegaard saying:

(1) I think, among other things, that Mozart is the greatest of all classics and that *Don Giovanni* deserves the first place among all classical productions,

and then:

(2) There is no doubt that music considered as a medium presents in all circumstances a very interesting problem. On the other hand it is doubtful if I am in a position to say anything satisfactory about it. I know quite well that I understand nothing about music. I admit freely that I am a layman. I shall not hide that I do not belong to the chosen class of musical connoisseurs . . . and though I feel that music is an art about which one cannot have a right idea without a high degree of experience I console myself with the thought . . . that Diana who had not herself given birth would come to the help of those giving birth; yes, that she had this gift from childhood . . . so that she was able to help her mother at her own birth.

I shall now leave Kierkegaard's general ideas and confine myself to some of his interesting remarks on the character of Don Juan in Mozart's opera. He says:

Don Juan is actually neither Idea – that is, Power, Life – nor individual; he hovers between both. This hovering is however the life of music. When the sea is in motion the foaming waves form all kinds of shapes like living beings and it seems then as if these beings wriggled into the waves whereas, on the contrary, the motion of the waves produces them. So Don Juan is an apparition that indeed comes into appearance but never condenses into firm shape, an Individual that constantly arises but never is finished, of whose history we learn no more than what the roaring of the waves tells us.

If one conceives of Don Juan thus everything becomes full of meaning and significance. If I think of him as a single individual . . . it seems funny that he has seduced one thousand and three maidens; for while he becomes an individual the accent falls on the wrong place: it matters, it is essential whom and how he has seduced. . . . If I conceive Don Juan musically I then have before me the power of nature, the daemonic which never wearies of seducing, which never stops – as little as the wind stops blowing, the sea rolling and the cataract tires of falling from a height. . . .

The number one thousand and three is, namely, odd and accidental and that is by no means unimportant for it gives the impression that the list is not closed, that Don Juan is still in swing. . . .

All this is true and is perfectly said. Kierkegaard goes on from this to point out a difference between spiritual and sensual love which I do not think sound – since he bases it on an incorrect *a priori* notion of individuality being in the one and not in the other. I shall therefore not discuss it here but pass on to another idea of his which is, that music does not express the singular but the general because music is too abstract to express differences. The reason Kierkegaard gives here is certainly unsound, because music can express many differences and extremely subtle ones. Surely the distinction is that music can express differences in mood, feeling, character, but not in intellectual concepts as such, i.e. music is not argument though it may be persuasion. His representation of Don Juan as not an individual but as the incarnation of Desire is excellent:

> The power of desire never grows weak and only when he desires is he in his right element. There he sits spreading joy like a god and drains the goblet, jumps up napkin in hand and is ready for the onslaught . . . his life foams and bubbles like the wine with which he refreshes himself.

If it be true that this Desire can be expressed more directly in music than in any other art it is because it is pure feeling without reflection. But I think also painting and sculpture and lyric poetry cannot be denied this power.

I shall now pass on to consider Kierkegaard's conception of the idea of the classical in art.

In every definition or description of the word 'classical' sooner or later the word or some such word as 'proportion' must appear. Everybody recognizes that works of art which we name classical are distinguished by a balance, a harmony of qualities which is what we mean by saying they have a just proportion. No one element or quality is apparently sacrificed to another in them, and this is the source of their harmony and the satisfaction they give.

I am inclined to believe that, on the other hand, all life – and thus, in works of art, all vitality – is due to disproportion, to a lack of balance, and that life itself is the effort to achieve this balance. This idea is in itself suggested by the very word 'static' which so readily associates itself with the word 'classical'. The idea of 'cold' is also very near the word 'classical' – a cold and classic beauty means essentially a beauty that one admires without passion.

The word 'romantic', on the other hand, is intimately connected with passion. Romantic love is in itself a description of this antithesis to classical admiration and suggests an element of extravagance, also one of temporariness, as if it were a state that could only exist until one had recovered one's balance. Works of art, when they are described as 'romantic', again suggest the presence of some element in excess or perhaps merely the neglect of certain qualities for the sake of others, and we love these works of art passionately when these particular qualities they display are what we long for or are in sympathy with at the moment. Should our mood change, we find we like them less and perhaps then not at all, or our intense liking may even become intense dislike.

These are common experiences both with regard to persons and to works of art. Now what has Kierkegaard to say on this matter? He says that 'classical' implies a divine collaboration of forces. It is, he says, 'a special luck that the most pregnant epic material was given to a Homer' and that 'the emphasis is as much on Homer as on the material, whence the deep harmony which informs every product we call classical'. He is writing actually about Mozart and he finds the same explanation in the fact that in *Don Juan* Mozart met the perfect musical subject and that this 'perhaps unique musical subject was given to no other than Mozart'. He reinforces the importance and singularity of this union between the maker and the subject by reminding us very aptly that if one were to think it were a mere lucky accident that Homer found such excellent epic material as the Trojan War and that Mozart found *Don Juan* we have to remember that what appears to us as the perfect epic material is only known to us through Homer. Similarly one might add that, essentially, we know only of *Don Juan* through Mozart and of *Faust* through Goethe.

It is significant from my present point of view that he regards this coming together of the poet and his subject or the musician and his subject as a marriage, and this marriage he regards as predestined. To repeat his words:

> It is for all mediocrities a marvellous consoling and soothing idea by which . . . they imagine that it is a pure mistake of Fate, a world-wide error that they have not become as excellent as certain others. Thus a universal optimism spreads. But to every high-minded person . . . this is naturally a horror whereas it is a holy bliss and delight to see united what belongs together.

It is a similar idealism which makes him repudiate the interpretation of those who 'take it as accidental that two lovers met, as accidental that they loved one another, there might be a hundred other maidens with whom he could have been just as happy, whom he might have loved just as tenderly'.

His comment on this is, that, if one thinks this, then 'one supposes that many a poet has lived who might have become as immortal as Homer if the latter had not first already used up this splendid material and many a composer just as undying as Mozart if only the opportunity had offered itself'.

The idea of a perfect marriage is not to be got rid of in the conception 'classical'. And I would go so far as to say that so intimately are works of art a part of life that the analogy is complete, and we shall find what applies to works of art applies also to the other creations of love.

But two important points have now to be considered. Let us first take the element of desire in love. Here again I recall something pertinent said by Kierkegaard:

> The poet desires his matter. To desire, one may say, is no art and it is quite true of a mass of weak poetic ideas. Rightly to desire is, on the contrary, a great art or rather it is a gift (latent). This is the inexplicable mystery of genius like the divining rod which never has its idea of desiring unless what it desires is there.

This is, in my opinion, profoundly true. But how are we to distinguish classical from romantic love in practice? How are we to tell the perfect from the imperfect marriage? Is there not a simple answer at hand? By its durability. Romantic passions may be extremely strong but they do not last. All experience is at one on this point. Nevertheless, it is necessary to add a reservation here which I have never seen made but which is all-important. Romantic passions do not last only when there is a discrepancy between the two factors. The attraction has been great but it has not been complete because some elements wanted by one are missing in the other. Hence dissatisfaction. But if the one did not require more of the other because it itself lacked what the other lacked and was not aware of the lack, then an imperfect marriage might be enduring. In that case how are we to distinguish between the romantic and the classical, since durability is our test?

My answer to this is that the majority do not distinguish and are incapable of so distinguishing – which is the reason why so many people confuse in one lot artists and works of art, as well as human beings, who really do not belong together. Wagner and Beethoven, Mozart and Cimarosa, are musical examples. If a classical work of art requires the perfect marriage of subject and master, so also the relationship between the work of art and the observer requires the same degree of matching, for one can only see in a work of art what one has to some degree within oneself. The reason why so many amateurs of music do not perceive the superiority of Beethoven and Mozart to, let us say, Wagner and Brahms is because they themselves are lacking in the qualities which Wagner and Brahms lack and therefore do not miss, are not aware of their absence. Now one can understand how a romantic passion may be durable. Also one can see that a true marriage is a marriage of sympathies and not at all complement-ary in its biological sense, i.e. a combination of opposites. The cheap idea of evolution, of progress by a biological combination of opposites, is seen to be not only superficial but contrary to the very nature of things. On the other hand, all nature and every artist strives at the perfect marriage in which there is complete unity. This unity in works of art is what we call the classical harmony. This classical harmony is actually neither cold nor static; it is only perceived as such by those who lack perception of much that is in the work. On the other hand, there is always a sort of unity where there is satisfaction and satisfaction may come

– as we have seen – by the mere unity of two sympathies. This is the explanation why so many inferior, lifeless, mediocre works have for a time been considered classics – all academic art belongs to this category. Its classicism is negative or exclusive, not inclusive.

Therefore when we get a great artist, like William Blake, saying that all beauty lies in excess we must understand that this is said, first of all, as a protest against the academic, the mere petty unity of small things. In great art there must be a degree of comprehensive vitality which will appear to the academics as diabolic. Actually we find this is the case and Mozart is a very good example of it. But Mozart is so comprehensive that this diabolic quality is not noticed by many people, just as in a well-proportioned face we are not particularly aware that there is a nose. The nose is there but it is not noticed unless it is out of proportion to the other features. Thus, in the same way, a well-proportioned object always looks smaller than it is. Therefore when the academics consider there is a certain too muchness or excess it will be either because they are unaware of or are blind to the other features which would give it due proportion or because it exists in disproportion in themselves.

The word 'classical' can only justly be applied to a work of art according to the definition Kierkegaard gives to it – which is, on the whole, the generally accepted definition – when a comprehensive unity has been achieved. We may well ask how are we to judge of the comprehensiveness of any unity or marriage? To which I can only reply that to make such judgments two things are necessary in him who judges: first, gift or talent; secondly, experience. Now these two factors, gift and experience, are in themselves also complex and not simple, and it is here that we are brought up against that unity in the observer of a work of art or in the partner to a marriage which is an essential to complete understanding of the other party. It may be seen by this that the very appreciation of works of art is in its way a marriage and that is why complete appreciation is relatively rare and why there are so many false judgments made by critics and why, furthermore, so many popular artists are of inferior quality.

CHAPTER TWENTY

Music and Dialectic

IT MAY BE said that every water-tight philosophical system conceived so far has foundered on the rock of aesthetics. There may be other rocks in the sea of thought upon which man's intellectual systems go to pieces, but this rock is the most dangerous and destructive of them all.

The sufferings of sensitive and subtle minds owing to the general shoddy use of literature which in the past has made writers like Kierkegaard and Walter Pater imagine that the art of music was ideally free from this taint and a purely abstract medium for pure expression, becomes more and more acute with the increasing vulgarization for utilitarian purposes of words. Today there are even writers who are so blind to the function of literature as an art that they maintain that its sole and whole duty is that of directly propaganding changes in the government of States; although they would repudiate indignantly the notion that the immediate duty of literature was to make men drink or abstrain from drinking alcoholic liquors, or from committing or not committing adultery.

Within the present century there has arisen as an expression and need of the age a perversion of the Hegelian dialectic which is known as dialectical materialism. The conception of art as a charmed and self-contained world was never one that commanded any general assent, and although the cry of art for art's sake had a certain validity as opposed to the narrow conception of art as the expression of a local and temporal morality or ethical passion, yet even this restricted validity is overlooked in the new puritanism which manifests itself in the political activity of the present age.

Everywhere in Europe and America today there is to be found

a group of critics who pretend to be revolutionary and to have a new and infallible criterion by which to determine the value of every artistic work. This criterion is political and, philosophically, it owes its origin to Hegel, who propounded that the will-process and the thought-process are essentially one, the former only being the latter on its objective side. Now we may think that Hegel's conception was true with the reservation – which I personally would make – that Hegel did not fully perceive how true it was and therefore that some of his conclusions and many of the details of his thought in general are incorrect. For example, Hegel did not give its proper importance to nature (which he considered inferior to thinking) or to art, which he also considered inferior and subordinate to philosophy and religion. But this was to deny the central truth of his own system, because nature and art (works of art) are both part and the largest and most important part of the phenomenal world – *not* politics or social systems, which are never actually objectified but always remain conceptual, i.e. an interpretation of an activity rather than an act or thing made. Hegel rightly says that when form and idea are so interfused as to become one the object is a work of art. I would prefer to put it in another way and say that then – when form and idea have become one – there is creation, i.e. something created. Romanticism – Hegel defined – is what happens when the idea is in excess of the form. But what happens when the form is in excess of the idea? Classicism. Well, instead of these two words we can use Revolutionary and Conservative in connection with the State. Now here we have to apply the Hegelian logic of thesis, antithesis and synthesis. But is there ever a perfect synthesis of thesis (say the revolutionary idea) and antithesis (the anti-revolutionary or reactionary idea) into a fixed social system? I should say Never! And there never could be, for that would be Utopia.

Now nature needs no Utopia or final perfection, neither does art; every creation has its own validity and the notion of progress in works of art or in nature is an illusion due to misconception. It may be that there is also no progress in society; indeed, if society, or the Hegelian state, is to be thought of as belonging also

M

to the phenomenal category of nature and art then this must be
so. In which case if ever a State deserves to rank as a creation of
the order of art and nature it can only be so by a complete synthesis of idea and form which thus precludes any revolutionary
(or reactionary) activity within it.

Now there has never been such a State. Every society known to
history has either been romantic (like the present) or classical,
like the eighteenth century; but always with the other element
more or less active.

But the very notion of thesis and antithesis in the Hegelian
and post-Marxian dialectic is based on the assumption that
thought is at the bottom of the Universe or that the fundamental
substance of the Universe is thought. And it seems Hegel and his
followers have thus started from an incorrect premise, which is
the source of all their difficulties. Nothing ever was created and
nothing ever can be created by thought. Who by taking thought
can add a cubit to his stature? it is love, not thought, which is the
creative power and fundamental substance of the Universe. Consequently it is in art, not in philosophy or science, that we may
find an objective creation analogous to nature. Creation does not
appear by the resolving of thesis and antithesis into synthesis; for
the simple reason that this operation is not to be achieved logically, that is by thought. The very process of thinking is in thesis
and antithesis. The synthesis is given, not arrived at by the mind
but presented through the senses, and is primary not derivative.
That is why society can only fluctuate from thesis to antithesis,
since society or the State is an intellectual conception, not an
organism, and all biological analogies on this point are deceptive
and invalid.

Hence we may see clearly that all attempts to criticize or judge
works of art by sociological criteria are erroneous. The intellectual conception of the Christian religion may be logically
destroyed without invalidating the frescoes of Giotto; whereas
our dialectical materialists would have us believe that the frescoes
of Giotto were not only the product of dogmatic Christianity
(which as works of art they are not) but also were dependant for
their virtue on the truth of Christianity. And by truth they must

mean absolute truth, for they cannot contend that Christianity only needed to be true for its time; if they do, how do they explain that then and now artists have thought Giotto's frescoes better than those of other equally Christian painters and also have thought this quite irrespective of whether the judges themselves have been Christians or not? Is a Jew *ipso facto* to be held incapable of understanding or experiencing fully the painting of Giotto? Well, then, a Christian is incapable of appreciating a Jewish Rembrandt and a dialectical materialist or a Communist is incapable of appreciating the works of art by non-Communists. If art is but the reflection of society or the expression of social needs, then when that society changes all previous works of art become valueless. Since the theory of dialectical materialism involves constant change, the oscillation from thesis to antithesis and back again, there can be – on this assumption – no works of art of permanent value to man. Or, shall we invent a new logical connection? Shall we say that when the society is classical the works of art that will be considered valuable will be romantic, and vice versa?

This alternation and correspondence is no doubt true of all man's intellectual contrivances and we may thus explain the vogue of fashion and the necessity of change; but it is exactly in their freedom from any connection with these social phenomena that works of art are what they are, namely, like nature, *creations*; not intellectual contrivances but creations whose value is timeless because they do not belong to any stage of the world conceived as a process of dialectical materialism.

This distinction becomes exceedingly clear when we consider the art of music. It is the hall-mark of the dilettante and the intellectual man of fashion to desire novelty in music or to find modern music fundamentally different from music of any other age. The historians of music are not perceptive musicians. It is the unfailing sign of a bad or imperfect musician to be interested in national or temporal characteristics in music. All the best music has this in common that it has neither date nor character, personal or national. On the contrary like nature, it is superpersonal, international and timeless. And this proceeds from the

M*

fact that it is a primary synthesis, a creation which we can only apprehend but cannot obtain by analysis. If by thinking we could analyse it, then also by thinking we could put it together; but this is just what we cannot do and it is because we cannot do this that we are entitled to call it a creation and its maker a creator and not merely an intellectual.

Applied to art or to nature the idea of thesis and antithesis is a mere logical conception and as such necessarily a falsification of its reality. Hegel's philosophy, like its offspring, dialectical materialism, is negative. It suffers from the same weakness as Darwin's theory of natural selection, it does not supply any motivating power. As was pointed out long ago, Darwin's theory would not have led to such confusion if it had been more accurately named as a theory not of natural selection but of natural rejection. Hegel's thesis and antithesis would long ago have come not to a synthesis but to a standstill if that were all there was in world or thought-process. It is precisely when music is not a creation that it may be described as a mere process of thesis and antithesis but, in the case of music, it is clear that this process is purely logical and has no relation with any world-process or objective reality. Music only achieves reality when, like nature, it is an organism with an inner life of its own which we can apprehend because it is connected with ours, or, in other words, has a meaning for us.

But this 'meaning' is not a syllogism for it can only be apprehended through our senses, otherwise it would be a mere abstraction, a figment of dialectical materialism.

Catalogue of Works

THE NUMBERS WITHOUT brackets are the original Köchel catalogue numbers; those within brackets are the new numbers assigned by Dr Einstein in the third edition of Köchel's catalogue published by Breitkopf and Härtel, Leipzig, 1937.

The works in each section are roughly in chronological order but the exact chronological order, according to the latest investigators, is given by the numbers in brackets and dates.

VOCAL MUSIC

Arias for Solo voice and Orchestra

K.				
21	(19ᶜ)	tenor	'Va dal furor portata'	1765
23		soprano and strings	'Conservati fedele'	,,
36	(33¹)	tenor	'Or che il dover'	1766
70	(61ᶜ)	soprano	'A Berenice'	1769
71		tenor	'Ah, più tremar	,,
74ᵇ		soprano	'Non curo l'affetto'	1771
77	(73ᵉ)	,,	Recit 'Misero me'; Aria 'Misero pargoletto'	1770
78	(73ᵇ)	,,	'Per pietà'	,,
79	(73ᵈ)	,,	'O temerario'	,,
82	(73ᵇ)	,,	'Se ardire'	,,
83	(73ᵏ)	,,	'Se tutti i mali'	,,
88	(73ᶜ)	,,	'Fra cento affanni'	,,
119	(382ʰ)	,,	'Der Liebe'	,,
143	(73ᵃ)	,,	Recit. 'Ergo interest'; Aria 'Quaere superna'	,,
146	(317ᵇ)	,,	'Kommet her'	1779
209		tenor	'Si mostra'	1775
210		,,	'Con ossequio'	,,
217		soprano	'Voi avete'	,,
255		alto	'Ombra felice'	1776
256		tenor	'Clarice cara'	,,

K.272	soprano	'Ah, lo previdi'	1777
294	„	'Alcandro lo confesso'	1778
295	tenor	'Se al labbro'	„
316 (300ᵇ)	soprano	'Popoli di Tessaglia'	„
368	„	'Ma, che vi fece'	1781
369	„	'Misera, dove son'	„
374	„	'A questo seno'	„
383	„	'Nehmt meinen Dank'	1782
416	„	'Mia speranza adorata'	1783
418	„	'Vorrei spiegarvi'	„
419	„	'No, no'	„
420	tenor	'Per pietà'	„
431 (425ᵇ)	„	'Misero! o sogno!'	„
432 (421ᵃ)	bass	'Così dunque'	„
433 (416ᶜ)	„	'Männer suchen'	„
435 (416ᵇ)	tenor	'Müsst' ich auch'	„
440 (383ʰ)	soprano	'In te spero'	1782
486ᵃ (295ᵃ)	„	Recit. 'Basta vincesti'; Aria, 'Ah, non lasciarmi'	1778–86
490	„	'Non più'	1786
505	„	'Ch'io mi scordi'	„
512	bass	'Alcandro lo confesso'	1787
513	„	'Mentre ti lascio'	„
528	soprano	'Bella mia fiamma'	„
538	„	'Ah, se in ciel'	1788
539	bass	'Ich möchte wohl'	„
541	„	'Un bacio di mano'	„
569		'Ohne Zwang' (only in M's catalogue)	1789
577	soprano	'Al desio'	„
578	„	'Alma grande'	„
579	„	'Un moto di goia'	„
580	„	'Schon lacht'	„
582	„	'Chi sà'	„
583	„	'Vado, ma dove'	„
584	bass	'Rivolgete a lui'	„
584ᵃ	soprano	'Donne vaghe'	„
612	bass	'Per questa bella mano'	1791
K.Anh.245(621ᵃ)	„	'Io ti lascio'	„

Canons

K. 89A1 (73¹) Canon for 4 voices	1770
89A2 (73ʳ) 4 Riddle Canons	„
228 (515ᵇ) Double Canon (4 voices)	1787

K.229 (382ᵃ)	'Sie is dahin'	1782
230 (382ᵇ)	'Selig, selig, alle'	,,
231 (382ᶜ)	'Leck mich im Arsch'	,,
232 (509ᵃ)	'Lieber Freistädtler'	1787
233 (382ᵈ)	'Leck mir den Arsch fein recht schön sauber'	1782
234 (382ᵉ)	'Bei der Hitz im Sommer'	,,
347 (382ᶠ)	'Lasst uns ziehen'	,,
348 (382ᵍ)	'V'amo di core'	,,
507	'Heiterkeit'	1786
508	'Auf das Wohl alter Freunde'	,,
508ᵃ	8 Canons	,,
553	'Alleluja'	1788
554	'Ave Maria'	,,
555	'Lacrimoso son' oi'	,,
556	'G'rechtelt's enk'	,,
557	'Nascoso è il mio sol'	,,
558	'Gehn ma in 'n Brada'	,,
559	'Difficile lectu'	1785-8
560ᵃ	'O du eselhafter Peierl'	1785
560ᵇ	'O du eselhafter Martin'	,,
561	'Bona Nox'	1788
562	'Caro bell' idol mio'	,,

Cantatas

K. 42 (35ᵃ)	Grabmusik (Passion Cantata)	1767
118 (74ᶜ)	*La Betulia Liberata*, solo voices, chorus and orchestra	1771
429 (420ᵃ)	'Dir, Seele des Weltalls.' Male voices and orchestra	1783
429ᵇ (420ᵇ)	'Dir, Seele des Weltalls.' Soprano, chorus and orchestra	,,
469	*Davidde Penitente*, based on the C minor, Mass K.427, with additions	1785
471	*Die Maurerfreude*. Tenor solo, male chorus and orchestra	,,
619	Eine kleine deutsche Kantate	1791
623	*Eine kleine Freimaurer-Kantate*. Male chorus and orchestra	,,

Kyrie, Te Deum, Veni, Regina coeli, Motets, Offertories, etc.

K. 20	Motet, 'God is our Refuge'	1765
33	Kyrie, F major, 4 voices and strings	1766

K.273	Graduale, F major, 'Sancta Maria', 4 voices, strings and organ	1777
276 (321^b)	Regina Coeli, C major, 4 voices, orchestra and organ	1779
277 (272^a)	Offertorium de b. v. Maria, 'Alma Dei', 4 voices, strings and organ	1777
322 (296^a)	Kyrie, E flat major, 4 voices, orchestra and organ	1778
323	Kyrie, C major, 4 voices, orchestra and organ	1779
324 (An.186^a)	Hymn, 'Salus informorum' (of doubtful authenticity)	
325 (An.186^b)	Hymn, 'Sancta Maria' (of doubtful authenticity)	
326 (93^d)	Hymn, 'Justum deduxit Dominus', 4 voices, bass and organ	1771
341 (368^a)	Kyrie, D minor, 4 voices, orchestra and organ	1781
343 (336^c)	Zwei deutsche Kirchenlieder, voice and bass *O Gottes Lamm* and *Als aus Ägypten Israel*	1779
615	Chorus 'Viviamo felici'	1791
618	Motet, 'Ave Verum', 4 voices, strings and organ	,,

Litanies, Vespers

K.109 (74^e)	Litaniae de B.M.V. (Lauretanae) for 4 voices, orchestra and organ	1771
125	Litaniae de venerabili altaris sacramento, 4 voices, orchestra and organ	1772
193 (186^g)	Dixit et Magnificat, C major, 4 voices, orchestra and organ	1774
195 (186^d)	Litaniae Lauretanae, D major, 4 voices, orchestra and organ	,,
243	Litaniae de venerabili altaris sacramento, E flat major, 4 voices, orchestra and organ	1776
321	Vesperae de Dominica, C major, 4 voices, orchestra and organ	1779
339	Vesperae solennes de confessore, 4 voices, orchestra and organ	1780

Masses

| K. 49 (47^d) | Missa Brevis, G major, 4 voices, strings and organ | 1768 |

K. 65 (61ᵃ)　　Missa Brevis, D minor, 4 voices, strings and
　　　　　　　　organ　　　　　　　　　　　　　　　　　　1769

　66　　　　　Mass, C major (Dominicus-Messe), 4 voices,
　　　　　　　　orchestra and organ　　　　　　　　　　　　"

115 (166ᵈ)　Missa Brevis, C major, 4 voices and organ　1773

116 (90ᵃ)　　Missa Brevis, F major, 4 voices, strings and
　　　　　　　　organ　　　　　　　　　　　　　　　　　　1771

139 (114ᵃ)　Missa Solemnis, C minor-major, 4 voices,
　　　　　　　　orchestra and organ　　　　　　　　　　　1772

167　　　　　Missa in honorem Smae Trinitatis, C
　　　　　　　　major, 4 voices, orchestra and organ　　　1773

192 (186ᶠ)　Missa Brevis, F major, 4 voices, strings and
　　　　　　　　organ　　　　　　　　　　　　　　　　　　1774

194 (186ʰ)　Missa Brevis, D major, 4 voices, strings and
　　　　　　　　organ　　　　　　　　　　　　　　　　　　"

220 (196ᵇ)　Missa Brevis, C major, 4 voices, orchestra
　　　　　　　　and organ　　　　　　　　　　　　　　　　1775

257　　　　　Credo-Missa, C major, 4 voices, orchestra
　　　　　　　　and organ　　　　　　　　　　　　　　　　1776

258　　　　　Missa Brevis, C major, 4 voices, orchestra
　　　　　　　　and organ　　　　　　　　　　　　　　　　"

259　　　　　Missa Brevis, C major, 4 voices, orchestra
　　　　　　　　and organ　　　　　　　　　　　　　　　　"

262 (246ᵃ)　Missa Longa, C major, 4 voices, orchestra
　　　　　　　　and organ　　　　　　　　　　　　　　　　"

275 (272ᵇ)　Missa Brevis, B flat major, 4 voices, strings
　　　　　　　　and organ　　　　　　　　　　　　　　　　1777

317　　　　　Krönungs Messe, C major, 4 voices,
　　　　　　　　orchestra and organ　　　　　　　　　　　1779

337　　　　　Missa Solemnis, C major, 4 voices,
　　　　　　　　orchestra and organ　　　　　　　　　　　1780

427 (417ᵃ)　Mass in C minor, 4 voices, orchestra and
　　　　　　　　organ　　　　　　　　　　　　　　　　　1782–3

626　　　　　Requiem, D minor, 4 voices, orchestra and
　　　　　　　　organ　　　　　　　　　　　　　　　　　　1791
　　　　　　　　(completed by Süssmayer)

Operas and other Stage Works

K. 35　　　　*Die Schuldigkeit des ersten Gebotes*, sacred
　　　　　　　　play, 1st part　　　　　　　　　　　　　1766

　38　　　　*Apollo et Hyacinthus*, Latin comedy with
　　　　　　　　music　　　　　　　　　　　　　　　　　1767

　50 (46ᵇ)　*Bastien und Bastienne*, German singspiel in
　　　　　　　　1 act (Weiskern)　　　　　　　　　　　　1768

K. 51 (46ᵃ) *La Finta Semplice*, opera buffa in 3 acts
  (Coltellini)   1768

  87 (74ᵃ)   *Mitridate, Re di Ponto*, opera seria in 3 acts
  (Cigna–Santi after Racine)   1770

111   *Ascanio in Alba*, Serenata teatrale in 2 acts
  (Parini)   1771

126   *Il Sogno di Scipione*, Serenata drammatica
  (Metastasio)   1772

135   *Lucio Silla*, Dramma per musica, 3 acts
  (Gamerra and Metastasio)   ,,

196   *La Finta Giardiniera*, opera buffa, 3 acts
  (Calzabigi)   1774

208   *Il Re Pastore*, dramma per musica, 2 acts
  (Metastasio)   1775

K.Anh.10 (299ᵇ) *Les Petits Riens*, Ballet Music   1778

344 (336ᵇ)   *Zaide*, singspiel, 2 acts (Schachtner) 1779

345 (336ᵃ)   *Thamos, König in Ägypten*, chorus and
  incidental music (Gebler)   ,,

366   *Idomeneo*, opera seria, 3 acts (Varesco) 1781

367   *Idomeneo*, ballet music   1781

384   *Die Entführung aus dem Serail*, singspiel, 3
  acts (Stephanie)   1782

422   *L'Oca del Cairo*, opera buffa (Varesco), unfinished   1783

430 (424ᵃ)   *Lo Sposo Deluso*, opera buffa, unfinished 1783

486   *Der Schauspieldirektor*, comedy with music,
  1 act (Stephanie)   1786

492   *Le Nozze di Figaro*, opera buffa, 4 acts
  (da Ponte after Beaumarchais)   1786

527   *Don Giovanni*, dramma giocoso, 2 acts (da
  Ponte)   1787

588   *Così fan Tutte*, opera buffa, 2 acts (da Ponte) 1790

620   *Die Zauberflöte*, grosse opera, 2 acts (Schikaneder)   1791

621   *La Clemenza di Tito*, opera seria, 2 acts
  (Mazzolà after Metastasio)   ,,

Oratorios (arrangements)

K.566   *Acis and Galatea* by Handel (newly instrumented)   1788

572   *Messiah* by Handel (newly instrumented) 1789

591   *Alexander's Feast* by Handel (newly instrumented)   1790

K.592   *Ode for St Cecilia's Day* by Handel (newly
              instrumented)   1790

Songs with Pianoforte

K. 52 (46ᶜ)	'Daphne, deine Rosenwangen'	1768
53	*An die Freude*	1767
147 (125ᵍ)	'Wie unglücklich'	1772
148 (125ʰ)	'O heiliges Band'	,,
149 (125ᵈ)	*Die grossmütige Gelassenheit*	,,
150 (125ᵉ)	*Geheime Liebe*	,,
151 (125ᶠ)	*Die Zufriedenheit im niedrigen Stande*	,,
152 (210ᵃ)	Canzonetta 'Ridente la calma'	(?) 1775
178 (125ᶜ)	Air for soprano 'Ah, spiegarti'	1772
307 (284ᵈ)	Ariette 'Oiseaux, si tous les ans'	1777
308 (295ᵇ)	Ariette 'Dans un bois solitaire' (de la Motte)	1778
349 (367ᵃ)	*Die Zufriedenheit* (Miller) ptfe or mandolin	1776
351 (367ᵇ)	'Komm, liebe Zither' (with mandolin)	1780–1
390 (340ᶜ)	'An die Hoffnung' (J. T. Hermes)	1780
391 (340ᵇ)	'An die Einsamkeit' (J. T. Hermes)	,,
392 (340ᵃ)	'Verdankt sei es dem Glanz' (J. T. Hermes)	,,
393 (385ᵇ)	Solfeggien (Vocal Exercises for his wife)	1782
441a	Ja! grüss dich Gott	1783
468	*Gesellenreise* (J. F. von Ratschky)	1784
472	*Der Zauberer* (C. F. Weisse)	1785
473	*Die Zufriedenheit* (C. F. Weisse)	,,
474	*Die betrogene Welt* (C. F. Weisse)	,,
K.Anh.26(475ᵃ)	'Einsam bin ich'	,,
476	*Das Veilchen* (Goethe)	,,
506	*Lied der Freiheit* (Blumauer)	(?) 1786
517	*Die Alte* (F. von Hagedorn)	1787
518	*Die Verschweigung* (C. F. Weisse)	,,
519	*Das Lied der Trennung* (K. E. K. Schmidt)	,,
520	*Als Luise die Briefe ihres ungetreuen Lieb-habers verbrannte* (G. von Baumberg)	,,
523	*Abendempfindung* (J. H. Campe)	,,
524	*An Chloe* (J. G. Jacobi)	,,
529	*Des kleinen Friedrichs Geburtstag*	,,
530	*Das Traumbild* (Hölty)	,,
531	*Die kleine Spinnerin*	,,
552	*Beim Auszug in das Feld*	1788
596	*Sehnsucht nach dem Frühlinge*	Jan. 1791
597	*Im Frühlingsanfang* (Sturm)	,, ,,
598	*Das Kinderspiel* (Overbeck)	,, ::

Vocal Duets, Trios, etc.

K.346 (439ᵃ)	Trio 'Luci care'	1783
389 (384An)	Duet 'Welch ängstliches Beben'	1782
434 (424ᵇ)	Trio 'Del gran regno'	1783
436	„ 'Ecco quel fiero instante'	„
437	„ 'Mi lagnerò'	„
438	„ 'Se lontan'	„
439	„ 'Due pupille'	„
441	„ 'Liebes Mandel'	„
(441ᵉ)	„ 'Liebes Mädchen'	„
479	Quartet 'Dite almeno'	1785
480	Trio 'Mandina amabile'	„
483	Song Tenor solo and chorus 'Zerfliesset heut''	„
484	Chorus 'Ihr unsre neuer Leiter'	„
489	Duet 'Spiegarti, oh Dio'	1786
532	Trio 'Grazie agl' inganni'	1787
549	Canzonetta, 'Più non si trovano', 2 sopranos and bass	1788
625 (592ᵃ)	Comic Duet 'Nun, liebes Weibchen' (doubtful)	1790
5An. (571ᵃ)	Comic Quartet 'Caro mio'	1789

Cadenzas

Mozart wrote numerous vocal cadenzas, also cadenzas for the concertos of other composers, namely, of J. C. Bach, J. S. Shroeters, L. Honauer and Beecke. He also wrote cadenzas for the following concertos of his own: K.175, K.246, K.271, K.365, K.382, K.413, K.414, K.415, K.449, K.450, K.451, K.453, K.456, K.459, K.488, K.595.

As Mozart was in the habit of improvising his cadenzas many of his finest concertos are without any written cadenzas of his. It is worth remarking that Beethoven wrote two superb cadenzas to Mozart's D minor pianoforte concerto (K.466), to the first and last movements respectively, which should be used by every pianist playing this work.

INSTRUMENTAL MUSIC

Church Sonatas

K. 67 (41ʰ)	for strings and organ	1767
68 (41ⁱ)	„ „ „ „	„
69 (41ᵏ)	„ „ „ „	„

K.144 (124ª)   for strings and organ   1772
 145 (124ᵇ)   „   „   „   „   „
 212   „   „   „   „   1775
 224 (241ª)   „   „   „   „   1776
 225 (241ᵇ)   „   „   „   „   „
 241   „   „   „   „   „
 244   „   „   „   „   „
 245   „   „   „   „   „
 263   for strings, 2 trumpets and organ   „
 274 (271ᵈ)   for strings and organ   1777
 278 (271ᵉ)   for strings, orchestra and organ   „
 328 (317ᶜ)   for strings and organ   1779
 329 (317ª)   for strings, orchestra and organ   „
 336 (336ᵈ)   for strings and organ   1780

Compositions for 2 Pianofortes and for pianoforte 4 hands

K. 19ᵈ   Sonata, C major (4 hands)   1765
 357 (497ª)   „   G   „   „   1786
 358 (186ᶜ)   „   B flat major   „   1774
 381 (123ª)   „   D major   „   1772
 401 (375ᵉ)   Fugue, G minor   „   1782
 426   „   C minor (2 pianofortes)   1783
 448 (375ª)   Sonata, D major   „   1781
 497   „   F major (4 hands)   1786
 501   Andante, G major, with 5 Variations (4 hands)   „
 521   Sonata, C major (4 hands)   1787

Minuets, Variations, etc. for Pianoforte

K. 1   Minuet and Trio, G major   1761–2
 2   Minuet and Trio, F major   1762
 3   Allegro, B flat major   „
 4   Minuet, F major   „
 5   Minuet, F major   „
 9ª (5ª)   Allegro, C major   „
 9ᵇ (5ᵇ)   Andante, B flat major   1763
 24   8 Variations on 'Laat ons juichen'   1766
 25   7 Variations on 'Willem van Nassau'   „
 94 (73ʰ)   Minuet, D major (doubtful)   1770
 153 (375ᶠ)   Fugue, E flat major (27 bars)   (?)   1782
 154 (385ᵏ)   Fugue, G minor (30 bars)   (?)   „
 179 (189ª)   12 Variations on Minuet by Fischer   1773
 180 (173ᶜ)   6 Variations on 'Mio caro Adone', from Salieri's
                      La Fiera di Venezia   „

K.236 (588ᵇ)	Andantino, E flat major	1790
264 (315ᵈ)	9 Variations on 'Lison dormait'	1778
265 (300ᵉ)	12 Variations on 'Ah, vous dirai-je Maman'	,,
315ᵃ (315ᵍ)	8 Minuets and Trios	1779
352 (374ᶜ)	8 Variations on March in Grétry's *Les Mariages Samnites*	1781
353 (300ᶠ)	12 Variations on 'La Belle Françoise'	1778
354 (299ᵃ)	12 Variations on 'Je suis Lindor' from an opera on Beaumarchais' *Le Barbier de Seville*	,,
355 (594ᵃ)	Minuet, D major	1790
398 (416ᵉ)	6 Variations on 'Salve tu, Domine', from Paisiello's *I filosofi immaginarrii*	1783
399 (385ⁱ)	Suite (Overture, Allemande, Courante, Sarabande)	1782
453ᵃ	Kleiner Trauermarsch	1784
455	10 Variations on 'Unser dummer Pöbel' from Gluck's *Die Pilgrime von Mekka*	,,
460 (454ᵃ)	8 Variations on 'Come un agnello' from Sarti's *Fra i due litiganti*	,,
500	12 Variations on an Allegretto	1786
573	9 Variations on a Minuet of Duporte	1789
574	*Eine kleine Gigue*	,,
613	8 Variations on 'Ein Weib ist das herrlichste Ding'	1791

Miscellaneous Compositions

K.356 (617ᵃ)	Adagio, C major for harmonica	1791
443 (385ⁱ)	Three-part Fugue	(?)1782
594	Adagio and Allegro, F minor for a mechanical organ	1790
608	Fantasy, F minor for a mechanical organ	1791
616	Andante, F major for a mechanical organ	,,

Pianoforte Trios, Quartets and Quintets

K.254	Trio (Divertimento) B flat major	1776
442	,, D minor-major	1783
452	Quintet, E flat major (oboe, clarinet, horn, bassoon and pianoforte)	1784
478	Quartet, G minor	1785
493	,, E flat major	1786
496	Trio, G major	,,

K.498	Trio, E flat major (clarinet, viola and piano- forte)	1786
502	„ B flat major	„
542	„ E major	1788
548	„ C major	„
564	„ G major	„
617	Adagio and Rondo, C minor-major for harmonica, flute, oboe, viola and 'cello	1791

Sonatas and Fantasias for Pianoforte

K.279 (189^d)	C major	1774
280 (189^e)	F „	„
281 (189^f)	B flat major	„
282 (189^g)	E „ „	„
283 (189^h)	G major	„
284 (205^b)	D „	„
309 (284^b)	C „	1777
310 (300^d)	A minor	1778
311 (284^c)	D major	„
312 (189^i)	Allegro for a Sonata, G minor	1774
330 (300^h)	Sonata, C major	1778
331 (300^i)	„ A „	„
332 (300^k)	„ F „	„
333 (315^c)	„ B flat major	„
394 (383^a)	Fantasia and Fugue, C major	1782
395 (300^g)	Capriccio, C major	1778
396 (385^f)	Sonata movement (with violin)	1782
397 (385^g)	Fantasia in D minor	„
399 (385^i)	Suite in Handel's style	„
400 (372^a)	First Movement of Sonata, B flat	1781
457	Sonata, C minor	1784
475	Fantasia, C minor	1785
485	Rondo, D major	1786
494	„ F „	„
511	„ A „	1787
511^a	„ B flat major (probably by Beethoven)	
533	Allegro and Andante, F major (added by Mozart to K.494 to make a Sonata)	1788
540	Adagio, B minor	„
545	Sonatina for beginners, C major	„
570	Sonata, B flat major	1789
574	Eine kleine Gigue	„
576	Sonata, D major	„

K.Anh.135 & 138ᵃ (547ᵃ) Sonata, F major   1788
K.Anh.136 (498ᵃ) Allegro and Minuet   1786

Sonatas, etc. for Violin and Pianoforte

K.	6		Sonata, C major	1762-4
	7	,,	D ,,	1763-4
	8	,,	B flat major	,,
	9	,,	G ,,	1764
	10	,,	B flat major	,,
	11	,,	G major	,,
	12	,,	A ,,	,,
	13	,,	F ,,	,,
	14	,,	C ,,	,,
	15	,,	B flat major	,,
	26	,,	E flat major	1766
	27	,,	G major	,,
	28	,,	C ,,	,,
	29	,,	D ,,	,,
	30	,,	F ,,	,,
	31	,,	B flat major	,,
	46ᵈ	,,	C major	1768
	46ᵉ	,,	F ,,	,,
	296	,,	C ,,	1778
	301 (293ᵃ)	,,	G ,,	,,
	302 (293ᵇ)	,,	E flat major	,,
	303 (293ᶜ)	,,	C major	,,
	304 (300ᶜ)	,,	E minor	,,
	305 (293ᵈ)	,,	A major	,,
	306 (300ˡ)	,,	D ,,	,,
	359 (374ᵃ)		12 Variations on 'La Bergère Célimène'	1781
	360 (374ᵇ)		6 Variations on 'Hélas, j'ai perdu mon amant'	,,
	372		Allegro of Sonata, B flat major	,,
	376 (374ᵈ)		Sonata, F major	,,
	377 (374ᵉ)	,,	F ,,	,,
	378 (317ᵈ)	,,	B flat major	,,
	379 (373ᵃ)	,,	G major-minor	,,
	380 (374ᶠ)	,,	E flat major	,,
	402 (385ᵉ)	,,	A major-minor	1782
	403 (385ᶜ)	,,	C major	,,
	404 (385ᵉ)	,,	C ,,	,,
	454	,,	B flat major	1784
	481	,,	E flat major	1785

| K.526 | Sonata, A major | 1787 |
| 547 | ,,   F   ,, | 1788 |

Concertos for Pianoforte and Orchestra

K. 37	F major (arrangements from Raupach and Honauer)	1767
39	B flat major (arrangements from Raupach and Schobert)	,,
40	D major (arrangements from Honauer, Eckardt and P. E. Bach)	,,
41	G major (arrangements from Honauer and Raupach)	,,
107 (21ᵇ)	3 Sonatas, by J. C. Bach, arranged as Concertos with strings	1765
175	D major	1773
238	B flat major	1776
242	F major for 3 pianofortes	,,
246	C major	,,
271	E flat major	1777
365 (316ᵃ)	E flat major for 2 pianofortes	1779
382	Konzert-Rondo, D major	1782
386	Konzert-Rondo, A major	,,
413 (387ᵃ)	F major	,,
414 (386ᵃ)	A ,,	,,
415 (387ᵇ)	C ,,	,,
449	E flat major	1784
450	B ,, ,,	,,
451	D major	,,
453	G ,,	,,
456	B flat major	,,
459	F major	,,
466	D minor	1785
467	C major	,,
482	E flat major	,,
488	A major	1786
491	C minor	,,
503	C major	,,
537	D ,,	1788
595	B flat major	1791

Concertos for Violin and Orchestra

| K.190 (166ᵇ) | Concertone for 2 Solo violins and orchestra, C major | 1773 |

K.207	B flat major	1775
211	D major	,,
216	G ,,	,,
218	D ,,	,,
219	A ,,	,,
261	Adagio for K.219	1776
268 (365ᵇ)	E flat major (uncertain authenticity)	1780
269 (261ª)	*Rondo Concertante* in B flat major	1776
271ª (271¹)	D major	1777
373	Rondo, C major	1781
470	Andante, A major	1785

Miscellaneous Concertos

K.191 (186ᵉ)	B flat major for bassoon	1774
293 (416ᶠ)	F major for oboe	1783
299 (295ᶜ)	C ,, ,, flute and harp	1778
313 (285ᶜ)	G ,, ,, flute	,,
314 (285ᵈ)	D ,, ,, ,, (oboe?)	,,
315 (285ᵉ)	Andante, C major for flute	,,
364 (320ᵈ)	*Sinfonia Concertante* for violin and viola with orchestra	1779
371	Rondo, E flat major for horn	1781
412 (386ᵇ)	D major for horn	1782
417	E flat major for horn	1783
447	E ,, ,, ,, ,,	,,
495	E ,, ,, ,, ,,	1786
622	A major for clarinet	1791
K.Anh.56 (315ᶠ)	D major for pianoforte and violin	1778

(There are unfortunately only 150 bars of this remarkably fine work)

String Duets and Trios

K.266 (271ᶠ)	Trio, B flat major (2 violas and bass)	1777
404ª	Six 3 part Fugues, arranged for violin, viola and bass, 3 from Bach's Wohltemperirte Klavier (I No. 8, II Nos. 13 and 14); 1 from Bach's Organ Sonata II; 1 from Bach's Kunst der Fuge, Contrapunctus 8; and 1 from a fugue of W. Friedemann Bach. Also, 6 introductory Adagios, of which 4 are by Mozart (in F minor, G minor, D Minor, F major)	1782

K.423	Duet, G major, violin and viola	1783
424	„ B flat major, violin and viola	„
563	Divertimento, E flat major, for violin, viola and 'cello	1788

String Quartets

K. 80 (73ᶠ)	G major	1770
155 (134ᵃ)	D „	1772
156 (134ᵇ)	G „	„
157	C „	„
158	F „	„
159	B flat major	„
160	E „ „	„
168	F major	1773
169	A „	„
170	C „	„
171	E flat major	„
172	B „ „	„
173	D minor	„
387	G major (Haydn set No. 1)	1782
405	Five four-part Fugues from Bach's Wohl-temperirte Klavier	„
421 (417ᵇ)	D minor (Haydn set No. 2)	1783
428 (421ᵇ)	E flat major („ „ No. 3)	„
458	B „ „ („ „ No. 4)	1784
464	A major („ „ No. 5)	1785
465	C „ („ „ No. 6)	1786
499	D „	„
546	Adagio and Fugue, C minor (Fugue same as K.426 for 2 pianos)	1788
575	D major (King of Prussia set No. 1)	1789
589	B flat „ („ „ „ No. 2)	1790
590	F major („ „ „ No. 3)	„

String Quintets

K.174	B flat major	1773
406 (516ᵇ)	C minor (originally composed as Serenade for wind instruments, K.388)	1787
515	C major	„
516	G minor	„
593	D major	1790
614	E flat major	1791

Miscellaneous Chamber Music

K. 61ᵍ	2 Minuets (2 violins, viola, 2 flutes and bass)	1769
61ʰ	6 Minuets (2 violins, 2 flutes, 2 oboes, 2 trumpets and bass)	,,
64	Minuet, D major, (2 violins, 2 horns and bass)	,,
65ᵃ (61ᵇ)	7 Minuets with trio (2 violins and bass)	,,
103 (61ᵈ)	19 Minuets, with and without trio (2 violins, 2 oboes, 2 horns and bass)	,,
285	Quartet, D major for flute and strings	1777
292 (196ᶜ)	Sonata, B flat major for bassoon and 'cello	1775
298	Quartet, A major for flute and strings	1778
370 (368ᵇ)	Quartet, F major for oboe and strings	1781
407 (386ᶜ)	Quintet, E flat major for horn and strings	1783
410 (440ᵈ)	Adagio, F major for 2 basset horns and bassoon	,,
411 (440ᵃ)	Adagio, B flat major for 2 clarinets and 3 basset horns	,,
487 (496ᵃ)	12 Duets for 2 basset horns	1786
581	Quintet, A major for clarinet and strings	1789
K.Anh.171 (285ᵇ)	Quartet, C major for flute and strings	1778

Symphonies

K. 16	E flat major		1764
19	D major		,,
22	B flat major		1765
43	F major		1767
45	D ,,		1768
48	D ,,		,,
73 (75ᵃ)	C ,,		1771
74	G ,,		1770
75	F ,,		1771
76 (42ᵃ)	F ,,		1767
81 (73ˡ)	D ,,		1770
84 (73ۿ)	D ,,		,,
95 (73)	D ,,		,,
96 (111ᵇ)	C ,,		1771
97 (73ᵐ)	D ,,		1770
102 (213ᶜ)	C ,,	(Finale only)	1775
110 (75ᵇ)	G ,,		1770
112	F ,,		1771
114	A ,,		,,

K.120 (111ª)	D major	(Finale)	1771
121 (207ª)	D „	(Finale)	1775
124	G „		1772
128	C „		„
129	G „		„
130	F „		„
132	E flat major		„
133	D major		„
134	A „		„

161 and 163 Symphony arranged from overture to
          Il Sogno di Scipione (K.126)   „

162	C major		„
181 (162ᵇ)	D „		1773
182 (166ᶜ)	B flat major		„
183	G minor		„
184 (166ª)	E flat major		„
199 (162ª)	G major		„
200 (173ᵉ)	C „		1774
201 (186ª)	A „		„
202 (186ᵇ)	D „		„
297 (300ª)	D „ ('Paris')		1778
318	G „		1779
319	B flat major		„
338	C major		1780
385	D „ ('Haffner')		1782
425	C „ ('Linz')		1783
444 (425ª)	G „ (Introduction by Mozart, the rest		
	by Michael Haydn)		„
504	D major ('Prague')		1786
543	E flat major		1788
550	G minor		„
551	C major ('Jupiter')		„

K.Anh.8 (311ª) Overture in B flat major   1778
K.Anh.9 (297ᵇ) *Sinfonia Concertante* for oboe, clarinet,
          horn and bassoon with orchestra   „

Divertimentos, Serenades, Cassations, etc. for Orchestra

K. 32	Galimathias musicum	1766
62	Cassation	1769
63	Divertimento (Final-Musik)	„
99 (63ª)	Cassation, B flat major	„
100 (62ª)	Serenade, D major	„
101 (250ª)	„ F „	1776

K.103 (61^d)	19 Minuets with and without trio	1769
104 (61^e)	Minuets	,,
105 (61^f)	6 ,,	,,
106 (588^a)	Overture and 3 Kontretänze	1790
113	Divertimento, E flat major	1771
122 (73^t)	Minuet, E flat major	1770
123	Kontretanz, B flat major	,,
131	Divertimento, D major	1772
136 (125^a)	,, D ,,	,,
137 (125^b)	,, B flat major	,,
138 (125^c)	,, F major	,,
164 (130^a)	6 Minuets	,,
166 (159^d)	Divertimento, E flat major	1773
176	16 Minuets	,,
185 (167^a)	Serenade, D major	,,
186 (159^b)	Divertimento, B flat major	,,
187 (159^c)	,, C major	,,
188 (240^b)	,, C ,,	,,
189 (167^b)	March, D major	,,
203 (189^b)	Serenade, D major	1774
204 (213^a)	,, D major	1775
205 (173^a)	Divertimento, D major	1773
206 (366)	March (used in *Idomeneo*)	1775
213	Divertimento, F major	,,
214	March, C major	,,
215 (213^b)	March, D ,,	,,
237 (189^c)	March, D ,,	1774
239	*Serenata Notturna* for 2 small orchestras	1776
240	Divertimento, B flat major	,,
247	,, F major	,,
248	March, F major	,,
249	,, D ,,	,,
250 (248^b)	Serenade (Haffner)	,,
251	Divertimento (Septet), D major	,,
252 (240^a)	,, F flat major	,,
253	,, F major	,,
267 (271^c)	4 Kontretänze	1777
270	Divertimento, B flat major	,,
286 (269^a)	*Notturno*, D major for 4 orchestras	,,
287 (271^b)	Divertimento, B flat major	,,
288 (271^h)	,, F major	,,
289 (271^g)	,, E flat major	,,
290 (173^b)	March, D major	1773
300	Gavotte, B flat	1778

K.610   Kontretanz   1791
    611   German Dance   „
K.Anh.226 (196ᵉ) Divertimento, E flat major   1775
    „   227 (196ᶠ) Divertimento, B flat major   „
    „   229 and 229ᵃ (439ᵇ) 5 Divertimentos   1783

Bibliography

Hermann Abert

W. A. Mozart, neu bearbeitete and erweiterte Ausgabe von Otto Jahns 'Mozart'. 2 volumes. Breitkopf und Härtel, Leipzig, 1955.

Georg Nikolaus von Nissen

Biographie W. A. Mozarts. Nach Originalbriefen, Sammlungen alles über ihn Geschriebenen, mit vielen neuen Beilagen, Steindrucken, Musikblättern und einem Faksimile. Nach des Verfassers Tode herausgegeben von Constanze, Witwe von Nissen, früher Wittwe Mozart. Breitkopf und Härtel, Leipzig, 1828.

Mozart. Briefe und Aufzeichnungen. Gesamtausgabe, gesammelt und erläutert von *Wilhelm A. Bauer* und *Otto Erich Deutsch*, Kassel, 1962/3.

Mozart und seine Welt in zeitgenössischen Bildern, begründet von *Maximilian Zenger*, vorgelegt von *Otto Erich Deutsche*, Neue Mozart-Ausgabe X/32, Kassel, 1961.

Mozart. Die Dokumente seines Lebens. Gesammelt und erläutert von *Otto Erich Deutsch*, Neue Mozart-Ausgabe X/34. Bärenreiter, Kassel 1961.
(English edition: *Mozart, a Documentary Biography*. Translated by *Eric Blom, Peter Branscombe and Jeremy Noble*. A. & C. Black, London, 1964.)

Edward Holmes

Life of Mozart, Chapman & Hall, London, 1845.

Lorenzo Da Ponte

Memorie die Lorenzo da Ponte da Ceneda scritte da esso. 4 Volumes. New York, 1823-7.

Edward J. Dent

Mozart's Operas: a critical study. Oxford University Press, London, 1955.

Chronologisch-thematisches Verzeichnis sämtlicher Tonwerke Wolfgang Amadé Mozart . . . von Dr L. R. v. Köchel. Sechste Auflage bearbeitet von Franz Giegling, Alexander Weinmann & Gerd Sievers. Breitkopf & Härtel, Wiesbaden, 1964.

Letters of Mozart and his family. Translated and edited by *Emily Anderson.* 3 Volumes. Macmillan and Co, London, 1938.

Théodore de Wyzewa et *Georges de Saint-Foix*

Wolfgang Amédée Mozart. Sa vie musicale et son oeuvre. Essai de biographie critique. 5 Volumes (Vols. 3–5: Saint-Foix alone). Desclée de Brouwer, Paris, 1912–46.

Eva and Paul Badura-Skoda

Mozart-Interpretation. Wancura, Wien, 1957.
(English edition: *Interpreting Mozart on the Keyboard.* Translated by *Leo Black.* Barrie and Rockliff, London, 1962.)

H. C. Robbins Landon and *Donald Mitchell*

The Mozart Companion. Rockliff, London, 1956.

Mozart-Handbuch. Chronik, Werk, Bibliographie. Herausgegeben von *Otto Schneider* und *Anton Algatzy.*

INDEX

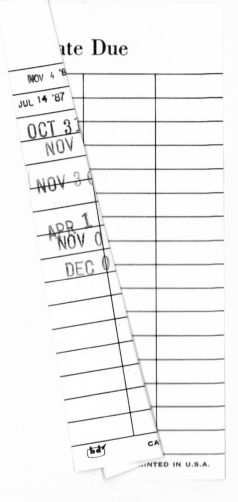

ate Due

NOV 4 '8		
JUL 14 '87		
OCT 31		
NOV		
NOV 3 0		
APR 1		
NOV 0		
DEC 0		

bd̄ CA

RINTED IN U.S.A.